"Kovalishyn takes us around the [...] two Bible interpreters. This work [...] graphical location affects interpretation. Familiar texts are discussed from unfamiliar perspectives, yielding new insights and deeper understandings for Western readers. These samples of 'situated exegesis' will be of interest to a broad audience, from pastors to students to scholars of hermeneutics. Highly recommended."

—**Karen H. Jobes**, Wheaton College (emerita)

"None of us reads the Bible neutrally. Whether we recognize it or not, we read and interpret the Bible from our own culture, experiences, and personal perspective. That is a bad thing if we assume we know everything but a good thing if we are willing to read Scripture with others and learn from each other's vantage points. These global readings are a gift of learning for those who want to better understand culturally diverse interpretations of the New Testament."

—**Nijay K. Gupta**, Northern Seminary

"The excellent scholarly essays in this important book, covering aspects of the New Testament from Matthew to Revelation, demonstrate the significance of contextual scriptural interpretation. Each chapter makes an important contribution, and the book as a whole is part of a seismic shift in the field of New Testament studies. I hope this volume is widely read by scholars and students alike."

—**Michael J. Gorman**, St. Mary's Seminary & University

"This a book I've been waiting for. In it, we listen to and learn from scholars across the majority world. Each author offers a close reading of a New Testament text in its context, alongside an exploration of their own cultural and social locations. The insights arising from this intersection are both fresh and compelling. I highly recommend this as a textbook for courses on the Bible."

—**Jeannine K. Brown**, Bethel Seminary

"I wish I were still teaching full-time so that I could use this as my main supplemental textbook in my New Testament introduction and survey courses. Many works have tried to show how crucial it is to read the Bible through the eyes of other cultures, nationalities, and ethnicities besides white American ones, but few have succeeded as well as Mariam Kovalishyn and her cadre of authors. Highly recommended!"

—**Craig L. Blomberg**, Denver Seminary (emeritus)

"This book truly is just as much a reformation as it is a revolution. It is not just new; in many ways it is a return to original hermeneutics. Modernist, white, Western ways of interpreting Scripture, which have held sway for much of church history, are not the only, or even the primary, ways of understanding the Bible. Our brothers and sisters from around the world provide cultural lenses that are much more similar to those of first-century readers. This is not a relativistic reading of the Bible; it is a more authentic one. This is an invaluable polycentric resource that forms a bridge between the ancient world and our modern global one."

—**Allen Yeh**, International Theological Seminary

THE NEW TESTAMENT
AROUND THE WORLD

THE NEW TESTAMENT AROUND THE WORLD

Exploring Key Texts from Different Contexts

EDITED BY

MARIAM KAMELL KOVALISHYN

Baker Academic

a division of Baker Publishing Group

Grand Rapids, Michigan

Published by Baker Academic
a division of Baker Publishing Group
Grand Rapids, Michigan
BakerAcademic.com

Printed in the United States of America

Library of Congress Cataloging-in-Publication Data
Names: Kovalishyn, Mariam Kamell, editor.
Title: The New Testament around the world : exploring key texts from different contexts / Mariam Kamell Kovalishyn, ed.
Description: Grand Rapids, Michigan : Baker Academic, a division of Baker Publishing Group, [2025] | Includes index.
Identifiers: LCCN 2024030896 | ISBN 9781540962966 (paperback) | ISBN 9781540968654 | ISBN 9781493449408 (ebook) | ISBN 9781493449415 (pdf)
Subjects: LCSH: Bible. New Testament. Classification: LCC BS2397 .N488 2025 | DDC 230/.0415—dc23/eng/20240823
LC record available at https://lccn.loc.gov/2024030896

Scripture translation use varies throughout and is noted in the footnotes for each chapter.

Cover design by Paula Gibson

Baker Publishing Group publications use paper produced from sustainable forestry practices and postconsumer waste whenever possible.

25   26   27   28   29   30   31   7   6   5   4   3   2   1

CONTENTS

PART 3 HEBREWS THROUGH REVELATION

INTRODUCTION

What if we took seriously the idea that our location affects our interpretation of the Bible? What if we saw this as something that could possibly lead us down unhelpful paths but could also provide avenues for hearing the text better? What if, as well, we took seriously that the church global is all Christ's body and that we need to learn from the eye, the foot, the hand (to play with Paul's metaphor in 1 Corinthians)?

Those are, in a nutshell, the questions that drove me to want to pull a book like this together. I'm a child of an Egyptian Coptic immigrant who married a missionary kid who grew up in the Philippines, and now I have married a Ukrainian immigrant to Canada; my interest in the global church is innate. As I progressed in my teaching, I wanted a book I could use in my classes and in my ministries that would introduce readers to scholars from all around the world, scholars who are part of the same body of Christ but whom we might not otherwise ever "meet." This book began during the Society of Biblical Literature's annual meeting in 2018, when presenters in my little study group spoke on interpreting the General Epistles (James–Jude) from their contexts. The James and two 1 Peter essays both began their lives there.[1] I wanted more: I wanted scholars to show me a sample of how their context affected their interpretation, and how their interpretation should affect their context, all across the New Testament. I didn't want a commentary; I wanted samples from the text of what I called "situated exegesis," wherein scholars would exegete the text with care and rigor, with an eye toward how their chosen passage or theme related with their context.

---

1. As an aside, it was Dennis Edwards's essay that convinced me I should have the two additional essays by people who explicitly identify as American minorities, whereas the main essays are by people whose first identity is not American.

The process was not easy. The initial essays came in early 2020, but we all know what happened as that year progressed. Committed authors had to drop out for reasons of family crises and illness; lockdowns and the abrupt move to online teaching added stress and extra burdens. Some PhD candidates had to withdraw so they could focus on completing their dissertations; others needed to withdraw because they needed the publication to come sooner. Everyone went with my blessing and ongoing prayers, and I am grateful and delighted with the group that has come together in this collection.

Unsurprisingly, there are overlaps and there are distinctives. While trying to bring the essays into a general format that would bring unity to the volume, I also wanted to keep the distinctives of the different authors' styles and interests. Some speak more broadly of "African" or "Asian" ways of interpreting; others interact very closely with a local translation of the Bible. I asked merely that they do their interpretation of the text with an eye on their context as well, something not always encouraged, particularly in evangelical interpretation. The results, I think, speak for themselves. Readers should be challenged to consider how their preferred interpretations may affect (or be affected by) their theological commitments, how Western cultural practices such as individualism and self-sufficiency may hinder our communal life as believers, and ultimately how our faith interacts with our culture and vice versa.

For the sake of accessibility, I decided to have all the Greek and Hebrew transliterated throughout, although at times the discussion hinges on technical words, and so some pages are sprinkled with italics more heavily than others. Other languages at times remain, whether in transliteration or in parentheses. Perhaps these will invite readers to consider how other languages are interacting with the biblical text we all revolve around.

I have also included an appendix with research data from the Pew Research Center drawing from their 2010 summary of global religions.[2] At times I found myself interested to know the religious landscape of the countries of the various authors: what were the dominant religions, which one held a majority, and so on. Several authors included similar data, drawn from their home country's censuses, but the Pew data gives some consistency in the date the data is drawn from. For those who are curious, we hope the appendix will be of use.

Finally, I must thank Langham Partnership, who provides scholarships for scholars around the world to be able to train and return to their home

---

2. "The Global Religious Landscape," Pew Research Center, December 18, 2012, https://www.pewresearch.org/religion/2012/12/18/global-religious-landscape-exec/. Unfortunately, the data has not been updated recently, and all they provide for 2020–50 are estimates.

countries to teach. The Langham Partnership supported the project from the beginning and put me in contact with a number of scholars. Any proceeds of this book will be donated to the Langham Partnership for ongoing scholarship support. I also thank Michael Evanson for his help with early drafts of the book and Jayden Behm for his work indexing, my sister Lisa Hough for working on final drafts doing copyediting, and Melisa Blok at Baker for her wonderful work as editor. And I thank my husband since, between starting vision and final project, we've added three kids to our household (four born between 2017 and 2023), and I am grateful for a partner who supported my ideas and my work on this. If I wrote on 1 Corinthians 7, I'd definitely have contextual thoughts about Paul's teaching on divided callings, and I'm glad mine is as painless as two busy professionals and parents can make it. And I am very grateful for Jim Kinney and Bryan Dyer at Baker Academic, who encouraged me to stick with this and bring this book to life. I hope and pray it is an encouragement to seeing the Bible as a relevant text to our lives and work.

Mariam Kamell Kovalishyn

ABBREVIATIONS

General

alt.	altered	et al.	*et alii*, and others
AT	author translation	etc.	*et cetera*, and so forth
c.	century	fig.	figure
ca.	circa	Grk.	Greek
cf.	*confer*, compare	Hb.	Hebrew
chap(s).	chapter(s)	i.e.	*id est*, that is
col(s).	column(s)	lit.	literally
e.g.	*exempli gratia*, for example	n.p.	no publisher
esp.	especially	p(p).	page(s)
ET	English translation	v(v).	verse(s)

Bible Versions

ESV	English Standard Version	NASB	New American Standard Bible
GNT	Good News Translation	NIV	New International Version
KJV	King James Version	NRSV	New Revised Standard Version
LXX	Septuagint	RSV	Revised Standard Version

Early Jewish and Christian Works

Avod. Zar.	Avodah Zarah	Pss. Sol.	Psalms of Solomon
b.	Babylonian Talmud	Sir.	Sirach
Did.	Didache	Tob.	Tobit
1–2 Macc.	1–2 Maccabees	Wis.	Wisdom of Solomon
Let. Aris.	Letter of Aristeas		

Dead Sea Scrolls

CD	Damascus Document	1QS	Serek Hayahad (Rule of the Community)
1QH	Hodayot (Thanksgiving Hymns)	11Q13	Melchizedek

Greek and Latin Works

Aelius Aristides
Or.   *Orations*

Aristotle
Ath. pol.   *Athenain politeia* (*Constitution of Athens*)

Cicero
Fin.   *De finibus bonorum et malorum* (*On the Ends of Good and Evil*)
Rep.   *De republica* (*On the Republic*)
Tusc.   *Tusculanae disputationes* (*Tusculan Disputations*)

Dio Chrysostom
Or.   *Orations*

Euripides
Hipp.   *Hippolytus*

Herodotus
Hist.   *Histories*

John Chrysostom
Hom. 1 Thess.   *Homilies on 1 Thessalonians*
Hom. Matt.   *Homilies on Matthew*

Josephus
Ag. Ap.   *Against Apion*
Ant.   *Jewish Antiquities*
J.W.   *Jewish War*

Julian
Ep.   *Epistles*

Justin Martyr
Dial.   *Dialogue with Trypho*

Lysias
Or.   *Orations*

Philo
Ebr.   *De ebrietate* (*On Drunkenness*)
Flacc. *In Flaccum* (*Against Flaccus*)
Leg.   *Legum allegoriae* (*Allegorical Interpretation*)
Legat. *Legatio ad Gaium* (*On the Embassy to Gaius*)

Plato
Gorg.   *Gorgias*
Leg.   *Leges* (*Laws*)
Phaed. *Phaedo*
Resp.   *Respublica* (*The Republic*)

Plutarch

Cat. Ma.	*Cato Major*
Cat. Min.	*Cato Minor* (*Cato the Younger*)
Conj. praec.	*Conjugalia praecepta* (*Advice to the Bride and Groom*)
Inim. util.	*De capienda ex inimicis utilitate* (*How to Profit by One's Enemies*)
Lib. ed.	*De liberis educandis* (*On the Education of Children*)
Mor.	*Moralia* (*Morals*)
Praec. ger. rei publ.	*Praecepta gerendae rei publicae* (*Precepts of Statecraft*)
Pyth. orac.	*De Pythiae oraculis* (*The Oracles at Delphi No Longer Given in Verse*)
Virt. mor.	*De virtute morali* (*On Moral Virtue*)

Virgil

Aen.	*Aeneid*

Xenophon

Lac.	*Respublica Lacedaemoniorum* (*Constitution of the Lacedaemonians*)

Inscriptions and Papyri

Agora	Woodhead, A. G. *The Athenian Agora, XVI*. Inscriptions: The Decrees. Princeton: American School of Classical Studies at Athens, 1997
AM	*Mitteilungen des deutschen Archäologischen Instituts: Athenische Abteilung.* Berlin: Deutsches archäologisches Institut, 1876–
CIL	*Corpus inscriptionum latinarum.* Consilio et Auctoritate Academiae Litterarum Regiae Borussicae Editum. Berlin: Georg Reimer, 1863–74
IDelta	Bernand, A., ed. *Le delta égyptien d'après les texts grecs 1: Les confines libyques.* 3 vols. Mémoires publies par les membres de l'Institut français d'archéologie orientale du Caire 91. Cairo: Institut français d'archéologie orientale, 1970
IEph	Engelmann, H., H. Wankel, and R. Merkelbach. *Die Inschriften von Ephesos.* IGSK 11–17. Bonn: Rudolf Habelt, 1979–84
IG 2^2	Kirchner, Johannes, ed. *Inscriptiones Atticae Euclidis anno anteriores.* 4 vols. Berlin: de Gruyter, 1913–40
IKios	Corsten, Thomas. *Die Inschriften von Kios.* IGSK 29. Bonn: Rudolf Habelt, 1985
JIWE	Noy, David. *Jewish Inscriptions of Western Europe.* Vol. 2, *The City of Rome.* Cambridge: Cambridge University Press, 1995
MAMA	Calder, W. M., E. Herzfeld, S. Guyer, and C. W. M. Cox, eds. *Monumenta Asiae Minoris antiqua.* 10 vols. London: Manchester University Press, 1928–93
PGM	Preisendanz, Karl, ed. *Papyri Graecae Magicae: Die griechischen Zauberpapyri.* 2nd ed. Stuttgart: Teubner, 1973–74
SEG	*Supplementum epigraphicum graecum.* Leiden: Brill, 1923–
*Syll*³	Dittenberger, Wilhelm, ed. *Sylloge inscriptionum graecarum.* 3rd ed. 4 vols. Leipzig: Hirzel, 1915–24

Secondary Sources

AB	Anchor Bible
ABCS	Africa Bible Commentary Series
ABSA	*Annual of the British School at Athens*

AF	*Anthropological Forum*
AJA	*American Journal of Archaeology*
AJEC	Ancient Judaism and Early Christianity
ANTC	Abingdon New Testament Commentaries
ARA	*Annual Review of Anthropology*
ASET	Africa Society of Evangelical Theology Series
ASM	American Society of Missiology Monograph Series
AUSTR	American University Studies, Series 7: Theology and Religion
BAGL	*Biblical and Ancient Greek Linguistics*
BBR	*Bulletin for Biblical Research*
BDAG	Danker, Frederick W., Walter Bauer, William F. Arndt, and F. Wilbur Gingrich. *Greek-English Lexicon of the New Testament and Other Early Christian Literature.* 3rd ed. Chicago: University of Chicago Press, 2000
BECNT	Baker Exegetical Commentary on the New Testament
BHGNT	Baylor Handbook on the Greek New Testament
BibAr	Biblia Arabica
BibInt	Biblical Interpretation Series
BNT	Die Botschaft des Neuen Testaments
BNTC	Black's New Testament Commentaries
BST	The Bible Speaks Today
BTB	*Biblical Theology Bulletin*
BTCP	Biblical Theology for Christian Proclamation
CBNT	Commentaire biblique: Nouveau Testament
CBQ	*Catholic Biblical Quarterly*
CCSS	Catholic Commentary on Sacred Scripture
CD	*Current Dialogue*
CNNTE	Contexts and Norms of New Testament Ethics
CNT	Commentaire du Nouveau Testament
Colloq	*Colloquium*
CP	*Classical Philology*
CRAI	*Comptes rendus des séances de l'Académie des inscriptions et belles-lettres*
CSSH	*Comparative Studies in Society and History*
DocPraeh	*Documenta Praehistorica*
DPL	*Dictionary of Paul and His Letters.* Edited by Gerald F. Hawthorne, Ralph P. Martin, and Daniel G. Reid. Downers Grove, IL: InterVarsity, 1993
EC	*Early Christianity*
EDNT	*Exegetical Dictionary of the New Testament.* Edited by H. Balz and G. Schneider. ET. 3 vols. Grand Rapids: Eerdmans, 1990–93
EGGNT	Exegetical Guide to the Greek New Testament
EKKNT	Evangelisch-katholischer Kommentar zum Neuen Testament
EMS	Evangelical Missiological Society
ExAud	*Ex Auditu*
FidRef	*Fides Reformata*
HCMR	History of Christian-Muslim Relations
HFTS	Helps for Translators Series
HNTC	Holman New Testament Commentary
HTR	*Harvard Theological Review*

HTS	Harvard Theological Studies
HvTSt	*Hervormde Teologiese Studies (HTS Theological Studies)*
ICC	International Critical Commentary
ICS	*Illinois Classical Studies*
IGSK	Inschriften griechischer Städte aus Kleinasien
IJPS	*Indian Journal of Political Science*
Int	*Interpretation*
IVPNTC	IVP New Testament Commentary Series
JAAR	*Journal of the American Academy of Religion*
JBL	*Journal of Biblical Literature*
JChS	*Journal of Church and State*
JECS	*Journal of Early Christian Studies*
JEH	*Journal of Ecclesiastical History*
JEMS	*Journal of the Evangelical Missiological Society*
JETS	*Journal of the Evangelical Theological Society*
JRAI	*Journal of the Royal Anthropological Institute*
JRH	*Journal of Religious History*
JSNT	*Journal for the Study of the New Testament*
JSNTSup	Journal for the Study of the New Testament Supplement Series
JSP	*Journal for the Study of the Pseudepigrapha*
LBRS	Lexham Bible Reference Series
LCL	Loeb Classical Library
LNTS	Library of New Testament Studies
MNTC	Moffatt New Testament Commentary
NABPR	National Association of Baptist Professors of Religion
NAC	New American Commentary
NBBC	New Beacon Bible Commentary
NCCS	New Covenant Commentary Series
NGS	New Gospel Studies
NICNT	New International Commentary on the New Testament
NIDNTT	*New International Dictionary of New Testament Theology.* Edited by Colin Brown. 4 vols. Grand Rapids: Zondervan, 1975–78
NIGTC	New International Greek Testament Commentary
NN	*Nations and Nationalism*
NovT	*Novum Testamentum*
NovTSup	Supplements to Novum Testamentum
NPNF[1]	*The Nicene and Post-Nicene Fathers*, Series 1. Edited by Philip Schaff. 1886–89. 14 vols. Reprint, Peabody, MA: Hendrickson, 2004
NTL	New Testament Library
NTS	*New Testament Studies*
NTT	New Testament Theology
OLA	Orientalia Lovaniensia Analecta
OS	*Ostkirchliche Studien*
PBM	Paternoster Biblical Monographs
PNTC	Pillar New Testament Commentary
PolTh	*Political Theology*
R&T	*Religion & Theology*

ResQ	*Restoration Quarterly*
RSSSR	*Research in the Social Scientific Study of Religion*
RTR	*Reformed Theological Review*
SBET	*Scottish Bulletin of Evangelical Theology*
SBFCMa	Studium Biblicum Franciscanum, Collectio maior
SBLDS	Society of Biblical Literature Dissertation Series
SBLMS	Society of Biblical Literature Monograph Series
SBLSBS	Society of Biblical Literature Sources for Biblical Study
SGBC	The Story of God Bible Commentary
SHBC	Smyth & Helwys Bible Commentary
SJPH	*Scandinavian Journal of Public Health*
SNTSMS	Society for New Testament Studies Monograph Series
SP	Sacra Pagina
TDNT	*Theological Dictionary of the New Testament*. Edited by G. Kittel and G. Friedrich. Translated by G. W. Bromiley. 10 vols. Grand Rapids: Eerdmans, 1964–76
THNTC	Two Horizons New Testament Commentary
TImp	*Testamentum Imperium*
TNTC	Tyndale New Testament Commentaries
TS	*Theological Studies*
TST	Toronto Studies in Theology
TTCSGNT	T&T Clark Study Guides to the New Testament
TX	*Theologica Xaveriana*
UBSHS	UBS Handbook Series
URM	*Ultimate Reality and Meaning*
USQR	*Union Seminary Quarterly Review*
WA	*World Archaeology*
WBC	Word Biblical Commentary
WLQ	*Wisconsin Lutheran Quarterly*
WMANT	Wissenschaftliche Monographien zum Alten und Neuen Testament
WTJ	*Westminster Theological Journal*
WUNT	Wissenschaftliche Untersuchungen zum Neuen Testament
WW	*Word and World*
ZECNT	Zondervan Exegetical Commentary on the New Testament
ZNW	*Zeitschrift für die neutestamentliche Wissenschaft und die Kunde der älteren Kirche*

Part 1

GOSPELS
AND ACTS

1

The Parable of the Sheep and the Goats as a Summons to Total Discipleship

Matthew 25:31–46 in Conversation with Integral Orthodoxy

BERNARDO CHO

At the conclusion of a long series of speeches preceding Jesus's last moments in Jerusalem, Matthew presents us with an unparalleled passage, traditionally known as the parable of the sheep and the goats (Matt. 25:31–46).[1] It begins with Jesus alluding to the vision of Daniel 7 so as to speak of "the Son of Man" who will sit "on his glorious throne" (Matt. 25:31) and finally judge "all the nations" (v. 32).[2] The parable then proceeds to describe how said judgment will take place. Just as a shepherd sets apart "the sheep from

---

1. On the genre of the passage, see John R. Donahue, "The 'Parable' of the Sheep and the Goats: A Challenge to Christian Ethics," *TS* 47 (1986): 9–11. On the closing of Matt. 24–25, see W. D. Davies and D. C. Allison, *Matthew 19–28: Volume 3*, ICC (London: T&T Clark International, 2004), 418; Dan O. Via, "Ethical Responsibility and Human Wholeness in Matthew 25:31–45," *HTR* 80 (1987): 84.

2. Unless otherwise noted, all translations of ancient texts, biblical passages, and modern sources in Portuguese are my own.

the goats," the end-time royal judge will distinguish the nations "from one another" (v. 32), with the result that "the righteous ones" will enter "eternal life" (v. 46), whereas the "accursed ones" will be sent to "eternal punishment" (vv. 41, 46). Most importantly, this climactic discourse reveals that the people inheriting the everlasting kingdom will be represented by those showing acts of compassion to "one of these least of my brothers" (v. 40), with whom the exalted Jesus closely identifies. The passage thus articulates the basis on which the eschatological destiny of the nations stands or falls: to feed, to welcome, to clothe, to nurse, and to visit the Son of Man's "brothers and sisters" (*adelphoi*) is to belong to him and his people, but to fail to do so is to exclude oneself from the protection of the apocalyptic shepherd-king.

Matthew 25:31–46 and Recent Debates in Brazilian Missiology

Despite its grammatical simplicity, the central point of the passage has rendered its theological appropriation rather elusive, especially for readers accustomed to setting the Pauline theme of justification by faith against Christian ethics (cf. Rom. 1–4; Gal. 1–3). If those suffering social dislocation are considered members of Jesus's own family, and works of justice are intrinsic to the identity of "the righteous ones," is the parable not blatantly teaching some degree of human merit as a means to salvation—whether by serving the outcast or by simply being in need? The fact that most technical discussions have focused on the referents of "these least of my brothers" and "the sheep" is surely indicative of how much is at stake.[3] Given that both groups are presumably counted among the saved, it seems crucial to determine precisely who they are in order for us to understand exactly how—or if—belief and practice are supposed to go together.[4]

Indeed, liberation theologians have famously tried to make sense of the implications of Matthew 25:31–46, resorting to it in defense of centering the principal thrust of Christianity not on its distinctive set of tenets but rather on its praxis of social justice.[5] Particularly in Brazil, reflections prioritizing socio-analytic categories, though not always overtly citing this parable, have given rise to the notion that the very presence of Jesus rests in the lives of the

3. See Klyne R. Snodgrass, *Stories with Intent: A Comprehensive Guide to the Parables of Jesus* (Grand Rapids: Eerdmans, 2008), 551–61, and the further references cited therein.
4. J. Ramsey Michaels, "Apostolic Hardship and Righteous Gentiles: A Study of Matthew 25:31–46," *JBL* 84 (1965): 27.
5. The most classic example is Gustavo Gutiérrez, *A Theology of Liberation* (Maryknoll, NY: Orbis Books, 1973), 191. See discussion in Ulrich Luz, *Matthew 21–28: A Commentary*, Hermeneia (Minneapolis: Augsburg Fortress, 2005), 267–70.

economically destitute, apart from any public confession of Christ's lord-ship.[6] Accordingly, it has become increasingly common to find, both in the literature and in popular understanding across the country, the downplaying of the doctrinal aspect of Christian proclamation, as if knowing the biblical gospel was of secondary relevance so long as one is busy alleviating the suf-fering of the oppressed.[7]

Influenced by the Lausanne movement and echoing the ideas advanced chiefly by Ecuadorian scholar René Padilla, many evangelical leaders in Bra-zil have countered by advocating a missiological approach, called "integral mission" (*missão integral*), which encompasses, among other things, both evangelism and social action.[8] Simply put, it proposes, on the one hand, that the announcing of the good news of Jesus must include a genuine preoccupa-tion with social justice—a principle demonstrably neglected by many Chris-tian communities, not least the so-called prosperity churches—and, on the other hand, that concern for the poor must not entail the diminishing of the normative content of the gospel.[9] In contrast to the jettisoning of proper proc-lamation by some liberation theologians, and also departing from a long-held assumption that good works are simply instrumental to preaching, integral mission has thus underscored the centrality of both conversionism *and* public engagements in eliminating economic injustice.[10] The following statement by the late Anglican bishop Robinson Cavalcanti, commenting on the 1974 Lausanne Covenant, represents a core concern by those holding this view: "As one notices, neither the reality of sin nor the need for conversion is in doubt, but rather the content of the converts' mission in this world, the extent of the implications of sin beyond the merely individual, as well as the scope and the means of the prophetic denunciation of [social injustice] by the Church."[11]

6. See Hugo Assmann and Jung Mo Sung, *Deus em Nós: O Reinado que Acontece no Amor Solidário aos Pobres* (São Paulo: Paulus, 2014).
7. E.g., José Comblin, *O Espírito Santo e a Libertação* (Petrópolis: Vozes, 1988), 31.
8. See C. René Padilla, *Mission between the Times: Essays of the Kingdom* (Carlisle, UK: Langham, 2013); Samuel Escobar, *A Time for Mission: The Challenge for Global Christianity* (Carlisle, UK: Langham, 2003). See also David C. Kirkpatrick, "C. René Padilla and the Origins of Integral Mission in Post-War Latin America," *JEH* 67 (2016): 351–71.
9. Recent treatments are Paulo Cappelletti, *Encontro das Teologias Latino-Americanas: Análise Histórico-Teológica da Teologia da Missão Integral versus Teologia da Libertação* (Londrina: Descoberta, 2019); Regina Sanches, *Teologia da Missão Integral: História e Método da Teologia Evangélica Latino-Americana* (São Paulo: Reflexão, 2009).
10. See David J. Bosch, *Transforming Mission: Paradigm Shifts in Theology of Mission* (Maryknoll, NY: Orbis Books, 1991), 40; David Bebbington, "Evangelicals and Reform: An Analysis of Social and Political Action," *Third Way* 6 (1983): 10–13. Both are cited in Kirkpat-rick, "C. René Padilla," 353.
11. Robinson Cavalcanti, *A Utopia Possível: Em Busca de um Cristianismo Integral* (Viçosa: Ultimato, 1997), 27.

The reception of this holistic approach, however, has been far from homogenous and has prompted critical responses from more conservative circles in subsequent years.[12] These debates have taken on a life of their own, making it impossible to parse the nuances here. Political preferences on both extremes of the spectrum have often set the tone for the conversation, leaving attempts at finding common theological ground unfruitful. What is more pressing for our purposes is that, while some proponents of integral mission have insisted that evangelism and social action are equivalent to two inseparable wings of a plane,[13] others have been accused of understating the place of orthodox thinking, thereby subsuming the message of the cross under a Marxist worldview, resembling their counterparts within liberation theology.[14] As a way forward, Pedro Dulci has recently argued for a methodological fine-tuning based on historic conceptions of the relation between nature and grace, in hopes of clarifying precisely how the two wings of Christian mission are to fly.[15] This revision has been termed "integral orthodoxy" (*ortodoxia integral*).[16]

As it shall become clear in what follows, in discussing the theological thrust of Matthew 25:31–46, one is struck by the same questions that have animated current missiological discussions within Brazilian evangelicalism. By bringing the idea of integral orthodoxy to bear in our interpretation of the passage,[17] I will argue that "these least of my brothers" and "the sheep" serve as paragons of total discipleship, entailing suffering and social action as visible expressions of faith in the teachings of Jesus. To that end, I will take the majority view as the most plausible exegetical explanation—namely, that both the ones inheriting the kingdom and those with whom the Son of Man identifies

12. See, for instance, Filipe Costas Fontes, "Missão Integral ou Neocalvinismo: Em Busca de Uma Visão Mais Ampla da Missão da Igreja," *FidRef* 19 (2014): 61–72. See also Guilherme Vilela Ribeiro de Carvalho, "A Missão Integral na Encruzilhada: Reconsiderando a Tensão no Pensamento Teológico de Lausanne," in *Fé Cristã e Cultura Contemporânea: Cosmovisão Cristã, Igreja Local e Transformação Integral*, ed. Leonardo Ramos, Marcel Camargo, and Rodolfo Amorim (Viçosa: Ultimato, 2009), 17–55.

13. According to Kirkpatrick ("C. René Padilla," 354), though Lausanne leader John Stott is often credited for the metaphor of the two wings, it actually goes back to Padilla.

14. The event that most notably triggered this controversy happened during the papal visit to Bolivia in 2015, when then president Evo Morales gave Pope Francis an image of Jesus hanging on the hammer and sickle, the symbol of Communism. A number of pastors in Brazil publicly praised the act as a representation of the Christian concern for the oppressed.

15. Pedro Lucas Dulci, *Ortodoxia Integral: Teoria e Prática Conectadas na Missão Cristã* (Uberlândia: Sal, 2015).

16. A similar approach has been advanced regarding theology and culture by James K. A. Smith in his *Introducing Radical Orthodoxy: Mapping a Post-Secular Theology* (Grand Rapids: Baker Academic, 2004).

17. Or, in good Gadamerian idiom, by "fusing the two horizons." See Hans-Georg Gadamer, *Truth and Method* (London: Continuum, 2011), 299–306.

represent authentic disciples—and contend that genuine empathy and concern for the outcast is what evinces true acceptance of God's unmerited favor. The burden of this chapter is to demonstrate that, while social action alone is not of ultimate soteriological consequence for Matthew, it is a nonnegotiable response from those who follow Jesus.

The Saved in the Parable as Models of Integral Orthodoxy

That the gathering of "all the nations" (Matt. 25:32) refers to the moment when the Son of Man will hold all humanity accountable—both Jews and gentiles—is indicated by Matthew's overall expectation that God will execute his universal judgment according to one's response to the authority of Jesus.[18] This theme is explicit in Matthew 5:17–20 and 7:21–23, which depict the Sermon on the Mount as determinative of true righteousness in contrast to the traditions of the Pharisees and the scribes,[19] and in the healing of a centurion's servant in Matthew 8:5–13, wherein faithful gentiles are said to be included "alongside Abraham, Isaac, and Jacob in the kingdom of heaven," as opposed to Jews who have rejected Jesus. Klyne Snodgrass is therefore correct to suggest that the other three instances in which "all the nations" occurs outside the parable likewise include both Jews and gentiles (Matt. 24:9–14; 28:18–19; cf. 4:8–9; 8:5–13; 16:27–28; 22:10–14).[20] Pride of place among these references belongs to the Great Commission, wherein the apostles of the resurrected Jesus are ordered to "make disciples of all the nations" (28:19), "until the consummation of the age" (28:20).

More significant is who "these least of my brothers" represent. Since it is apparent that this group belongs to the Son of Man, the simple fact that there is a distinction between them and "the sheep" forces us to discern their identities in relation to one another as well as to all humanity.[21] The motif of God's concern for the outcast has been invoked to support the reading of "these least of my brothers" as the poor in general. For instance, Proverbs 19:17 says that "showing favor to the helpless" is comparable to "lending to

---

18. This is a reinterpretation of Jewish tradition, which envisages the judgment of the nations apart from Israel (e.g., Joel 3:2; Zech. 14:2; Pss. Sol. 17; 4 Ezra 7). See Sherman W. Gray, *The Least of My Brothers: Matthew 25:31–46; A History of Interpretation*, SBLDS 114 (Atlanta: Scholars Press, 1989), 255–57. Compare Snodgrass, *Stories with Intent*, 554–55; Kathleen Weber, "The Image of Sheep and Goats in Matthew 25:31–46," *CBQ* 59 (1997): 59.

19. Jonathan T. Pennington, *The Sermon on the Mount and Human Flourishing: A Theological Commentary* (Grand Rapids: Baker Academic, 2017), 144; Scot McKnight, *Sermon on the Mount*, SGBC (Grand Rapids: Zondervan, 2013), 31.

20. Snodgrass, *Stories with Intent*, 554.

21. Michaels, "Apostolic Hardship," 27.

Yahweh."[22] But, while there is nothing in Matthew contradicting such a trope, three aggregate points suggest more eloquently that the phrase "these least of my brothers" is a reference to persecuted followers of Jesus, whose path was trodden by the apostles themselves.

First, when "brother" (*adelphos*) does not stand for a literal relative in Matthew, it usually refers to the primary audience's fellow Israelites (or members of the church; cf. Matt. 18), never human beings universally. The Sermon on the Mount, with its focus on the eschatological community of the Messiah, provides strong evidence for this (5:22–24, 47; 7:3–5).[23] Second, though the parable is the only place where "brother" occurs beside "least" (*elachistos*, 25:40), the Matthean Jesus consistently uses the expressions "my brothers" (12:48–50) and "one of these little ones" (*hena tōn mikrōn toutōn*, 10:40–42; 18:1–14) to describe early believers in his message (cf. Mark 9:37, 41; Luke 9:48; 10:16; John 13:20).[24] Significantly, some of these instances also bespeak the end-time consequences of welcoming the disciples—that is, people "should not despise them" (Matt. 18:10), because even giving them "a cup of cold water" will count in the end (10:42). Third, in the apocalyptic vision of Daniel 7, the Son of Man not only participates in the universal judgment of the nations (Dan. 7:9–10) but also vindicates the oppressed people of God (7:25). Given that Matthew 25:31–46 assumes the same picture, it is very probable that, as with the Son of Man—who identifies himself with the "saints of the Most High" in Daniel 7:27 (cf. 7:13–14)—the royal judge in the parable regards the suffering disciples as his own relatives.[25] Granted, parables do not always have precise historical counterparts; in this case, the role of "these least of my brothers" would be simply literary, so as to determine the criteria of judgment, not to provide "a basis for an exempt group."[26] Nevertheless, if the saying is to be intelligible, we must consider the possible connections between the specific entities within the passage and the larger

22. For references outside the Hebrew Bible, see Sigurd Grindheim, "Ignorance Is Bliss: Attitudinal Aspects of Judgement according to Works in Matthew 25:31–46," *NovT* 50 (2008): 315–19. For the practice of charity in early Judaism, see Pieter W. van der Horst, "Organized Charity in the Ancient World: Pagan, Jewish, Christian," in *Jewish and Christian Communal Identities in the Roman World*, ed. Yair Furstenberg, AJEC 94 (Boston: Brill, 2016), 120–23.

23. *Pace* Snodgrass, *Stories with Intent*, 556.

24. See Graham Foster, "Making Sense of Matthew 25:31–46," *SBET* 16 (1998): 128–39; Donahue, "'Parable' of the Sheep and the Goats," 3–28; J. M. Court, "Right and Left: The Implications for Matthew 25:31–46," *NTS* 31 (1985): 223–33; A. J. Mattill Jr., "Matthew 25:31–46 Relocated," *ResQ* 17 (1974): 107–14; Lamar Cope, "Matthew XXV:31–46: 'The Sheep and the Goats' Reinterpreted," *NovT* 11 (1969): 32–44; Michaels, "Apostolic Hardship," 27–37.

25. Compare with R. T. France, *Matthew: An Introduction and Commentary*, TNTC 1 (Downers Grove, IL: InterVarsity, 1985), 360–62.

26. Snodgrass, *Stories with Intent*, 558.

narrative world of Matthew.[27] And, once that is done, understanding "brothers" as disciples proves most compelling.[28]

As for "the sheep," what warrants their partaking in the kingdom is their visible actions toward the destitute in the parable, not their subscription to some abstract system of thought. Against the claims that the passage purports some way of acceptance into eternal life without allegiance to Jesus, however, it is important to bring to mind the prominent Matthean theme of the justice of the heavenly kingdom as something that, in the words of Jonathan Pennington, is actualized "by and through the grace that alone comes from Jesus's saving work" (cf. Matt. 5:3).[29] In short, Matthew never entertains the possibility of earning eschatological deliverance apart from the lordship of the messiah. The question that follows, then, concerns the scope of said benevolent acts, since, as concluded above, the phrase "these least of my brothers" is a cipher for suffering disciples. A number of commentators have concluded that the purpose of the parable is to anticipate the judgment of the nations strictly based on expressions of kindness to the emissaries of Jesus.[30] It is indeed puzzling that "the goats" are reproached not so much for a supposed lack of good works as for their failure to assist those with whom the Son of Man identifies. But this implies that "the sheep" inherit the kingdom simply by being kind to Christian missionaries. The problem with limiting the good deeds, as though significant only when done to the disciples, is that it finds absolutely no corroboration elsewhere in Matthew. Attentive readers of the Gospel would know that the followers of Jesus are called to transcend religious parochialism, seeking the well-being of all, including their own pagan enemies (cf. Matt. 5:43–48; see also Luke 10:25–37).

All things considered, both the identity of the sheep and their good works toward "these least of my brothers" are best interpreted in the context of the

27. As narrative critics have reminded us. See Stephen D. Moore, *Literary Criticism and the Gospels* (New Haven: Yale University Press, 1989).

28. In this regard, it is striking that the otherwise excellent treatment by Snodgrass (*Stories with Intent*, 556), while correctly pointing out that the use of "the little brothers of Jesus" in Matthew is varied, does not mention a single passage wherein the term refers to the poor in general.

29. Pennington, *Sermon on the Mount*, 159. For faith as allegiance, see Matthew W. Bates, *Salvation by Allegiance Alone: Rethinking Faith, Works, and the Gospel of Jesus the King* (Grand Rapids: Baker Academic, 2017).

30. E.g., Michaels, "Apostolic Hardship," 27–37; Donald A. Hagner, *Matthew 14–28*, WBC 33B (Nashville: Nelson, 1995), 744–47; Craig S. Keener, *The Gospel of Matthew: A Socio-Rhetorical Commentary* (Grand Rapids: Eerdmans, 1999), 605. Compare with David L. Turner, *Matthew*, BECNT (Grand Rapids: Baker Academic, 2008), 609. Indeed, in Did. 12.1, one finds a similar concern: "Let everyone coming in the name of the Lord be welcomed" (*pas de ho erchomenos en onomati kyriou dechthētō*; cf. Did. 11.2). See Court, "Right and Left," 231.

overarching leitmotif of discipleship in Matthew, which finds its closure in the very last pericope of the Gospel (Matt. 28:16–20).[31] The Great Commission, as John Donahue points out, provides a bridge between the ending of the historical career of Jesus and the ending of history itself. If the parable of the sheep and the goats is a portrait of the close of the age, the Great Commission is a mandate for church life prior to that close. The church is to be a community in mission that is to prepare for the coming of Jesus. The disciples are to baptize in the name of the Father, Son, and Holy Spirit and to teach the gospel of the kingdom as disclosed in the life and teaching of Jesus.[32]

In other words, Matthew 25:31–46 depicts the consummation of the age that 28:16–20 envisions: "the sheep" epitomize the people from "all the nations" who take heed of the risen Christ's imperative "to keep all things that I commanded" (28:20). Simply put, "the sheep" are called "the righteous ones" because their deeds attest that they are genuine disciples—they receive Jesus's teachings and keep his commandments. This interpretation coheres with the importance attributed to ethical responsibility in the final speeches uttered by Jesus in Jerusalem (cf. 24:1–25:30),[33] and the portrayal of "the sheep" in the parable neatly fits the overall Matthean characterization of people who live by the righteousness of the kingdom: not only are they generous and hospitable (cf. 5:38–42; 10:40–42),[34] but their lack of recognition of any merit before the Son of Man betrays the quality of self-forgetfulness (cf. 6:1–18).[35] By contrast, the fact that "the goats" are surprised at their own condemnation parallels those in the end of the Sermon on the Mount who call Jesus "Lord"—and even boast some impressive miraculous achievements—but in the end are said to have fallen short of doing "the will of the Father" (7:21–23).

So how does this address the current theological controversies in Brazil? In addition to being the most plausible way of understanding the passage against the backdrop of the Gospel of Matthew as a whole, taking both "these least of my brothers" and "the sheep" as examples of followers of Jesus also helps us to navigate biblically some of the discussions surrounding the mission of the church. The aforementioned approach known as "integral mission" has made some invaluable contributions in retrieving the central place of social action alongside the Christian duty to preach the good news to the world. This

---

31. See Michael J. Wilkins, *The Concept of Disciple in Matthew's Gospel as Reflected in the Use of the Term* Μαθητης, NovTSup 59 (Leiden: Brill, 1988), 222.

32. Donahue, "'Parable' of the Sheep and the Goats," 13–14.

33. For details, see discussion in Via, "Ethical Responsibility," 90. See also Davies and Allison, *Matthew*, 432–33.

34. See Joshua W. Jipp, *Saved by Faith and Hospitality* (Grand Rapids: Eerdmans, 2017), 6.

35. Compare with Grindheim, "Ignorance Is Bliss," 319–24.

is consistent with our exegesis of Matthew 25:31–46 and provides a potent instantiation of the holistic character of the mission of the church. But, as explained in the previous section of this essay, a major point of contention has been the proper relation between evangelism and social action. If the two are inseparable, what is the conceptual framework that should bind them together? One realizes the urgency of this question from the simple fact that, as some socially conscious Brazilian evangelicals have recently abandoned the importance of gospel proclamation, a few leaders who are more doctrinally minded, reacting against what they regard as a mild form of apostasy, have fallen once more into the pitfall of overemphasizing preaching over works.

Precisely on this stroke, bringing together Matthew 25:31–46 and integral orthodoxy has the potential to move the conversation forward. Borrowing especially from thinkers of Dutch and Swiss Reformed traditions—not least, Abraham Kuyper, Herman Dooyeweerd, Herman Ridderbos, and André Biéler—and recognizing the real advancements that the best proponents of integral mission have promoted in Brazil, Dulci suggests that a more principled way of understanding evangelism and social action as one single enterprise is found in the relation between nature and grace.[36] Debates over this issue are ancient, cross-denominational, and at times convoluted, but Dulci's survey can be summarized in quite simple terms: he insists that Christ is Lord over the entire cosmos (grace), and hence the witness of the church must engender transformation in all aspects of human society (nature).[37] He contends that "to say that socio-cultural transformation is not part of God's mission in the world through his Church implies a dire disregard for the scope of his kingdom over creation," and so genuine orthodoxy must be integral and point to the renewal of the whole of our societies.[38] Here, of course, Dulci is in continuity both with some of the ideals of the early Reformers and with the main tenets of the Lausanne movement and integral mission.[39] What is particularly

36. See Dulci, *Ortodoxia*, 119–72. Dulci engages extensively with some (unpublished) ideas of Lutheran missiologist Valdir Steuernagel. Furthermore, it is important to clarify that the concepts of integral mission and integral orthodoxy encompass every aspect of human existence, not only evangelism and social action—e.g., the arts, the sciences, the marketplace, and creation care. See Christopher J. H. Wright, *The Great Story and the Great Commission: Participating in the Biblical Drama of Mission* (Grand Rapids: Baker Academic, 2023), 60–74.

37. Dulci, *Ortodoxia*, 140. See also Abraham Kuyper, *Lectures on Calvinism* (Grand Rapids: Eerdmans, 1943).

38. Dulci, *Ortodoxia*, 188.

39. Previous attempts at bringing the Reformed tradition to bear in current conversations in the majority world have been done by Sri Lankan missiologist Vinoth Ramachandra, who suggests that John Calvin, with his emphasis on the concrete implications of the gospel, may be considered to some degree the first liberation theologian (Ramachandra, "Reformed Amnesia?," *Vinoth Ramachandra* [blog], March 28, 2013, https://vinothramachandra.wordpress.com/2013/03/28

helpful about Dulci's approach is the specific way he frames the holistic nature of Christian witness. He states, "*The relation between preaching and
social action is not one of partnership, complementarity, or miscellaneous
priorities.* Rather, it is *an imperatival relation, namely, the responsibility for
social transformation as an imperative of the gospel proclamation.* . . . We
need to go beyond the simple realization that the proclamation of the gospel
and the struggle for social justice are related. It needs to be explained how
this connection takes place."[40] In brief, social action is the imperative—the
command—that results from the indicative—the reality—of the lordship of
the risen Christ. Believing and announcing the latter culminates in living out
the former.

It remains to be seen whether Dulci's proposal will remedy the old "evangelism versus social action" dichotomy in Brazil, and this is not the place to offer
a detailed critique of his work as a whole. But, in any case, imagining the
Christian mission in terms of the gospel's indicative and imperative is useful,
given that this is how Matthew also understands the dynamics of discipleship.[41]

In the Sermon on the Mount, for example, all the commandments constituting the messianic law (cf. Matt. 5:21–48) are predicated on the more fundamental reality of the identity of the disciples. In Matthew 5:3–12, Jesus
describes his followers in terms of kingdom makarisms—namely, poverty in
spirit, mourning, meekness, hunger and thirst for justice, mercy, purity of heart,
peacemaking, and persecution—and, in 5:13–16, he affirms that their raison
d'être is to reflect God's character in the world. And these claims are further
justified in 5:17–20 by the authority of Jesus vis-à-vis torah.[42] The disciples are
to obey the imperatives of the kingdom, because this is what it looks like to be
rooted in its indicative: flourishing in the likeness of the one who came to fulfill
the law and the prophets.[43] To quote from the Matthean Jesus himself, to be a
disciple is to be "complete—integral [*teleioi*]—as the heavenly Father" (5:48).

/reformed-amnesia/). See also Samuel Escobar, "A Evangelização e a Busca de Liberdade, de
Justiça e de Realização pelo Homem," in *A Missão da Igreja no Mundo de Hoje: As Principais
Palestras do Congresso Internacional de Evangelização Mundial Realizado em Lausanne, Suíça*,
ed. Billy Graham et al. (São Paulo: ABU, 1982), 173–94. The best recent treatment on this topic
from the anglophone world is found in Wright, *Great Story*, 1–73.

40. Dulci, *Ortodoxia*, 209–10 (emphasis original).

41. See Dale C. Allison Jr., *The Sermon on the Mount: Inspiring the Moral Imagination*
(New York: Herder & Herder, 1999), 29–30.

42. On Matthew's portrayal of the relationship between Jesus and torah in the Sermon on
the Mount, see Bernardo Cho, "To Keep Everything Jesus Commanded: Teaching as Modeling
Obedience in the Gospel of Matthew," in *It's about Life: The Formative Power of Scripture;
Essays in Honour of Rikk E. Watts on the Occasion of His Seventieth Birthday*, ed. Bernard
Bell et al. (Vancouver, BC: Regent College Publishing, 2023), 34–41.

43. See Pennington, *Sermon on the Mount*, 41–68.

So, Matthew is adamant that the righteousness of the kingdom involves an orthodoxy that is irreducibly integral—so integral that even the motivation for our actions counts (cf. Matt. 6:1–18). By using the anachronistic word "orthodoxy" with reference to the Gospel of Matthew, of course, we are simply translating the evangelist's central concern that discipleship means faithfulness to the teachings of Jesus. On the one hand, service to the poor is not a substitute for accurate belief in what Jesus says, since he never intended "to destroy the law and the prophets" (5:17). On the other hand, a correct understanding of "the law and the prophets"divorced from concrete acts of mercy is not correct at all. Evangelism and social action belong together, and their relation is regulated by the fact that the latter demonstrates the truthfulness of the former. For Matthew, obedience to the imperatives of the gospel is what proves prior acceptance of its indicative. Or, according to another biblical author, "just as the body without spirit is dead, so also the faith without works is dead" (James 2:26). Though body and spirit are equally essential to human existence, one animates the other.[44]

Indeed, as Christopher Wright has recently demonstrated, such an emphasis on the integral character of God's people's vocation—which encompasses correct worship *and* obedience to divine justice—is found not only in Matthew but also across the whole biblical story.[45] "The Bible," Wright states, "is a declaration of the single overall mission of God—to rid his whole creation of evil and create for himself a people redeemed from every tribe and nation of humanity as the population of the new creation."[46] So the injunction in the Great Commission for the disciples "to teach" others "to keep" what Christ ordained (Matt. 28:20) not only takes us back to the Sermon on the Mount's integral orthodoxy but also represents the actual pinnacle of what God always intended for his people: "God wanted his people Israel to be *like God* by showing compassion and seeking justice for the poor and needy, for the homeless, the family-less, the landless. . . . So then, in the same way and in the same tone of voice, Jesus is effectively saying to his disciples, 'Your mission is to make disciples and to teach them to obey what I have commanded you, which, as you know, is deeply rooted in all that God commanded his people in our Scriptures, reflecting my Father's own character as the God of compassion and justice.'"[47]

---

44. Craig L. Blomberg and Mariam J. Kamell, *James*, ZECNT (Grand Rapids: Zondervan, 2008), 141.

45. Wright, *Great Story*, 1–37. See also Christopher J. H. Wright, *The Mission of God: Unlocking the Bible's Grand Narrative* (Downers Grove, IL: IVP Academic, 2006); and Bernardo Cho, *The Plot of Salvation: Divine Presence, Human Vocation, and Cosmic Redemption* (Carlisle, UK: Langham , 2022).

46. Wright, *Great Story*, xii.

47. Wright, *Great Story*, 95 (emphasis original). See also Cho, "To Keep Everything Jesus Commanded," 42–45.

Consequently, "the sheep" represent true disciples who learned to be integrally orthodox through the fulfillment of the Great Commission, and they remind us that the mission of the church is accomplished by people transformed by the compassion of God himself, as fully demonstrated in the ministry of Jesus. The outcome is that "the nations" (Matt. 28:19) are also taught to be compassionate (cf. 18:21–35). Hence, "the sheep" are called "the righteous ones" because they do not contemplate the preposterous separation between faith and works: "the sheep" inherit the eternal kingdom as integrally orthodox, total disciples of Jesus.

And a similar point should be made regarding "these least of my brothers." They too are models of integral orthodoxy. But the key contrast with "the sheep" is found in their circumstances. Whereas "the sheep" are in the position to serve and welcome the outcast, "these least of my brothers" *have become* the outcast as a result of the righteousness of the kingdom.[48] This indicates that, if hunger and thirst for justice and mercy are transparently evident in the former (cf. Matt. 5:6–7), it is the makarism of being persecuted for the sake of Christ that stands out in the latter at the moment of the Son of Man's final enthronement (cf. 5:10–12). From this perspective, the revelation of "the sheep" unwittingly serving the end-time royal judge as they assisted "these least of my brothers" envisages something even more profound than the undeniable importance of Christians caring for fellow persecuted believers.[49] The reality to which this points is that the true followers of Jesus are so deeply shaped by his self-giving way of life (cf. 16:21–28) that they either strive to alleviate the suffering of the marginalized or find themselves among the many others who are despised by the powers of this passing age (cf. James 2:6–7).[50] "The sheep" encounter the Son of Man in "these least of my brothers" because both groups are walking on the cruciform road of total discipleship, where the risen Christ himself is present "until the consummation of the age" (Matt. 28:20).

A Summons to Total Discipleship

We may conclude that Matthew 25:31–46 not only provides comfort for suffering disciples but also forcefully challenges other Christian readers to take a stance toward the most vulnerable.[51] The immediate implication is twofold:

48. See Michaels, "Apostolic Hardship," 37; compare with Keener, *Matthew*, 606.
49. Donahue, "'Parable' of the Sheep and the Goats," 25.
50. Compare with Alicia Vargas, "Who Ministers to Whom: Matthew 25:31–46 and Prison Ministry," *Dialog* 52 (2013): 128–37.
51. Compare Michaels, "Apostolic Hardship," 36–37; Donahue, "'Parable' of the Sheep and the Goats," 30–31. Again, to say that Matt. 25:31–46 encourages the reader to assist persecuted disciples is obviously not to claim that acts of mercy should be restricted to Christian

the tendency to diminish the importance of biblical teaching remains untenable, and the view that the Great Commission is merely about imparting doctrinal truths must be deemed reductionistic.

For obvious reasons, Bible-centered Protestants, who presumably form the main readership of this essay, may find the latter statement a bit disturbing.[52] Yet, when read from the standpoint outlined above, the parable forces us to ask how we could teach someone "to keep all things" that Jesus commanded (Matt. 28:20) if our orthodoxy is not integral. As the classic work by Rodney Stark and the more recent study by Pieter van der Horst have demonstrated, one of the features that most clearly differentiated Christians from pagans in antiquity was their significant expanding of the practice of organized charity, originally inherited from Judaism.[53] The fourth-century emperor Julian famously complained to the pagan high priest Arsacius, "When no Jew ever has to beg [*metaitei*] and the impious Galileans [Christians] support not only their own poor, but ours as well, everyone can see that our people lack aid from us" (*Ep.* 22.430C–D).[54] This gives testimony to the early understanding of the Christian identity in terms of total discipleship—or integral orthodoxy, with indicative ending in imperative, belief leading to obedience, evangelism producing social action.

Furthermore, if our reading of Matthew 25:31–46 has any cogency, then the passage is also about the place where the church is called to locate itself within the power structures of society. Political grandeur is not what characterizes "these least of my brothers," and it is irrelevant in the Son of Man's estimation whether or not some of "the sheep" belonged to the elite. This is not to say that the mission of the church is restricted to the lowly. Rather, at the final manifestation of the eschatological royal judge, the true disciples will be found imitating their crucified King, regardless of their social status. By doing so they will assume a critical stance toward injustice, bringing on themselves opposition from those who claim to rule the world. If the New Testament portrayal of the challenges faced by the earliest Jesus movement

---

missionaries. It is simply to affirm a key concern of this particular passage. As Wright puts it, "Christian works of compassion or social righteousness" must be "*modeled*" within the church but never "*confined* to believers in the church" (*Great Story*, 104, emphasis original).

52. Dulci himself (*Ortodoxia*, 184–86) gives some examples of the prevalence of such a notion among mainstream evangelical churches in the West. Compare with Kevin DeYoung and Greg Gilbert, *What Is the Mission of the Church? Making Sense of Social Justice, Shalom, and the Great Commission* (Wheaton: Crossway, 2011).

53. Rodney Stark, *The Rise of Christianity: How the Obscure, Marginal Jesus Movement Became the Dominant Religious Force in the Western World in a Few Centuries* (San Francisco: Harper, 1997), 73–94; van der Horst, "Organized Charity," 127–28, 145–46.

54. Translation from van der Horst, "Organized Charity," 116 (notes and emphasis original). See also Stark, *Rise of Christianity*, 84.

is credible (cf. Acts, 2 Corinthians, Revelation), then we may infer that the suffering of "these least of my brothers" is a direct consequence of their insistence that Jesus Christ alone is Lord.

This makes us ponder how integrally orthodox our engagement in politics has been. In recent decades, the evangelical movement in Brazil has been known much more for its lust for political influence than for its real interest in the well-being of all.[55] As with some of our brethren in North America, Christians on the left have tolerated all sorts of atrocities in the name of taking the place of the rich, and right-wing Christians have effusively applauded politicians who, despite citing biblical verses in their public speeches, have a long record of authoritarianism. As a result of this polarization, the same people who profess the lordship of Christ over the cosmos have divided the church on the basis of ideological preferences, and orthodoxy has been defined in terms of whom one votes for. And worse yet, all of this is to secure primacy in the public sphere. It is unsurprising that missiological conversations in Brazil have foundered on these problems. When one sees this state of affairs through the lens of Matthew 25:31–46, it is difficult not to notice the deep gulf separating this mindset from the character of the Matthean Jesus himself, who in utter dependence on the Father refuses to worship the devil in exchange for hegemony (cf. Matt. 4:1–11).

In this regard, those referred to as "the sheep" and "these least of my brothers" have something important to teach followers of Jesus in the twenty-first century. If Brazilian Christians—or Christians in general—are really to participate in the Great Commission, we must never forget that, at the end of the day, the only "left" and "right" distinction that matters is the one that sets apart the total disciples of the crucified and risen Christ from the rest of humanity.

55. See Paul Freston, *Evangelicals and Politics in Africa, Asia and Latin America* (Cambridge: Cambridge University Press, 2001), 9–58; and Andrea Dip, *Em Nome de Quem? A Bancada Evangélica e Seu Projeto de Poder* (Rio de Janeiro: Civilização Brasileira, 2018), who is significantly more critical of evangelicals.

2

Seeing the Divine Beauty on the Way to the Cross

Reading the Transfiguration in Mark from a Russian Perspective

VIKTOR ROUDKOVSKI

> Beauty will save the world.
>
> —F. M. Dostoyevsky, *The Idiot*

Mark's emphasis on discipleship as following Jesus on the way to the cross has long been recognized as an integral part of Mark's literary and theological strategy.[1] Mark's Gospel is a call to a cruciform loyalty to Jesus: "If anyone wants to follow me, let him deny himself and take up his cross and let him follow me" (Mark 8:34).[2] This strategy becomes particularly pronounced when one considers the situation of the Markan audience, that of persecution and the events surrounding the Jewish-Roman war of AD 66–70. Numerous

---

Please note that this chapter was written before the Russian invasion of Ukraine, and its claims are even more pertinent in the context of the war.

1. See Ernest Best, *Following Jesus: Discipleship in the Gospel of Mark*, ed. Ernst Bammel, JSNTSup 4 (Sheffield: JSOT, 1981).

2. All translations of the biblical text are the author's own.

studies address the date, location of the audience, and purpose of the Gospel of Mark—and most of them in some way or fashion engage with the question of persecution and the events of the Jewish-Roman war as the situation of Mark's audience.[3] The transfiguration narrative plays an important function in Mark's discipleship section (8:22–10:52). As Mark presents Jesus and his followers on the "way" to Jerusalem, the cruciform nature of following Jesus is a predominant theme. While the disciples have difficulty understanding the notion of the crucified Messiah, in the transfiguration event they "see" the future crucified Messiah as a glorified divine Jesus. In the context of the persecution of Mark's audience, the theme of following Jesus on the way to the cross constitutes a significant part of Mark's pastoral strategy. Furthermore, in the context of the Jewish-Roman war, the question of how Christians should respond and with whom they should align would be of paramount importance. I contend that Mark's message to his audience in the aftermath of the Neronian persecution and during the Jewish-Roman war can have a powerful resonance with and impact on many faithful Christians of various traditions in the Russian context and that the transfiguration narrative, given the passage's influence on the Orthodox faith, serves as an important vehicle of Mark's call to faithful discipleship.[4]

The Memory of the Soviet Past and New Russia

Winston Churchill once famously said that Russia is "a riddle, wrapped in mystery, inside an enigma."[5] While the context of this statement had to do with the imminent events of World War II, his statement can be applied to a long and complex history of Russia.[6] One of the characteristics of Russia is its enormous landmass, and part of Russian history is filling that land with people of diverse ethnic backgrounds. In the nineteenth century, the Russian

3. See H. N. Roskam, *The Purpose of the Gospel of Mark in Its Historical and Social Context*, ed. M. Mitchel and D. Moessner, NovTSup 114 (Leiden: Brill, 2004), 27–74; David Rhoads, "Social Criticism: Crossing Boundaries," in *Mark and Method: New Approaches in Biblical Studies*, ed. Janice Anderson and Stephen Moore (Minneapolis: Fortress, 1992), 135–59.

4. It is also worth noting that while in the West the Feast of Transfiguration is a festival of secondary rank, in the East it is one of the most beloved and popular of the Twelve Great Feasts of the Church (see Timothy [Kallistos] Ware, *The Orthodox Church*, new ed. [London: Penguin Books, 1997], 298–99). Moreover, in the event of the transfiguration, the entire convergence of the "logic" of Eastern Christian theology, devotion, worship, mysticism, and iconography takes place. See Solrunn Nes, *The Uncreated Light: An Iconographical Study of the Transfiguration in the Eastern Church* (Grand Rapids: Eerdmans, 2007).

5. Transcript of BBC broadcast, London, October 1, 1939, https://www.bbc.com/history ofthebbc/anniversaries/october/winston-churchills-first-wartime-broadcast.

6. While certain elements of this paper can also be appropriated in many republics of the former Soviet Union, the focus of this essay is on the Russian Federation.

poet Fyodor Tyutchev wrote, "Who would grasp Russia with the mind? For her no yardstick was created; Her soul is of a special kind, by faith alone appreciated."[7]

Whether one characterizes Russia as a mystery or as something that cannot be comprehended, Orthodox faith is one feature that can help in understanding Russia. Ever since Prince Vladimir baptized Russia into Orthodoxy in AD 988, the Russian Orthodox Church not only has exercised enormous influence in the Russian land but also, since the fall of Constantinople to Islam in 1453, has seen itself as a protector of Christian faith in the world, and Moscow as the "third Rome."[8] Obviously, the events of the Communist revolution in 1917 and the subsequent program of militant atheism impacted Christian faith in Russia a great deal.

Soviet Communism was committed by its fundamental principles to an aggressive and militant atheism. The situation that Christians in the Soviet Union found themselves in has no exact precedent in earlier history. Although the Roman Empire persecuted Christians, it was not an atheist state. The Ottoman Turks gave the church a certain measure of toleration. But under the Soviets, many Christians died. Many churches were destroyed. Many priests and clergy members were imprisoned or executed. Monasteries, seminaries, theological academies, parochial schools, homes for the aged, and hospitals, with a few exceptions, were ordered to close.[9] In schools, the Soviet teacher "must be guided by the principle of the Party spirit of science; he is obliged not only to be an unbeliever himself, but also to be an active propagandist of godlessness among others, to be the bearer of the ideas of militant proletarian atheism."[10] In addition to the program of militant atheism, World War II left much devastation and loss of life, which had an impact on Christian faith as well.

As the land of Russia has emerged from the collapse of Communism, it now faces new challenges and new realities. Orthodoxy has returned to prominence. Churches are being rebuilt. Many Russians have a renewed interest in Christian faith. At the same time, the events of the "terrible nineties"—namely, the corruption and weak economy—left a negative impact on Russia and continue to do so. In the aftermath of the collapse of Communism, the

---

7. Fyodor Tyutchev, *Selected Poems*, trans. John Dewey (Gillingham, UK: Brimstone, 2014), 113.

8. See Ware, *Orthodox Church*, 102–4.

9. See Ware, *Orthodox Church*, 161–63. For the history of the life and persecution of Protestant Christians during the Soviet period, see Tatyana K. Nikolskaya, *Russian Protestantism and State from 1905 to 1991* (St. Petersburg: European University Press, 2001).

10. F. N. Oleschuk, in *Uchitelskaya Gazeta* [*The teacher's newspaper*], November 26, 1949, as quoted in Ware, *Orthodox Church*, 147. Oleschuk was a secretary of the League of Militant Atheists.

constant geopolitical struggle with the West, the enormous influence of the Orthodox religious system, and the memories of struggles during Communism have left many faithful followers of Christ in a delicate situation of facing choices about loyalties.

Protestant Christians in particular have found themselves in a very complex situation. The well-known 1997 Law on Freedom of Conscience and Religious Associations, designed to curtail the full equality granted to all religious groups by the 1990 Law on Religious Freedom, acknowledges, in its preamble, "Christianity, Islam, Buddhism, Judaism, and other religions as constituting an inseparable part of the country's heritage." Earlier, the preamble recognizes "the special contribution" of Orthodoxy to the country's history and to the establishment and development of its spirituality and culture.[11] Obviously, the historical and cultural dominance of Orthodoxy puts Protestant Christians in a disadvantageous situation.[12] The recent 2016 Yarovaya Law, which has anti-evangelism and anti-missionary provisions, was clearly designed to target non-Orthodox groups and prompted outcry of concern and opposition from Russia's Protestant minority.[13] Claiming their historical heritage from the West, the Protestant Christians often struggle in the culture that gives Orthodoxy a special status. Furthermore, a geopolitical struggle with the West puts Protestant Christians in a delicate situation. Should they be loyal to the West, where their religious heritage comes from? Or should they follow the state? Or should they align themselves with the dominant Christian expression of Russian Orthodoxy? For Protestant Christians especially, Mark's call to the cruciform loyalty to Jesus is of special significance. Several options for loyalty exist: (1) to the West, with all its promises of progress and bright and just society; (2) to the Russian state, with its promise of protection, independent sovereignty, and strength; (3) to alignment with the seemingly cultural Christianity of Orthodoxy; or (4) to Jesus, the crucified and risen Lord. How does Mark—and specifically the transfiguration narrative—help Russian believers as they navigate this maze of competing loyalties? Before

---

11. "Federal Law No. 125-F of September 26, 1997, on the Freedom of Conscience and Religious Associations," Legislation Online, Office for Democratic Institutions and Human Rights, accessed September 7, 2021, https://web.archive.org/web/20210708031115/https://www.legisla tionline.org/download/id/4379/file/RF_Freedom_of_Conscience_Law_1997_am2008_en.pdf.

12. See Wallace L. Daniel and Christopher Marsh, "Editorial: Russia's 1997 Law on Freedom of Conscience in Context and Retrospect," *JChS* 49, no. 1 (2007): 5–17.

13. See Sarah Zylstra, "Russia's Ban on Evangelism Is Now in Effect," *Christianity Today*, July 21, 2016, https://www.christianitytoday.com/news/2016/july/russia-ban-evangelism-effect .html. The law is named after Irina Yarovaya, a Deputy Chairman of the State Duma. The law is presented to combat terrorism. The legislation requires religious groups and missionaries to obtain government permission to operate and restricts missionary activity of nonregistered churches, which mostly includes evangelicals and religious minorities.

delving into the text of the narrative, a few words are in order about Mark's context of persecution and war.

Mark's Audience: Persecution and War

Although for a long time the identity of Mark's audience has been debated, the prevailing view has held that the evangelist addressed his Gospel to the community to which he belonged, most probably in Rome.[14] If so, then the events of the persecution and Jewish-Roman war would fit well with Mark's emphasis on cruciform discipleship (Mark 8–10) and Jesus's critique of the doomed temple establishment (11:11–25), including the temple's demise (13:1–2).

David Rhoads presents a very plausible scenario relative to the question of Mark's Gospel and the Jewish-Roman war of AD 66–70.[15] In AD 66, the Jews expelled the Roman troops from Israel and rallied for independence. Diverse groups from all over Israel joined the war movement: lower-class groups resisting economic oppression, sectarian groups fighting for the first commandment prohibition against any lord but God, and high-priestly groups seeking better terms in the Roman relationship. Of course, in the end, the Romans defeated all these efforts, destroyed Jerusalem, and razed the temple in AD 70. In Rhoads's estimation, Mark wrote his story during or after the war, about the Messiah who had come in person and who spoke about the events preceding the war, the Jewish leaders' downfall, and the temple's demise.[16] I would add that for Christians living in Rome in the aftermath of the Neronian persecution, the Jewish-Roman war would present uncertainties about their future and their very existence. Should they align themselves with Rome against their Savior's people? Perhaps this would win some type of favor with the Romans and spare many of their

14. Galilee and Syria have also been proposed. For examination of questions related to the location of Mark's audience, see Dwight H. Peterson, *The Origins of Mark: The Markan Community in Current Debate*, BibInt 48 (Leiden: Brill, 2000). Richard Bauckham and others have challenged this consensus. Bauckham and his coauthors argue that the Gospels were written not for a specific church or group of churches but rather for an unspecified Christian audience and could be read in any and every Christian community in the late first-century Roman Empire. See Richard Bauckham, "For Whom Were the Gospels Written?," in *The Gospels for All Christians: Rethinking the Gospel Audiences*, ed. Richard Bauckham (Grand Rapids: Eerdmans, 1998), 9–48. For a critique of Bauckham's views, see Roskam, *Purpose of the Gospel of Mark*, 17–22. For a mediating position that the Gospels were written for a specific audience but with an eye toward a wider readership, see Ben Witherington III, *The Gospel of Mark: A Socio-Rhetorical Commentary* (Grand Rapids: Eerdmans, 2001), 29–30.

15. See Rhoads, "Social Criticism," 138.

16. Rhoads, "Social Criticism," 138.

lives. Should they join the war movement against Rome in defense of the temple, as many Jews had done for varying reasons? Maybe this would bring Mark's Christians a certain degree of honor from the Jewish communities worldwide. Or maybe it was too late, the temple would be destroyed, and Mark's Christians needed to be loyal to Israel no matter what, even in the aftermath of the destruction. The suffering of Mark's Christians under Nero and now the choices of alignment with either Rome or Israel/temple may explain Mark's focus on cross-bearing discipleship and the strong critique of the temple's religious establishment (including its demise), respectively. The temple would be destroyed as Jesus predicted (Mark 13:1–2), and loyalty to Jesus (as a new temple) is what was necessary.[17] In the Russian context, for Christians tempted by power and prestige that may come from the West or by a cultural Orthodoxy, the message of Mark, and the transfiguration in particular, is very appropriate: "Listen to him" (9:7).

Transfiguration in Mark's Literary Context: The Suffering One as a Transfigured One

The transfiguration passage comes at a strategic point in Mark's narrative. In the larger context of Mark's story, the passage forms a bridge between Jesus's public ministry in Galilee and his passion in Jerusalem. The first eight chapters of Mark present the powerful Jesus who triumphs over demonic forces, over illness, over the critics of religious establishment, and over nature itself. Even demonic powers recognize Jesus's sonship and are overcome (Mark 1:1; 5:1–12). The turning point in the narrative is the announcement of the passion in 8:31–32, which creates a crisis of the powerful Messiah becoming a defeated, crucified Messiah. Before Mark narrates the events of Jesus's Jerusalem ministry and his passion in Mark 11–16, the central section of the Gospel that presents Jesus and the disciples "on the way" (8:22–10:52) to Jerusalem develops the notion that the powerful Messiah of Mark 1–8 is a suffering Messiah, and not only do those who follow him need to understand that messianic identity and suffering are inseparable, but they too should follow in Jesus's footsteps.

The material in this section is presented in a widely recognized deliberate structural pattern: three passion predictions (Mark 8:31; 9:31; 10:32), followed

17. See Donald Juel, *Messiah and Temple: The Trial of Jesus in the Gospel of Mark*, SBLDS 31 (Missoula, MT: Scholars Press, 1977); P. W. Walker, *Jesus and the Holy City: New Testament Perspectives on Jerusalem* (Grand Rapids: Eerdmans, 1996); Emilio Chávez, *The Theological Significance of Jesus' Temple Action in Mark's Gospel*, TST 87 (Lewiston, NY: Mellen, 2002); Timothy Gray, *The Temple in the Gospel of Mark: A Study in Its Narrative Role*, WUNT 242 (Tübingen: Mohr Siebeck, 2008).

by three failures of the disciples to understand the importance of messianic identity as a suffering one and their destiny as participants in that suffering (8:32–33; 9:32; 10:35–41), followed in turn by three didactic sections in which Jesus instructs the disciples on the cruciform shape of discipleship (8:34–38; 9:35–37; 10:42–45).[18] The spiritual blindness of the disciples, highlighted by the bracketing of the central section with two accounts of healing the blind (8:22–26 and 10:46–52), is a dominant motif. In the transfiguration narrative, these "spiritually blind" disciples see and experience the glory of the transfigured Jesus.

The Disciples' Experience

The text of the transfiguration story has many rich theological elements that converge and contribute to its overall meaning and interpretation. The significance of the phrase "after six days"; the location of the event on "the mountain"; the choice of Peter, James, and John for the ascent; the appearance of figures from the past, Elijah and Moses (Mark's order); the symbolism of white raiment; the significance of the heavenly voice; and Peter's reaction are only several elements that contribute to the theological richness of the passage. What stands out in Mark's account is how much Mark wants to focus on the disciples. The disciples, in the words of the author of 2 Peter, become "partakers of the divine nature" (2 Pet. 1:4). Mark (followed by Matthew), but not Luke, has a statement that perhaps gives us a clue that the passage is an integral part of Mark's discipleship theme: "He was transfigured before them" (Mark 9:2; Matt. 17:2).[19] Then, one observes that the focus of the event is on the disciples, with third-person and first-person plural personal pronouns: "He took them on the high mountain" (Mark 9:2); Elijah and Moses were seen "by them" (9:4); Peter's reply, "It is good for us to be here" (9:5); "Let us make three tabernacles" (9:5); "They were afraid" (9:6); "A cloud overshadowed them" (9:7); and "They looked around and they saw no one" (9:8). The disciples are not mere spectators but participants in the event. While the nature of exactly what they participated in and witnessed is a great mystery, Orthodox theology provides instructive clues that resonate with Christians in the Russian context.

---

18. While christological themes that pertain to Jesus's identity are of paramount significance in Mark's central section, the theme of discipleship is not far behind. Best's insight is instructive: "The nature of discipleship emerges out of an understanding, not of the teachings of Jesus (though Mark instructs), but of Christ and what he did." See Best, *Following Jesus*, 15–16.

19. Luke does not have "before them," although the disciples play a significant role as well. See Luke 9:28–36.

Seeing the Divine Jesus: The Beauty of the Liturgical Experience

Many Western commentaries on the transfiguration passage rightly focus on Jesus's divine status and the disciples' experience of seeing the divine Jesus before the events of the final week as central to the meaning of the event. Eastern Orthodox theology, and liturgical texts dedicated to this event, hermeneutically go even further to focus on the disciples' experience of seeing the splendor of God's glory, otherwise known as *theoria*. Orthodox theology teaches that on Mount Tabor, the divine glory shone through Christ's humanity. His humanity, without ceasing to be humanity, was transformed by and suffused with divine glory. Christ's humanity was deified.[20]

According to the teaching of Orthodox Christianity, the purpose and goal of human existence is to attain *theosis*, or "deification," understood as "likeness to" or "union with" God. This *metamorphosis* (see Mark 9:2) results from a deep love of God, pure life, and contemplation. According to Orthodox teachings, the Christian life involves the following: (1) *katharsis* (purification); (2) *theoria* (illumination); and (3) *theosis* (deification).[21] *Theoria,* then, refers to illumination, where one becomes aware of God and that all that is and is not has ontology in God. Both *katharsis* and *theoria* are an integral part of the *theosis* process.[22] The disciples experienced *theoria,* and this passage with its parallels (Matt. 17:1–13; Luke 9:28–36) has been foundational not only in the formation of *hesychast* ascetic practices[23] but also with calling Christians to the right (*orthos*) liturgy (*doxa*). Orthodox faith is a liturgical faith that focuses on the experience of seeing and contemplating the beauty of the divine. The disciples experienced the beauty of Jesus's "dazzling white" garments, "whiter than anyone could bleach them" (Mark 9:3), which is a reference to something unnatural and transcendent.[24] For Russian Christians, this would evoke not only the divine status of Jesus

---

20. See James Payton, *Light from the Christian East: An Introduction to the Orthodox Tradition* (Downers Grove, IL: InterVarsity, 2007), 137–52.

21. See Paul Evdokimov, *Orthodoxy* (Hyde Park, NY: New City, 2011), 100–105; Vladimir Lossky, *The Vision of God* (Crestwood, NY: St. Vladimir's Seminary Press, 1963); Stanley Harakas, "Eastern Orthodox Christianity's Ultimate Reality and Meaning: Triune God and Theosis—an Ethician's View," *URM* 8, no. 3 (1985): 212–15.

22. While *theosis* is a goal, humans partake in *theosis* in this life, as well as experiencing *katharsis* and *theoria.*

23. The disciples' experience of "Taboric" or "uncreated" light became the central feature of the Hesychast controversy. Barlaam, representing the Western scholastic tradition, and Gregory of Palamas were two key figures involved in the controversy. See Ware, *Orthodox Church*, 61–72.

24. For interpretive options as to the significance of Jesus's clothing and appearance at the transfiguration, see Craig Evans, *Mark 8:27–16:20*, WBC 34B (Nashville: Nelson, 2001), 37–38; Dorothy Lee, "On the Holy Mountain: The Transfiguration in Scripture and Theology," *Colloq* 36, no. 2 (2004): 143–59.

but also the beauty of the liturgical experience. Transfiguration was the disciples' experience of heaven on earth.

When Prince Vladimir wanted to embrace one religion for the Russian land, he sent emissaries to different parts of the world to discover and bring the right faith for the land. Only after visiting Constantinople's great church of the Holy Wisdom (*Hagia Sophia*) did the emissaries discover what they desired. Albeit legendary, for many Russians the emissaries' report constitutes an important moment in the origins of Orthodoxy in the land: "We knew not whether we were in heaven or on earth, for surely there is no such splendour or beauty anywhere upon earth. We cannot describe it to you, only this we know, that God dwells there among humans, and that their service surpasses the worship of all places. For we cannot forget that beauty."[25]

The disciples' experience of divine beauty at the transfiguration would be foundational in the theological understanding that Orthodox liturgy functions as a "field of vision wherein all things on earth are seen in their relation to things in heaven, first and foremost through liturgical celebration."[26] The Markan focus on the disciples as participants in the event of the transfiguration, where they beheld the splendor of the divine beauty coupled with the heavenly voice saying, "Listen to him" (Mark 9:7), would resonate with Christians in the Russian context as a call to liturgy that challenges all other competing narratives that would call for allegiance.

Elijah and Moses: Encouragement from Those Who Withstood Tyrants

Mark makes explicitly clear that the disciples also saw "Elijah and Moses" (Mark 9:4). Mark's reversal of the order in which these two great men appear in Jewish history has been the subject of some debate.[27] The significance of Elijah being mentioned first may have something to do with the fact that the subsequent dialogue with the disciples in Mark 9:11–13 focuses on Elijah. Moreover, the appearance of Elijah according to Malachi 4:5 would be connected to the dawning of the eschaton. By reversing the order, Mark did not intend to communicate the precedence of one figure over another. Instead,

---

25. *The Russian Primary Chronicle: Laurentian Text*, trans. S. Cross and O. Sherbowitz-Wetzor (Cambridge, MA: Mediaeval Academy of America, 1953), 111.

26. George Every, *The Byzantine Patriarchate* (London: SPCK, 1947), 9.

27. Some view Moses and Elijah as representing the Law and the Prophets. See R. T. France, *The Gospel of Mark: A Commentary on the Greek Text*, NIGTC (Grand Rapids: Eerdmans: 2002). Many Orthodox commentaries on the transfiguration passage and iconography note that Elijah represents the living and Moses represents the dead, as "the dead and the living" acclaim Jesus as the divine Messiah. See Leonid Ouspensky and Vladimir Lossky, *The Meaning of Icons* (Crestwood, NY: St. Vladimir's Seminary Press, 1982), 212.

Mark wanted to put an emphasis on the eschatological orientation of the event. What Elijah's name could have pointed to in the disciples' minds is the promise of the eschaton, as Elijah was considered to be the "deathless" one because of his translation to heaven (2 Kings 2:11). As the one who has not tasted death, he would be a logical figure to appear in the eschaton.[28] Mark may have communicated that his readers would find in this fact a sign that points to Jesus's coming victory over death. Moreover, there is one other element with Moses and Elijah worth mentioning that would resonate with the Russian context. John Chrysostom, one of the most important saints of Orthodoxy, related the reasons for the appearance of Moses and Elijah in his homily on the Matthean transfiguration. After mentioning the fact that Moses and Elijah represent the Law and the Prophets as well as the dead and the living, thus informing the disciples that Jesus had power over death and life, Chrysostom points out that both Moses and Elijah had to deal with rejection and tyrants: "For both the one and the other had courageously withstood a tyrant: one the Egyptian, the other Ahab; and this on behalf of a people who were both ungrateful and disobedient: and by the very persons who were saved by them, they were brought into extreme danger; and each of them wishing to withdraw men from idolatry."[29] For Chrysostom, Elijah and Moses were not only discussing the exodus of Jesus (Jesus's passion/departure; see Luke 9:31) but providing consolation to the disciples in their dread of the suffering of Jesus. The disciples, along with the Markan audience, would be encouraged by the vision of a transfigured Jesus with figures who withstood the dread of tyranny and suffering. The Russian Christians with the collective memory of the tyranny of the Soviet past and perhaps the current present would be encouraged as well to follow in the footsteps of Elijah, Moses, and Jesus.

Remember the Future: The Kingdom Having Come in Power

The disciples participated not only in the experience of the splendor of the divine beauty but in the eschatological realization that the kingdom of God spoken of in Mark—both in the beginning (Mark 1:14–15) and particularly

---

28. According to 4 Ezra 6:25–26, one of the signs of the end of the age is that those who are left will "see those who were taken up, who from their birth have not tasted death; and the heart of the earth's inhabitants shall be changed and converted to a different spirit." Later rabbinic interpretations combined the reference to Moses's death, "no one knows . . . his grave" (Deut. 34:6), with the passage "and [he] was there with the LORD" (Exod. 34:28) to conclude that Moses was taken to heaven without death, like Enoch and Elijah. This may have been a popular belief in Jesus's time. Their translation to heaven meant that they were believed able to return to earth. See France, *Gospel of Mark*, 351–52.

29. John Chrysostom, *Hom. Matt.* 56.3 (*NPNF*[1] 10:346).

in the promise that comes immediately before the transfiguration narrative ("Some of you standing here will not taste death until they see the kingdom of God having come in power," 9:1)—has become a present reality. The disciples experience the future eschaton in the present. Mark's note that the event happens "six days" later (9:2) is instructive, as it is not only a chronological statement but a theological one. "Six days" is a statement that would evoke the creation story of Genesis 1 and undoubtedly would communicate that the seventh day—the day of transfiguration—is a preview of God's new creation.

For many Orthodox Christians, the eschatological orientation of their theology is evident not only in liturgical practices but in iconography. One of the most significant conventions in writing icons is their eschatological orientation. The images of saints and events from the Bible, as well as saints and events from Christian history, are portrayed from the perspective of the future. For example, the Orthodox icon of crucifixion depicts Christ crucified from the perspective of the future in a deified state emphasizing his victory over death, while the Western crucifix has Christ in agony, focusing on Christ the victim. As Greek Orthodox theologian John Zizioulas, following St. Irenaeus and St. Maximus the Confessor, asserts, "Everything, including especially the human being, was meant to grow into perfection; their truth lay in the end, not in the beginning. Since the end decides finally about the truth of history, only those events leading to the end will be shown to possess true being."[30] The disciples experienced the splendor of God's future kingdom in the present. Mark's audience in the context of persecution and the Jewish-Roman war would be encouraged to continue in their loyalty to Jesus by this vision of God's new creation and the splendor of the divine Jesus and his kingdom. In the Russian context, the preview of God's future kingdom would encourage Christians to continue to be loyal to Christ and his kingdom and participate in the transfiguration here and now.

Peter's Reply: Celebration of God's Faithfulness

Most commentators view Peter's response to the experience in a negative light.[31] Peter says, "'Rabbi, it is good for us to be here, and let us make three tabernacles, one for you, one for Moses, and one for Elijah,' for he did not know what to answer, for they were afraid" (Mark 9:5–6). While Peter's response to Jesus's transfiguration on the surface may appear insufficient, the phrases "he did not know what to answer" and "they [the disciples] were

30. John Zizioulas, "Towards an Eschatological Ontology" (paper given at King's College, London, 1999), 1.
31. See France, *Gospel of Mark*, 353–54; Evans, *Mark 8:27–16:20*, 36–37.

afraid" do not need to point to the inappropriateness of Peter's response. Nor does Peter attempt to put Jesus on par with Elijah and Moses by requesting the same three tabernacles. Instead, one may argue that the request to build tabernacles recalls the exodus. To commemorate that event, the Jews celebrated the Feast of Tabernacles by living in small booths or huts for seven days (Lev. 23:42–44; Neh. 8:14–17). The Feast of Tabernacles celebrated God's provision, protection, and faithfulness to his people during the excruciatingly hard times in the wilderness.

Perhaps Peter's proposal to celebrate God's faithfulness to his people, after seeing the transfigured Jesus, is appropriate after all. Moreover, if Peter's proposal is seen in light of Jesus's announcement of the inauguration of the eschaton (Mark 1:14–15), and if the transfiguration is the disciples' experience of the kingdom, as has been argued above, then not to celebrate God's faithfulness would be inappropriate.[32] God's presence on earth should always elicit Peter's response, "It is good for us to be here" (9:5). In the Russian context, Peter's response, "It is good for us to be here" and "Let us make three tabernacles," should be the response not only to the liturgical experience of seeing the divine beauty but to seeing the divine beauty in the daily grind of the liturgy of life. Peter's response that evokes God's faithfulness to his people should resonate with many Russians (and non-Russians in the Soviet Union) whose families experienced persecution, hardship, and oppression due to their Christian identity.

Voice from Heaven and Descent: A Call to Loyalty

The transfiguration scene concludes with God's dramatic *entrée*: "And the cloud appeared overshadowing them, and a voice out of the cloud came, 'this is my beloved son, listen to him'" (Mark 9:7). The cloud indicates the motif of theophany. R. T. France points out, though, that this particular mention of the "cloud" echoes Sinai narratives (Exod. 16:10; 24:15–16).[33] If so, then Exodus 19:9 would be instructive, as God's speaking to Moses out of the cloud was intended for the Israelites as well. The Lord said to Moses, "I am going to come to you in a dense cloud, in order that the people may hear when I speak with you and so trust you ever after" (19:9). The phrase "This is my beloved son" here also echoes the baptism scene earlier in the narrative, in Mark 1:11: "You are my beloved son." Here God's voice is clearly intended

---

32. What is instructive is that because of the daily solemn outpouring of water during the festival (Num. 28:7), Tabernacles came to be associated with eschatological hopes. See Zech. 14:16–19.

33. France, *Gospel of Mark*, 354–55.

for the disciples. At two strategic places, baptism and transfiguration, God's voice enters the narrative strategically to affirm Jesus's messiahship—at the baptism, to Jesus, and at the transfiguration, to the disciples.

The command "Listen to him," echoing Deuteronomy 18:15 to "listen" to the voice of Moses, is intended to convey the notion of listening as loyally following Jesus's teachings. As the people were to trust Moses as the spokesman for God, here the disciples are to trust Jesus as the Messiah, the beloved Son. Alluding to Psalm 2:7, God's voice declares Jesus as royal Son of God, and the disciples are commanded to listen and obey him. All of the teachings of Jesus are in view here, but especially those that deal with the cruciform nature of discipleship. As the Markan audience confronted the challenge of choosing loyalties in the midst of persecution and war, so does the Russian audience confront the choice of loyalties today. The call to loyalty is clear: "Listen to him."

All Synoptic accounts of the transfiguration end with the note of descent from the mountain (Matt. 17:9; Mark 9:9; Luke 9:37). All Synoptic accounts are followed with the story of exorcism (Matt. 17:14–21; Mark 9:14–29; Luke 9:37–42). In all accounts, the disciples' failure to perform exorcism is noted (Matt. 17:19; Mark 9:18; Luke 9:40). Only Mark, though, has the father's statement, "I believe, help my unbelief" (Mark 9:24). This arrangement of transfiguration and descent into exorcism, coupled with the disciples' failure and the father's statement about belief and unbelief, is the evangelists' way of telling their respective audiences that the vision of transfiguration must be lived out here on earth even in the context of challenges like exorcism, albeit by imperfect followers of Christ.

Conclusion

May 9 is a very special day for the Russian people because it is a national holiday that celebrates the Victory Day over Nazi Germany in 1945 and the end of the Great Patriotic War. For many Russians, this is an emotional day because every family today in some way or fashion has been impacted by that war. Many lost close relatives and friends. Many were wounded. Many heroic acts were accomplished. The highlight of the Victory Day on May 9, among many festivities and celebrations, has always been the parade. Recently, as many veterans have died, the procession of the eternal regiment (*bessmertniy polk*) was created, in which relatives of those who died in the war and the veterans who died after carry their pictures and images in their honor. The parade, though, is the most colorful and celebratory festivity not only of that day but of the whole year. On May 9, 10 a.m. Moscow time, for many Russian people time stands still as the parade begins in Moscow's Red Square at a

Figure 2.1. Honor Guard of *Preobrazhensky* Regiment

place known as the *Voskresenkie Vorota* (Resurrection Gates), which functions as an entry point into the Red Square. The parade is meant to evoke a
strong sense of national identity, celebration over the end of the horrors of evil
enacted by Nazism, honor for the veterans, and the display of military might.
The parade, which is a "must see" ritual for most Russians, begins with the
emotional procession led by the Honor Guard of *Preobrazhensky* Military
Regiment. This regiment begins the parade by carrying and processing the
Russian flag and the Soviet flag (replica), which was put over the Reichstag
to bring the end to Nazism. The orchestra plays the famous arrangement of
Svyashennaiaya Voina (Sacred War) as the regiment processes.

The name of this regiment since 2013, *Preobrazhensky*, means in Russian
"belonging to transfiguration." As I watched the parade in 2015 celebrating
the seventieth anniversary of victory over Nazism, and the seventy-fifth anniversary in 2020 (postponed until July due to COVID), I observed how the
Transfiguration Regiment began the military parade in Moscow's Red Square
with the strong display of Russian weaponry and military personnel in the
most beautiful and choreographed way. With all that majestic pomp and
festivity, it is hard not to notice the surroundings of many Russian Orthodox
cathedrals in the Kremlin complex with their easily noticeable onion-shaped
domes. As a Christian, I found it hard not to think about Christian faith and

our relationship to the state, to the military, to the enemy, and to Orthodoxy, the dominant expression of Christianity in Russia.

Two very different images are commonplace in the Russian context: the image of a military parade led by the "Belonging to Transfiguration" Regiment (see fig. 2.1) and the icon of the transfiguration (an image of a very popular Orthodox feast; see fig. 2.2). These present Russian Christians with two different options of where to place their ultimate loyalties. One is the parade of military might, and the other is the transfigured Jesus, who will soon be crucified and vindicated by the resurrection, with the beauty of the eschaton. In the context of challenge and uncertainty, the account of the transfiguration calls believers to loyalty in the powerfully transfigured and suffering divine Messiah, who invites us to put our loyalties in him, not in the state or the institution, and it is a quest to see, taste, experience, and participate in the beauty of God's presence "on earth as it is in heaven."

Public Domain / Wikimedia Commons

Figure 2.2. Icon of the transfiguration

3

Power and Exorcism in Luke

An Indonesian Reading

DANY CHRISTOPHER

A story goes that there was a person being possessed by a demon. The people tried everything to cast it away but to no avail. Finally, a Christian minister came and successfully exorcised the demon. Upon seeing this, the people responded, "No wonder, it is a Christian demon." This story, whether it actually happened or not, fittingly describes the Indonesian view of the spirit-world.

For most Indonesians, the main question regarding spirits and demons is not whether they exist.[1] The question, rather, is *which* demon or spirit, and, consequently, how to deal with the many spirits that intertwine and affect the human world. This contrasting worldview inevitably results in a different emphasis or interpretive impulse when reading the biblical text.[2] In a more secular context such as the West, the focus is on proving the plausible existence of the spirit-world[3] or interpreting such phenomena in a different way (e.g.,

---

1. The skepticism toward the supernatural has been part of the Western mindset for quite some time. See, e.g., Giovanni B. Bazzana, *Having the Spirit of Christ: Spirit Possession and Exorcism in the Early Christ Groups* (New Haven: Yale University Press, 2020), 5–9; Stephen C. Barton, "Thinking about Demons and the Demonic," *Theology* 111 (2008): 83–92.

2. Matthew R. Malcolm, "Contextual Biblical Interpretation and Indonesian Readers," in *Sola Scriptura in Asia*, ed. Yongbom Lee and Andrew R. Talbert (Eugene, OR: Pickwick, 2018), 36.

3. From the New Testament front, see Craig Keener, "Spirit Possession as a Cross-Cultural Experience," *BBR* 20, no. 2 (2010): 215–36.

symbolically or psychologically).[4] In Indonesia, the emphasis is on the manner of dealing with the spirit-world and its beings, especially the evil spirits. There is a sense of fear when facing malign spirits. Such fear requires the service of someone who has the knowledge and power to protect the people from harm. It is within this context that the notion and story of Jesus's power to exorcise demons have great significance.

The goal of this chapter is to read Luke 4:33–37 in light of a spirit-world perspective in line with the context of Indonesia. I will begin by describing how Indonesians understand the spirit-world. Then I will explain in brief how Luke depicts Jesus's encounter with the activities of the malign spirits. Finally, I will discuss our particular passage, which records the first exorcism of Jesus. In discussing Luke 4:33–37, I will also venture to other spirit-encounter stories in Luke and Acts to see whether consistent patterns can be found.

The Spirit-World Perspective in Indonesia

In general, belief in the spirit-world among Indonesians can be summed up in three statements.[5] First, spirits are everywhere. They dwell in a variety of places: buildings, rocks, trees, rivers, mountains, seas, traditional weapons, and even humans. Historically, such belief can be traced back to the many indigenous religions in Indonesia. Many Indonesians were animistic, believing that there is spirit in everything.[6] Another factor that causes such belief to thrive is the influence of Hinduism with its pantheon of deities, demi-gods, and spirits. Hinduism flourished in Indonesia before the arrival of Islam in the thirteenth century.[7]

Although fewer and fewer Indonesians officially adhere to animism, this worldview still holds strong.[8] This is mainly because Indonesia, as a nation, sees itself as a religious state. The first principle of *Pancasila*, Indonesia's

---

4. E.g., spirit possession as a power struggle by marginalized women (I. M. Lewis, *Ecstatic Religion: A Study of Shamanism and Spirit Possession*, 3rd ed. [London: Routledge, 2003], 26–28) or indicating dissociative identity disorder (*Diagnostic and Statistical Manual of Mental Disorders*, 5th ed. [Washington, DC: American Psychiatric Association, 2013], 300.14).

5. There are numerous subcultures in Indonesia. Anthropological studies in Indonesia usually focus on one particular subculture (e.g., Javanese, Balinese, Batak, and others). Nevertheless, some findings from those studies can generally be applied to the broader Indonesian context.

6. Bernard H. M. Vlekke, *Nusantara: A History of Indonesia*, rev. ed. (Brussels: Manteau, 1961), 14.

7. Clifford Geertz, *The Religion of Java* (Chicago: University of Chicago Press, 1960), 5; Denni Boy Saragih, "Religion in Indonesia: A Historical Sketch," *RSSSR* 30 (2020): 56–57.

8. Robert W. Hefner, "Introduction: Indonesia at the Crossroads: Imbroglios of Religion, State, and Society in an Asian Muslim Nation," in *Routledge Handbook of Contemporary Indonesia*, ed. Robert W. Hefner (London: Routledge, 2018), 9.

official philosophical foundation, is One Lordship (*Ketuhanan yang Maha Esa*). Officially, there are six accepted religions, with Islam as the majority (87.2 percent), followed by Christianity, both Protestantism and Catholicism (9.8 percent) and three other religions.[9] In such a climate, animism is often assimilated into the more established religious system. Thus, it is not uncommon to find someone, even among Christians, who believes in the existence of jinn ("spirits" in the Islamic belief system) as well as local guardian spirits (part of the indigenous belief system).

There are many types of spirit-beings, each with its own characteristic and power. For example, according to Indonesian folk tradition, *tuyul* appears childlike and bald; *genderuwo* is huge, dark, and hairy; *kuntilanak* comes across as a beautiful woman, with a fragrant flowery scent.[10] Many believe that spirit-beings are territorial, dwelling in or ruling certain places or regions. Some are thought to be spirits of ancestors, while others are spirits of animal deities. Some are benevolent; others are malevolent. However, even a neutral or benevolent spirit can be hostile, depending on situations and human responses. These spirit-beings are also hierarchical. One of the most famous and deeply revered spirits is the Queen-spirit of the South Sea (*Ratu Laut Selatan*; Javanese: *Nyi Roro Kidul*).[11] Usually the power of these spirits is restricted to territories or places where they reside. Outside of their territorial stronghold, they are considerably weaker and even powerless. Other spirits are foreign categories assimilated into Indonesian culture. For example, from Islam one learns about the presence of jinn, spirit-beings living in the spirit-world. They can be Muslim jinn, who believe in Allah, and can also be stray jinn who believe in other gods.[12]

Second, the human world is intertwined with and affected by the spirit-world and its beings. On the one hand, some spirit-beings are considered dangerous. They can inflict harm and devastation. Humans must be careful not to offend them. So, for example, one must be polite and show respect when passing the territory of those beings. On other occasions one might need to appease them to avoid disturbance or even death. There are different ways to show respect or to appease these spirits: giving a mere spoken request for permission when passing their territories, giving appropriate

9. "Agama," Indonesia.go.id, accessed January 9, 2020, https://www.indonesia.go.id/profil /agama.

10. For more-detailed references, see Geertz, *Religion of Java*, 16–29.

11. Geertz, *Religion of Java*, 28–29.

12. See, for instance, M. Quraish Shihab, *Yang Tersembunyi: Jin, Iblis, Setan dan Malaikat dalam Al-Qur'an-As-Sunnah serta Wacana Pemikiran Ulama Masa Lau dan Masa Kini* (Jakarta: Lentera Hati, 1999), 81–91.

offerings, and in some cases, performing certain rituals, which might include sacrifices.[13]

On the other hand, some spirit-beings are considered neutral or even good. Humans can borrow their power for personal gain. Such personal gain ranges from political power to protection to finances to love. Even some in the political seats try to gain and maintain their position with the help of and power from the spirit-world.[14] The greater the political seat, the stronger the spirit with which a person will try to make a pact. It is believed that one with a stronger guardian spirit will overcome those with weaker spirits. Historically, it is said that the Javanese kings are tied to one of the great spirits of Java, the Queen-spirit of the South Sea.[15] The late sultan Hamengku Buwono IX, the descendant of the Javanese king, a former governor of the province of Jogjakarta, used to perform an annual public ritual, with offerings thrown to the South Sea.[16] Even Abdurrahman Wahid (Gus Dur), one of the most renowned leaders of moderate Islam, held a ritual at the southern coast of Java, seeking permission and blessing from the Queen-spirit when he was running for president.[17]

Third, the presence of spirits will sometimes result in spirit possession. Spirit possession can be defined as "an invasion of the individual by a spirit."[18] Usually the invasion or indwelling takes place because the spirit is more powerful than the human host.[19] Such a phenomenon is common in many subcultures in Indonesia. Many recount people possessed by evil spirits, causing illness and harm, who need exorcism. In order to exorcise, one asks the help of a *dukun* (traditional healer), who is believed to have the ability to contact, summon, and order spirit-beings to follow his or her commands. So, when someone is possessed or harmed by an evil spirit, a *dukun* must first decipher which spirits and magical power caused the harm.[20] A *dukun* will usually ask the spirit a few questions: (1) the spirit's name; (2) where it comes from; (3) why the spirit has come; and (4) what it wants. Afterward the

---

13. Mark Woodward, *Java, Indonesia and Islam* (New York: Springer, 2011), 89; Charles E. Farhadian, *Christianity, Islam, and Nationalism in Indonesia* (New York: Routledge, 2005), 112.

14. Nils Bubandt, "Sorcery, Corruption, and the Dangers of Democracy in Indonesia," *JRAI* 12 (2006): 413–31. See also Bubandt, *Democracy, Corruption and the Politics of Spirits in Contemporary Indonesia* (London: Routledge, 2014).

15. Woodward, *Java, Indonesia and Islam*, 88.

16. Mita Cut, "Mixing Religious Rituals and Mystical Experience with Modern Democracy: Indonesia's Sultan Hamengku Buwono IX," *PolTh* 10, no. 4 (2009): 609–10.

17. Karen Strassler, "Seeing the Unseen in Indonesia's Public Sphere: Photographic Appearances of a Spirit Queen," *CSSH* 56, no. 1 (2014): 103–6.

18. Lewis, *Ecstatic Religion*, 40.

19. Janice Boddy, "Spirit Possession Revisited: Beyond Instrumentality," *ARA* 23 (1994): 407.

20. Woodward, *Java, Indonesia and Islam*, 91.

dukun might give something for the spirit to eat, as a way to appease it, and ask the spirit to go home once the meal is finished.[21] For a more severe case, a *dukun* might perform certain rituals and sacrifices. To defeat evil spirits, a *dukun* must harness great power and/or receive help from powerful spirits.[22]

It should be noted that spirit possession does not always refer to possession by demons or evil spirits for malevolent purposes. Sometimes, people are possessed by spirits that are regarded as benevolent. In some Indonesian cultures, people purposely invite spirits to possess them for a variety of reasons. In one traditional dance, *kuda lumping* (horse dance), each dancer must be possessed by a spirit in order to dance accordingly. The spirit can be an animal spirit— usually a horse spirit—or ancestor spirits, or even jinn. A spiritual guardian (*pawang*) is there to ensure the well-being of the spirits as well as the dancers.[23] In another Indonesian subculture, a human host invites spirits of ancestors to speak or to heal, often exhausting the host.[24] In a Chinese-Indonesian ritual in West Kalimantan, a parade of people being possessed by spirits is held as a sign of unity or togetherness of the gods of the land (the earth-gods of Chinese, Malay, and Dayak tribes) and the brotherhood between the people.[25] In other cases, spirit possession indicates the presence of a higher power or authority to solve a problem within the community.[26]

Thus, from remote villages to metropolitan cities, many Indonesians believe in the spirit-world and its great impact on human lives. One common response among Indonesians when dealing with spirits is fear. Many fear not only the demonic spirits but other neutral spirits as well, since they might also harm people who fail to treat the spirits properly and respectfully. Christians in Indonesia often read the biblical text with the aforementioned spirit-world perspective in the background. This is especially true when dealing with passages on demons, spirit possession, and exorcism, such as Luke 4:33–37. Thus, it is important that our reading of Luke 4:33–37 can answer some questions regarding Christian faith and the common beliefs and practices rooted in the Indonesian spirit-world perspective.

21. Geertz, *Religion of Java*, 20.
22. Woodward, *Java, Indonesia and Islam*, 91.
23. Paul Christensen, "Modernity and Spirit Possession in Java: Horse Dance and Its Contested Magic," *DORISEA Working Paper* 2 (2013): 3–4.
24. Dimitri Tsintjilonis, "Monsters and Caricatures: Spirit Possession in Tana Toraja," *JRAI* 12 (2006): 551–67.
25. Margareth Chan, "The Spirit-Mediums of Singkawang: Performing 'Peoplehood,'" in *Chinese Indonesians Reassessed: History, Religion and Belonging*, ed. Siew-Min Sai and Chang-Yau Hoon (London: Routledge, 2013), 138–42.
26. Robert Wessing, "When the Tutelary Spirit Objected: Conflict and Possession among the Using of East Java, Indonesia," *AF* 26, no. 4 (2016): 355–75.

Encountering the Spirit-World in the Gospel of Luke

In general, the Gospel of Luke displays a strong spirit-world perspective. This is especially true in terms of Jesus's encounter with evil spirits. The two most common groups of examples of this encounter are the ministry of exorcism and the ministry of healing.[27] Exorcism is clearly one of Jesus's main ministries. Jesus casts out demons in Capernaum (Luke 4:33–36, 40–41). He releases Mary Magdalene from seven evil spirits (8:2). He sets the Gerasene man free from many demons (8:27–39). He restores a boy from a violent demon (9:37–43). He also casts out a mute spirit (11:14). Luke reports a number of short accounts of Jesus's ministry of healing and exorcism (6:18; 7:21). When sending his disciples out, Jesus transfers his power and authority to heal and cast out demons (9:1–2), who submit to the name of Jesus (10:17). The casting out of demons is the sign of the coming of the kingdom of God (11:20). When Jesus is threatened by Herod, Jesus replies, "Look, I drive out demons and perform healings today and tomorrow, and on the third day I complete my work"[28] (13:32). Jesus's first clash is not with the people but with the devil/Satan (4:1–13). In Luke, Satan is the real enemy. Hence, Satan attempts to foil Jesus's mission by tempting Judas (22:3). However, Jesus's successful mission results in Satan's fall (10:18).

Luke also emphasizes the reality of the spirit-world through the blurring of the boundary between healing and exorcism. At times, healing and exorcism seem to be intertwined. In Capernaum, Jesus rebukes demons, and they come out of their human hosts (Luke 4:35, 41). In the passage that follows, he rebukes not a demon but a fever suffered by Simon's mother-in-law, and it leaves its human host (4:39). Similarly, a woman who is crippled and bent over is said to be afflicted by a spirit and bound by Satan (13:11, 16). Yet, Jesus releases her from her sickness (13:12), causing her to be healed (13:14). In other passages, Jesus is said to heal those who have diseases and those who are affected by evil spirits (6:18; 7:21; 8:2; cf. 9:42: Jesus rebukes the evil spirit and heals the boy). This juxtaposition is akin to the spirit-world perspective in which physical illness is somehow connected to the activity of evil spirits, and hence there is no real distinction between illnesses of physical causes and those of spiritual causes.

Jesus's ministry of exorcism and healing is important in Luke's overall narrative and theology. For Luke, the spirit-world is real, and evil spirits wreak

27. Graham Twelftree, *In the Name of Jesus: Exorcism among Early Christians* (Grand Rapids: Baker Academic, 2007), 132–36; John C. Thomas, *The Devil, Disease and Deliverance: Origins of Illness in New Testament Thought* (Sheffield: Sheffield Academic Press, 1998), 191, 227.

28. All biblical translations are my own.

havoc on human life. The coming of Jesus, therefore, is important to release the people from that bondage. For Luke, the only way to be free from evil spirits is through Jesus. With that background, we now look closer into Luke 4:33–37.

Jesus and the Exorcism in Luke 4:33–37

Our pericope is important for a number of reasons. First, it is the first exorcism story recorded in Luke. In fact, it is the first mighty deed performed by Jesus, which shows the centrality of the exorcism ministry of Jesus. Second, it places the singular "demon/spirit" (Luke 4:33, 35) and the plural "spirits" (4:36) side by side. The fate of the particular spirit in this pericope represents the fate of all evil spirits. Thus, this pericope serves as a blueprint for later spirit encounters and exorcism. I will focus on two themes: (1) the demon's acknowledgment of Jesus; and (2) the relation between Jesus's power and spirit possession.

I Know Who You Are: The Significance of the Demon's Acknowledgment

In this pericope, Luke introduces the demonized man with a peculiar phrase. The man is said to have "a spirit of an unclean demon" (*pneuma daimoniou akathartou*, Luke 4:33). It is the only occasion in which Luke employs such a phrase. Later in the pericope, Luke uses the more common words "demon" (*daimonion*, 4:35)[29] and "unclean spirits" (*akathartois pneumasin*, 4:36).[30] All these terms refer to the same spirit-being that possesses the man.

Luke states that the incident takes place on the Sabbath day, at the synagogue (Luke 4:31, 33). Sabbath and the synagogue are supposed to be sacred.[31] For the Jews, the Sabbath is a sacred day, a boundary marker indicating that they belong to the Lord. Yet, not only does the demon present itself there and then, but it also attacks Jesus verbally, expressing its hostility. One should wonder why the demon takes the initiative. Does the hostility toward Jesus indicate an attempt to intimidate? Luke does not say. But, by initiating the contact, the demon shows that it refuses to back off and tries to "fight" Jesus.

---

29. Cf. Luke 4:35, 41; 7:33; 8:2, 27, 29, 30, 38; 9:1.

30. Cf. Luke 4:36; 6:18; 8:29; 9:42. Another common term is "evil spirit" (e.g., 7:21; 8:2; 11:26).

31. While the sacredness or ritual purity for a synagogue gathering is debated (Joel B. Green, *The Gospel of Luke*, NICNT [Grand Rapids: Eerdmans, 1997], 222), the sacredness of Sabbath for the Jews is generally acknowledged (Daniel K. Falk, "Sabbath," in *The Eerdmans Dictionary of Early Judaism*, ed. John J. Collins and Daniel C. Harlow [Grand Rapids: Eerdmans, 2010], 1174–79).

In Luke 4:34, the demon begins by aggressively shouting toward Jesus ("Ha!"), expressing its displeasure at him.[32] Then the demon questions Jesus: "What is there between me and you?"[33] The answer, according to the demon, is nothing. Jesus is not welcome at all. The demon then asks again, "Have you come to destroy us?" This question is important because this is the main reason why the demon shows hostility toward Jesus. The coming of Jesus equals the destruction of demons. The plural ("us") indicates that such a fate will fall upon not only this particular demon but also all other demons as well (cf. 8:27–33).[34]

The reason why the demon cannot oppose its destruction is because of the identity of Jesus. While the demon addresses Jesus as "Jesus of Nazareth," it knows very well the true identity of Jesus. In the final part of the verbal harassment, the demon states, "I know who you really are: The Holy One of God." A number of interpreters understand this as an attempt to control Jesus. According to early Greco-Roman writers, by knowing the true identities and names of the deities, a person is able to control them.[35] But of no less importance is the emphasis on the fact that the demon truly understands who Jesus really is and how this affects its fate.

This is not the only incident in which demons know the true identity of Jesus. A few verses later, Luke reports that many demons, as they are being cast out, shout toward Jesus, "You are the Son of God!" (Luke 4:41). Here we have the motif of acknowledgment, minus any clear attempt to control Jesus. A few chapters later, in the Gerasene incident, a demon also shouts with fear, "What is there between me and you, Jesus, Son of the Most High God?" (8:28). Here, the demon explicitly begs Jesus for mercy ("I beg you, do not torment me"). In these instances, there is hardly any attempt to control Jesus. Rather, these passages emphasize the fact that the demons know who Jesus really is. All acknowledge Jesus as the one from God, and all of them are powerless before him.

This motif of acknowledgment can also be found in the book of Acts. When Paul is in Philippi, a slave girl with a divination spirit speaks of Paul and his

---

32. Green, *Luke*, 223; cf. Joseph Fitzmyer, *Luke I–IX*, AB 28 (Garden City, NY: Doubleday, 1981), 545; François Bovon, *Luke 1: A Commentary on the Gospel of Luke 1:1–9:50*, Hermeneia (Minneapolis: Augsburg Fortress, 2002), 162.

33. Literally, "What to us and to you?"

34. Fitzmyer, *Luke I–IX*, 545–46; Green, *Luke*, 223.

35. This notion is found in some Greek magical spells (e.g., *PGM* VIII.6–7, 13). See Green, *Luke*, 224; John Carroll, *Luke: A Commentary*, NTL (Louisville: Westminster John Knox, 2012), 119; I. Howard Marshall, *The Gospel of Luke*, NIGTC (Grand Rapids: Eerdmans, 1978), 193; cf. Hans Dieter Betz, ed., *The Greek Magical Papyri in Translation* (Chicago: University of Chicago Press, 1986).

companions as "slaves of the Most High God" (Acts 16:17). Here, the spirit of divination (lit., spirit of *pythōn*) refers to the same spirit possessing the priestess of the Apollo temple at Delphi.[36] Even though the spirit is within its territorial stronghold, it is helpless when Paul, in the name of Jesus, orders the spirit to come out of the slave girl (16:18). There is also an incident in which an evil spirit responds to some Jewish exorcists, "Jesus I know, Paul I recognize; but you, who are you?" (19:15). These incidents show that, regardless of the identities and locations of the evil spirits, whether within the land of Judea or in pagan territory, all of them know who Jesus really is.

Such understanding is important for the context of Indonesia. With so many alleged types of demons and spirits, each with its own power and dominion, many Christians fear that the power of Jesus is limited to certain areas or spirits. In some places, they might think they need additional rituals or even help from the local *dukun* to appease those spirits. The Lukan passage above shows that Jesus's power is not limited to "local" demons. Every single demon and spirit, far and near, knows who Jesus truly is, and every single one of them is powerless before him. There is no need for any offerings to appease those spirits. Thus, there is no need to fear.

No Other Spirit: The Relation between Power and Spirit Possession

After the demon shouts, Jesus immediately rebukes it and commands it to come out from the man (Luke 4:35). The demon has no choice but to obey. Even when it tries to throw its human host down, Luke notes that he suffers no harm. After the exorcism takes place, the crowd is astonished by the power and authority of Jesus (4:36). The amazement is not so much about Jesus's ability to cast out the demon but rather about the manner in which he does it. For the Jews, the common method of exorcism involved some sort of ritual (e.g., calling the name of Solomon and using his incantations) or medium (e.g., tree root or fish innards).[37] Jesus uses none of those things. He simply commands the demon, and it has no other choice but to obey. In short, Luke depicts Jesus as qualitatively different from other exorcists.

But where do Jesus's power and authority come from? For Luke, they stem from the anointing of the Holy Spirit.[38] One way to highlight the significance

---

36. Ben Witherington III, *The Acts of the Apostles: A Socio-Rhetorical Commentary* (Grand Rapids: Eerdmans, 1998), 493–94; Craig S. Keener, *Acts: An Exegetical Commentary*, vol. 3, *15:1–23:35* (Grand Rapids: Baker Academic, 2014), 2422–29; Dany Christopher, "'The Spirit of Jesus' in Acts 16.7: An Ethnographic Reading," *JSNT* 46, no. 1 (2023): 3–18, esp. 13.

37. Josephus, *Ant.* 8.46–49; Tob. 6:8; 8:2–3.

38. Fitzmyer, *Luke I–IX*, 547; John Nolland, *Luke 1:1–9:20*, WBC 35A (Dallas: Word, 1989), 208; Green, *Luke*, 224; Carroll, *Luke*, 118.

of the relation between Jesus and the Holy Spirit is through the concept of spirit possession. When we discuss spirit possession in Luke, the common assumption is that possession is caused by evil spirits. Yet, as shown above, in the spirit-world perspective, demonic possession is only one part of the larger phenomenon of spirit possession. Pieter Craffert laments, "Except for demon possession, possession is a neglected and under-researched topic in New Testament studies in general and Jesus research in particular."[39]

One factor that we do not often take into account regarding spirit possession in Luke is the indwelling of the Holy Spirit. It can be argued that Luke presents Jesus as someone who possesses a Spirit, which is above all other spirits. Jesus's authority and power derive from the indwelling of the Holy Spirit.[40] In light of the spirit-world perspective, Luke's presentation seems necessary. The Greco-Roman readers at that time were familiar with the notion and language of spirit possession. One who is possessed by gods or spirits might be bestowed with supernatural power. As stated by Eric Eve, "In an age when causality tended to be seen in terms of agency, the performance of superhuman deeds naturally required the aid of superhuman agents; if not gods, then demons."[41] In the case of Jesus, the indwelling of the Holy Spirit enables Jesus to perform his teachings and deeds with divine power and authority. With the Spirit of God in him, Jesus is able to overpower all other spirits.[42]

The description above might explain why, from the beginning of his Gospel, Luke shows that the Spirit is at work, both in Jesus and in God's chosen people. Not only is the phenomenon of spirit possession abundant, but it is necessary as a sign of God's power at work. The angel Gabriel prophesies that John the Baptist will be filled with the Spirit (Luke 1:15). The same angel informs Mary that she, though a virgin, will conceive through the work of the Spirit (1:35). Elizabeth is filled with the Spirit (1:41), and it causes her to utter a blessing. The baby in the womb of Elizabeth miraculously reacts to the coming of Mary (1:44; presumably also the work of

39. Pieter F. Craffert, "Spirit Possession in Jesus Research: Insights from the Anthropological Study of Possession," *R&T* 25 (2018): 111.

40. Fitzmyer, *Luke I–IX*, 543; Marshall, *Luke*, 192.

41. Eric Eve, *The Healer from Nazareth: Jesus' Miracles in Historical Context* (London: SPCK, 2009), 24.

42. Here, spirit possession does not necessarily mean that Jesus is overpowered, forced, or enslaved by the Spirit, akin to demon possession. Rather, the Spirit of God empowers Jesus without him losing his own consciousness. Luke uses different words to distinguish possession by demons and empowerment by the Spirit of God. For demons, he mainly uses "have" (Luke 4:33; 7:33; 8:27; cf. Acts 16:16; 19:13). For the indwelling of the Holy Spirit, he often uses "filled with" (Luke 1:15, 41, 67; cf. Acts 2:4; 4:8, 31; 7:55; 9:17) and "full of" (Luke 4:1; cf. Acts 6:5; 11:24).

the Spirit?). Simeon has the Holy Spirit upon him, and he is informed and led by the Spirit (2:25–27).

Such spirit possession also characterizes Jesus and his mission. At Jesus's baptism, the Holy Spirit descends on him (Luke 3:22). He is said to be full of the Spirit, led by the Spirit (4:1), and in the power of the Spirit (4:14). In his mission manifesto, Jesus declares that he is the chosen one on whom the Spirit of the Lord has descended (4:18, 21). He rejoices in the Spirit (10:21) and baptizes others with the Holy Spirit (3:16). It can be said that Lukan Christology is primarily a Spirit Christology. Luke frames his Gospel and the ministry of Jesus with the presence of the Holy Spirit. In the last chapter of Luke, Jesus states that he will send his disciples what God the Father has promised and that they should wait until they are "clothed with power from on high" (24:49)—a clear reference to the "spirit possession" at Pentecost (Acts 2:4). Such a dense reference to the indwelling of the Spirit and its power working through Jesus should frame our reading of the rest of the Lukan Gospel, especially Jesus's exorcism of other spirits. Thus, in Luke 4:33–37, Jesus is able to overpower the demon because the Spirit that "possesses" Jesus is stronger than the spirit that possesses the man (cf. Luke 11:21–22).

For the Indonesian context, the indwelling of the Holy Spirit is an important teaching. Many who fear the demonic spirits might search for the help of a stronger guardian spirit for protection. Luke shows that no other spirit is stronger than the Spirit that is in Jesus, since it is the Spirit of God himself. Therefore, a Christian should not be afraid of the power of all other spirits. Moreover, the Spirit that descends on and empowers Jesus also resides within the people of God (cf. Luke 11:13).

Conclusion

Indonesians have a spirit-world perspective that is quite different from a secular Western view. This, in turn, affects the way Indonesians read and interpret passages on demons and exorcism, such as Luke 4:33–37. For many Indonesians, fear, not skepticism, is the common attitude when dealing with spirits. Hence, it is important for many Indonesian Christians to know that spirit-beings, wherever they are, know clearly who Jesus is, and all of them submit to him. Jesus's power to exorcise is not limited to supposedly "Christian" or "local" demons. It is a call not to fear the many types of spirits and demons with their fearsome power throughout the archipelago. It is also important for many Indonesian Christians to know that Jesus is the one who possesses the Spirit above all spirits. One should seek help only from Jesus and not from the *dukun* or even other powerful spirits.

The Indonesian awareness of the spirit-world is instructive to those who approach these texts with skepticism or reach for a "scientific" explanation. Luke clearly presents the spirit-world as active and opposed to Jesus. For Luke, the exorcism by Jesus demonstrates that the Spirit within Jesus, and within those who believe, is stronger than any other spirits. Just as there is no other name but Jesus, likewise there is no other spirit but the Holy Spirit.

4

"For God So Loved Hong Kong / Hongkongers"

A Literary and Territoriality Reading of John 3:16–21

JOSAPHAT TAM

"For God so loved the world . . ." This is perhaps the single most beloved verse of Christians in modern days. This is also one of the most "simple" and frequent pieces of Scripture Hong Kong people have heard, whether they are Christians or not. But there are problems and implications as it has been understood by Hong Kong people over time. In the Chinese language, the word "world" in John 3:16 is translated as 世人 (shìrén)—that is, "people in the world." The Chinese word excludes the meaning "place"; it can only mean "people." As a result, this verse is understood individualistically. This is problematically coupled with the history of Hong Kong. Most residents are immigrants from mainland China, many of whom fled to British Hong Kong to escape the Cultural Revolution in China. To these refugees, Hong Kong was not their permanent home; they knew the British rule would end in 1997. Hong Kong was called "Borrowed Place, Borrowed Time" in those

Disclaimer: This chapter was written in early 2020 and represents the author's view at that time. The author declares that he has no intention to violate any current law where he is now located.

colonial days,[1] affecting people's sense of place. Their predominant concern was with their own selves. No one loved this "place" as much as his or her own possessions, whether assets or money.

But toward and after 1997 and the handover of sovereignty back to China, things changed for those who chose to stay. The sense of public space has grown, as Hongkongers were promised "Hong Kong people ruling Hong Kong." This chapter is not the place to track all the social changes, but in recent years—as the Chinese Communists altered their policy and stressed their "overall jurisdiction" over Hong Kong—resistance from "Hongkongers" surfaced. The notion of Hong Kong as a "place" really owned by Hongkongers is cherished and defended by the newer generations. A deep sense of belonging to this place is felt by people born and living there.

In light of this context, we revisit this favorite passage, John 3:16–21. From a literary and a territoriality perspective, I attempt to recover some of the exegetical aspects that have been neglected by Hong Kong Christians. In recent scholarship, the "world" is seen as a character cherished by God that plays a key role in this so-called monologue section. Its dual role as both people and place shows a complexity that is often missed. Recent studies on territoriality in the field of human geography also help to bring new insights as to how we can understand the message of John 3:16–21. Seeing how people and place are intertwined and affect each other, we can reflect on the significance of this best-known passage in the Bible in light of Hong Kong's own context.

2019: Hong Kong and Hongkongers through Our Own Eyes

Hong Kong is a cosmopolitan city. There are 1.2 million Christians among a population of over 7 million.[2] After over 150 years of British colonial rule and having returned to China, Hong Kong now struggles in the "one country, two systems."[3] The Anti-Extradition Law Amendment Bill movement (Anti-ELAB movement hereafter)[4] started in June 2019 and is ongoing at the time of writing (January 2020). Together with the "Umbrella movement" in 2014, they

1. This oft-used epithet originates from Richard Hughes, *Hong Kong: Borrowed Place, Borrowed Time* (London: Andre Deutsch, 1968).

2. "Hong Kong 2018: The Facts," The Government of the Hong Kong Special Administrative Region, https://www.yearbook.gov.hk/2018/en/pdf/Facts.pdf.

3. A constitutional model pledged by China to give Hong Kong a high degree of autonomy from the mainland. On its erosion, see Brian C. H. Fong, "Stateless Nation within a Nationless State: The Political Past, Present, and Future of Hongkongers, 1949–2019," *NN* 26 (2020): 1069–86; B. Y. T. Tai, "Hong Kong No More: From Semi-Democracy to Semi-Authoritarianism," *Contemporary Chinese Political Economy and Strategic Relations* 4 (2018): 395–430.

4. For a detailed review of events, see Francis L. F. Lee et al., "Hong Kong's Summer of Uprising: From Anti-extradition to Anti-authoritarian Protests," *China Review* 19, no. 4 (2019): 1–32.

reveal a deep dissatisfaction of Hong Kong's people with China's tightening grip. The Anti-ELAB movement shows considerable Christian participation; some protesters come from churches that hold a more conservative view of the separation of church and state. "Sing Hallelujah to the Lord" became the hymn sung by protesters, whether believers or nonbelievers. At the same time, a deep rift also is opening up in the society and tearing Hong Kong apart because of the movement. Very broadly speaking, older generations tend to support the local government controlled by the Communists and its police force oppressing the demonstrations. Younger generations, identifying with the students in *Les Misérables*, support the protesters, demanding greater democratic freedoms and an independent investigation of police misconduct during the movement.

Due to extensive media coverage, continued police brutality toward the protesters has caused a collective trauma. To the general public, the masked and unnamed protesters, not to mention the dead youngsters, represent faceless sufferers that could be your children. Sympathy toward these unarmed, injured youngsters has fostered a greater solidarity among the public and a stronger sense of "Hongkongers" as a result.[5] Although people worry about the future, they find their identity rooted in this place they do not wish to leave, even if some seek the freedom of another passport. A sizable number of Hongkongers are determined to fight for freedom until the end.

Literary Perspective on John 3:16–21: The "World" as a Character in Johannine Studies

With the aforementioned Hong Kong context, we revisit John 3:16 from two perspectives. The first arises from the field of literary criticism and the second from human geography. They supplement each other in enriching our understanding.

Character studies have been the subject of popular research in literary criticism. Treating the "world" as a character means that it is different from a mere object in a story. It has mental and moral qualities, style and characteristics, expressions/attitudes, and reactions/responses toward other characters.

---

5. Though 92 percent of the population is ethnic Chinese ("Race Relations Unit: Demographics," Home Affairs Department of the Government of the Hong Kong Special Administrative Region, January 16, 2018, https://www.had.gov.hk/rru/english/info/demographics.htm), people's sense of identity is definitely "Hongkonger." As reflected in a poll (June 2019), 52.9 percent of people consider themselves "Hongkongers"; only 10.8 percent describe themselves as "Chinese." See "Categorical Ethnic Identity Table," HKU Public Opinion Programme, last accessed June 26, 2019, at this link: https://www.hkupop.hku.hk/english/popexpress/ethnic/eidentity/poll/datatables.html (site is no longer available).

Both Cornelis Bennema and Christopher Skinner have studied the "world" (*kosmos*) as a character in John.[6] Bennema identifies the world as "personified, functioning as Jesus' major opponent and interacting with him through its people," displaying "ignorance . . . , intolerance . . . , hatred, wickedness, being unreceptive (1:11; 14:17), and hostility (persecution and murder [16:2]). . . . It does not know God, Jesus, or the Spirit (1:10; 14:17; 16:3; 17:25), it rejects Jesus (1:11), loves evil (3:19), hates (7:7; 15:18–19; 17:14), (falsely) presumes (16:2), and rejoices (16:20)."[7] To Skinner, the world "represents the human forces that stand in opposition to Jesus, and in this way, functions even if surreptitiously, as the story's primary antagonist. . . . [It] carries the promise of great things but consistently betrays that promise for a darkened perspective that opposes rather than celebrates the plans and purposes of God."[8]

This characterization of the world is correct to a certain degree, but Bennema and Skinner did not consider that all the believing characters in John are also members of the world.[9] These members of the world are shown to know God in a generally positive sense. Current Johannine character studies on the "world" do not distinguish the role the world plays in the monologues from that in the larger storyline of the Gospel (the narrated events). In fact, monologues (as well as narrative asides) express the viewpoints of the narrator, which could be at variance with the viewpoints found in the narrated events. In another work, I postulate that John 1:1–5, 9–18 and 3:16–21, 31–36 should be treated as a framework of preamble and monologues, guiding the reader in their understanding of the Gospel.[10] The role that the world plays thus deserves a closer look.

6. Cornelis Bennema, *Encountering Jesus: Character Studies in the Gospel of John* (Milton Keynes, UK: Paternoster, 2009), 31–37; Christopher W. Skinner, "The World: Promise and Unfulfilled Hope," in *Character Studies in the Fourth Gospel*, ed. Steven A. Hunt, D. François Tolmie, and Ruben Zimmermann, WUNT 314 (Tübingen: Mohr Siebeck, 2013), 61–70. Similarly, see Stanley B. Marrow, "Κόσμος in John," *CBQ* 64 (2002): 90–102; Lars Kierspel, *The Jews and the World in the Fourth Gospel: Parallelism, Function, and Context*, WUNT 2/220 (Tübingen: Mohr Siebeck, 2006).

7. Bennema, *Encountering Jesus*, 37.

8. Skinner, "World," 70.

9. For instance, the Samaritans, the Samaritan woman, the blind beggar, Mary, Martha, and, most obviously, the disciples. Francis J. Moloney called such use of the world "neutral." See Moloney, "God, Eschatology, and 'This World': Ethics in the Gospel of John," in *Johannine Ethics: The Moral World of the Gospel and Epistles of John*, ed. Christopher W. Skinner and Sherri Brown (Minneapolis: Fortress, 2017), 210. Ironically, a similar tension in the function of the world was observed by Rudolf K. Bultmann, *The Gospel of John: A Commentary*, trans. G. R. Beasley-Murray, R. W. N. Hoare, and J. K. Riches (Philadelphia: Westminster, 1971), 55.

10. Josaphat C. Tam, *Apprehension of Jesus in the Gospel of John*, WUNT 2/399 (Tübingen: Mohr Siebeck, 2015), 46.

John 3:16–21: Structure and Function

The monologue here is a mini-story within the larger story of John. It can be broken into two smaller parts. The first, 3:16–18, concerns three characters—namely, "God," his "Son," and the "world," composed of those who believe or not. The second part, 3:19–21, concerns people's reactions to the light and darkness in the world, revealing their own judgment. Characters involved are "light," "darkness," and people who are either evildoers or truth-doers. Through these two parts, the timeless gospel truth of God's love is met by people's responses. The implied reader is now informed of these "spiritual" principles, which John conveys after 1:19–3:15. The phenomenon described in this mini-story will be replayed and manifested in more detail as the Gospel unfolds.

John 3:16–18 and 3:19–21: Focuses and Traits

In John 3:16–18, God is the focus. The narrator explains to the reader God's own attitudes and actions toward the world through the Son. The world as a character acts mainly on a cosmic level here, as the recipient of God's action. The "faith" language in verses 16–18 is used to describe people's attitudes toward God (see fig. 4.1). For the part of the world that does not believe, its condemnation is clear (3:18). But that is not God's desire. His will is to save, not to condemn, the world (3:17). The world is cherished by God, whose love is demonstrated in the giving and sending of his only Son.

In John 3:19–21, attention is put on the people of the world. The name "Son" is not used and is replaced by "light" instead (cf. 1:4–5, 7–9). In 3:19a, the "world" occurs not as a character but as a place (*eis ton kosmon*), while the character is represented by the "people" (*hoi anthrōpoi*). Further, in verses 20–21, "faith" language is replaced with "works" language, which describes people's responses toward Jesus: "evildoers" (*ho phaula prassōn*) and "truth-doers" (*ho poiōn tēn alētheian*). As in the Gospel narratives that are going to unfold, the world is composed of nonbelievers and believers, expressed as those doing wickedness (3:20) or doing truth (3:21).

Through these more concrete portrayals, the narrator foresees the phenomenon of people's different reactions toward the "light"—that is, Jesus, "the light of the world" (as in John 8:12; 9:5; 11:9; 12:46). The traits of these two opposite groups of the world portrayed here reflect that the "world" is itself an umbrella term composed of conflicting subgroups, not merely antagonists or protagonists.

Figure 4.1. The phrasing of John 3:16–21

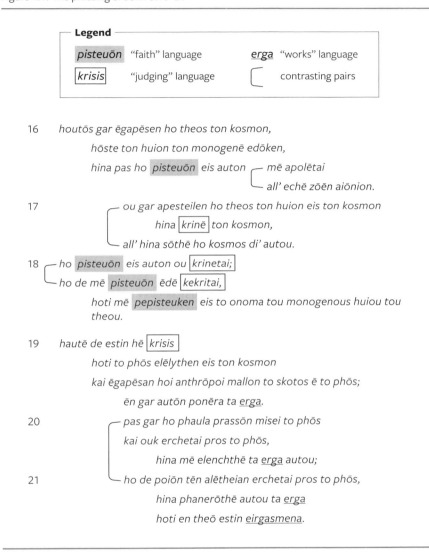

"World" as Both Place and People

Furthermore, as "into the world" (*eis ton kosmon*) is used in both John 3:16–18 (v. 17) and 3:19–21 (v. 19), the vacillation between *kosmos* denoting people and denoting place deserves closer attention. In verses 16–17, *kosmos* occurs three times in relation to a verb, receiving the action of "love" (*agapaō*), "judge" (*krinō*), and "save" (*sōzō*). In these cases, *kosmos* obviously refers to people. However, in verses 17 and 19, because of the verbs of motion (*apostellō*, v. 17; *erchomai*, v. 19), it makes the most sense that the phrase *eis ton kosmon* refers to place. The multiple mentions of *kosmos* in such close proximity, one referring to place while the other three refer to people, appears deliberate. Obviously, John has a choice to use different words that differentiate place from people. The multiple mentions suggest that, from John's perspective, the two separate denotations belong to the same core conceptual idea.[11] At the least, John wants his reader to notice that the two aspects of *kosmos* are closely connected. *Kosmos* is a dual people/place concept.

"World" in John 3:16–21 and in the Subsequent Chapters

In Johannine studies, it is often claimed that the "world" is represented by "the Jews," especially in light of Jesus's controversies with them in John 5–12, where the two are virtually synonymous.[12] But, given our focused analysis on 3:16–21, the world is not necessarily bound by any people or ethnic groups. Rather, the world has a strong universal flavor in the monologues, of which "the Jews" portrayed in later chapters are only a partial manifestation.[13] The world represents "a sinful humanity estranged from God," as Bennema observes, and was put "on trial" by Jesus's testimony, as Andrew Lincoln describes.[14] Yet, at the same time, the world remains the target of God's supreme love. This universal love motif goes beyond what the cosmic trial motif can contain in John 5–12.

From a macroperspective, especially in John 5–12, a negative portrayal of the world is present. If the "crowd" is a faceless character there, then the "world" is a similar collective character, appearing in one place as the "Jews" and in another as the anonymous crowd or other characters. Yet, in John's

---

11. This is in contrast to a double entendre, where the single occurrence of a word carries double meanings. Now the multiple occurrences of a word with distinct senses carry one core concept.

12. Bultmann, *Gospel of John*, 86–87; Wayne A. Meeks, "Man from Heaven in Johannine Sectarianism," *JBL* 91 (1972): 69–71; John Ashton, "The Identity and Function of the Ἰουδαῖοι in the Fourth Gospel," *NovT* 27 (1985): 40–75; Klaus Wengst, *Bedrängte Gemeinde und verherrlichter Christus: Ein Versuch über das Johannesevangelium*, 4th ed. (München: Kaiser, 1992), 57; Stephen Motyer, *Your Father the Devil? A New Approach to John and "the Jews,"* PBM (Carlisle, UK: Paternoster, 1997), 57; Bruce J. Malina and Richard L. Rohrbaugh, *Social-Science Commentary on the Gospel of John* (Minneapolis: Fortress, 1998), 246. Against all these, see Adele Reinhartz, *Befriending the Beloved Disciple: A Jewish Reading of the Gospel of John* (London: Continuum, 2001), 25; Kierspel, *Jews and the World*, 155–213.

13. Marrow rightly notes that even so, in John 13–17, the "world" resumes its usage and role as nonbelievers instead of "the Jews" in John 5–10. Marrow, "Κόσμος in John," 100.

14. Bennema, *Encountering Jesus*, 32; Andrew T. Lincoln, *Truth on Trial: The Lawsuit Motif in the Fourth Gospel* (Peabody, MA: Hendrickson, 2000).

monologue of 3:16–21, the world remains a treasured character in a scene in which God plays a key loving role throughout. This portrayal of the world is in tension with its later portrayals. Based on our analysis above, categorization of the world as either a mere antagonist or a mere protagonist is too crude for this Gospel. The world in John possesses more complex traits. There appears to be a deliberate tension between the general unbelieving attitude of the world and the hopeful and genuine conversion of the world. God's promises made in John, though unfulfilled in regard to some members of the world, are definitely fulfilled in regard to others of the world. This special relationship between the monologues and the subsequent narratives should not be missed.

Summary

From a literary perspective, I argue that the "world" in John should be understood as a people/place dual concept. It is a collective persona, the recipient of God's love; it is also the place or realm where God's Son came as the "light." In Chinese Bible translations, this cannot be expressed, because Chinese language separates the world as place, 世界 (shìjiè), and the world as people, 世人 (shìrén). This is unfortunate, as we cannot easily see the duality of the Johannine concept of *kosmos*.

Furthermore, the "world" is itself an umbrella term, not just referring to antagonists or protagonists. In the narrative, the world is represented by "the Jews" and "the crowd" as well as by some believing characters. The differentiation wholly depends on whether they have faith and works, as stated in John 3:16–18 and 3:19–21. Thus, the monologue here reveals the author's plan. It can be called an "indirect interior monologue"—that is, the narrator "presents unspoken material as if it were directly from the consciousness of a character and, with commentary and description, guides the reader through it."[15] Consequently, it has an important bearing on understanding the Gospel as a whole, especially in setting the cosmic and soteriological backdrop of Jesus's mission as well as reconstructing John's own strategy to use the world to influence readers.

The same case applies to our reading of John 3:16–21. The "world" in our world never consists of simple constituents. "Characters" (people) in this world are always complex. In a society deeply divided by political leanings, like Hong Kong, it is difficult not to oversimply issues and label people hastily. Yet the consistent and predominant trait of God to love the world reminds us to always go beyond people's differentiations and labeling and look through the Father's heart, through his eyes, as John shows in his monologue.

15. Robert Humphrey, *Stream of Consciousness in the Modern Novel* (Los Angeles: University of California Press, 1954), 29.

Territoriality Perspective on John 3:16–21: The "World" Understood in Three Realms

If the "world" refers not merely to people and not merely to place, then the dynamic between them deserves closer attention. Therefore, studies in human geography become helpful to understand the people/place dynamic. Since the 1980s, the idea of human territoriality has been given increasing focus by scholars of various fields,[16] including biblical studies.[17] As Robert David Sack explains, human territoriality is "the act of delimiting and controlling an area of space," so as to control place and things. On the one hand, a territory bounds and controls who is in and out, itself an expression of power.[18] This is experienced in relation to our "self" as we are influenced by the place surrounding us. On the other hand, a territory exhibits two levels of forces that construct the idea of territoriality centered on the place of the self. These are "forces of realms" and "forces of perspectives" (see fig. 4.2).[19] "Forces of realms" entail the realms of social relations, of nature, and of meaning, while "forces of perspectives" entail "the human ability of metaphysical elevation above the place of one's standing" as the self reflects on these different realms.[20] Sack's model of territoriality deserves application to our text to see how John 3:16–21 might be understood in light of these interactions.

16. Jean Gottman, *The Significance of Territory* (Charlottesville: University of Virginia Press, 1973); Robert David Sack, *Human Territoriality: Its Theory and History* (Cambridge: Cambridge University Press, 1986); Sack, *Homo Geographicus* (Baltimore: Johns Hopkins University Press, 1997); Edward W. Soja, *Thirdspace: Journeys to Los Angeles and Other Real-and-Imagined Places* (Cambridge, MA: Blackwell, 1996); Soja, *Seeking Spatial Justice*, Globalization and Community 16 (Minneapolis: University of Minnesota Press, 2013); Claude Raffestin, "Could Foucault Have Revolutionized Geography?," in *Space, Knowledge and Power: Foucault and Geography*, ed. Stuart Elden and Jeremy W. Crampton, trans. Gerald Moore (Aldershot, UK: Routledge, 2007), 129–37; Alexander B. Murphy, "Entente Territorial: Sack and Raffestin on Territoriality," *Environment and Planning D: Society and Space* 30 (2012): 159–72.

17. For instance, Bruce J. Malina, "Apocalyptic and Territoriality," in *Early Christianity in Context: Monuments and Documents*, ed. Frédéric Manns and Eugenio Alliata, SBFCMa 38 (Jerusalem: Franciscan Press, 1993), 369–80; Kalinda Rose Stevenson, *The Vision of Transformation: The Territorial Rhetoric of Ezekiel 40–48*, SBLDS 154 (Atlanta: Scholars Press, 1996); Jerome H. Neyrey, "Spaced Out: 'Territoriality' in the Fourth Gospel," *HvTSt* 58 (2002): 632–63; Neyrey, "Spaces and Places, Whence and Whither, Homes and Rooms: 'Territoriality' in the Fourth Gospel," in *The Gospel of John in Cultural and Rhetorical Perspective* (Grand Rapids: Eerdmans, 2009), 58–84; Ksenija Magda, *Paul's Territoriality and Mission Strategy: Searching for the Geographical Awareness Paradigm behind Romans*, WUNT 2/266 (Tübingen: Mohr Siebeck, 2009).

18. Sack, *Human Territoriality*, 5, 19; David Storey, "Territoriality: Geographical," in *International Encyclopedia of the Social and Behavioral Sciences*, ed. James D. Wright, 2nd ed., 25 vols. (Amsterdam: Elsevier, 2015), 20:221–26.

19. Sack, *Homo Geographicus*, 27–59.

20. Magda, *Paul's Territoriality*, 50.

Figure 4.2. The relational geographical framework

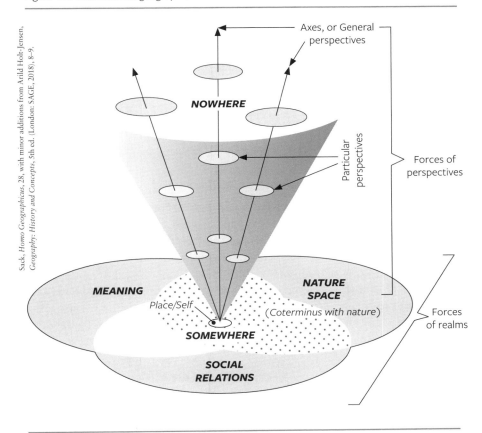

Sack, *Homo Geographicus*, 28, with minor additions from Arild Holt-Jensen, *Geography: History and Concepts*, 5th ed. (London: SAGE, 2018), 8–9.

Realm of Social Relations ("In / Out of Place" Loop)

For the realm of social relations, Sack suggests that, based on social rules, in any place there is an "in / out of place" loop, which is like constantly active currents. Within this loop, some elements are appropriate ("in place") in some places but unacceptable ("out of place") in others. Translating this into the Gospel of John, for instance in 1:4, from the perspective of the authorial monologue (1:1–5), the element "life" is in place with "in him [the Word]" (being a kind of "space"), whereas in 1:5 "light" is out of place with "in the darkness."

Bringing such geographical awareness to John 3:16–21, we see the "world" is a place where God establishes his relationship with the "world" as people. The vocabulary reveals the social relations: "love," "give," "save," "condemn/

judge," "believe," and "hate." The verbs that show God establishing a relationship with the world are particularly noteworthy: God loves the world, gives them his Son, wants to save the world, and is not willing to judge or condemn them. Especially significant is how the author emphasizes God's unwillingness to judge and God's desire to save (see fig. 4.1, above). By linking judgment to people's decision not to believe, the out of place element of judgment in God's relationship with people is largely mitigated, for it is attributed to an individual's unbelief: people can choose to avoid judgment. Thus, the author attempts to set various actions as "in place" with the "world" so that the reader in their "world" may come to understand.

Realm of Nature ("Spatial-Interaction" Loop)

Another "loop" of forces concerns the realm of nature. Sack calls it the loop of "spatial-interaction," which is interconnected with the "in / out of place" loop mentioned above. Elements in a place are examined for how they relate to the place through interaction with the material conditions set in the physical world.[21]

John 3:16–21 involves elements in the realm of nature. Both the world and God are not only characters; they "exist" in the realm of nature in the narrative. Through the monologue, contact between the two spheres—namely, the earthly and the divine—is said to have occurred. Verbs of movement ostensibly involve spatial interactions: the Son is "*sent into* the world" (*apesteilen . . . eis ton kosmon*, 3:17); the light has "*come into* the world" (*elēlythen eis ton kosmon*, 3:19). As a result of this, "the evildoer does not *come to* the light" (*ho phaula prassōn . . . ouk erchetai pros to phōs*, 3:20), whereas "the truthdoer *comes to* the light" (*ho . . . poiōn tēn alētheian erchetai pros to phōs*, 3:21).[22] Of course, these verbs of movement do have a deeper metaphorical meaning, as will be discussed in the next section, but they reflect a clear spatial interaction: God's Son/light comes, and some people come to him, while others refuse to. If we take the world as a place, these physical movements, or spatial interactions, anticipate what will happen in Jesus's ministry later, showing the principle of the nature of the world. It tells readers what God has done and what the world's possible responses are. This principle is true not merely for the narrated time of Jesus but also in the reader's time.

In addition to the above, John 3:16–21 is also reminiscent of the preceding preamble and monologues (1:1–5, 9–18), naturally recalled when 3:16–21 is heard. The loop of spatial-interaction applies in both:

21. Sack, *Homo Geographicus*, 94.
22. All Scripture translations in the chapter are the author's own.

- Already in 1:1–5, 9–18, the "world" is connected to "God." The God who loves the world (3:16–21) is the God/Word who created the world "in the beginning" (1:1, 3, 10).
- The "light," representing the Son in 3:19, has already appeared in 1:5, where it is said that it shines in the darkness (1:5). The idea that the true light was coming into the world (3:19a) has its precedent in 1:9 (*erchomenon eis ton kosmon*) and 1:11 (*eis ta idia ēlthen*).
- For those who believe in his name, they become "children of God" (*tekna theou*) (1:12), which is analogous to the Son in 3:16. Yet, for this Son, the reader has already learned his uniqueness. He is "the only one from the Father" (*monogenous para patros*, 1:14) and "the only God who is in the bosom of the Father" (*monogenēs theos ho ōn eis ton kolpon tou patros*, 1:18).

Thus, regarding the identity of God and the Son/light, 1:1–5, 9–18b provides the necessary background for the reader's apprehension. The reader cannot misunderstand their identity and confuse Jesus with the other "gods" of the Greco-Roman times as they read. The preamble and monologue are a few chapters away, yet the easy-to-recognize subgenre binds them together. Through them, the spatial-interaction loop between God and the world sets a frame of reference that provides the Gospel with a universal scope, in terms of both place and people. Humanity and the Divine are connected, spatially and relationally, in a unique way distinct from any other religion of the day.

John 3:16–21 demonstrates the nature of the world in relation to the coming of God's Son. It proclaims not only the identity of God and his Son but also what the Son has done, as well as the outcomes of response or rejection. In order for the world to be able to become "sons and daughters" of God (1:12), God sacrificed his "only Son" (3:16). Judgment, elaborated on in 3:19–21, is already (*ēdē*) made in verse 18 on the basis of the people's response to the universality of the event.

Realm of Meaning ("Surface/Depth" Loop)

A third "loop" of forces active in a place concerns the realm of meaning. Sack calls it the loop of "surface/depth," and it questions the other two loops to see if any reality is hidden under artificially constructed realities, and whether they are external or the internal workings of the mind. It initiates "awareness and reflexivity."[23] Johannine scholarship concurs that the author

23. Sack, *Homo Geographicus*, 95.

often conveys ideas of transcendent reality by using physical symbols.[24] This also applies to portrayals involving spatial dimensions. The vocabulary used relates to sacrifice and emotion.

Surface: Sending and Giving; Depth: Sacrifice

In John 3:16–17, "giving" (*didōmi*) and "sending" (*apostellō*) both take "the Son" as object. The indirect object, the "world," is inferred from the text. These actions done for the world have profound meaning for the reader. First, *didōmi* signifies the act of a gift from God, done as a result of his supreme love (*houtōs gar ēgapēsen . . . hōste*). Second, *apostellō* signifies a directional dimension, showing where the Son in the world is originally from. This spatial movement from God has a purpose: "to save the world" (*hina sōthē ho kosmos*). Thus, both spatial actions ("giving" and "sending" of the Son), with their reason and purpose stated, carry deeper theological meaning that invites the reader's reflection. Using straightforward vocabulary, these actions are linked to Jesus's sacrifice as it is hinted at in the lifting up of the serpent in verse 14. They prepare the reader to look forward to the climax of the Gospel—namely, the death and resurrection of Jesus.

Surface: Coming and Not Coming; Depth: Contrasting Emotions and Works

Similarly, the use of "coming to" (*erchomai*) language in John 3:19–21 is significant. At first sight, the coming of the light into the world in 3:19 (*to phōs elēlythen eis ton kosmon*) signifies simply the arrival of Jesus. This parallels the sending of the Son in 3:17 (*apesteilen ho theos ton huion eis ton kosmon*). As we discussed above, in the loop of "spatial-interaction," such language entails the willingness or unwillingness to come. But more, the coming of the light is responded to with emotions, including love and hate. Some people (the world's evildoers) love (*agapaō*) darkness and hate (*miseō*) the light. Conversely, the truth-doers come to the light. The contrasting responses entail not only contrasting emotions but also contrasting works. The works of the truth-doers are accomplished through God (*en theō estin eirgasmena*, v. 21b), while the works of the evildoers are evil (*autōn ponēra ta erga*, v. 19b). This "works" language echoes the "believing" / "not believing" language used in verse 18.

---

24. For instance, C. H. Dodd, *The Interpretation of the Fourth Gospel* (Cambridge: Cambridge University Press, 1953), 133–43; Saeed Hamid-Khani, *Revelation and Concealment of Christ: A Theological Inquiry into the Elusive Language of the Fourth Gospel*, WUNT 2/120 (Tübingen: Mohr Siebeck, 2000); Craig R. Koester, *Symbolism in the Fourth Gospel: Meaning, Mystery, Community*, 2nd ed. (Minneapolis: Fortress, 2003).

Thus, the "coming" language brings in deeper implications of love and hate, and righteous and evil works as a result of belief and unbelief. What is described on the surface reveals deeper spiritual truth underneath. For John, "coming" is no casual term.

Summary

In the above analysis, the territoriality perspective reveals the significance of the spatial dimensions in John 3:16–21. The "in / out of place" loop in the realm of social relations shows how God attempts to establish relationship with the world intentionally. The "spatial-interaction" loop in the realm of nature shows the reader the principle/nature of God's "sending" and the Son's "coming" as bringing forth salvation and judgment, connecting humanity with the Divine in universal terms. The "surface/depth" loop in the realm of meaning shows how verbs of spatial movements on the surface ("sending" and "giving," "coming" and "not coming") give deeper theological meaning to the Son's sacrifice, revealing people's emotions and works as a result of the coming of the light.

Reading the text through these lenses calls for a greater sensitivity to the implications of the world as space *and* people. We cannot understand the Gospel story fully without such an awareness. John carefully constructs the idea of the "world" and sets it in relation to the people and place he creates in the storyline.

Discussion and Relevance to Hongkongers

With the help of Sack's idea of territoriality, we probed into John's "perspective" as an insider ("somewhere" in fig. 4.2). As readers, we reflect on John's message. Rooted in the place of our "self," we form our own "contextualized perspective" ("particular perspectives" in fig. 4.2) as we conduct critical evaluations in relation to what is happening in the society in Hong Kong.

With the complex traits of the "world" as a people/place dual concept, we see that our place, Hong Kong, is very relevant to what is expressed in the gospel message. People of this city are used to pursuing money as a life goal. Economic development is the primary concern of the government and the people. Everything is measured in monetary and pragmatic terms. Secularism affects not only the society but also the churches. Claiming to be urban churches, they believe in quantitative growth, in terms of both attendance and revenue. Successful church leaders boast about their church size or the number of churches they have planted (of course, such boasting is wrapped in spiritual terms). The testimonies of celebrities or high-ranking government officials receive much attention. But with the ongoing social turmoil, people are starting to treasure and hold a more relational view of the society here. We all live in Hong Kong, and we are Hongkongers. People and place affect each other closely. Hongkongers, though diverse, hold core values, like freedom, human rights, democracy, rule of law, and clean governance, which become all the more indispensable when undermined.

Love and peace are what Hong Kong churches can bring to society (this "world") through the gospel message. As we gain a greater sense of belonging, as profound interactions between place and people are felt, we need to tell our fellow Hongkongers that they are not alone in caring for and loving this place. God loves the world. He loves Hong Kong and Hongkongers, to the point that he sends his children to be with them, to tell them that his salvation has been achieved by his only Son, Jesus Christ, and that reconciliation is possible in Christ as we love the light and do the truth. Every Hongkonger, as well as Hong Kong itself, is beloved by God. God on high, hear the prayer of your children who sing out in protest: "Bring him peace, bring him joy, he is young. . . . If I die, let me die, let him live, bring him home, bring him home."[25]

25. Quoting from the musical *Les Misérables*.

5

Empowering Place and Expanding Eden

A Batak Reading of the Theology of the Land in the Book of Acts

CHAKRITA M. SAULINA

The historical significance of the book of Acts in shaping biblical theology is paramount. As the second volume of Luke's writing, Acts chronicles the expansion of Jesus's movement and its proclamation of God's redemptive plan to the ends of the earth. This agenda led to the gentile missions and their inclusion among Jesus's followers. The book also underscores the outpouring of the Holy Spirit, and with this power the disciples perform things that mimic what Jesus does in his ministry, most notably miraculous healings. Thus, together with Luke's Gospel, Acts is an "elaborate historical, geographical, and social concretization [of] . . . the good news concerning Jesus as the savior of the last and lowly, the emerging church, and the saving acts of God in human history."[1]

Moreover, Acts offers insight into the construction of the social identity of the early followers of Jesus as God's covenant people in connection to—and in

---

1. John H. Elliott, "Temple versus Household in Luke-Acts: A Contrast in Social Institutions," in *The Social World of Luke-Acts: Models for Interpretation*, ed. Jerome H. Neyrey (Peabody, MA: Hendrickson, 1991), 211–40.

contrast with—the Jews who oppose them. This opposition correlates with the partings of the ways of the early Christians from Judaism,[2] in which the Jewish followers of Jesus undergo complex social dynamics. Although this group is deeply rooted in their Jewish heritage, their devotion to Jesus's teaching necessitates a new way of living and a reworking of their religious identity. The book of Acts portrays this tension and its implications, including the connection that Jewish followers of Jesus have to the Holy Land and the land's theological significance in shaping their identity amid opposition from their fellow Jews.

In Acts, the Jews construct their identity vis-à-vis three main components: kinship, the law, and the temple (21:28; 25:8). The incident of Paul's arrest in the temple underlines connections between these three elements and how the Jews use them to draw boundaries that separate them from others (e.g., gentiles and early followers of Jesus). Here, Paul is seen only as part of the second group, despite his Jewish ancestry. The Jews from Asia accuse him of bringing the Greeks into the temple (kinship and the temple are linked), thus defiling the holy place (referring to the law). Focusing on spatial elements in this identity formation, we can see that Jerusalem is strongly associated with the vitality of the temple as the locus of the Jewish religious establishment, and the city often denotes a unified and hostile force rejecting the message proclaimed by Jesus's disciples (9:2; 21:11–13; 22:5).

The role of the land in shaping the identity of early Jesus followers has been debated, however. In many cases, Acts describes the continuing role of the temple and the city in the life of the disciples. These disciples participate in the temple cult—for example, maintaining the daily prayer times (3:1; 5:42; cf. 5:21, 25) and the purification law (21:23–26). Nevertheless, some argue that Jerusalem and the temple lost their theological significance among the early Christians, as suggested by the expansion of Christian missions to gentile areas. Furthermore, some consider the geographical description in Acts 1:8 to function rhetorically to refer to ethnic identities.

In contrast, this essay offers a fresh way of understanding the theology of the land in Acts through the lens of the precolonial Toba Batak (a tribe in Sumatra, Indonesia). The Toba Batak construct and project their identities using many elements that can also be found in the social and religious values of the Jewish followers of Jesus. These parallels enable a "conversation" between the two groups. The Batak synthetic way of constructing their cosmology provides a starting point and emphasis that is distinct from those of

---

2. See James D. G. Dunn, *The Partings of the Ways: Between Christianity and Judaism and Their Significance for the Character of Christianity* (London: SCM, 1991). See also Judith Lieu, *Neither Jew nor Greek? Constructing Early Christianity*, 2nd ed., Cornerstones (London: Bloomsbury T&T Clark, 2016).

modern historical and social-anthropological approaches, leading to a unique way of evaluating spatiality in identity formation. This concept allows a fresh approach to reading spatiality in Acts.

The Toba Batak: Anthropological Data

The Toba Batak are an ethnic group that resides in the northern part of Sumatra island, within the western region of Indonesia. Along with the Simalungun, the Angkola, the Karo, and the Dairi, they form a community known as the Batak. The Toba Batak inhabit the area surrounding Lake Toba and within Samosir Island. Records about Sumatra can be found as early as the sixth century in Chinese and Arabian sources.[3] The earliest record of the Batak can be found in the record of Venetian Niccolò de' Conti (1395–1469), who resided for a year on the island as part of his journey from Damascus to Eastern Indonesia (1414–39).

In the late eighteenth century, during fierce competition between the British and the Dutch to obtain natural resources from the island of Sumatra, a more comprehensive study of its inhabitants began. William Marsden published the first monograph in 1783, *The History of Sumatera*, and allocated more than thirty pages to explaining the Batak.[4] Regarding foreign penetrations of the Batak land (and expansion from the interaction on the coastland), the efforts of the European and American missionaries in the early 1800s are worth noting. Two British missionaries began their missions in 1824, followed by two American missionaries in 1834. However, it was not until 1864 that significant Christian influence in the Batak land started through the work of Ludwig Ingwer Nommensen, a German missionary.[5]

Social Identity Formation: The Batak and Judeo-Christians in Conversation

From an anthropological perspective, humans bring order and avoid chaos in navigating their daily lives through the construction of a symbolic universe.[6]

---

3. Achim Sibeth notes, "Venetian Marco Polo and the Arab Ibn Battuta and the Franciscan Odorich of Portenau all visited Northern Sumatra in the course of their journeys in the 13th and 14th Centuries." See Achim Sibeth, Uli Kozok, and Juara R. Ginting, *The Batak: Peoples of the Island of Sumatra; Living with Ancestors* (New York: Thames and Hudson, 1991), 16.

4. Sibeth, Kozok, and Ginting, *Batak*, 16.

5. See Chakrita M. Saulina, "Salvation through Jesus's Sahala: A Batak Reading of Jesus's Victory over the Devil and Death in the Letter to the Hebrews," in *Reading Hebrews and 1 Peter from Majority World Perspectives*, ed. Sofanit T. Abebe, Elizabeth W. Mburu, and Abeneazer G. Urga, LNTS (London: Bloomsbury Academic, 2024).

6. Jerome H. Neyrey, "The Symbolic Universe of Luke-Acts: 'They Turn the World Upside Down,'" in Neyrey, *Social World of Luke-Acts*, 273.

Within this, people define themselves according to the world where they belong and how they interact with it. Jerome Neyrey writes, "A cosmos is fundamentally preferable to chaos. People, then, seek to find order or to impose it on their world so as to give it intelligibility and to define themselves in relation to it. In this they are seeking and producing socially shared meanings. By erecting imaginary and/or real lines, people define 'my' or 'ours' in relation to what is 'yours' and 'theirs,' which is the function of city walls, fences, boundaries, and the like."[7]

This description conveys the complex process of understanding and establishing one's identity, with many variables at work.[8] This essay is interested in analyzing the social aspect of identity formation, which has been overlooked by modern Western thought in favor of individual identity. In social identity formation, one understands one's identity through interactions with others and one's particular membership in a social group (or groups), along with the principles, values, and emotional implications that spring from that membership.[9]

In constructing their social identity, the Batak and the Judeo followers of Jesus utilize parallel elements. Both groups recognize the importance of kinship and ancestry, the role of communal sacred law in governing their everyday life, and the sacred connection between God the creator, people, and the land (cf. Acts 21:28; 25:8). Despite the fact that the groups exist at different times and in different geographical locations, these corresponding notions enable a dialectical analysis and provide a distinctive way of reading the book of Acts through the lens of the Batak.

Divine Ancestral Covenants

The Batak and the Judeo followers of Jesus underline the importance of kinship and ancestry vis-à-vis God the creator and the divine realm. The Toba Batak place significant value on their ancestral lines. Johannes Keuning states, "The kinship with its interwoven bonds of affinal relationships was and is of primary importance."[10] The prominence of familial bonds correlates with the Batak concept of a divine bloodline. They believe that all the Batak

7. Neyrey, "Symbolic Universe," 273.

8. Aaron J. Kuecker, *The Spirit and the "Other": Social Identity, Ethnicity and Intergroup Reconciliation in Luke-Acts*, LNTS (London: T&T Clark International, 2011), 25.

9. Kuecker, *Spirit and the "Other,"* 27; see also Henri Tajfel, *Social Identity and Intergroup Relations*, European Studies in Social Psychology (Cambridge: Cambridge University Press, 1982), 2.

10. Johannes Keuning, *The Toba Batak, Formerly and Now*, Modern Indonesia Project (Ithaca, NY: Department of Far Eastern Studies, Cornell University, 1958), 5.

people are the descendants of one divine figure, Si Radja Batak, to whom all Batak last names (*marga*) are connected.[11] This figure is believed to be the son of a god,[12] and this belief forms the foundation for their ancestral worship. The Toba Batak practice a patrilinear kinship system; however, both sides maintain knowledge regarding their ancestral lines from one generation to the next.[13] A Batak person may be able to trace his or her ancestral line as far as fifteen to twenty generations back.[14] As J. C. Vergouwen aptly describes, "This patrilinear kinship system is the backbone of Batak society, which is built up of lineages, *marga* and tribal groups all connected with each other in the male line. Men form the kinship groups: the women create the affinal relationships because they must marry into other patrilinear groups."[15]

A similar idea can also be found in the Judeo-Christian communities in Acts. For the Jews, God's covenants with Abraham and David are focal points in the theological emphasis of their genealogies, and Luke emphasizes this ancestral covenant as he points out the significance of Jesus's life and works within God's redemptive plan (Luke 1:55, 72–73; 3:8; Acts 3:13, 25; 4:25; 7:2). God "adopted" Abraham to be the progenitor of God's "family," through whom God birthed a new society. This group begets a new nation designated for God's divine purpose of blessing the entire world. The miraculous births of Isaac, Esau, and Jacob underline the notion of a divine bloodline.[16] God's creative power is the essence behind the Israelites' origin and flourishing as a nation, granting their status as God's people.[17] Nevertheless, in the new era of God's redemptive story, Luke demonstrates that the effects of God's salvific work through Jesus's life and ministry (including his death, resurrection, and ascension) expand the boundaries of this ancestral covenant and bring forth a new covenantal relationship (i.e., the faith-based covenant in Jesus). This new affiliation enables the inclusion of gentiles through their faith in Jesus and their divine adoption into God's family through the power of the Holy Spirit (Acts 10:44–48; 11:15–18).

11. J. C. Vergouwen, *The Social Organisation and Customary Law of the Toba-Batak of Northern Sumatra* (Hague: M. Nijhoff, 1964), 21.

12. Vergouwen, *Social Organisation*, 21.

13. Vergouwen, *Social Organisation*, 17–21.

14. Vergouwen, *Social Organisation*, 18.

15. Vergouwen, *Social Organisation*, 2.

16. The covenant includes the matriarchs, whose barrenness is strikingly highlighted in the first three generations (Gen. 18:9–15).

17. Jonathan Sacks emphasizes the notion of descendants and land as gifts from God in the life of the Israelites. To the patriarchs (Abraham, Isaac, and Jacob), God repeatedly promises children and land, promises that get delayed with the infertility of the matriarchs and Israelite life as nomads and foreigners in Egypt. Jonathan Sacks, *The Great Partnership: Science, Religion, and the Search for Meaning* (New York: Schocken Books, 2011), 177–79.

The Sacred Law

One of the most distinctive features of the precolonial Batak is their cosmology, which is intertwined with their theology. The Toba Batak believe in God the creator, called Ompu Mulajadi Nabolon.[18] As the creator, Mulajadi is omnipresent, and his power can be seen everywhere in his creation as he sustains the universe. Alongside Mulajadi are his three sons (Bataraguru, Mangalabulan, and Soripada). They govern the three layers of the cosmos: the upper-, middle-, and underworld. Besides these three sons, Mulajadi also begets three daughters who become his sons' wives; their union provides the origin of the earth and humankind.

The relationship between Mulajadi and his sons carries a complex ontological connection. Some add another god to the list: Asiasi, although the role of this god is unclear. Waldemar Stohr says, "There is some evidence that Debata ["god" in Batak language] Asiasi can be seen as the balance and unity of the trinity of gods [i.e., the three sons of Mulajadi]. In this sense, he is nothing more than a manifestation of the highest god, Mulajadi."[19] Some others, however, claim that Mulajadi himself is the direct manifestation of the unity of his three sons, which is crucial for establishing the harmony of the cosmos.[20]

Batak cosmology is fundamentally different from the modern worldview, which often distinguishes between elements of the cosmos and the force that creates and sustains it (which P. H. Tobing describes as an analytical way of understanding cosmology); the Batak see the former in unity with the latter. The elements are part of the microcosmos whose quality does not merely represent the macrocosm but also carries the totality of the macrocosm. Tobing depicts this as synthetical construction of cosmology.[21] Further explaining this concept, he suggests:

> As a consequence of this mentality the way in which things are experienced, no matter how large or small they are, is of a totalitarian character. . . . They [the Toba Batak] experience the cosmos, the community, the individual, etc.

18. The name literally means "the big and powerful one, the origin of the genesis." See Bungaran Antonius Simanjuntak and D. Sinaga, *Arti dan Fungsi Tanah Bagi Masyarakat Batak Toba, Karo, Simalungun*, rev ed. (Jakarta: Yayasan Pustaka Obor, 2013), 16–17.

19. Quoted in Sibeth, Kozok, and Ginting, *Batak*, 65.

20. Basyral Hamidy Harahap and Hotman Siahaan, *Orientasi Nilai-Nilai Budaya Batak: Suatu Pendekatan Terhadap Perilaku Batak Toba dan Angkola-Mandailing*, Nilai budaya Batak (Jakarta: Sanggar Willem Iskandar, 1987), 64; Philip Oder Lumban Tobing, *The Structure of the Toba-Batak Belief in the High God* (Macassar: South and South-East Celebes Institute for Culture, 1963), 35.

21. Tobing, *Structure of the Toba-Batak Belief*, 28.

each as a totality. By this we mean a unity of functionality heterogeneous entities, cooperating for the sake of a totality, but which can only exist and be conceived within and because of this totality. . . . The Toba Batak conceive the whole cosmic space as the totality of under-, middle-, and upperworld. In this totality, each of these three worlds has a function, through which the harmony and the existence of the universe is possible. The elimination of one of these worlds would mean the annihilation of the universe as well as of the existence of each of them.[22]

Batak synthetic cosmology requires a different way of evaluating human activities vis-à-vis the divine: people see themselves as part of the cosmos and align themselves with the law of the divine force. I refer to this way of life as "the Divine Way," as the Batak always seek to hear God / the gods' voice(s) and value the elements of their lives—including how they use and settle in their land—as a place of encounter between the mortals and the divine and in connection with how the gods reveal themselves through these elements.

This way of thinking is certainly different from most approaches in modern social science and anthropology, which focus on human experiences to explicate realities (both physical and/or spiritual existence).[23] In contrast, in the theocentric way of conducting life, religious motives and conceptions take precedence in almost all aspects of life, both personal and social.[24]

The Batak begin with the view that they are part of a larger "ecosystem" and that the physical and social realities on earth mirror the divine reality where Mulajadi reigns. Paul Pedersen describes the connections between the three layers of the cosmos vis-à-vis the presence and authority of Mulajadi: "Batak mythology described a tree of life, reaching out from the underworld to the upper world, symbolic of the High God in uniting all existence and representing the totality of cosmic order. The fate of every man was recorded on this tree of life from which all life originated."[25]

Therefore, it is not far-fetched to find areas of Batak society where there are other instances of their effort to mirror their life on earth with the structure of the cosmos. Besides their theology and cosmology, the trinitarian principle can also be seen in the Toba Batak's anthropology and social structure. Every Toba Batak considers himself or herself a manifestation of the High God and

---

22. Tobing, *Structure of the Toba-Batak Belief*, 28–29.

23. Paul B. Pedersen, *Batak Blood and Protestant Soul: The Development of National Batak Churches in North Sumatra*, A Christian World Mission Book (Grand Rapids: Eerdmans, 1970), 22; Harahap and Siahaan, *Orientasi*, 66, 69.

24. Vergouwen, *Social Organisation*, 67; Harahap and Siahaan, *Orientasi*, 67–69.

25. Pedersen, *Batak Blood*, 21.

considers human existence to consist of three distinct elements: life (*hosa*), blood (*mudar*), and flesh (*sibuk*).[26] In addition to these three, humans also carry three potent inner elements: *tondi*, *sahala*, and *begu*. *Tondi* and *sahala* are given by Mulajadi.[27] *Tondi*, in some ways, corresponds to the notion of the human soul. It functions as the invisible force behind a living human being and enables the body to move. *Sahala* is the potent force of the *tondi*. The Batak describe physical death as the time when the *tondi* leaves the body forever. When someone dies, his or her *begu* is set free. Here, *tondi* is seen as a "life-soul" and *begu* as "death-soul."[28] In some ways, begu is analogous to a ghost in popular culture.

Toba Batak customary law (*adat*) also applies a trinitarian structure called *Dalihan Na Tolu* (lit., "the three stones"[29]), the foundation of how society operates.[30] This social philosophy is composed of three components: Hula-hula/Mora, Dongan Sabutuha, and Boru. All three statuses are created through marriage. The Hula-hula is the family of the bride, and they are superior over Dongan Sabutuha and Boru. They hold the power and authority within their family line. They are also the protector and sustainer of the family's stability. The Dongan Sabutuha are those who hold the same marga (family name), and the Boru is the groom's family, whose marga cannot be the same as the marga of the bride's father. The Boru serve the needs of Hula-hula, and they should be willing to make sacrifices on their behalf.[31] Within this system, every married Batak man (in his patriarchal lineage) may hold the three statuses with respect to his in-laws and extended family.

Parallel to the Batak, the two religious groups in the book of Acts practice a theocentric way of life. In ancient Jewish society, the symbolic system centers around God and God's covenant with the Israelites. In this covenant relationship, God's commandments given through Moses are the way to maintain their status before God as God's people. In their daily lives, God's holiness is central to how they construct their identity as a distinctive group.

Neyrey suggests that in establishing social boundaries, people, including the Jews mentioned in Acts, consider six areas concerning God's holiness:

26. Harahap and Siahaan, *Orientasi*, 65.

27. Jonar Situmorang, *Mengenal Agama Manusia* (Yogyakarta: Penerbit Andi, 2017), 149. For more on *Sahala* and *Tondi*, see Saulina, "Salvation through Jesus's Sahala."

28. Sibeth, Kozok, and Ginting, *Batak*, 66.

29. The stones here refer to the structure of their traditional stove formed by the three stones. This symbolic notion signifies the importance of this trinitarian principle as these people's daily sustenance.

30. Harahap and Siahaan, *Orientasi*, 46–47, 55–57. Cf. Sibeth, Kozok, and Ginting, *Batak*, 46.

31. Harahap and Siahaan, *Orientasi*, 48.

Figure 5.1

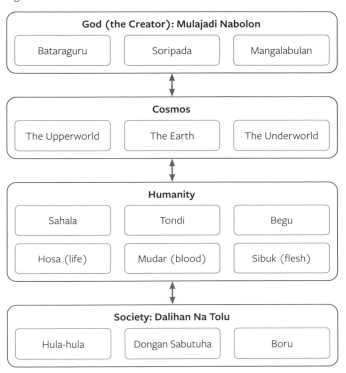

the self, others, nature, time, space, and God.[32] Within these elements, they conduct three categories of actions in forming their identity:

1. Establishing boundaries: the Jewish community determines who is in and who is out. For them, there is a clear boundary between those who are part of God's covenantal people and those outside (Acts 10:28; cf. Lev. 20:26; John 4:8), which manifests in their everyday activities (e.g., kosher diet and Sabbath observance).

2. Building structure: the Jewish community maps, categorizes, and stratifies different elements in one's life. We can see this principle in how they classify time, places, and people in relation to their status as God's people (e.g., in the temple cult and the classifications of people's status, such as priests, Levites, laymen, and women).

32. Neyrey, "Symbolic Universe," 273, 75–85. Cf. Bruce J. Malina, *The New Testament World: Insights from Cultural Anthropology* (Atlanta: John Knox, 1981), 25.

3. Identifying margins: in relation to the previous two principles, at times a society faces people who cannot be put into a certain category or places that cannot be mapped. To deal with these issues, a community locates such people or conditions at the margins, and they often become suspect. For instance, in the purity system, some situations and conditions were considered to create impurity and were perceived as dangerous or threatening.[33]

The Sacred Space and Social Identity

The importance of space in forming one's identity is often neglected as modern Western thought focuses on human influence over a spatial environment while forgetting the impact of this environment on its inhabitants.[34] Margaret Rodman claims that "there is little recognition that place is more than locale, the setting for action, the stage on which things happen. . . . It is time to recognize that places, like voices, are local and multiple. For each inhabitant, a place has a unique reality, one in which meaning is shared with other people and places. The links in these chains of experienced places are forged of culture and history."[35]

For many ethnic groups, identity and geographical location are not separable. This close association between place and people creates an "environment of trust" in kinship, social interactions, cosmology, and tradition that is place based.[36] A corresponding idea is also found in the Toba Batak's socioreligious belief system, as they have a theocentric approach to time and space. They view the earth as the result of divine grace and protection, as delineated in the myth of Si Boru Nadeak Parujar, the daughter of Bataraguru (one of the sons of Mulajadi).[37] She was forced into marriage with Siraja Odapodap, Mangala Bulan's son. She refused to follow the order and then fled the upperworld to a watery middleworld. She found herself having nowhere to rest. Out of compassion, Mulajadi gave her a handful of soil to have a place to set her feet and rest. This piece of land then turned into a much larger area. However, the dragon, the underworld ruler who lived in the water, opposed the fact that the landmass had spread over his head. The

---

33. Neyrey, "Symbolic Universe," 281.

34. Margaret C. Rodman, "Empowering Place: Multilocality and Multivocality," *American Anthropologist* 3, no. 94 (1992): 640–56.

35. Rodman, "Empowering Place," 643.

36. Rodman, "Empowering Place," 647–48.

37. Hesron H. Sihombing, "The Batak-Christian Theology of Land: Towards a Postcolonial Comparative Theology," *Cross Currents* 73 (2023): 42–63. Cf. Sibeth, Kozok, and Ginting, *Batak*, 65.

dragon was unsettled and rolled around, and he aimed to destroy the earth with his movement. With the help of Mulajadi, Boru Parujar overcame the dragon of the underworld by sticking a sword over his body and imprisoning him with an iron block.

With this theological understanding of land as a divine gift, the Batak view their native land as sacred. Space was never a neutral element but holds an intrinsic value and supernatural power that can influence human life.[38] Pedersen states, "The Toba Batak did not emphasize quantitatively measurable time but experienced every space of time qualitatively and concretely."[39] They always seek God's blessing whenever they open a new village (*huta*).[40] *Huta* is the foundation of Batak society, organizing economic, social, and political resources and entities. The theological significance of the land and *huta* has several implications, including their ecological conscience. Delineating this notion, Hesron Sihombing states:

> The Batak people believed that every space had its own spiritual occupant, so they should treat every space with respect for divine blessings to materialize. Soil and land could not be treated as merely a tool for economic fulfillment. Forests could not be exploited irresponsibly. People had to conduct religious rituals before taking wood from the forest, and only selective wood was allowed to be taken. Trees around a water source, such as a lake, could not be cut down. It is evident that the Batak people's concerns with ecological sustainability were closely entwined with their understanding of God, religion, and community.[41]

Spatial Elements in Acts

The significance of spatiality in biblical narratives is often overlooked. Geography is viewed as part of the background (as location/setting) without any intrinsic value. Matthew Sleeman argues that this phenomenon represents a wider issue in Western thought that marginalizes the spatial aspect of reality.[42] In Luke-Acts studies, for instance, the study of geography is reduced to cartography or ontological dualism.[43] Regarding the latter, some argue that one

38. Pedersen, *Batak Blood*, 21; Sihombing, "Batak-Christian Theology," 50.

39. Pedersen, *Batak Blood*, 21.

40. Sihombing, "Batak-Christian Theology," 50; Simanjuntak and Sinaga, *Arti*, 24–25.

41. Sihombing, "Batak-Christian Theology," 50.

42. Matthew Sleeman, *Geography and the Ascension Narrative in Acts*, SNTSMS 146 (Cambridge: Cambridge University Press, 2009), 22. Vine Deloria Jr. comes to a similar assessment. The modern Western world is what he calls a time-based culture. Deloria distinguishes time-based cultures from place-based cultures. Vine Deloria Jr., *God Is Red: A Native View of Religion* (Wheat Ridge: Fulcrum, 2023), 55–69.

43. Sleeman, *Geography*, 29. See further discussion on pp. 33–35.

element of the early Christians that is distinct from the Jews is their detachment from the promised land, as they no longer view it as having special status. Gary Burge, for instance, argues, "Early Christian mission did not see itself limited to the province of Judea that gave it its birth. The Christian community did not interpret its identity as linked to Judea or even to Galilee as Jesus had done."[44] Jesus's response to the disciples' question in Acts 1:6 bolsters this claim: the mission is not about restoring the kingdom of Israel with Jerusalem as the center of its "universe." As Burge further states, "The early Christians possessed no territorial theology. Early Christian preaching is utterly uninterested in a Jewish eschatology devoted to the restoration of the land."[45]

Corresponding to this argument, scholars also suggest symbolic functions of the geographical descriptions in the programmatic statement of the disciples' mission in Acts 1:8: "You will be my witnesses in Jerusalem, in all Judea, Samaria, and to the ends of the earth" (NIV). These areas serve as rhetorical devices referring to the growing scope of influence of Jesus's early followers and their numbers; these spatial descriptions do not have their own intrinsic force. As David Bauer suggests, "The geographical areas mentioned here are ciphers for ethnic groups: 'all Judea and Samaria' for 'quasi-Jews,' and 'the end of the earth' for gentiles, including those gentiles who have no association with Jews or Judaism."[46] Therefore, the spatial details have no theological importance but denote the early Christians' focus on international and multiethnic missions.

In contrast, I propose that the distinctive perspective of the Batak synthetic cosmology provides a fresh way of evaluating the role of geography in Acts by underlining what I have referred to as earlier as the Divine Way. This principle signifies the people's unified devotion to conduct their lives according to the divine will (God's rules over the cosmos). The Divine Way heightens the necessity of understanding the spatial elements in the book through a theocentric approach. In this framework, readers of the book are drawn to divine proclamations, commands, and evaluations, which manifest in and influence human activities, including how God's people should value their lands. I will use this theme to examine Luke's spatial elements in Acts in relation to the early Christians' identity formation, focusing mainly on Acts 1–15.

This theocentric approach to evaluating space is built on Sleeman's "Third-space" framework. In his book, *Geography and the Ascension Narrative in*

44. Gary M. Burge, *Jesus and the Land: The New Testament Challenge to "Holy Land" Theology* (Grand Rapids: Bakar Academic, 2010), 58.

45. Burge, *Jesus and the Land*, 59.

46. David R. Bauer, *The Book of Acts as Story: A Narrative-Critical Study* (Grand Rapids: Baker Academic, 2021), 74; see also Kuecker, *Spirit and the "Other,"* 99.

Acts, Sleeman argues against devaluing space without understanding Luke's geography. Using the three-grid schema of space (First-, Second-, and Third-spaces), Sleeman produced a comprehensive spatialized reading method for Acts.[47] His work is built on Soja's work in categorizing three ways of evaluating space.[48] "Firstspace" is an objective way of understanding space as it points to the external and material (physical) aspects of space. This describes the mappable elements of geography in our world.[49] Unlike this objective understanding, "Secondspace" refers to the mental projection of spatiality or the "imaginative geography" that is usually presented in written design or architectural plans.[50] From a modern perspective, these two terms encompass a complete spectrum of evaluating space and human geography, as the two ideas complement and oppose each other. To this dichotomy, Soja introduces "Thirdspace," which allows for aspiration amid spatiality's concrete and imaginative nature.

Thirdspace enables the third way of perceiving human spatiality as "simultaneously real [Firstspace], imagined [Secondspace], and more (both and also)."[51] According to Sleeman, "Thirdspace, as Other, continually undermines any claim of a settled firstspace-secondspace binary relationship, and opens up new ways of seeing space, being in space and ordering space. . . . It is politically charged space that resists the power plays and closure of materialist firstspace and ideational secondspace, being space wherein alternative territorialities and worldviews are explored. *Thirdspace resides in visionary vistas that imagine new meanings or possibilities for shaping spatial practices.*"[52]

Looking closely at Acts, the importance of spatial aspects starts with Luke's frequent references to Jerusalem and the temple, more references than any other New Testament author uses.[53] These data highlight the continuing role of the temple and the city in the life of the disciples in Acts. As mentioned earlier, these disciples actively participate in the temple cult—for example, maintaining the daily prayer times (Acts 3:1; 5:42; cf. 5:21, 25) and the purification law (21:23–26). The disciples also remain in Jerusalem for a certain period; the dispersion starting in Acts 8:1 is triggered by an external

---

47. Sleeman, *Geography*, 43–56.
48. Edward W. Soja, *Thirdspace: Journeys to Los Angeles and Other Real-and-Imagined Places* (Cambridge, MA: Blackwell, 1996).
49. Soja, *Thirdspace*, 10, 74–75.
50. Soja, *Thirdspace*, 10, 79.
51. Sleeman, *Geography*, 44–45. Cf. Soja, *Thirdspace*, 10–11, 81.
52. Sleeman, *Geography*, 45 (emphasis added).
53. *Naos* (temple), *ouikos* [*thou theo*] (house of God), and *hieron* (the holy place) occur fourteen times in Luke and twenty-four times in Acts, the highest number of references to the temple in the New Testament. Cf. Elliott, "Temple versus Household," 218–19.

force—persecution—rather than the disciples' actual intention to migrate. Nevertheless, the apostles continue to be present in Jerusalem. These decisions should not be overlooked; they are part of the response to Jesus's commands and indicate the continuing significance of the city.

Additionally, the first and second spaces in Sleeman's work signify an anthropocentric view of geography, and this framework is insufficient to assess (if not incompatible with) the Christocentric world of Acts, which produces a new cosmology. The book necessitates a "third" method of spatial evaluation due to the two major events described at the beginning of the book that also frame the entire following narrative: (1) Jesus's ascension and (2) the coming of the Holy Spirit.

These two events link heaven and earth in a way that they haven't been since Adam and Eve's rebellion; these events bring eschatological space and time to the earth with all its restorative expectations and implications. Jesus's ascension conveys the notion of Christ's lordship over the universe and enlarges the disciples' spatial imagination so that they live in this new reality.[54] Similarly, the coming of the Holy Spirit signifies the disciples' new identity, authority, and power on earth. Their identity as Christ's witnesses enables them to "alter" the natural world, having the same ability to perform miraculous deeds as Jesus did. They participate in the cosmic saga as they turn people's eyes from darkness to light and from the power of Satan to God (Acts 26:18; cf. Luke 4:6[55]). The coming and presence of the kingdom of God on earth requires a new perspective to understand God's geography, where the link between heaven and earth is properly acknowledged and examined. An Edenic view of space aptly fits these criteria.

Empowering Place: The Edenic Theology of the Land

Scholars have pointed out the parallel between elements presented in Acts 2:1–13 and the Tower of Babel.[56] The Tower of Babel episode highlights the significance of the spatial aspect of God's calling to humanity, as presented in Adam and Eve's commission to fill the earth (Gen. 1:26–28). The violation of this commandment results in the scattering of people all over

54. Sleeman, *Geography*, 74–75.
55. Luke is the only Gospel that describes Satan's claim of having authority over all the inhabited world (his cosmology), which provides the background for the cosmic war between the kingdom of God and the power of darkness.
56. Michael S. Heiser, *Supernatural: What the Bible Teaches about the Unseen World—and Why It Matters* (Bellingham, WA: Lexham, 2015), 63; G. K. Beale, *The Temple and the Church's Mission: A Biblical Theology of the Dwelling Place of God*, New Studies in Biblical Theology 17 (Downers Grove, IL: Apollos, 2004), 203.

the face of the earth, a geographical notice (Gen. 11:9). This scattering is also associated with the notion of God divorcing the nations while giving a special place to the Israelites as God's own portion (Deut. 32:8–9).[57] In Acts 2, however, Luke shows that the coming of the Holy Spirit reverses the separation.[58]

Examining the tower in Genesis 11 through ancient Mesopotamian cultic rituals is especially enlightening. As G. K. Beale persuasively suggests, "The judgment at Babel occurred as a result of the people uniting to build a temple tower in order to force God to come down from heaven in blessings. Such cultic towers were typical of the time in ancient Mesopotamia. Their purpose was to serve as a gateway between heaven and earth whereby the god could come down and even refresh himself on the way to the earthly temple. . . . Like Babel's temple tower, the Jerusalem Temple was intended to be the link between heaven and earth."[59] In Genesis 1 and 2, Eden is seen as the place where heaven and earth collide. With this theological background in mind, we can see that the violation of God's command is not only people's refusal to spread out over the earth but also the human effort in erecting the tower, as it signifies human endeavor in bringing back "Eden" (here, heavenly power manifests on earth) on their terms.

In Luke's Gospel and Acts, however, Luke tells the story of how God brings back Edenic reality in a fresh way through the work of Jesus, the coming of the Holy Spirit, and the ministry of the disciples. This Edenic theology consists of three aspects: (1) the new magnitude of the link between heaven and earth, manifested first in Jerusalem; (2) the restoration of God's call for humanity, as God's imagers[60] and caretakers of the earth; and (3) the expansion of the scope of this second Eden to the end of the earth. These three notions convey God's agenda for the universal restoration (*apokatastaseōs pantōn*, Acts 3:21).

The ascension of the resurrected Jesus to heaven and the coming of the Holy Spirit on earth create a new spatial reality where God's power reigns like never before. The coming of the kingdom of God is certainly part of this claim. Jesus proclaims the coming of the kingdom, and it can be seen and experienced in his teachings, healings, and exorcisms (esp. Luke 9:1–6; 11:14–23; cf. Matt. 12:22–32). Here, the Batak synthetic cosmology can be very helpful in understanding the significance of this phenomenon. The Batak see the micro-cosmos (life on earth) not only as mirroring the macro-cosmos

57. Michael S. Heiser, *The Unseen Realm: Recovering the Supernatural Worldview of the Bible* (Bellingham, WA: Lexham, 2015), 113–14.
58. Cf. Beale, *Temple*, 202.
59. Beale, *Temple*, 203.
60. This term is coined by Heiser. See Heiser, *Unseen Realm*, 43.

(the entire universe, the seen and unseen realms) but also as a place where the full quality of the macro-cosmos can be experienced. For instance, the power of Mulajadi that sustains the cosmos can also be experienced fully (not just its partial quality) in even the smallest communal entity (e.g., a Batak *huta*). A similar (but not identical) idea can also underline the extent of God's kingdom on earth. The manifestations should not be seen as merely a representation or foretaste of God's earthly reign. Rather, they are the visual and experiential quality of this new reality, where evil loses its power and the disciples are endowed with power and authority over the enemy (Luke 10:18–19). Jesus also sees his body as the replacement of the temple "during his ministry and more climactically at his resurrection (John 2:19–22; Matt. 26:61; 27:40; Mark 14:58; 15:29)."[61] Through Jesus, his disciples experience God's presence freshly and more powerfully.

The Divine Way, through the Batak lens, also helps readers of Acts grasp a new way of understanding the role of the temple. Stephen's defense of the accusations in Acts 6:11 and 13, which results in his murder as the first recorded martyr in Acts,[62] is often used to demonstrate the annulment of the significance of this sacred space. The accusation in 6:13 is certainly revealing, since the false witnesses testify that Stephen rejects the temple and the law of Moses (cf. 21:28).[63] In Luke's narrative development, the vital function of Stephen's speech cannot be ignored. First, it is the longest speech recorded in Acts. Second, the public response to his speech provides the background for how the gospel spreads beyond Jerusalem. Dunn argues that the speech has two main themes: (1) the temple not being seen as the center of God's presence and purpose and (2) the reoccurring acts of rejection toward God's messengers.[64] Stephen's response thus marks the beginning of the Christian critique of the temple, which develops into the two contrasting positions between Christianity and Judaism vis-à-vis the temple's centrality for religious observance.[65]

Contrary to the idea that Jesus's followers no longer consider Jerusalem and the temple as having theological significance, Stephen's speech shows

---

61. Beale, *Temple*, 203.

62. It can be argued that Stephen's death mirrors Jesus's death; see Craig C. Hill, "Acts 6.1–8.4: Division or Diversity?," in *History, Literature, and Society in the Book of Acts*, ed. Ben Witherington (Cambridge: Cambridge University Press, 1996), 138. More comprehensively, see Hill, *Hellenists and Hebrews: Reappraising Division within the Earliest Church* (Minneapolis: Fortress, 1992).

63. It is important to note that what the opposition brings to Stephen is a false accusation and is not representative of Stephen's true attitude about the temple. Hill, "Acts 6.1–8.4." See also Neyrey, "Symbolic Universe," 272.

64. Dunn, *Partings of the Ways*, 87–88.

65. Dunn further notes that Stephen's critique applies only to the temple, not to the tabernacle. Dunn, *Partings of the Ways*, 90, 92.

that believers strive for reform, including a new way of valuing these sacred places.[66] First, Stephen's high view of the covenant and the law is shown by his repeated references to the phrase "our ancestor" (nine times)[67] and Moses's name (also nine times). Stephen reminds the council that God's revelations to and covenant with his people are what make places holy (e.g., God's original promise of the promised land, Acts 7:5, 30–33, 38). The places mentioned in the speech are both outside and inside the boundaries of the Holy Land. For instance, God's glory appears in Mesopotamia (7:2; cf. 7:49).

Second, contrary to other gods whose presence and dwelling places are built by human hands (Acts 7:41, 43), God's decision to include a special place to signify his presence and to be a place of worship originates from his divine prerogative and commands (7:44, 46–47). Thus, the theological significance of the temple attaches directly to God's own authority and is not from human invention. People's obedience is mandatory to show their respect to the holy place. Instead of showing respect, God's people made repeated offenses, which led to their exile and the destruction of the temple (7:43). Stephen's speech, just like Jesus's oracle (Luke 21:5–6), indicates the possible destruction of the temple as God's judgment (see Acts 7:51–53 in relation to 7:43).

The Synoptic Gospels agree that Jesus prophesied the destruction of the temple's "walls" (Matt. 24:1–2; Mark 13:1–2; Luke 21:5–6). Through the Divine Way of evaluating spatiality, demolishing the walls can be interpreted as both literary and symbolic. Vis-à-vis the former, the destruction of the temple is seen as God's judgment on the sins of the Jews. However, the collapse of the walls can also be considered through a more positive lens. Reading this event through the Divine Way may signify how the boundaries of the temple, as the place where heaven and earth collide, are expanding. This idea is vital for Luke, particularly. The Lukan Jesus opens the gate of paradise, often associated with Eden, for a repentant sinner (Luke 23:43).[68] Correspondingly, the tearing of the temple's curtain may be viewed as indicating fresh and profound access to God's throne.

Stephen's entire speech, therefore, debunks the false accusation against him and opens a fresh way of understanding the early Christian ways of reforming the law and the temple. As Neyrey aptly suggests, "To their observant

66. Neyrey, "Symbolic Universe," 272.

67. This phrase underlines Stephen's inclusion of himself as part of the covenant people. It is striking, however, that in Acts 7:51–53, the phrase "our ancestors" turns into "your ancestor."

68. For a comprehensive discussion on the link between the temple and Eden, see J. T. A. G. M. van Ruiten, "Eden and the Temple: The Rewriting of Genesis 2:4–3:24," in *Paradise Interpreted: Representations of Biblical Paradise in Judaism and Christianity*, ed. Gerard P. Luttikhuizen, Jewish Early, and Conference Christian Traditions (Leiden: Brill, 1999), 63–94.

Jewish neighbors, they indeed 'turned the world upside down,' for they did not respect or observe the value orientation (God's holiness-as-separation) or its major symbolic and structural expressions. Thus they were perceived. . . . Maintaining their rootedness in Israel's scriptures and in worship of Israel's God, they disputed with observant Jews over where to draw the lines and how to classify persons, *places*, things and times. They offered a reformed system, but a concern for 'purity' nonetheless."[69] Purity, however, took a broader meaning of placing one's heart in obedience to God's command rather than only following the purity laws (Acts 10:1–33). The Judeo-Christian communities theocentric construction of their identity included the land.

Jerusalem bears a new theological significance in this process. In this area, the Batak's understanding of their native land brings new insights. For the Toba Batak diaspora, their native land always holds a special status, regardless of migration. Reading Acts through the Divine Way leads us to a similar notion about Jerusalem. "The ends of the earth" (Acts 1:8) does not replace the status of Jerusalem as the birth place of the new reality. Treating Jerusalem as merely a political entity or territory also impoverishes this status. God's kingdom on earth cannot be reduced to a political agenda. God's transformative power requires the disciples to see their lives differently and to arrange them appropriately to align with the new reality where heaven and earth collide. Through their devotion to Christ, the disciples bring "Eden" with them everywhere they go.

The Divine Way also transforms Jerusalem's theological status. James Dunn claims that the city holds its substantial status only due to the temple, but Jerusalem is still important in Acts because Luke perceives it as "the focal point of the eschatological climax of God's purpose for Israel" (cf. Acts 1:6, 21–22; 3:21).[70] Indeed, some apostles remained in Jerusalem even after the persecutions began.[71]

However, Acts also underlines Jerusalem's vitality apart from the temple's physical presence. Jerusalem's status fits within Luke's continued interest in valuing the city in his Gospel, which begins and ends in Jerusalem. Strikingly, while Luke includes the temple and many crucial events at the beginning of his Gospel, he concludes with God's interest in Jerusalem despite the impending destruction of the temple (Luke 19:41–44). Luke's Gospel emphasizes Jesus's status as the son of David, the heir of God's promise that the Davidic kingdom will have no end. God's covenant with David

---

69. Neyrey, "Symbolic Universe," 303 (emphasis added).
70. Dunn, *Partings of the Ways*, 77–78.
71. Hill, "Acts 6.1–8.4," 137.

precedes and precludes the necessity of the temple's existence. Jerusalem's eschatological status may not include the physical temple. Luke provides several hints that lead his readers to a new way of seeing the temple (23:45) and points to new "temples"—the disciples—with the coming of the Holy Spirit (Acts 2:1–12).

From the perspective of the Divine Way, the divine commands and proclamations hold the highest position in evaluating the function of the spatial elements in Acts. This is clear starting at the beginning of the book, which provides both the introduction and the framework from which the narrative in the book should be evaluated. Jesus first asks the disciples not to leave Jerusalem until the Holy Spirit comes (1:4), and Jesus says that the Spirit will empower them to be his witnesses in Jerusalem, Judea, Samaria, and to the ends of the earth (1:8). Furthermore, the angel's proclamation in 1:11 likely includes Jerusalem as the place where Jesus will return. Thus, Jerusalem is the beginning of the new Eden, even as its border is expanding.

The powerful force of God through the work of the Holy Spirit leads to the rediscovering of God's call for humanity. Just like the Batak always see their connection with the cosmos, the disciples are called to see themselves as part of God's new reality. This special role leads to two further implications: ecological concerns and ethics. Vis-à-vis the former, the Edenic theology reminds the disciples that the earth, let alone the land, belongs to God (Acts 14:15–17; 17:24–28). Regarding ethics, as Paul urges in Lystra and in Athens, living in God's land means acknowledging Christ's lordship and despising evil. Through the lens of the Divine Way, there is also a healthy dynamic between lamentation and hope, where lamentation acknowledges the presence of evil in the world and hope arises because evil is not part of God's original creation (Gen 1:12, 18, 21, 25, 31), nor is it part of the new Eden. The presence of evil does not mean that God is not in control or that the kingdom of God has failed to manifest. The strong bond between heaven and earth after Jesus's ascension and the outpouring of the Holy Spirit rejects this dualistic worldview. The disciples are called to resist evil, and God's power within them is enough to do so. The delay of God's judgment over evil may be seen as grace: God's kingdom awaits the fullness of the nations responding to the good news.

The day of Pentecost denotes the expansion of this new Eden. As Beale argues, "The divine Spirit from the heavenly temple has descended and rested on God's people who become part of the heavenly temple on earth."[72] The Spirit empowers the disciples to be Christ's witnesses (Acts 1:8; 2:40; cf. Rev.

---

72. Beale, *Temple*, 208.

11:3–5). Just like Jesus's, the disciples' presence and testimonies transform the spatial reality where they belong. Thus, the list of geographical places in Acts 1:8 should be seen as expanding the new Edenic reality. "What would appear to be the building of the new spiritual temple at Pentecost included symbolic representatives of all the nations because this temple will not fail to fulfill the intention of Eden's and Israel's temples to expand its borders until the entire earth comes under its roof."[73]

73. Beale, *Temple*, 208.

Part 2

PAULINE EPISTLES

6

Reading Romans in the Midst of Empire

Chinese Readers Grappling with Romans 13:1–7

SZE-KAR WAN

The controversial passage in Romans 13:1–7 that appears to enjoin unquestioned obedience to authorities continues to bedevil modern readers habituated to the ideals of democratic governance. From nineteenth-century American abolitionists to twentieth-century anti-Nazi partisans to legions of resisters to tyrants and totalitarian regimes, they all have had to contend with this seemingly insuperable impediment. But, in fact, not only are the sentiments expressed in this passage atypical of the general thoughts expressed in Romans, they actually gainsay what Paul says consistently in his extant writings—that this world along with its earthly institutions is passing away and stands at the precipice of a divine wrath about to be unleashed on this passing age.[1] The beginning of Romans 12, which counsels readers not to

---

1. So Neil Elliott, "Romans 13:1–7 in the Context of Imperial Propaganda," in *Paul and Empire: Religion and Power in Roman Imperial Society*, ed. Richard A. Horsley (Harrisburg, PA: Trinity Press International, 1997), 186: "The pagan world is characterized as hostile and shameful [within the eschatological context of Rom. 12–13] *except* for the governing authorities as they are presented in 13:1–7, who are benevolent and to be regarded with 'honor' (*timē*, 13:7)"

conform to this world, would flatly contradict a defense of earthly authorities and an injunction to submit to them. If Paul ever spoke so glowingly about the government or magistrates, there is no evidence of it outside Romans 13. This incongruity is so jarring that several proposals have seriously entertained the possibility that this passage is either an interpolation by later scribes reconciling themselves with Roman rule or an adaptation of an older Hellenistic Jewish wisdom saying to the present context.[2] It of course escapes no one's attention that this passage is included in a consequential missive being dispatched to the very seat of the Roman Empire.[3]

Whether Paul personally composed this pro-government passage matters little to modern readers grappling with its weighty implications, especially those who are trapped by its apologies or justification for totalitarian regimes. For such readers, this short passage, carefully unmoored from its literary context and Paul's larger eschatological reasoning, represents the totality of Romans. Nowhere is this clearer than in the case of Hong Kong churches struggling with a centralized government over universal suffrage. Since the former British colony came under Chinese rule in 1997, an intense debate has arisen on the legitimacy of taking part in a political process marked by threats and violence. For readers who take Western liberal democracy for granted, the debate reveals just how fraught the hermeneutical task of appropriating an ancient text for the modern world is. Chinese interpreters read this passage not in the comfort of their studies, or from the podium of their classrooms, but in the field, with one ear close to the ground and the other trained on the cries of their friends and colleagues. In two previous contributions, I studied the exegetical issues of Romans 13:1–7 within the larger context of Paul's thoughts; here I concentrate on being in conversation with Hong Kong interpreters.[4]

(emphasis original). See also, by way of comparison, Victor P. Furnish, *The Moral Teaching of Paul* (Nashville: Abingdon, 1979), 117, who calls Rom. 13 a "monumental contradiction" in Paul's thought.

2. On the passage being a later interpolation, see James Kallas, "Romans xiii, 1–7: An Interpolation," *NTS* 11 (1965): 365–74.

3. The history of interpretation on Rom. 13:1–7 is predictably enormous. Positions and issues are helpfully sketched out in David W. Pao, "The Ethical Relevance of New Testament Commentaries: On the Reading of Romans 13:1–7," in *On the Writing of New Testament Commentaries: Festschrift for Grant R. Osborn*, ed. S. E. Porter and E. J. S. Schnabel (Leiden: Brill, 2013), 193–213.

4. Sze-kar Wan, "Coded Resistance: A Proposed Rereading of Romans 13:1–7," in *The Bible in the Public Square*, ed. C. B. Kittredge, E. B. Aitkin, and J. A. Draper (Minneapolis: Augsburg Fortress, 2008), 173–84; S.-k. Wan, *Romans: Empire and Resistance*, TTCSGNT (London: Bloomsbury T&T Clark, 2021), 79–102. I want to thank the Rev. Leo Kwan for providing me with references to many of the Hong Kong articles.

Daniel Ng: Piety Divorced from Society

There is no better example to illustrate the impact of this passage on the modern world than Nazi Germany, where we find political supporters and opponents alike wrestling with it. Pro-Nazi pastors preached "tens of thousands of sermons up and down the country" on Romans 13, which "became one of the glues that held the Third Reich together."[5] The German theologian Otto Dibelius appealed to Martin Luther's reading of Romans 13 to counsel not only submission but even active support: "From Rev. Martin Luther we learned that the church should not be allowed to interfere with legitimate state power if it does what it is called to do, *even if it turns hard and ruthless*."[6] Submission to the governing authorities, according to Nazi supporters, is absolute and is independent of the character of the state. Resisters to the Nazi regime found the appeal to Romans 13 oppressive, but they did little to dispute this surface reading. In his last conversation with his cousin on a lonely train platform a few days before his death, Weimar officer Heinrich Graf von Lehndorff confessed to being crippled by Paul's foreboding words: "Must a Christian in his responsibility for his fatherland really have to put up with everything? Must he continue to look on idly as a madman ripped the people into pieces? One thing became clear to us at least: the Apostle Paul gave us no handle if we were to call on his letter to the Romans to save our own salvation. He only let us know how heavy weighed the decision with which we saw ourselves confronted. There was only the choice between guilt and guilt."[7]

This same struggle over Paul's words in the face of unjust laws and policies can be observed in the American antebellum debate over slavery, the South African struggle against apartheid, or Japanese Christians' quiet but insistent opposition to the Pacific War.[8] It now dominates the hermeneutical discussion in China over Hongkongers' demand for universal suffrage. As the relationship between the semiautonomous Special Administrative Region and the central Chinese government threatened to collapse, a Hong Kong Evangelical Free Church pastor, Daniel Ng (吳宗文, *Wu Zongwen*), delivered a sermon on

5. Thomas Weber, "When Romans 13 Was Invoked to Justify Evil," CNN, June 22, 2018, https://www.cnn.com/2018/06/22/opinions/jeff-sessions-bible-verse-nazi-germany-opinion-weber/index.html.

6. Weber, "When Romans 13 Was Invoked to Justify Evil."

7. Hans Graf von Lehndorff, *Ostpreussisches Tagebuch: Aufzeichnungen eines Arztes aus den Jahren 1945–1947*, 13th ed. (Munich: Biederstein, 1961), 93. Unless otherwise indicated, all translations in this chapter are my own.

8. For a brief account of how the passage was used to justify and vilify the American War of Independence, to support and reject slavery during the American Civil War, and to support Nazi Germany, see S.-k. Wan, *Romans*, 79–89. For Japanese efforts, see Mitsuo Miyata, *Authority and Obedience: Romans 13:1–7 in Modern Japan*, AUSTR 294 (New York: Peter Lang, 2009).

Romans 13, in which he suggests that believers must not use "unjust political means" to achieve good. Instead, believers should follow the examples of Jesus and Paul, who, Ng suggests, attempted to "reform and construct society [only] by means of their faith and values." They did so, accordingly, because their revolution began with the "inner heart" (內心, *neixin*), the depths of one's personal life. Only when these are reformed "could a spiritual kingdom that does not belong to this world be constructed." Ng concludes that believers must submit to the authorities because their governance is ordered by God, respect officials because they are God's servants appointed to mete out rewards and punishments, and pay their taxes because that is an obligation stipulated by God.[9]

Ng's emphasis on believers and not on either the church or society is no accident, for he sees the individual as the only agent for social reform. He leaves no room for civil institutions between the state and individuals or what sociologists call "mediating structures" that make a modern democracy possible. Ng goes further, however, in discouraging activism. He cites Karl Barth in support of his position that all revolutions are "negative" because true transformation lies only with God.[10] Little does Ng realize that Barth's negative assessment applies primarily to the church, as he makes clear in his formulation of the "existing order" in terms of state, church, law, and society, not merely individuals. Barth made that explicit in his later publication.[11]

Ng attempts to turn Barth's negative into a positive (積極, *jiji*): "Believers must assist a relatively just government to fulfill its God-ordained mission." They could do so by abandoning their "superstition in political system," by refusing to worship the false idols of "democracy, freedom, human rights, and rule of law," and most of all by acknowledging and affirming the historical reality that the Chinese central government exercises its sovereignty and administrative authority over Hong Kong. In other words, Ng counsels Hong Kong Christians to accept Barth's alleged fatalism in human revolution and to work toward aiding a "relatively just" government to maintain a stable and prosperous society. If that means accepting the loss of freedoms, the rule of law, human rights, and such—all by-products of decaying realities in Ng's estimation—so be it.[12]

9. Daniel Ng, "為香港求平安祈禱會" [Peace in Hong Kong prayer meeting], *Christian Weekly* 2373, February 14, 2010, http://www.christianweekly.net/2010/ta20295.htm.

10. Karl Barth, *The Epistle to the Romans*, 6th ed., ET (London: Oxford, 1933), 481–84.

11. Karl Barth, *Church and State* (London: SCM, 1939). The English title accurately expresses the content of the original, whose German title was *Rechtfertigung und Recht* [Justification and justice].

12. Ng, "Peace in Hong Kong."

Remarkable in Ng's sermon is the lack of any explicit or implicit reference to the Chinese government. It focuses exclusively on the division and contentiousness that result from Hong Kong Christians taking different political positions. One reason for the absence might be strategic. Ng thinks a historic task lies before Christians: "To make China change its mind about Christianity and to transform Christianity into a force that can move Chinese civilization forward."[13] But the more pernicious reason is a naivete concerning authoritarian systems and the political process, born of and sustained by an individualistic understanding of faith. Once Christianity is reduced to individual piety and personal belief, the systemic impact of all political structures—including authoritarianism and totalitarianism—on all aspects of life cannot but be minimized. The spiritual and the political are seen as occupying mutually exclusive planes, so that for Ng it is not a problem ignoring the hulking presence of the central government. This silence on the government and its flip side stress on obligation to obey the authorities belie an unspoken but clear demand for absolute obedience to the state irrespective of whether the state is just in its laws or their execution.

Li Xinyuan: The Autonomy of a Christianized Confucian Conscience

Around the same time when Ng's sermon was delivered, a mainland Chinese, Li Xinyuan (李信源), published a short study on Romans 13 in a magazine known to be critical of the religious policies of the Chinese government.[14] In a verse-by-verse commentary on Romans 13:1–7, Li accepts the conclusion that submission to the governing authorities should be part of Christian obligations, because those who hold civil authority have been so ordained by God. Along the same line, Li insists that opposition to civil authorities is tantamount to opposing God's commandment (Rom. 13:2), because God is the ultimate authority standing behind all civil government. The Chinese Union Version, on which Li bases his reading, renders the last line of 13:2, *hoi de anthestēkotes heautois krima lēmpsontai*, as "those who resist deserve punishment" (抗拒的必自取刑罰).[15] "Deserve" here is literally "will self-select" (必自取, *bi ziqu*) in the Chinese Union Version, thus stressing the wrongdoers'

13. Ng, "Peace in Hong Kong."
14. Li Xinyuan, "基督徒與執政掌權者—羅馬書13:1–7釋義" [Christians and governing authorities—exegetical notes on Romans 13:1–7], 生命季刊 52 [*Christian Life Quarterly*] (2009): 13–20.
15. The NRSV has "those who resist will incur judgment," giving little weight to the reflexive *heautois*. By contrast, the KJV reads, "they that resist shall receive *to themselves* damnation" and the NIV, "those who do so will bring judgment *on themselves*." The Greek, however, should be rendered literally, "Those who oppose will receive punishment upon themselves." Both the NRSV and the Chinese Union Version ignore the reflexive *heautois*.

deserts to the point of granting them agency in meting out their own punishment. This Li accepts, and as a result he takes the passage to mean that the just punishment received for opposing the state has a "theological" rather than a "political or social" cause.

This subtle distinction signals a critical step in Li's reading. In suggesting that punishment is a matter purely between the offender and God, Li effectively removes the right of judgment from the state, thereby refusing to grant the government absolute control over its citizenry. He further observes that *krima* literally means "judgment" (審判, *shenpan*), which according to Paul is God's prerogative alone (Rom. 2:2; 2 Cor. 5:10). If a state punishes a citizen for crimes, it does so as God's intermediary at God's instruction. Li finds support for this reading in the opening line of 13:4, *theou gar diakonos estin*, in which *theos* takes the emphatic position and the government official is interpreted as "God's *servant*" (上帝的用人, *shengdi de yongren*) in the Chinese Bible. The meaning of *diakonos* is controversal: the KJV translates it as "minister," while the NRSV and NIV have "servant."[16] Li does not dwell on the ambiguity, however; instead, he takes the Chinese translation as indicating that civil authorities are little more than lowly servants whose natural functions are to follow the master's orders in discharging appointed responsibilities. The result is a reading that explicitly rejects the state's absolute authority.

Li further reduces the state's imputed supremacy by denying it as an independent arbiter of morality, the judge of good and evil, by giving more weight to *syneidēsis* ("conscience," Rom. 13:5) than Paul intended. Conscience, according to Li, is not just a marker of guilt after the fact but a positive, constructive moral guide to individual action:

> In fact, "conscience" here refers not to the guilty conscience as a result of having committed evil deeds but to our 良心 (*liangxin*) that, with supreme peace before God, is capable of preemptively reminding (預先提醒, *yuxian tixing*) us not to sin. Such is Christian conscience, which, working in tandem with common sense (常識, *changshi*), can also exercise moral judgment on right and wrong. What sets it apart from what common folk (世人, *shiren*, lit., "people of the world") call "conscience" is that Christians' *liangxin* is controlled by the Holy Spirit, uses God's 道 (*dao* or "Way") as standard, and possesses an integrity (完整性, *wanzhengxing*). If we submit to the authorities in accordance with God's commandments, we will maintain peace and integrity of the conscience.[17]

16. See S.-k. Wan, "Coded Resistance," 180–81, where I suggest that both senses might well have been intended by Paul.

17. Li, "Christians and Governing Authorities," 16. Li uses 良心 (*liangxin*) in both occurrences, but since he puts it in quotes the first time, I decided to translate the first with the English and the second with Chinese transliteration.

Without acknowledging it, Li in reality relies on the traditional Confucian concept of conscience, 良心 (*liangxin*; lit., "good or virtuous heart-mind"), or 良知 (*liangzhi*; lit., "good or virtuous knowledge"), to make this hermeneutical move. On *syneidēsis* being used primarily as a negative marker, Li has ancient lexical support. As C. Maurer has amply documented, the word from the fifth to second century BC onward was used in the context of pointing out what someone has done wrong.[18] Philo struggles to interpret *syneidēsis* positively but ultimately does not escape the Old Testament idea of its being marshaled as an accuser of crooked deeds. The best he can manage is to interpret "conscience [as] an instrument in God's hand to bring men to conversion."[19] Paul's usage in his extant corpus betrays no systematic development but largely retains its original sense of accusatory judgment for having done something wrong.[20] While he uses the term in the sense of "conscientiousness" or "self-awareness" in 1 Corinthians 8 and 10,[21] in Romans 13:5 the term probably means something like "moral consciousness or conscience,"[22] referring to our "inner authority that recognizes the necessity of obedience."[23] Paul's sense of conscience here and elsewhere is remarkably content-free and is close to the preverbal intuition that prompts us to follow what common sense tells us is right. The next verse makes this explicit: "For this reason you also pay taxes, for the authorities are God's ministers devoted to this very thing" (Rom. 13:6). The exercise of *syneidēsis* "involves agreement with God's will. . . . [*Syneidēsis*] is responsible awareness that the ultimate foundations both of one's own being and also of the state are in God."[24]

If that is what lies beneath Paul's use of "conscience," Li goes beyond him, indeed beyond the whole Greek and Hellenistic tradition, in imputing to *syneidēsis* not only the responsibility of "preemptively reminding us not to sin" but especially the power of a creative principle that "is controlled by the Holy Spirit, uses God's *dao* as standard, and possesses an integrity."[25] What enables Li to extend Paul's conception of conscience is the Neo-Confucian notion of 良知 (*liangzhi*), which contains within itself the necessary and sufficient ground for self-perfection. Human nature being inherently good and capable of self-development and self-perfection, one's highest moral obligation is

18. C. Maurer, "συνείδησις," *TDNT* 7:902–4.
19. Maurer, *TDNT* 7:913.
20. G. Lüdemann, "συνείδησις," *EDNT* 3:302.
21. "It is man himself aware of himself in perception and acknowledgment, in willing and acting," which is closer to self-awareness. Maurer, *TDNT* 7:915.
22. BDAG, 968.
23. Lüdemann, *EDNT* 3:302.
24. Maurer, *TDNT* 7:916.
25. Li, "Christians and Governing Authorities," 16.

to extend the innate goodness in one's heart-mind to encompass Supreme Goodness (致良知, *zhi liangzhi*; lit., "to extend good or virtuous knowledge"). Contrary to the thin notion of conscience as intuitive prompting toward some vague sense of doing the right thing, conscience in the Mencian line of Neo-Confucianism is equipped with moral content. Embedded within this innate goodness is the potentiality for self-perfection, even self-transcendence, thus giving it an almost religious status. The Confucian conscience, at least in theory, is capable of critiquing state corruption and all forms of ideological captivity.[26] This is the step Li takes.

In rejecting the inviolability of the state, however, he makes sure that the Confucian *liangxin* is properly converted to Christianity by subordinating it to the Holy Spirit and imbuing it with God's *dao*.[27] Once the Christian foundation is laid, criticism against the state can now be erected thereon. In Li's reading, the state is superseded not just by God but also by a Christian-ized Confucian conscience, thus giving extraordinary autonomy and agency to the believer over against the state.

The believer's agency in choosing between obedience and defiance can be summed up in Li's reading of Titus 3:1: "Remind them to submit to governing authorities, to obey, to be prepared for every *good work*." On "good work," Li contends that "if the commands of government officials or civil authorities do not contradict God's will, Christians should follow, from submissive (順服, *shunfu*) disposition to obedient (順從, *shuncong*) acts, all for the purpose of doing what God deems to be 'good work.' On the other hand, if the authorities' commands violate the will of God, we would be doing 'evil work' if we submit to them."[28] The power of faith naturally impels a Christian to stand with the sanctity of the law, Li contends, but if the government were to promulgate laws and regulations impeding the Christian faith, then "good work" can only mean opposing the state and refusing to follow its corrupt ordinances.[29]

Li's contention that Christian submission to the state is conditional on the justness of the law and his insistence on imputing to the conscience the responsibility of examining the morality of the state set him apart from Ng.

---

26. See, e.g., Tu Weiming, *Centrality and Commonality: An Essay on Confucian Religious-ness*, rev. ed. (Albany: SUNY Press, 1989); and in critique, Sze-kar Wan, "The Viability of Confucian Transcendence? Grappling with Tu Weiming's Interpretation of the *Zhongyong*," *Dao* 7 (2008): 407–21. It must be said, however, that such potentiality was seldom realized in Dynastic China.

27. *Dao* is expansive in meaning. It ranges from "road" to "teaching" to "principle" to the moral order of things. Its enormous breadth makes it the perfect candidate for the translation of John 1:1: "In the beginning was the *Dao*" (太初有道, *taichu you dao*).

28. Li, "Christians and Governing Authorities," 18.

29. Li, "Christians and Governing Authorities," 19.

Not only does Ng place no limit on the state's authority, but he even proposes that obedience to those in authority be absolute. Enlisting Barth, he goes so far as to suggest that all human endeavors to right governmental wrongs are futile and should be avoided. Li, by contrast, eschews blind loyalty to the state and urges Christian vigilance in judging whether the state is faithfully discharging its responsibility as a servant of God, and he does so on the basis of a transformed, Christianized Confucian conscience. This difference can perhaps be explained by Li's experience of having lived under the Communist regime as a Christian minority and his religious liberty being restricted by Chinese laws. Ng, on the other hand, lived his whole life in Hong Kong, where religious freedom was guaranteed first by the British colonial government and later by the Basic Laws, a set of quasi-constitutional measures to ensure rule of law in Hong Kong. That experience, combined with an understanding of Christian faith as no more than personal piety, produces a view of the state that borders on wishful thinking.

Despite their differences, however, Ng and Li share a common assumption that the government is fundamentally good and would do the right thing given the opportunity. Li counsels compliance with the state as long as it accords with conscience. If a citizen does good, he contends, the state could be trusted to do the right thing, "to reward good behaviors while punishing bad" (賞善罰惡, *shangshan fa'e*).[30] Li uses Paul's words to gesture toward a public morality that is self-evident to anyone willing to examine its contents and that is acceptable to both citizens and state. Li seems sanguine about a state's police functions because of his confidence that the state would readily recognize goodness in the individual when present and that observance of the law is self-evident. He simply assumes that the state and citizens subscribe to the same moral code of behaviors, so that the state can be trusted to mete out rewards and punishments correctly and justly by a simple application of the self-evident standards.

Submission to (Unjust) Government

Events in Hong Kong would soon challenge this optimistic view of the state. In 2012, a China-initiated proposed change to the high school curriculum aimed at instilling a more "patriotic" view of Communist China prompted a protest movement across the city. What made Paul's words in Romans 13 so contentious was that many leaders of that movement, teenagers all, prominently highlighted their Christian faith in opposing the proposal. The

---

30. Li, "Christians and Governing Authorities," 19.

protest, accompanied by massive demonstrations and widespread classroom walkouts, forced the Hong Kong government to withdraw the proposal. Two years after that victory, emboldened pro-democracy activists pushed for a universal suffrage that had been codified in the Basic Laws. This time the protesters were rebuffed. Despite broad participation by the citizenry—an estimated one million protesters, a seventh of the total population, took to the street—China stood firm. Three months after protesters occupied the financial district, Hong Kong police broke up the movement by force, dashing hopes for a general election. In the summer of 2019, a protest against an extradition law escalated into a second round of demonstrations for universal suffrage. Despite near-universal support, the protests succeeded only in brutal repression and tighter control by the central government. With the passage of the National Security Act in 2020, the government forged a legal weapon to arrest and prosecute anyone deemed seditious and dangerous. And prosecute it did. Pro-suffrage activists were promptly rounded up and jailed, news outlets critical of the Hong Kong government were shuttered, and dissenting voices were silenced—all done legally and, in Chinese parlance, "patriotically." These events proved once and for all that confidence in good deeds being self-evident and autocratic power wielding its sword justly had been hopelessly misplaced.

Open confrontation between protesters and government led, ironically, to a cessation of debate over Romans 13. It was partly the result of antigovernment activists simply acting out their biblical reading by participating in the protests. Their action, wittingly or unwittingly, advanced a biblical hermeneutic that grounded the passage in the larger context of biblical justice. Supporters of the government, for their part, doubled down on a literal reading of submission. Ng, in response to the arrest of nine activists, many of whom were prominent church leaders, advocated "excommunicating" Christians and pastors who had taken part in civil disobedience. He did so on the basis of Romans 13:1, that all should submit to the governing authorities.[31] This argument brings to light a troubling assumption, however—that the state and ecclesial ordinances are so identified that protest against the state represents a violation against the church. His colleague Lü Yuanxin (呂元信) makes that connection explicit by suggesting that Christians who oppose the government in fact oppose God.[32] Humility, Lü argues, dictates that we follow the plain meaning of Romans 13: even tyrannical governments come

31. Chapman Chen, "Romans 13:1 Abused by Pro-CCP Hong Kong Pastor to Censure Occupy Leaders," Hong Kong Bilinguál News, May 14, 2019, https://www.hkbnews.net/post /romans-13-1-abused-by-pro-ccp-hong-kong-pastor-to-censure-occupy-leaders-chapman-chen.
32. "播道神學院院董呂元信恐嚇反送中信徒:反對政府就是反對神" [Evangel seminary trustee Lü Yuanxin intimidates the anti-extradition Christians: Opposing government is opposing God],

from God and must be obeyed. Just as Peter and Paul submitted to unjust authorities and refrained from mounting a revolution even as they were sentenced to death, so Christians must follow suit. Christians can oppose the government only if it forces them to betray such biblical principles as prayers and evangelization. Otherwise, they must view tribulation under a tyrannical government as a spiritual exercise that can purify believers for the will of God. Opposing civil authorities is therefore tantamount to opposing God, he concludes. Individual Christians might voice their opinions with humility, but they are categorically forbidden to take part in antigovernment demonstrations.

Underlying these supporters' harsh rhetoric is a tacit admission that the government is unjust. They counsel humility and silent endurance but otherwise make no effort to address the power imbalance between an autocratic regime and its citizens or the question of the state's raison d'être. Confucian classics make philosophical arguments for opposing tyrannical and corrupt governments, but that is lost on critics who elevate submission to the level of an ontological absolute. This turn of events presents difficulty for moderates who oppose demonstrating against the government except for principled and pragmatic reasons. Su Yingrui (蘇潁睿) for example, opposes a church's participation in political activism but allows for individual involvement based on his view of separation of state and church.[33] Because the church's mission is evangelism, not transformation of political systems, he concludes that it is inappropriate for a church to be involved in politics, even though he does allow for church members taking part in political change. Su even goes so far as to admit that there is no biblical mandate against civil disobedience. If a government turns out to be the devil's tool and abdicates its role as a just arbiter of good and evil, believers cannot afford to be silent in good conscience but are morally bound to voice their opposition to tyranny and corruption, as long as they do so peacefully. The church under no circumstances is allowed to take part in politics because of a supposed unbridgeable gulf between the church and the state. It might be countered that Su's assessment of the church-state relationship could be more nuanced, but it is clear that he begins with the assumption that the state is corrupt. The question for him is how to overcome the "plain meaning" of Romans 13. More than six decades earlier, the same question also haunted von Lehndorff to his death.

Apostlesmedia.com, September 18, 2019, https://apostlesmedia.com/2019/09/18/播道神學院院董呂元信：反對政府代表反對神/.

33. 蘇潁睿 [Su Yingrui], "基督徒可否參與抗爭政府行動" [Can Christians take part in resisting government?], *Christian Times*, January 7, 2020, https://christiantimes.org.hk/Common/Reader/News/ShowNews.jsp?Nid=160805&Pid=104&Version=0&Cid=2052&Charset=big5_hkscs.

Popular speaker and author Milton Wan finds himself equally disturbed by the political upheaval.[34] He recognizes government overreach as well as the propagandist use of Romans 13 to support an authoritarian regime—even though all that is left unsaid—for he goes out of his way to stress the radicalness of Paul's position within the Roman imperial context: to say that all earthly authorities are appointed by God is to place a Roman Empire that claims supremacy and a Caesar who calls himself a son of god (*filius divi*) under the sovereignty of Yahweh. To underscore Wan's point, one might note that Paul's words would have been highly seditious, worthy of capital punishment even, if only the imperial censors had known what he was peddling. Wan's observation is intended to rescue Paul from his critics and to mollify those who deem Paul a sellout to the state; it is not designed to chart a course for engaging the state. But that begs the question: If Paul was so radical in his approach to the Roman state, what stops us from following his example in opposing regimes we know to be tyrannical or corrupt? To answer the question for himself, Wan retreats to the private realm of "personal calling." He is called, he tells his audience, not to political activism but to dialogue with Chinese intellectuals. Possibility for that dialogue would be foreclosed if he were caught opposing the government. Whether or not that is a viable strategy, his views are clear: he will not publicize his opposition to a corrupt regime with an open act of civil disobedience—for pragmatic reasons. As to what the audience should do, he leaves the matter to individual choices.

Conclusion

Despite the different approaches to Paul's words in Romans 13 and the diverse political and ideological assumptions, several points of convergence emerge from this brief survey. First, Chinese interpreters of Romans 13 assume that engagement with the state is to be pursued only by individuals, not by the church as a corporate body. There is little or no reflection on how the church as an institution or as a mediating structure between the state and individuals might play a part in the construction of civil society. The call for universal suffrage, on which so much energy has been spent and for which so many lives have been expended, is defined narrowly in terms of individual ballots. Their discussion betrays an ignorance of how a representative democracy functions. Hong Kong had never developed a democratic culture, which the

---

34. Milton Wan (溫偉耀, *Wen Weiyao*), "從聖經看政權與社會公義 (羅馬書13:1–7)—(包括唯一的一次回應香港「佔領中環」與「公民抗命" [Biblical view on political authority and social justice (Rom. 13:1–7)], sermon delivered on February 22, 2015, YouTube, February 27, 2016, https://www.youtube.com/watch?v=aEkurQUbY8o.

British overlord refused to foster until it was too late and which their current neocolonists would never allow.

This brings up my second observation. Every author and speaker surveyed here expresses, explicitly or implicitly, a resignation that the current government is incapable of transformation. This pessimism is no doubt honed by the collective memory of millennia-long political impotence of ordinary citizens, but it is still remarkable that they all show a willingness to accept the current government as an irreducible given. In this regard, they are not so different from Romans who bought into Caesar's narrative that the Roman commonwealth was favored by the gods and was predestined to rule the peoples of the world, that their form of government represented the best possible, and that they were foreordained to occupy a privileged place in a divinely ordered hierarchy.[35] Contrary to his modern interpreters in Hong Kong, Paul decisively rejects Roman supremacy by appealing to the author and creator of nature, for God alone is the sole source of absolute authority. All earthly authorities are secondary and derivative. True, Paul himself couched such seditious language in biblical imagery inaccessible to imperial censors, but at least Paul intended to convey that message to his audience unambiguously.[36]

The failure to appreciate the differences between Paul's time and ours is the third problem shared by all Hong Kong interpreters. It takes a Taiwanese, Zhang Sicong (張思聰) veteran of the 2013 Taiwan Sunflower Revolution, to state the obvious: to use Romans 13 to counsel blind obedience to a corrupt state ignores the plain fact that Paul was writing at a time of imperial autocracy, whereas modern Taiwan is a multiparty representative democracy. If authority is ultimately derived from God, then the modern locus of authority resides with the constitution and not with any autocrat, so that submission to authority can only mean submission to the constitution. Even so, in both the biblical narrative and the modern world, there are innumerable positive antigovernment examples: Moses being saved as a result of the midwives defying Pharaoh's order, prophets criticizing their rulers, revolts of African American slaves, the American Civil Rights Movement, and so on.[37] All this points to the need for what Brian Walsh and Sylvia Keesmaat call a "double immersion": "We must be immersed in the biblical narrative . . . and we must be immersed in the world" before we can discern, on the one hand, the most

35. Cicero, *Rep.* 6.13; Virgil, *Aen.* 6.851–53. See discussion in S.-k. Wan, *Romans*, 7–8.
36. For Paul's openness and concealment, see S.-k. Wan, "Coded Resistance," 174–83.
37. Sicong Zhang (張思聰), "由「學生反服貿運動」看基督徒的權柄與順服," [Assessment of Christian authority and submission from students against the Inter-Strait Movement], Haleluya Christian Community, May 9, 2014, http://haleluya.cc/c/document_library/get_file?p_l_id=70 96979&folderId=6693217&name=DLFE-67580.pdf.

productive steps forward with regard to our participation in the world and, on the other, our most faithful reading of the biblical text.[38] Only by taking account of the integrity of the ancient context and our quotidian concerns in the world we live in can we hope to move forward. That we must do with utmost seriousness, for lives depend on it.

38. Brian J. Walsh and Sylvia C. Keesmaat, *Colossians Remixed: Subverting the Empire* (Downers Grove, IL: IVP Academic, 2004), 136. See also how the same method is applied to a study of Romans in Sylvia C. Keesmaat and Brian J. Walsh, *Romans Disarmed: Resisting Empire, Demanding Justice* (Grand Rapids: Brazos, 2019), 34.

7

Spoilage of *Jang-Yu-Yu-Seo*

Paul's Response through 1 Corinthians 11:17–34

JIN HWAN LEE

The Corinthian Christ group suffered schisms among its group members (cf. 1 Cor. 1:10–13). Their segregation even came to the fore at their periodic communal meal, an original form of Eucharist. What we hear in 1 Corinthians 11:17–34 is Paul's polemic and teaching over the schisms at the table. If verse 21 is to be read as the heart of Paul's polemic on the issue, then verse 33 is his ultimate resolution for the issue. Based on current major English Bible translations, the two verses can be paraphrased as follows: "When eating, each of you *takes* your meals *first*, one goes hungry, another gets drunk" (v. 21); "therefore, my brothers, when you come to eat for a communal meal, *wait for* each other" (v. 33, emphasis added).

The Greek words whose translations are emphasized in those two verses are *prolambanō* and *ekdechomai*, respectively. The current English versions adopt a temporal interpretation of the two Greek verbs. This is also true for the New Korean Revised Version. Its implication is clear: certain members proceeded to eat first, which eventually resulted in schisms at the table. They were socially stronger members who were the minority in the group (cf. 1 Cor. 1:26). They were relatively more educated, had more resources, and were more able to exercise social privilege than the majority. Paul's polemic, then, has to do with the time difference in eating between the socially stronger and socially weaker members.[1] By implication, commentators describe the socially stronger members as impatient, greedy, and inconsiderate.[2] Their eating prior to the socially weaker members appears to be against the spirit of loving one another, which brought schisms and humiliation to the whole group.

However, such a reading might sound questionable, especially when heard by a reader whose culture considers diners eating out of order disrespectful in certain circumstances. South Korea is one of the countries in East Asia where the oldest person or the socially strongest person begins eating first, at which point the meal starts. A particular meal setting or context may be required for such a way of dining, but most Koreans consider this normal for Korean dining etiquette. Rather than what to eat or where to eat, Koreans are concerned more about with whom to eat and how to eat. That is because Korean dining manners are deeply rooted in Korean culture, and people are unconsciously governed by this culture in daily life. Depending on with whom people are eating, meal etiquette at the table may be expected. The Korean perspective of dining manners might provide a different light for reading 1 Corinthians 11:17–34, especially since Greco-Roman meal culture is somewhat similar to the meal etiquette in Korea. I will briefly discuss meal etiquette in Korea and Greco-Roman meal etiquette and then return to 1 Corinthians 11.

Jang-Yu-Yu-Seo in Korean Dining Etiquette

Confucianism has heavily influenced Korean culture and society. Its first official adoption into Korean history traces back to the fourth century CE during the period of the Three Kingdoms of Korea (first century BC to seventh century AD).[3] The Han dynasty of China conquered Gojoseon, the former state of the proto–Three Kingdoms of Korea, in 108 BC. Confucian philosophy was then gradually introduced in the Kingdoms. By the fourth century AD, its influence had increased as the Kingdoms adjusted their cultural and political standards based on Confucianism. As a result, spheres of

1. This reading has consistently been argued with the late arrival of the weaker members to their communal meal.

2. E.g., Gerd Theissen, *The Social Setting of Pauline Christianity: Essays on Corinth*, trans. John H. Schütz (Philadelphia: Fortress, 1982), 145–74; Jerome Murphy-O'Connor, *St. Paul's Corinth: Texts and Archaeology*, 3rd ed. (Collegeville, MN: Liturgical Press, 2002), 185; Hans Josef Klauck, *Herrenmahl und hellenistischer Kult: Eine religionsgeschichtliche Untersuchung zum ersten Korintherbrief* (Münster: Aschendorff, 1982), 291; Peter Lampe, "The Eucharist: Identifying with Christ on the Cross," *Int* 48, no. 1 (1994): 36–49.

3. James Huntley Grayson, *Korea: A Religious History* (Oxford: Clarendon, 1989), 61; Jennifer Oldstone-Moore, *Confucianism: Origins, Beliefs, Practices, Holy Texts, Sacred Places* (Oxford: Oxford University Press, 2002), 19.

art, literature, education, and philosophy underwent substantial changes. However, its influence hardly affected the social sphere.[4] The entrenchment of Confucian social mores and values in Korean society did not take place until the reign of Joseon, the last dynasty of Korea (AD 1392–1897). Joseon adopted Neo-Confucianism as the new state ideology. Henceforth, Korea became a stable Confucian society, and the ideals of Confucianism have generally continued to underpin Korean society to the present day. Both in name and in reality, Korea advocates Confucian ideals as its "traditional values."[5]

Ul-Ho Lee explains why Confucianism has significantly influenced Korean culture and society. He draws attention to similarities of essential teachings between Confucianism and the Korean folk philosophy of *Han* (lit., "one" or "oneness" in Korean).[6] The idea is driven from the myth of *Dan-Goon*, one of the foundational myths of Korea. The myth emphasizes three human relations: (1) between the god of heaven, *Hwan-In*, and his son, *Hwan-Woong*, who was sent to the human world; (2) between *Hwan-Woong* and his subordinates; and (3) between *Hwan-Woong* and the Bear, who became a female and married *Hwan-Woong*. These three human relations are representative of relationships between (1) father and son; (2) ruler and subject; and (3) husband and wife, respectively. Members of a pair stand on opposing ends and represent different social statuses, but *Han* ideology predominantly teaches the *harmony* that upholds each relationship. It emphasizes unity within differences. Strife, conflict, discord, or anything that breaks harmony and unity has no place in the myth of *DanGoon*.[7] This harmonic concept is called *Um-Yang* (Yin-Yang), which is the symbol on the Korean national flag (see fig. 7.1). Lee finds this Korean folk philosophy comparable to the "five ethical principles" in Confucianism, known as *Oh-Ryun* in Korean. It teaches five moral rules in human relations: (1) love between father and son; (2) loyalty between ruler and subject; (3) distinction between husband and wife; (4) order between adult and child; and (5) trust between friends. These relationships contain hierarchy. A central Confucian virtue is to behave appropriately according to one's rank with good intent, by which society stands in harmony with order.[8] The first three of the five Confucian teachings are very similar to the three teachings of the Korean folk philosophy.

4. Grayson, *Korea*, 62–64.
5. Oldstone-Moore, *Confucianism*, 58.
6. Ul-Ho Lee, 한국 개신 유학사 시론 [Poetry of Korean Reformed Confucianism] (Seoul: Pakyoungsa, 1980), 11–29.
7. Grayson, *Korea*, 61.
8. Oldstone-Moore, *Confucianism*, 53.

Figure 7.1. The national flag of South Korea, *Tae-Geuk-Ki*

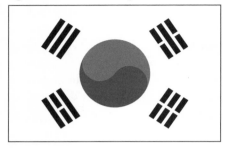 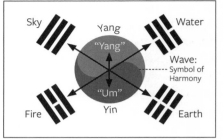

Confucius's teaching on *Oh-Ryun* was later developed for political purposes into *Sam-Gang-Oh-Ryun*, probably the most influential Confucian ideals embedded in Korean culture and society, and which became the heart of Neo-Confucianism. In addition to *Oh-Ryun*, three teachings, known as *Sam-Gang* (lit., "three bonds"), are added to the first three human relations of *Oh-Ryun*. *Sam-Gang* discusses rightful behavior between (1) ruler and subject; (2) father and son; and (3) husband and wife. It teaches that the latter ought to be subordinate to the former in each relation. The hierarchical dimension in those three human relations is highly fostered and promoted. The Confucian influence on Korean society officially ended with the end of the Joseon dynasty.[9] Nonetheless, its residual legacy, the so-called Confucian tradition, has lasted insofar as Korean culture and society continue to be patriarchal, and hierarchy overflows with authoritarianism in nearly all spheres of life.

Among these *Sam-Gang-Oh-Ryun*, the fourth moral rule of *Oh-Ryun* requires further attention. This rule, called *Jang-Yu-Yu-Seo* in Korean, teaches about the relationship between adult and child. Its literal meaning is "order must be preserved and honored between adult and child." However, this order is not strictly limited to that between adult and child but is also applicable to all stages of life and all human relations. That is, anyone who is older than the other, or anyone who is socially stronger than the other, takes authority and priority in their social relations. The former case would best apply to familial or neighbor relations, whereas the latter case is observable in workplaces or social clubs. Hence, the heuristic definition of "colleague" or "coworker" in the workplace is very narrow in Korea. Even if an assistant employee and associate employee work together in the same department of a company, they do not label each other as colleagues, because they hold different levels of status. It is also true for the heuristic definition of "friend" in Korea. Koreans rarely think that an older person and a young child can

9. Grayson, *Korea*, 213.

be friends. Koreans often define their friends based on being the same age, which provides an egalitarian base. Otherwise, most Korean social relations convey hierarchism.

Jang-Yu-Yu-Seo has been influential on dining contexts to the point that Korean meal etiquette has been historically developed based on Confucianism.[10] Past generations of scholars produced books and texts discussing social norms during the reign of the Joseon dynasty. *Nae-Hoon* teaches that home education must start from the earliest stage of life, and its first lesson should be on dining etiquette—namely, how to eat and behave at the table when eating with adults/seniors.[11] *Sa-So-Jeol*, written by Deok-Moo Lee in 1775, discusses a number of table etiquette best practices, such as dining with one's right hand, eating with self-control, not slurping loudly, not shouting, not insulting anyone, not fighting, and many more. There are also dining instructions, such as how to use spoon and chopstick, how and where to put them on the table, how to display food, what to eat first and last, and so forth.[12] Rather than provide a full list of the etiquette guidelines, I will discuss a selection of Korean dining etiquette rules that many would consider relevant today. However, the implied dining context needs to be carefully defined. What follows is generally applicable to either familial meals eaten with seniors such as (grand)parents or official communal meals of workplaces eaten with socially stronger people such as a manager, executive, or CEO. The rules may not be applicable to other dining contexts, such as eating with friends or colleagues.

Seating Position

When eating with seniors at home, people gather *around* them and eat. Seniors, therefore, sit on the middle seat(s) at the table, not on the very end seat. It is a way of honoring seniors, making them as comfortable as possible and making them the central figure at the table. Of course, it is hard to apply this to a situation in which four or fewer people are dining at a square table; but when five or more people are dining together at a rectangular table, most Koreans would know where the seat of honor would be (fig. 7.2). The case for eating at a restaurant is the same. The inside seat that is farthest from the

10. Chung Hee Chung and Eun Seul Choi, "밥상머리 교육을 통한 인성교육의 방향 고찰" [Study for learning direction of character education in light of dining table education], *Journal of Child Education* 25, no. 3 (2016): 395–400.

11. Young Ae Ju and Miyeon Won, "Consideration of the Courtesy Education at the Dining Table in the Books of Social Norms of Joseon Dynasty Era," *Family and Environment Research* 54, no. 4 (2016): 417.

12. Deok-Moo Lee, *Sa-So-Jeol*, trans. Jong-Kweon Kim (Seoul: Myeongmundang, 1993), 56–60, 278–316.

Figure 7.2. Possible seat(s) of honor in Korean dining

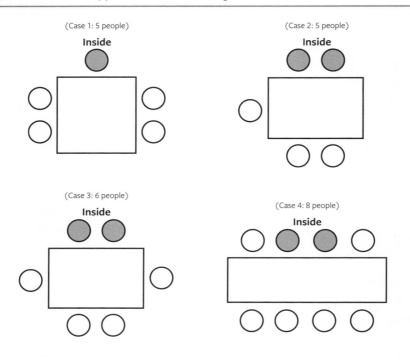

entrance, or the center seat at the table, is known as the seat of honor. People are used to letting older people or socially stronger people of a workplace take the seat of honor.

Food Allotment

Unlike the Western dining custom in which dishes are served in order of course, such as progressing from salad/soup to the main meal and ending with dessert, Korean dining is set all at once. Meals contain both main dishes and side dishes. Main dishes are often better in quality, as they are fresher than side dishes. Koreans usually make a large amount of various side dishes at a time (such as *kimchi*), storing them in a refrigerator and serving them at every meal little by little, accompanying the main dishes of a meal. Because people eat around seniors or socially stronger people, naturally the main dishes are served around them. Arranging main dishes around seniors demonstrates respect. That said, seniors do not necessarily eat *more* than other people at the table. Serving better food in front of seniors is a matter of honor. In return, seniors encourage younger people to eat main dishes (better food) more. There is a mechanism of respect going on at the table on each side.

Beginning a Meal

There is no official way of beginning meals. Depending on religious background, some people may start with their religious rite; for example, Christians begin their meals with a prayer to God. However, regardless of religious background, Koreans typically uphold that the oldest person or socially strongest person ought to start eating first, at which point the meal begins and other diners start eating. This dining etiquette practice is the most culturally embedded one in Korean society. It has been historically encouraged from generation to generation, conveying the most precise sense of *Jang-Yu-Yu-Seo*.

Ending a Meal

Just like the beginning of a meal, there is no set way of ending a meal. Everyone leaves the table once finished eating. But Koreans normally consider that the practical closure of the meal comes when the oldest or socially strongest person finishes. In the context of eating with a boss for work, leaving the table when the boss is still eating would be socially inexcusable unless the person has a particular reason to leave early.

As Korean society tends to be an evolving nuclear-familial society, it is difficult to say that these four dining etiquette practices are universal standards in every family; nonetheless, these four are the most deeply embedded in Korean dining customs and are practically treated as common dining etiquette.

Spoilage of Jang-Yu-Yu-Seo

Before I move on, let me briefly discuss an issue that Korean society is currently facing: the ugly spoilage of *Jang-Yu-Yu-Seo*. As I discussed earlier, its original idea, along with the other four moral principles, is to seek harmony in society, but its application has illuminated a severe social malady. It has transformed into a culture, called *Gahp-Jil*, that encourages socially stronger people or groups to overemphasize an arrogant and bossy attitude toward socially weaker people in their social relations. The infamous "nut rage" incident of Korean Air in 2014 is a typical case for the *Gahp-Jil*.[13] There are indeed many similar cases happening in Korea. Conflicts between generations have grown more than ever as well. Such an issue reveals that society suffers from the spoilage of *Jang-Yu-Yu-Seo*. A sense of entitlement overflows while respect of people diminishes in human relations.

A Korean linguist, Hyun-Yong Cho, stresses a paradoxical implication of "order" in *Jang-Yu-Yu-Seo*. He suggests that the implied meaning of order is "consideration" or "care."[14] Hence, when an older person or socially stronger one wants to stand on his or her privilege over younger or socially weaker people, he or she is supposed to *respect* them first. This is a far more accurate rendering of the teaching of *Jang-Yu-Yu-Seo* on which Korean society might restore harmony and unity.

Dining Etiquette in Greco-Roman Private Associations

In the following discussion, I will draw attention to dining etiquette with relevant meal practices in Greco-Roman private associations. I have argued elsewhere that meal practices of private associations provide the archetype of communal meals that Christ groups practiced in their formative stage.[15] They ran their communal meals periodically with mostly predetermined members, and so did private associations. Such a meal type was different from other meal types, such as familial meals, everyday ad hoc party meals, marriage meals, or patronage meals, even if they all generally share the so-called Greco-Roman meal tradition.[16] Membership practice, provisioning and distributing meals, menus, and many more practices in the Christ groups find their origin in association meals.

Various inscriptions and papyri from associations discuss table etiquette as part of their communal rules. Many associations reinforced table manners by

13. While traveling from New York JFK airport to Incheon airport as a first-class passenger, the vice president of Korean Air, Hyun-Ah Cho, demanded that the plane return to the gate at New York JFK airport because a flight attendant's service failed to reach Cho's expectation. The attendant served her macadamia nuts in a bag, but Cho wanted them on a plate. She demanded the removal of the attendant from the flight, which resulted in the delay of the flight. For more details, see "'Nut Rage' Delayed Korean Air Plane," BBC News, December 8, 2014, https://www.bbc.com/news/world-asia-30375004.

14. Hyun-Yong Cho, 우리 말의 숲에서 하늘을 보다 [Looking at the sky in our language forest] (Seoul: Hawoo, 2015), 106.

15. Jin Hwan Lee, *The Lord's Supper in Corinth in the Context of Greco-Roman Private Associations* (Lanham, MD: Lexington Books / Fortress Academic, 2018).

16. For further discussion on the Greco-Roman common meal tradition, see Dennis Edwin Smith, *From Symposium to Eucharist: The Banquet in the Early Christian World* (Minneapolis: Fortress, 2003), 1–13; Matthias Klinghardt, *Gemeinschaftsmahl und Mahlgemeinschaft: Soziologie und Liturgie frühchristlicher Mahlfeiern* (Basel: Francke, 1996), 45–152.

levying fines or penalties for dishonoring table rules. The Iobakchoi inscription (*IG* 2².1368; Athens, AD 164/5) is an excellent example:[17]

> If anyone begins fighting;
>> or if anyone is found acting disorderly;
>> or lying down on someone else's seat;
>> or insults or abuses someone else . . . (lines 73–76)

> The one who insulted and abused is responsible for paying twenty-five light drachmas to the treasury; and the one who caused the fighting is responsible for paying the same twenty-five light drachmas; otherwise, he shall not come to the Iobakchoi meeting until paying off the debts. (lines 79–83)

Associations seemed likely to enact such table manners for a practical reason: assumedly those listed misbehaviors frequently occurred at communal meals. Fines and penalties support the case.

It is worth paying further attention to the table rule against lying down on someone else's seat. Seating practice, in general, was one of the crucial elements in Greco-Roman dining customs. The social status of each diner was the key to determining his or her seating position. Socially stronger people reclined on seats that were far from the entrance of a *triclinium* (a typical Greco-Roman dining place), while socially weaker people reclined close to the entrance. Food allotment varied accordingly. Anyone who reclined on higher seats enjoyed better and more food than those who reclined on lower seats. Greco-Roman dining practice inevitably displayed a hierarchical atmosphere. Accordingly, conflict over seating was intense because where to recline defined a person's social level. In Lucian's *Symposium* 9, we see Zenothemis and Hermon compete against each other for the second-most honorable seat. Luke 14:7–11 is another example of the intensity of conflict over seating. The pericope teaches humility, but it also reveals rivalry in the seating practices involved in banqueting of the day.

But what exactly does it mean to recline at someone else's seat in associations? It presupposes a situation in which conflict occurs when each member's seat is predetermined. To get a fuller understanding of the rule against taking someone else's seat, we must understand a peculiar banqueting custom in association meals regarding the incumbency of functionaries, which generated a system called "flat hierarchy."

---

17. Unless otherwise noted, translations are mine. The inscription in its original language is from John S. Kloppenborg and Richard S. Ascough, *Attica, Central Greece, Macedonia, Thrace*, vol. 1 of *Greco-Roman Associations: Texts, Translations, and Commentary* (Berlin: de Gruyter, 2011), 242–45.

Many inscriptions from associations reveal that each group had its ruling authorities. For example, the Iobakchoi association had the priest, vice-priest, *archibakchos*, treasurer, secretary, and many more (*IG* 2².1368, lines 122–27). These roles were never intended as permanent positions but were meant to be held for a year or two: "The Iobakchoi shall choose [a treasurer] by vote every two years" (lines 146–47).[18] Associations *rotated* functionaries. By serving as a functionary, a member could enjoy social benefits within his or her association; most significant for this study, they benefited from elevated status in associations. The given status was, of course, fictive, as it was valid only for the duration of incumbency. As associations rotated their functionaries, socially weaker members could get a chance to enjoy elevated status by taking offices. This so-called flat hierarchy created an opportunity in associations whereby socially stronger members might have to recline at lower seats at communal meals when they were not in office. At the same time, the socially weaker members with an office reclined on higher seats, enjoying better and more food. In other words, associations assigned members' seats by their fictive ranks, a practice that could never happen outside of associations.[19] Accordingly, conflict often occurred in associations when the socially stronger members without offices were not willing to step down to lower seats.

Association meals began with offering a libation to the deity of the group. Association data specifically reveal that the libation duty was placed on functionaries, not on ordinary members. Furthermore, functionaries enjoyed more and better food than ordinary members at communal meals. For example, the *collegium* of Diana and Antinous in Lanuvium (*CIL* 14.2112) indicates that the newly selected president (*quinquennalis*) received a "double share" and the secretary (*scriba*) and the messenger (*viator*) received "a share and a half" from all distributions.[20] This adds a reason for the socially stronger members' unwillingness to recline on lower seats. It might be that fighting, insulting, and abusing other members occurred with their arrogantly taking

18. Cf. *IG* 2².1369 (Liopesi, 2nd c. AD); *AM* 66.228 no. 4 (Athens, 138/7 BC); *SEG* 2.9 (Salamis, 243/2 BC); *IKios* 22 (Kios, late Hellenistic or early imperial period).

19. John S. Kloppenborg, "Collegia and Thiasoi: Issues in Function, Taxonomy and Membership," in *Voluntary Associations in the Graeco-Roman World*, ed. John S. Kloppenborg and S. G. Wilson (London: Routledge, 1996), 18, 26.

20. *CIL* 14.2112, col. 2.17–20: *Item placuit, ut quisquis quinquennalis in hoc collegio factus fuerit, is a sigillis eius temporis,* | *quo quinquennalis erit, immunis esse debebit, et ei ex omnibus divisionibus partes dupl[as]* | *dari. Item scribae et viatori a sigillis vacantibus partes ex omni divisione sesquip[las]* || *dari placuit.* See also, for example, *IDelta* 1.446 (Psenamosis, 67–64 BC); *SEG* 40.688 (Tenos, 300 BC); *SEG* 58.1640 (Tlos, or Xanthos, 150 BC–100 BC); *SEG* 31.122 (Liopesi, early 2nd c. AD); *Agora* 16.161 (Athens, early 3rd c. BC); *IEph* 4337 (Ephesos, AD 19–23); *CIL* 14.2112 (Lanuvium, AD 136); *CIL* 6.10234 (Rome, AD 153); *IG* 2².1366 (late 2nd or early 3rd c. AD).

seats that were for functionaries. Conflict over seating was intense in association meals, instigated by the socially stronger members. Their disrespectful
attitude and sense of entitlement—not welcoming socially weaker members
as their functionaries and an unwillingness to recline on lower seats—were
the source of the conflict.

Let us now turn our attention to how meal etiquette in private associations is comparable to the Korean dining etiquette discussed earlier. First,
both concern respectful behavior at the table. Disorderly behaviors at the
table, such as insulting, fighting, or loudly speaking when eating, are generally treated dishonorably. Second, both dining customs display hierarchical
dimensions, although private associations added fictive characteristics to it.
Whether through order or levels of honor, certain people occupied better
seats and had easier access to more and better food than others at the table.
Third, both meals start with the highest person in rank at the table. Korean
dining begins when a socially stronger person starts eating. Association meals
started with a libation offering to a deity by one of the functionaries. Finally,
one might make a tangential comparison to the concept of the spoilage of
privilege briefly examined above with regard to Korean dining. The ideology of *Jang-Yu-Yu-Seo*, which undergirds both Korean culture and dining
etiquette, has the potential risk of harming a society. A similar risk existed
in the hierarchical societies of the Greco-Roman world, especially in a social
club or religious group where a flat hierarchy was the norm. The Greco-Roman
banquet, including that of private associations, was a social institution. It
represented a small society.[21] In both Greco-Roman private banqueting practices and typical Korean dining practices, socially stronger people have often
advocated their social powers and privileges, causing conflicts in human relations; thus, a sense of entitlement and disrespect remain risks to social order.

1 Corinthians 11:17–34 Revisited

As I mentioned in the introduction of this essay, current Bible translations
accept a temporal reading of *prolambanō* and *ekdechomai*. Such an interpretation leads to the conclusion that the socially stronger members in the
Corinthian Christ group eating earlier caused schisms in the group. According to the discussions in the previous sections, however, eating before others
may not be the full problem, especially where (flat) hierarchism exists. First
Corinthians 12:28–30 reveals a hierarchical dimension of the Christ group.

21. Smith, *From Symposium to Eucharist*, 1–12; see also Dennis E. Smith and Hal E. Taussig,
Many Tables: The Eucharist in the New Testament and Liturgy Today (Philadelphia: Trinity
Press International, 1990), 21.

Some scholars have proposed an alternative reading of the two verbs. They suggest nontemporal readings of *prolambanō* and *ekdechomai*, meaning, "take" (eat, consume, devour) and "welcome," respectively.[22] Two arguments are critical. First, *prolambanō* is a compound verb composed of the preposition *pro*, meaning, "before," and the verb *lambanō*, meaning "take." Its literal translation, "take in advance," is, of course, possible. Some suggest that according to a lexicographic point of view, however, the prefix (*pro*) in *prolambanō* had lost its temporal force by the first century.[23] The nontemporal translation "take" (eat, devour) is, therefore, appropriate for *prolambanō* in 1 Corinthians 11:21. The other argument has to do with Paul's use of *synerchomai* (come together) in 1 Corinthians. Including its verbal participle forms, this verb is used five times in 11:17–34 (vv. 17, 18, 20, 33, and 34). This verb also appears twice in 14:1–40 (vv. 23 and 26). Some scholars have brought attention to the fact that Paul's repeating uses of this verb in both pericopes, in fact, presuppose the presence of the entire membership at the table.[24] In this context, then, Paul's edification in 1 Corinthians 11:33 (*ekdechomai*, "welcome") has to do with meal etiquette, and his polemic in verse 21 (*prolambanō*, "take, devour") concerns misbehavior of socially stronger members *at* the table.

How, then, does the nontemporal reading apply to the communal gathering of the Corinthian Christ group? Scholars who propose the nontemporal interpretation of the two verbs often point to the socially stronger members' inhospitality.[25] Their unwillingness to share meals with other members who had nothing to eat at the table caused schisms. Much emphasis is on different quality and quantity of food consumption between the socially stronger members and weaker members at the table. The former devoured and got drunk while the latter remained hungry.

22. E.g., Hans Conzelmann, *1 Corinthians*, trans. James W. Leitch, Hermeneia (Philadelphia: Fortress, 1969), 192, 195n22; Bruce W. Winter, "The Lord's Supper at Corinth: An Alternative Reconstruction," *RTR* 37, no. 3 (1978): 73–82; Ottfried Hofius, "The Lord's Supper and the Lord's Supper Tradition: Reflections on 1 Corinthians 11 23b–25," in *One Loaf, One Cup: Ecumenical Studies of 1 Cor 11 and Other Eucharistic Texts: The Cambridge Conference on the Eucharist, August 1988*, ed. Ben F. Meyer, NGS 6 (Macon, GA: Mercer University Press, 1993), 91; Richard A. Horsley, *1 Corinthians*, ANTC (Nashville: Abingdon, 1998), 158.

23. Bruce W. Winter, *After Paul Left Corinth: The Influence of Secular Ethics and Social Change* (Grand Rapids: Eerdmans, 2001), 146. Cf. the second-century inscription *Syll*³ 1170, which illustrates the loss of temporal meaning; see also *MAMA* 4.279 (Phrygia, AD 2–3); *SEG* 21.534.

24. Hofius, "Lord's Supper," 94; Horsley, *1 Corinthians*, 158. See also Valeriy A. Alikin, *The Earliest History of the Christian Gathering: Origin, Development and Content of the Christian Gathering in the First to Third Centuries* (Leiden: Brill, 2010), 31.

25. See, e.g., Conzelmann, *1 Corinthians*, 192, 195n22; Winter, "Lord's Supper at Corinth"; Hofius, "Lord's Supper," 91; Horsley, *1 Corinthians*, 158.

However, I want to draw attention to the fact that food consumption itself was not the main problem for Paul. The focal point of his polemic is not a matter of food consumption or improper sharing per se. Instead, Paul was against members exercising a sense of entitlement in Christ groups that could make a member think more of himself or herself than others. The conflict at periodic communal meals of the Corinthian Christ group was deeply rooted in the community's context of heterogeneous social strata (cf. 1 Cor. 1:26), which affected its seating practice. Socially stronger members thought themselves to be better than the rest because they enjoyed better social privileges than other members in their daily lives outside of the group. Likely, some of them, especially those who were not in a leadership position, attempted to take higher seats, which were for selected leaders of the group; indeed, their conduct would be another case for *Gahp-Jil*. Such behavior was disrespectful as well as harmful to the Christ group. It could destroy the system of flat hierarchy, making the periodic communal meal as ordinary as everyday private meals.

Paul expresses his consternation in 1 Corinthians 11:20. His sarcastic questions in verse 22 ("Don't you have houses to eat and drink in? Or do you show contempt for the church of God and humiliate those who have no house?") and his proper suggestion in verse 34 ("if you are hungry, eat at home") reflect the problem of the socially stronger members lording their social privileges over others. Paul encourages the group to be united, reminding them that the death of the Christ was not just for the socially privileged but for all (11:23–26). He thus practically asks the socially stronger members to *welcome* (*ekdechomai*, 11:33) the selected leaders to recline on higher seats, even if some of them are from lower social strata. Paul's overall interest in structuring God's community is to get rid of any privilege associated with a member in his or her social life, particularly when members gathered together in the name of the Lord Jesus Christ. First Corinthians 11:17–34 instructs the socially stronger members to stand with the socially weaker members.

Epilogue: Churches, Then and Now

History repeats itself. If not the same one, similar social issues or conflicts recur from time to time. One of the problems of the church in Corinth involved the overexercising of social privilege within its communal gatherings by socially stronger members. Greco-Roman society was hierarchical; thus, to some extent, such social behavior was tolerated or even reinforced. However, in a church gathering context where a system of self-government is in place, and people from different social levels coexist as holy ones of God, such behavior becomes highly problematic. Paul perceived it as disrespectful and tried to convince members to respect each other. Telling them that their association is the body of Christ, he encouraged them to seek unity and harmony so that the death of Christ would not be in vain. This message is still relevant to the current day, particularly to churches in Korea.

A sense of entitlement prevails in Korean society, and it is sadly true that some churches in South Korea have also taken ill in the same way as the church in Corinth. A social malady caused by *Jang-Yu-Yu-Seo* appears among ministers. While this is not the case for every church in Korea, it is indisputable that distorted hierarchism and authoritarianism often exist among ministers. The office is often regarded as a status, not as a role. The more a church grows, the more strictly hierarchical order is maintained. A lead minister's request often appears to be something that following ministers should carry out; otherwise, he or she could be laid off (another example of *Gahp-Jil*). Paradoxically, however, they call each other coworkers of the Lord, and brothers and sisters of the Lord. Many times, lower ministers are less respected but forced to sacrifice their own time or family time in the name of serving God. Such disrespectful treatment, in fact, exists in various relationships in a church. It can also apply to minister-laypeople relations, elder-deacon relations, adult-youth relations, and even relationships between men and women. What would Paul say if he were to hear about *Gahp-Jil* in the Korean church? Although its particular situation of conflict is different from that of 1 Corinthians 11:17–34, his overall implied response would be the same: *Get rid of your sense of entitlement! Respect others! Seek a state of unity!*

8

Sin, Pollution, and Cleansing in 2 Corinthians 7:1

An African Perspective

J. AYODEJI ADEWUYA

An African reading of the Bible is a diverse, complex, and challenging process. In part, this is because the African sociocultural, political, and religious context is, in itself, complex and multifaceted. However, there are some commonalities that bind the people of the continent and allow an interpreter to speak of an African reading or perspective. Two of these often-intertwined commonalities are brought to bear on the interpretation of 2 Corinthians 7:1 in this essay. First is the significant role of the community in spiritual and identity formation. Second is the well-known fact that Africans are by nature profoundly religious, and the existence of God, with the attendant requirement of purity in approaching the Deity, is accepted without question. It is with these two prevalent ideas in view that this essay seeks to elucidate 2 Corinthians 7:1 within the African context. It attempts to show how the reading of 2 Corinthians 7:1 from an African perspective enhances the understanding of the text, an example of the "inculturation biblical hermeneutic,"

This chapter is adapted from a previously published work: *1 & 2 Corinthians*, ed. Yung Suk Kim (Minneapolis: Augsburg Fortress, 2013). Reproduced by permission of Augsburg Fortress.

an approach by which interpreters consciously and explicitly seek to interpret the biblical text from sociocultural perspectives of different people.[1]

Furthermore, this approach contends that "ordinary" African readers of the Bible do not dwell on a passage as somebody else's text to be read and analyzed; instead, they see the text as intended to provide them with a framework to look at their own lives. As such, they immediately appropriate a particular text and situate themselves inside of it, trying to understand what it expects of them. Thus, discussing a text really means discussing the life of the people without making any significant distinction between method and content. Reality and the biblical text merge, each shedding light on the other and competing for attention. Hence, culture is understood as a "hermeneutic for reading Scripture."[2]

Paul's Call for Purification

In discussing Paul's call for cleansing in 2 Corinthians 7:1, the interpreter must first address the function and purpose of the passage in its immediate context of 6:14–7:1 and 2 Corinthians as a whole.[3] One must then proceed to examine Paul's pollution language, his usage of the purification metaphor, and how these fit into a life of holiness that is motivated by the fear of God.

In its immediate context, 2 Corinthians 7:1 is Paul's conclusion of his appeal to holiness in 6:14–7:1. The opening inferential particle, "therefore" (oun), indicates that this verse sums up the preceding appeals (6:14, 17). Paul draws out the practical and ethical implications of his extended quotations. He goes on to enumerate the promises of the separation he has urged, and, based on those promises, Paul reformulates and expands the command of 6:14. Paul has appealed to his readers to avoid unequal yokes. He now expresses his command for separation in verse 14 in terms of cleansing from defilement of flesh and spirit, a way of referring to the total person. Notably, in 7:1 he addresses the Corinthians as "beloved," a term frequently used by Paul for those with whom he enjoys a close and congenial relationship.[4]

---

1. This is a term coined in Justin S. Ukpong, "The Parable of the Shrewd Manager (Luke 16:1–13): An Essay in Inculturation Biblical Hermeneutic," *Semeia* 73 (1996): 190.

2. John S. Pobee, "Bible Study in Africa: A Passover of Language," *Semeia* 73 (1996): 166.

3. Although some scholars continue to argue that 2 Cor. 6:14–7:1 is an interpolation, in agreement with others I have argued that the passage is to be seen as an integral part of the letter, specifically contending that the passage is part of Paul's argument for communal holiness in the Corinthians correspondence. See J. Ayodeji Adewuya, *Holiness and Community in 2 Cor. 6:14–7:1: Paul's View of Communal Holiness in the Corinthian Correspondence* (Eugene, OR: Wipf & Stock, 2011).

4. Frank G. Carver, *2 Corinthians: A Commentary in the Wesleyan Tradition*, NBBC (Kansas City, MO: Beacon Hill, 2009), 219.

In 2 Corinthians 7:1, Paul urges the Corinthians to "cleanse yourselves" (*katharisōmen heautous*) of pollution or impurities. So far, Paul has argued that the Corinthians should live separated lives in contradistinction to the society in which they are located. However, with 7:1, he raises the notion of separation to a higher dimension than external behavior or actions. The call to cleansing is an appeal to the Corinthians, whom Paul has designated as both God's temple and God's people, to live as befits their calling. His contention is that sin—which he refers to as pollution—whether physical or psychological, leaves the residue of guilt and spiritual pollution. How can we remove this from ourselves? It is by appropriating the provision that God has made for our cleansing. Christians deal with sins by repentance and confession; God applies the value of Christ's death and shed blood to us, and he forgives us. Because the Corinthians, as members of the new church of God in Christ Jesus, have now become the recipients of these promises from God, they are likewise confronted with the responsibility to effect complete ethical and religious renewal per the directives of their God. Every aspect of the Corinthians' lives must be affected in the Corinthians' efforts to make themselves clean. In doing so, they will increasingly become like Christ. Paul summons the Corinthian church to stop inappropriate relationships with iniquity, the powers of darkness, Belial, unbelievers, and idols (2 Cor. 6:14–16). Paul's exhortation to holiness and a call for separation in 2 Corinthians 6:14 is now formulated in terms of cleansing from defilement of both flesh and spirit, a circumlocution for both the community and the total person.

One must not fail to notice Paul's juxtaposition of the plural "yourselves" (*heautous*) with the singular "flesh and spirit" (*sarkos kai pneumatos*, 2 Cor. 7:1), something that suggests the relationship between the individual and the community of faith. On the one hand, the community must cleanse itself. On the other hand, the individual as an integral member of the community has the obligation of cleansing himself/herself. This is reminiscent of Paul's exhortation in Romans 12:1–2 to present their bodies (plural) as a single sacrifice. As succinctly stated by Richard Hays:

> Thus, the primary sphere of moral concern is not the character of the in-
> dividual but the corporate obedience of the church. Paul's formulation in
> Romans 12:1–2 encapsulates the vision: "Present your bodies [*somata*, plural]
> as a living sacrifice [*thysian*, singular], holy and well-pleasing to God. . . .
> And do not be conformed to this age, but be transformed by the renewing
> of your mind." The community, in its corporate life, is called to embody
> an alternative order that stands as a sign of God's redemptive purposes in
> the world. . . . The coherence of the New Testament's ethical mandate will
> come into focus only when we understand that mandate in *ecclesial* terms

when we seek God's will not by asking first, "What should I do," but "What should *we* do?"[5]

Paul uses a word that rarely occurs in the Pauline corpus for "cleanse" (*katharizō*, 2 Cor. 7:1). This verb and the cognate adjective *katharos* are used in the Septuagint Priestly materials concerning making persons, things, or places ceremonially fit for participation or use within the cultus (cf. Num. 9:13; 18:11, 13; Lev. 4:12; 6:11; 11:36–37; 12:8; 13:13, 17, 37). In Psalm 51:2, 7, 10, for example, the adjective and verb are used in the prayer for ethical purity in the entire person. In its general usage, the word group denotes physical, religious, and moral cleanness or purity in such senses as "clean," "free from stains or shame," and "free from adulteration." Purification in the Old Testament usually has to do not simply with a dedication to holy use but with the removal of ceremonial uncleanness (or ritual impurity), which occurred in several ways. Isaiah 52:11, a passage to which Paul alludes in 2 Corinthians 6:17, mentions purification in anticipation of the return from the exile. This need for purification, along with the usual purification for holy service, was probably in mind as the priests and Levites purified themselves (Ezra 6:20) and then the people and the rebuilt city gates (Neh. 12:30) after the exile (cf. 12:45; 13:22). In the New Testament, the term *katharizō* is linked to cultic settings (cf. Mark 7:19; Acts 10:15; 11:9). It is used in the Gospels to heal leprosy (Matt. 8:2–3; 11:5; Mark 1:42; Luke 4:27), but its scope includes moral cleansing (cf. James 4:8; Heb. 9:14; 1 John 1:7).[6] Thus, the notion of separation to a dimension beyond the external is implicit in the idea of purification. Cleansing in this passage has to do with proper use of the temple, the dwelling place of the Holy Spirit through which God is to be glorified (1 Cor. 6:19–20).

Paul's choice of the word for "defilement" (*molysmos*, a New Testament *hapax legomenon*) in 2 Corinthians 7:1 is striking. It signifies the full range of cleansing that he evidently has in mind. In 1 Esdras 8:80, it is used to denote the pollution created by the inhabitants of the land with their idolatry. In 2 Maccabees 5:27, Judas Maccabee retreats to the desert to escape the idolatry and pollution of the temple imposed by Antiochus Epiphanes. It denotes cultic as well as ethical defilement in both contexts (see also Isa. 65:4). The word also appears in a judgment oracle against the false prophets for the defilement they have brought to Jerusalem that was worse than Sodom and Gomorrah's (Jer. 23:15 LXX). The close association of *molysmos* with idolatry suggests that Paul might be thinking especially of defilement that comes from dining

5. Richard B. Hays, *The Moral Vision of the New Testament* (San Francisco: HarperCollins, 1996), 196–97.
6. Carver, *2 Corinthians*, 219.

in the local temples, membership in the pagan cults, ritual prostitution, active engagement in pagan worship, and the like. This brings the argument in the paragraph back full circle to Paul's opening injunction to stop entering into unequal partnerships with unbelievers (2 Cor. 6:14). When Paul demands the cleansing of "flesh and spirit" (*sarkos kai pneumatos*, 7:1), he is referring both to the physical body[7] and to the "seat of emotion and will."[8] Here, he uses two terms in a popular manner to comprehend the whole person viewed physically and spiritually. Paul calls for a thorough moral cleansing that will affect the Corinthians' entire existence (see 1 Cor. 7:34; 1 Thess. 5:23).[9] Every aspect of the believer's life is to be rendered free from any pollutant or contaminant that would disrupt his/her relationship with God. Furthermore, "making holiness perfect" (2 Cor. 7:1), as Paul urges, is not a second process that is done alongside making oneself personally clean; it is something that results from making oneself personally clean. When believers have cleansed themselves from every defilement, they will thereby have made holiness perfect.

Paul's call to cleansing will undoubtedly ring a bell for a traditional African, as he/she not only is familiar with purification rites but also understands the underlying reasons for such acts. There are various kinds of purification rites in Africa tied to multiple events and for different reasons.[10] As Oyin Ogunba's study shows, traditional African festivals of purification also have sociopolitical significance.[11] Nevertheless, religious purification rites are concerned explicitly with each society's relationship with its members and the Deity. In such cases, the significant grounds for purification are taboos that cause the rupture of cosmic harmony and interpersonal relationships, the holiness of God, and relationship with the Deity (God). Ogunba notes that "the physical presence of supernatural beings at festivals of all categories is regarded as laden with purification possibilities, and people take advantage of their own benefit."[12] He further argues that people use such occasions to purge themselves "of all the accumulated filth of the old year in order to enter the

---

7. Cf. Rudolf Bultmann, *Theology of the New Testament*, trans. Kendrick Grobel (New York: Scribner's Sons, 1951), 1:200, who calls attention to 1 Cor. 6:16; 2 Cor. 4:10–11; 12:7; Gal. 6:17; and 4:13 as illustrations of Paul's occasional interchangeable and neutral use of *sōma* and *sarx*, under the influence of the LXX's rendering of *rsb* by either term with no difference in meaning.

8. Cf. Ernest De Witt Burton, *Galatians*, ICC (Edinburgh: T&T Clark, 1921), 486–90.

9. Carver, *2 Corinthians*, 219–20.

10. See Benjamin C. Ray, *African Traditional Religions: Symbol, Ritual and Community* (New Jersey: Prentice Hall, 1976), 90–100.

11. Oyin Ogunba, "Yoruba Occasional Festivals," in *Yoruba Language and Literature*, ed. A. Afolayan (Ile-Ife: Obafemi Awolowo University, 1982), 36–56.

12. Ogunba, "Yoruba Occasional Festivals," 36.

New Year a chastened, reborn person."[13] As such, purification rites constitute a positive approach to the cleaning and removal of sin and pollution, involving an outward act that is consequently believed to have an inner spiritual cleansing.[14] If, for example, one is aware or made aware by a diviner that he/she has committed an offense that has resulted in the disruption of peace, he/she will have to undergo a ritual cleansing. The cleansing may include ritual shaving of the hair followed by ritual bathing in a flowing stream. The sinner undertakes the "washing off" of stains under the guidance of a priest, providing what the priest directs him/her to bring for the "washing." The whole event is symbolic and dramatic. Sin is portrayed as a stain and a filthy rag that can be washed off and cast off, respectively, bringing new life as the rejuvenated person takes on a clean white cloth and casts off the old one.

The significance of purification among many African societies is also evident in the words that are used. Among the Zulus, purification is called either *ukuhlambulula* or *ukusefa*, which means "to make thin" or "to make a person free, loose, unbound"; they derive from the word *ukuhlamba*, which means "to wash."[15] In Zulu, traditional life purification rites are understood as the process through which a person is made "free and refined of dross and imperfection."[16] From the practice of ritual regarding impurity, the concept of guilt develops, and as a result, purification becomes atonement. It is also evident that ritual and ethical reflection often merge without a break in the sphere of purification. The common Swahili word for cleansing is *utakaso*, a word that is translated as "cleansing" or "sanctification." It is used for both moral and ritual purification, referring to the total removal of evil. For example, it is used for rituals such as the cleansing of evil spirits and the removal of a curse. It applies to the cleansing of the widow or widower after the death of the spouse. It is used in contrast to *kusafisha*, which, although translated as "cleaning" or "washing," is applied when cleaning a house, washing clothes, and so on. The wide range of meaning of *utakaso* fits well with the multifaceted nature

---

13. Oyin Ogunba, "Yoruba Festivals: The Past, the Present and the Future" (paper delivered at the 10th Odunjo Memorial Lectures, May 2, 2002), cited in Gbemisola Remi Adeoti, "Traditional Cleansing Rites and State Reconstruction in Contemporary Nigerian Drama," in *Ìbà: Essays on African Literature in Honor of Oyin Ogunba* (Ile-Ife: Obafemi Awolowo University, 2014), 90.

14. J. Omosade Awolalu, "Sin and Its Removal in African Traditional Religion," *JAAR* 44, no. 2 (1976): 284.

15. Bengt G. M. Sundlker, *Bantu Prophets in South Africa*, 2nd ed. (London: Oxford University Press, 1961), 210.

16. Alfred T. Bryant, *A Zulu-English Dictionary with Notes on Pronunciation: A Revised Orthography and Derivations and Cognate Words from Many Languages; Including Also a Vocabulary of Hlonipa Words, Tribal-Names, etc., A Synopsis of Zulu Grammar and a Concise History of the Zulu People from the Most Ancient Times* (1905; repr., Charleston, SC: BiblioBazaar, 2015), 239.

of holiness articulated by Paul in 2 Corinthians 6:14–7:1. In addition to the preceding, purification is a social process for traditional Africans. To belong to a group requires one to conform to its standard of purity—the outsider, the uninitiated, and the rebel are considered unclean. Therefore, the emotionally charged activities that accompany purification or cleansing constitute a ritual demonstration.

Molysmos and the African Concepts of Sin and Taboos/Pollution

An important word in 2 Corinthians 7:1, as noted above, is *molysmos*, a word that in its simplest sense means "pollution." Paul's choice of it is notable. When an "ordinary" African reader reads of pollution or contamination in this verse, the concepts of sin and taboos readily come to mind. This is because, concerning human behaviors and attitudes, they constitute, on the one hand, what could be referred to as moral demands and, on the other, what results in the default of such demands. Diedrich Westermann rightly notes that "the many taboos which a man has to observe are not to be regarded as things mechanical which do not touch the heart, but that the avoidance is a sacred law respected by the community. In breaking it, you offend the divine power."[17] Moreover, the behavior of the individual determines what happens to all. As a result, sin is not a private matter. Taboos may bring honor and prestige. At the same time, it may bring shame, dishonor, and even destruction. Africans tenaciously hold the belief that moral values are based on the recognition of the divine will and that sin in the community must be expelled if perfect peace is to be enjoyed.

Taboos generally have to do with forbidden conduct. They are recognized as actions that go against the good and well-being of other individuals, the community, and the gods. Thus, if there will be harmonious person-to-person, person-to-community, and divine-person relationships, these actions must be forbidden. Among the Yoruba, taboo is referred to as *eewo* (things forbidden). On the whole, taboo embraces everything that could be considered sin.[18] Invariably, there are many forms of taboos in accordance with the multifaceted activities of African society. It must also be indicated that taboos differ from one culture to another in Africa. In fact, what is a taboo in one African community may be permitted in another one. What is important, however, is that taboos are to be kept with all seriousness. To break a taboo is to bring disorder not only on oneself but on the whole community, which may entail severe

---

17. Diedrich Westermann, *The African Today and Tomorrow* (London: Oxford University Press, 1949), 65.

18. D. B. Jacob, *A Text Book on African Traditional Religion* (Ibadan: Aromolaran, 1977), 240.

penalties. Taboos are also crucial to the African because they teach spiritual and moral values, which are the hallmarks of African religion. Their observance promotes the needed sense of mutual responsibility and communality on which the African culture and religion are solidly built. Thus, in Yoruba beliefs, *eewo* are essentially religious rules associated with spiritual beings.

The breach of prohibitions (taboos) is an abomination. Generally, abominations are serious offenses that are believed to threaten the natural, cosmic, and social order. A case in point is incest, which is a taboo in Africa. Among the Nuer, for example, *rual* (incest) is regarded as the greatest sin. If two people involved in incest "are very closely related, death may follow possibly within a few days."[19] Among the Yoruba of southwestern Nigeria, if a person commits incest, those involved in the immoral act are exposed to ridicule and are required to offer propitiatory sacrifice to assuage the anger of the ancestral spirits. The breach of *eewo* incurs a state of pollution and the threat of supernatural sanctions. Only purification rites can rectify this situation.

The discussion about holiness in traditional African life takes into account the concept of ritual dirt and ensuing purification. For example, for the Yoruba, *ìrìra* (pollution, or abomination) is essentially a religious phenomenon, not merely a sociocultural phenomenon. If one were to tell the Yoruba that a particular writer says that *ìrìra* is "dirt," and the "reflection on dirt involves reflection on the relation of order to disorder, being and non-being, form to formlessness, life to death," they would probably say that he/she must be speaking metaphorically. "Dirt" implies a set of ordered relations and the subsequent contravention of that order. Contrary to anthropologists who might suggest that dirt simply implies something out of place, the often-lethal punishments for sins such as incest and adultery are externally imposed by the Deity in the interest of maintaining social structure and cohesion. Hence, one might conclude that "pollution in Yoruba religion is both spiritual and material in nature."[20] *Ìrìra*, "dirt," is both "like and unlike" ordinary dirt. It is better described as "ritual dirt" or "religious dirt," which means far more than mere filth. The Yoruba see "ritual dirt" essentially as a religious phenomenon.

In the same vein, speaking of the Igbo tribe of Nigeria, Emefie Ikenga Metuh argues that "ritual dirt" is a religious phenomenon and that it is to "be sought primarily in its meaning as a mythico-symbolic pattern of expression, rather than in the type of society in which it occurs." Furthermore, drawing

19. E. E. Evans-Pritchard, *Nuer Religion* (London: Oxford University Press, 1956), 18.
20. W. B. Kristensen, *The Meaning of Religion*, trans. J. Carman (The Hague: Martinus Nijhoff, 1960), 445.

his insight from the Igbo religious worldview, he explains that "Igbo ideas about 'Ritual Dirt' and purification see them essentially as a religious phenomenon. Their ideas about pollution and prohibitions have wide-ranging psychological and socio-cultural functions, but they are not to be reduced to a mere psychosociological or cultural phenomenon."[21] Understanding pollution thus leads to the conclusion that purification rites done among the Yoruba and Igbo are essentially religious. They promote access to the gods for acceptable worship.

The Fear of God

In 2 Corinthians 7:1, Paul suggests "the fear of God"[22] as the motivation for holiness. The NIV translation of *en phobō theou* as "out of reverence for God" is on target.[23] Holiness is predicated on a relationship with God. In 2 Corinthians 7:1, believers are made holy by the cleansing of every defilement while living a life of reverence for God—that is, submission to his lordship. The eschatological significance of this concept is well-stated by Euichang Kim. She writes that the fear of God in 2 Corinthians 7:1 derives "from the recognition that an eschatological judgment will come to all people and that it is thus this fear that motivates believers to live a holy life."[24] This resonates with the African understanding of eschatological judgment held among some Africans, such as the Yoruba, who believe in the existence of *Orun Rere* (good heaven) or *Orun Apaadi* (a "heaven" that is full of potsherds, something that portends burning). It is believed that good people are destined for the former and the wicked for the latter. Most Africans would not have a problem associating judgment with God. However, unlike in traditional Christian theology, where all judgment is in the future, Africans make room for punishment here and now. Ethics and morality are correspondingly important in the here and now. Paul would have concurred.

An unspoken awareness of the sinless perfection of God permeates traditional Africa. On the one hand, such awareness is evident in the various names that are used for God in different parts of Africa. The Yoruba people speak of God as *Oba pipe ti ko labawon* (the perfect King who is without blemish) or

---

21. See Emefie Ikenga Metuh, *African Religions in Western Conceptual Schemes: The Problem of Interpretation* (Bodija: Pastoral Institute, 1985), 73–74.

22. Euichang Kim, *The Fear of God in 2 Corinthians 7:1: Its Meaning, Function, and Eschatological Context*, LNTS 605 (Edinburgh: Bloomsbury T&T Clark, 2019), not only discusses in detail several aspects of "the fear of God" in the Pauline corpus in general but specifically focuses on its significance in 2 Cor. 7:1.

23. This sense is present in the Wisdom literature; see, e.g., Pss. 2:11; 5:7; Prov. 1:7, 29; 8:13.

24. Kim, *Fear of God*, 168.

Oba mimo (the holy God). On the other hand, the awareness of God's holiness is demonstrated by the strict rules that must be followed during rituals having to do with God. To get into and maintain a relationship with God, a person must necessarily enter into a covenant with divinity.[25] Such a covenant is usually based on several demands and sanctions. This is accompanied by a strong belief that fulfilling or not fulfilling the demands of the covenant relationship produces consequences that affect not just the individual but the whole community. On the whole, it may be said that as far as African religion is concerned, morality arose because of one's consciousness of belonging to the Divine Being. Consequently, moral values are seen as the offspring of religion. If it is agreed that morality embodies the will of God, then it is what religion (which is the practical demonstration of God's relationship with humankind) approves as being moral that society must also approve, and what religion condemns must also stand condemned by society. In other words, as S. A. Adewale points out, "the ethics of Yoruba (indeed all Africans) from one to another is religious."[26] It is thus clear that, above all things, the basis of holiness is one's relationship with God. J. Estlin Carpenter notes, "The historical beginning of all morality is to be found in religion; or that in the earliest period of human history, religion and morality were necessary correlates of each other."[27] Robertson Smith cautiously affirms that "in ancient society all morality, as morality was then understood, was consecrated and enforced by religious motives and sanctions."[28] Africa is not an exception.

The point here is clear. For Africans, morality is not independent of religion.[29] The African view of the holiness of God—and its implications just described—is in line with Paul's use of *hagiōsynē* ("holiness," 2 Cor. 7:1) concerning God. Paul uses *hagiōsynē* to express that essential character of

25. Bolaji Idowu, *Olodumare: God in Yoruba Belief* (London: SCM, 1962), 145.

26. S. A. Adewale, *The Religion of the Yoruba: A Phenomenological Analysis* (Ibadan, Nigeria: University of Ibadan Press, 1988), 70.

27. J. Estlin Carpenter, *Comparative Religion* (London: Williams & Norgate, 1913), 196.

28. W. Robertson Smith, *The Religion of the Semites* (London: A&C Black, 1914), 267.

29. Contra A. B. Ellis, *The Tshi-Speaking Peoples of the Gold Coast of West Africa* (London: Chapman and Hall, 1847), passim. In his discussion about the sense of sin and morality among the Twi-speaking people of the Gold Coast (now Ghana), he wrongly asserted that "religion is not in any way allied with moral ideals" and that the two only come together "when man attains a higher degree of civilization." He claimed that "among the people of the Gold Coast sin is limited to insults offered to the gods, and neglect of the gods. Murder, theft, and all offenses against the person or against property, are matters in which the gods have no immediate concern and in which they have no interest. The most atrocious crimes, committed as between man and man, the gods can view with equanimity" (280). Ellis's view is not a true representation of the sense of sin among these people. See also Carl F. H. Henry, *An Introduction to the Philosophy of Religion* (New Jersey: Prentice Hall, 1985), 131, who argues strongly for a morality of good and evil that is intrinsically independent of God.

God as separateness from all evil as well as for his just dealings in his relationship with humanity, the likeness of which character the believer will possess in greater or lesser degrees in proportion to his/her conformity to the will of God. As believers cleanse themselves in body and spirit, it will become increasingly possible to describe them by the term *hagiōsynē*—"holiness." When Paul urges the Corinthians to bring holiness to completion, he is not suggesting the possibility of holiness as ethical purity, which is somehow not wholly pure. To the contrary, he is exhorting believers to pursue an ethical purity that is limited but not tainted, an ethical purity that reflects only a portion of the holiness of God and must come to reflect ever more of God's holiness. Holiness may expand—indeed it must—as the believer comes to be more in the likeness of Christ through a greater awareness of what constitutes defilement of flesh and spirit and subsequently cleanses himself/herself of that defilement. For Paul, the perfecting of holiness is the purpose of the Christian life (cf. Rom. 6:19). It is "the grand object of a genuine Christian pursuit."[30] One may rightly conclude with Stanley Porter that *hagiōsynē* as used in 2 Corinthians 7:1 is not "merely a static condition, a holiness obtained by the observance of cultic practices. . . . The context is not one of resting content with an unholy life . . . but one of acting out one's status in Christ."[31] Africans uphold the strong belief that God and the divinities have set the standard of holiness. This implies that a person's moral actions stem from religion and cannot be separated. One cannot but concur with Egudu that "since good attitude or behavior towards fellow men is one of the essential conditions for religion, it has to follow naturally and logically too that there cannot be any morally good attitude or act which does not to that extent share in the nature of religion."[32]

Summary

The biblical text's claim to universal validity demands its appropriation by readers with different orientations in different contexts. This endeavor requires fresh ways of expressing the universal truth of the biblical text and its message while at the same time giving due recognition to another religious ethos as a positive expression of the common religious thought, which in this case is the subject of holiness. As John Carman succinctly states, "The universal human religion is by a circuitous route derived from early and later Christian

---

30. Carver, *2 Corinthians*, 220.
31. For more details, see S. E. Porter, "Holiness, Sanctification," *DPL*, 400.
32. R. H. Egudu, "Can There Be Morality without Religion?," *Faith and Practice* 1, no. 2 (1972): 47.

confidence in the universal comprehensibility of the Christian message and the universal applicability of Christian piety. The divine Word can be expressed in differing human words because that divine word is somehow behind every human being capable of uttering words."[33] African purification rites and symbols can serve as tools to both illuminate our interpretation of 2 Corinthians 7:1 and communicate the subject of holiness in an African setting. In African religion, holiness is the nature of God, derives from him, is demanded by him, and is based on a covenant relationship with him. Purification rites are required to remain in closeness with God. Implicit in the purifications rites is the demand for ethical purity. This is the idea Paul presents in 2 Corinthians 7:1. Cleansing, in this passage, has to do with proper use of the body, as it is regarded as a temple, a dwelling place of the Holy Spirit and through which God is to be glorified (cf. 1 Cor. 6:15–20). There is no aspect of the Corinthians' lives that is to be ignored in their efforts to make themselves clean. This is the essence of purification among traditional Africans. Maintaining a covenant relationship with the Deity requires the total removal of pollution.

33. J. B. Carman, "Religions as a Problem for Christian Theology," in *Christian Faith in a Religiously Plural World*, ed. D. C. Dawe and J. B. Carman (New York: Orbis Books, 1978), 96.

9

Redefining Identity

A Kenyan Reading of Galatians 3:1–14

ELIZABETH (LIZ) W. MBURU

The Problem of Identity

If you ask any Kenyan, "Who are you?" the answer may be surprising. For too long, Kenyans, and indeed Africans in general, have been defined by the West—first by the missionaries (who brought a Westernized gospel), then by the colonialists (whose colonial processes undermined the systems, values, and views of entire cultural worlds and stripped the Kenyan colonized peoples of their identities),[1] and now by globalization (which has opened us up to a staggering number of identity options). Our identity has long been a projection of how we are perceived by others.

Galatians is a popular letter that is often used to teach against legalistic practices and a works mentality. However, a Kenyan contextual reading reveals that Galatians is not primarily about this. The underlying issue in this letter is that of identity: the distinguishing character or personality of an individual. A clearly perceived and articulated identity is important for economic, social, political, and spiritual progression. Several issues contribute to the subversion and disintegration of a genuine Christian identity. However, a major issue is

---

1. Eugene Hillman, *Toward an African Christianity: Inculturation Applied* (New York: Paulist Press, 1993), 5.

syncretism. This is "the unresolved, unassimilated, and tension-filled mixing of Christian ideas with local custom and ritual."[2] In a rejection of the identity imposed by "others," many Kenyan Christians seek to redefine their identity by looking back to African traditional religious practices and worldviews. One author refers to this phenomenon as "double loyalty" or "dual belonging" and argues that "African Christianity is incurably pluralistic."[3]

This chapter provides a rereading of Galatians 3:1–14 from the perspective of a Kenyan reader. Paul is raising the following question: What are the identity markers that confirm that one is a Christian? The main identity markers in Judaism at the time consisted of shared ethnicity, culture, and religion. Circumcision, observance of the Sabbath, and keeping the Mosaic law were badges of identity peculiar to the Jewish people.[4] The Galatian believers, misled by false teachers, insisted on circumcision and the law as the main identity markers that showed they belonged to the people of God. Paul corrects their wrong thinking by arguing that one's Christian identity is grounded in Christ through an act of faith. Faith and the Spirit, rather than circumcision and the law, are the main identity markers for a believer.

Background

Kenya is a country in East Africa with a population of about 47.5 million.[5] It is found on the equator, bordered by Ethiopia, Somalia, Tanzania, Uganda, and South Sudan. The Indian Ocean runs along the southeast border. It is very diverse, with over forty tribes. The official languages are Kiswahili and English, with most people speaking both. Since ethnic identity is so important, most people also speak their traditional languages. The different peoples of Kenya have different religious and cultural beliefs and practices. By 2009, the main religions in Kenya included Christianity—with Protestants in the majority—Islam, Hinduism, and Traditionalism.

As in most of Africa, religious spaces in Kenya are fluid. We are capable of "participating in Islam, one form or another of Christianity, and African traditional rituals all in one day without fear of self-contradiction."[6] The

---

2. Lamin Sanneh, *Whose Religion Is Christianity? The Gospel beyond the West* (Grand Rapids: Eerdmans, 2003), 44.

3. Joseph Galgalo, *African Christianity: The Stranger Within* (Limuru: Zapf Chancery Publishers Africa, 2010), 27.

4. G. W. Hansen, "Galatians, Letter to the," *DPL*, 327.

5. "2019 Kenyan Population and Housing Census Results," Kenyan National Bureau of Statistics, November 4, 2019, https://www.knbs.or.ke/2019-kenya-population-and-housing -census-results/.

6. Galgalo, *African Christianity*, 27.

belief in a retribution theology, intermediaries, spiritual powers, and witchcraft that is so evident in our churches betrays a theological framing that is more aligned with African traditional religious worldviews than a biblical worldview.[7] Many Kenyan pastors can be compared to witchdoctors in the way they practice their craft. Christian objects such as crosses and anointing oil, as well as other objects, such as handkerchiefs, are used as amulets, fetishes, and talismans and are believed to have power in themselves to bring about healing or deliverance.

Kenyan Christians instinctively recognize that Christianity as it was handed down to us has a foreign flavor that does not quite mesh with who we are. It therefore has to be reshaped. Contextual theologizing is vital for the healthy growth of Christian identity. Unfortunately, a failure to interrogate the assumptions underlying our traditional religious beliefs and practices has meant that they are uncritically incorporated into daily life. For instance, traditional burial rites, which ensure that the dead successfully pass on to the realm of the ancestors, may sometimes be practiced alongside a Christian burial service, without any visible conflict. Clearly, the very gospel we claim to believe in stands endangered as we embroil ourselves in syncretistic doctrines and practices. Many Kenyan Christians are confused as to what is truly biblical faith and practice. While an outsider might be critical of the way in which such practices are reshaping Christian identity in Kenya, and indeed the syncretistic end products ought to be shunned, an insider recognizes the yearning within to "find ourselves."

This is further complicated by a rapidly changing digital and globalized context. According to one source, Kenya is the leading consumer in Africa of smartphone and internet usage.[8] This implies that the digital space has as much of an impact on Kenyans as the geographical space in which we live. This means that a young woman in the village uses social media even as her grandmother in the same homestead continues to cook with firewood. Clearly, redefining identity in this complex landscape is a challenging task.

Exegesis of Galatians 3:1–14

Galatians 3:1–14 is found in the main body of the letter, which begins at 1:6 and ends at 6:15. In order to understand Paul's message, it is important to set 3:1–14 within its historical, theological, and literary contexts.

7. Joseph Galgalo, "Syncretism in African Christianity: A Boon or a Bane," in *African Contextual Realities*, ed. Rodney L. Reed, ASET (Carlisle, UK: Langham Global Library, 2018), 84–85.

8. Kevin Namunwa, "Kenya Leads Africa in Smartphone Usage," *Business Today*, March 11, 2019, https://businesstoday.co.ke/kenya-leads-africa-smartphone-usage/.

The apostle Paul identifies himself as the author (Gal. 1:1; 6:11). Although his later fame was as the apostle to the gentiles (Gal. 2:8; Eph. 3:8), Paul began his religious journey as a Hellenistic Jew with a deep knowledge of Judaism, the Septuagint, and the Greek style of writing. This is evident in the letter. The recipients were Galatian Christians (Gal. 1:2; 3:1), and depending on whether one opts for the southern province or the northern ethnic group, this can affect dating.[9] Our conclusions either way, however, do not affect its core message.

What was Paul's purpose for writing this letter? There was conflict in the Galatian church, and there were accusations that Paul was preaching a defective gospel. Scholars identify the troublemakers as Judaizers. Judaizers argued that keeping the law of Moses was essential for salvation (cf. Acts 15:1). They also insisted that the law on its own was able to restrain sinful conduct, while others argued that it did not matter if believers sinned because they are saved by faith alone. Paul writes to refute these Judaizers and to provide the Galatian believers with the proper foundation for a genuine Christian identity.

The genre of Galatians is an occasional letter to specific recipients. The immediate literary context is a defense of Paul's apostleship as well as a theological defense of his gospel. In the section under study, Paul refutes the Judaizers' teachings with various arguments from the Galatians' experience (3:1–5) and Scripture (3:6–9). He concludes with the truth that righteousness is found only through faith in Christ and not the law (3:10–14). This section grounds our understanding of Paul's argument to the Judaizers about what constitutes the key identity markers of Christianity. In the next section, Paul provides an argument from history that contrasts law and promise.

Galatians 3:1–5: The Galatians' Experience

Many commentators agree that Galatians 3:1–5 is the central message of the letter, clarifying the nature of justification. Paul therefore presents the indisputable truth that the reception of the Spirit is *the* identity marker that confirms one is a Christian. In this section, Paul uses an argumentative style popular in his day that includes vivid images, rhetorical questions, and intense reasoning.[10]

3:1 O *foolish Galatians! Who has bewitched you? [Before whose] eyes Jesus Christ was publicly portrayed as crucified.*[11]

9. Thomas R. Schreiner, *Galatians*, ZECNT (Grand Rapids: Zondervan, 2010), 31.
10. Craig S. Keener, *The IVP Bible Background Commentary: New Testament*, 2nd ed. (Downers Grove, IL: IVP Academic, 2014), 528.
11. The text from Gal. 3:1–14 is my own translation.

Paul begins with language that is shocking to the ear. With a harsh exclamation and a rhetorical question, he vividly expresses his incredulity at their actions. Paul is questioning either their moral inclinations (not their intellectual capacities) or their lack of spiritual discernment.[12] Paul's choice of the more formal "Galatians," instead of "brothers" or "beloved," alerts them to the seriousness of the situation. Coupling "foolish" with "bewitched" (*baskainō*) emphasizes the gravity of the situation. This can also be understood in the sense of practicing magic. Whether literal (real demonic influence) or figurative, this word suggests that the Galatians were under an evil spiritual influence.[13] Ultimately, Satan is the deceiver. Like in the parable of the soils, their quick desertion implies that the roots of the gospel had not sunk deep enough (cf. Matt. 13:1–23).

This opening statement resonates with the Kenyan belief in intermediary spirits as well as witchdoctors. Witchcraft is one of the major manifestations of syncretism, and witchdoctors openly advertise their services. The worldview of dynamism means that people seek power to gain control over diverse circumstances. This power is acquired from spirit-beings.[14] Establishing communication with the spirit-world and even vying for power to control this unseen realm through witchcraft are common.[15] Nevertheless, what Paul is talking about is not the same as practicing black magic. It may also look as if Paul is endorsing magic; he is not. He uses the language of the day to express his astonishment: their falling away looks like bewitchment.

What does "publicly proclaimed as crucified" signify? Rather than a physical portrayal of Christ's death, Paul may be pointing to the vivid communication of the significance of Christ's death on the cross.[16] He may also be pointing to himself as one who "acted out the crucifixion through his own lifestyle (2:20)."[17] Both interpretations are applicable.

3:2 *This only I wish to find out from you: Did you receive the Spirit by works of the law or by means of hearing [the message] by faith [i.e., trusting God]?*

Paul uses a series of rhetorical questions as a dialogical device to ensure that the Galatians identify personally with the issue and recognize their error. The first has to do with how they received the Spirit. For Paul, this is not

12. Schreiner, *Galatians*, 180; Richard N. Longenecker, *Galatians*, WBC 41 (Nashville: Nelson, 1990), 99, 103.

13. Douglas J. Moo, *Galatians*, BECNT (Grand Rapids: Baker Academic, 2013), 181.

14. Elizabeth Mburu, *African Hermeneutics* (Carlisle, UK: HippoBooks, 2019), 52.

15. Yusufu Turaki, *Foundations of African Traditional Religion and Worldview* (Nairobi, Kenya: WordAlive, 2006), 35.

16. Schreiner, *Galatians*, 181–82; see also Longenecker, *Galatians*, 101.

17. Keener, *Bible Background*, 529.

some event subsequent to coming to faith in Christ; rather, the Spirit is the identifying characteristic of the Christian.[18] This is the main issue and the most important question in this section.

Little wonder, then, that Paul introduces the phrase "works of the law" (*ergōn nomou*). Observance of the law—in this case, circumcision—was one of the Jewish identity markers. The law had for centuries defined the Jewish people and played a significant role in their social and religious identities. Likewise, the pagan culture of the gentile Galatian believers had also been a significant part of their social and religious life. Walter Hansen suggests that "they may well have felt a loss of identity since their faith in Christ excluded them from both their pagan temples and from the Jewish synagogues."[19] No wonder their past had so easily been revived by the false teachers! Nevertheless, this "Christ and . . ." doctrine was essentially a corruption of the gospel.

As with the Galatians, tradition plays a major role in ordering Kenyan life, with the past being used to determine how one lives in the present.[20] The traditional Kenyan conception of time acknowledges a long past, a present, and no future (or at least the future is only the present extending forward). The past is the most important dimension and very difficult to let go—a reality often seen in our churches.

Paul uses the phrase "works of the law" in sharp contrast to "hearing by faith" (*ex akoēs pisteōs*), a kind of antithesis often used by speakers in forceful argumentation.[21] "Hearing" can refer to either the act of hearing or the message heard, and "faith" can refer to either trusting God or the content of what is believed.[22] The best alternative, reinforced by the preposition, is "hearing by means of trust in Christ." No amount of human effort can enable one to receive the Spirit. It is a gift.

3:3 Are you so foolish? Having begun in the Spirit are you now being perfected in the flesh?
Going back to his original indictment, Paul again refers to the Galatians as foolish. In the same way that he has just contrasted "works of the law" and "hearing by faith," he now makes it explicit that he is really comparing the Spirit and the flesh. Flesh (*sarx*) here refers not to the physical body but

18. Scot McKnight, *The NIV Application Commentary: Galatians* (Grand Rapids: Zondervan, 1995), 138.
19. Hansen, "Galatians," 327.
20. Mburu, *African Hermeneutics*, 57.
21. Keener, *Bible Background*, 529.
22. Schreiner, *Galatians*, 183.

to "the human nature in itself, the human without the divine."[23] Or, viewed another way, Spirit and flesh "are two different domains under which a person chooses to live or, . . . two different periods of time . . . (before Christ and after Christ), two worlds that war against one another (5:16–18)."[24] Many Jewish teachers taught that, although salvation was by grace, those Jews who rejected the law were lost. Consequently, gentiles who had converted to Judaism would need to prove that they were genuine by obeying every detail of the law.[25] This is probably what was behind the Judaizers' thinking. However, as Paul argues, the law is limited as to what it can achieve.

Much as with many Kenyans today, the Galatians' desire to establish their new sense of identity had been derailed by their past beliefs and practices. However, with this rhetorical question, Paul makes it clear that the experience of the Galatians did not need to be supplemented with anything more. With the coming of Christ, the law, which had served its purpose, needed to be put aside. Paul's questions have a clear answer. Their new identity was founded on a new reality, and their previous identity markers had been superseded by faith and the Spirit.

3:4 *Did you suffer so many things without cause—if indeed it is without cause?*

Paul is not yet done. He asks another rhetorical question that challenges them to interrogate the value of their new allegiance in light of their personal experience. This is not only rhetorically more effective but would also be the ultimate eyewitness argument.[26] The verb "suffer" (*paschō*) used here has been translated in various ways. Some commentators translate it as "experienced" (which includes positive experiences), whereas others translate it as "suffered." Those who prefer "experienced" argue that the context of Galatians does not indicate any suffering on their part. However, others argue that Galatians 4:29 suggests the Galatians experienced some persecution. Other texts in Galatians also seem to support this (1:10; 5:11). Whatever the case, it is almost certain that the Galatians were not exempt from the discrimination and verbal abuse that were a staple of the early Christian experience.[27] Paul phrases this like a question, but it also implies a condition and a warning. If the Galatians are so foolish as to follow the Judaizers, then their suffering has been in vain.

23. Herman N. Ridderbos, *The Epistle of Paul to the Churches of Galatia*, NICNT (Grand Rapids: Eerdmans, 1953), 114.

24. McKnight, *Galatians*, 141.

25. Keener, *Bible Background*, 529.

26. Keener, *Bible Background*, 529.

27. Schreiner, *Galatians*, 185.

3:5 *Therefore does the one who provides you with the Spirit and who works miracles among you do so by works of the law or from hearing [the message] by faith [i.e., trusting God]?*

Beginning with the inferential conjunction "therefore" (*oun*), Paul asks his final rhetorical question, essentially a summary of verses 2–4. "The one who provides" and the one "who works" point to the same person (i.e., God).

With regard to miracles, some commentators suggest that Paul merely describes the impact of his own ministry among the Galatians.[28] Others argue that the working of miracles means that the charismatic and powerful work of the Spirit is ongoing (cf. 1 and 2 Corinthians).[29] The belief in miracles in an increasingly secularized world is rare. However, in Kenya, healings and deliverance are experienced daily through the power of the Holy Spirit. Nevertheless, one must be discerning, as some of these so-called miracles are merely a front for unscrupulous people.

Regardless of one's position, the answer to this last question is obvious. The first part of the question has already been answered—the reception of the Spirit is clearly by means of faith and not works. By implication, the second part requires a similar answer. The working of miracles can be only by faith and not by works of the law.

Galatians 3:6–9: The Testimony from Scripture

Having successfully concluded from the Galatians' own experience that justification is by faith, Paul now turns to the testimony from Scripture. This provides an even more powerful argument because of the important role of Scripture. The main issue of identity comes in this section. The question Paul seeks to answer is "Who are Abraham's children?" The Judaizers argue that it is those who are circumcised. However, Paul refutes this position, arguing that believers, although not circumcised, are the children of Abraham and have received the blessing.

3:6 *Just as Abraham believed God, and it was accounted to him as righteousness . . .*

Beginning with a comparative conjunction, "just as" (*kathōs*), that ties the Galatians' own experience of faith to Abraham's experience, Paul begins with a popular Old Testament Jewish proof text that was used to show how Abraham modeled faith (Gen. 15:6). Some commentators argue that this conjunction should be understood to mean Abraham had the Spirit. However, this

---

28. Schreiner, *Galatians*, 186.
29. Longenecker, *Galatians*, 105.

cannot be the case since the Spirit is a gift of the new age inaugurated in and by Christ.[30] While the Spirit did come upon certain individuals to empower them for certain tasks (and certainly this was also possible in Abraham's case), it was not the permanent indwelling experienced by New Testament believers.

Paul uses Abraham as the model because he is the progenitor of Israel.[31] This makes sense within the Kenyan worldview, for the authority of an ancestor, a parent, or an elder in the community is unquestioned. In addition, since Jewish teachers regarded Abraham as the model convert to Judaism, any argument that referenced him was more likely to be respected by the Judaizers.[32] It is also probable that the Judaizers had referenced Abraham and probably argued, on the basis of Scripture, that for one to be justified, one must be a child of Abraham.[33] This naturally implied circumcision and observance of the law.

Jewish tradition emphasized Abraham's obedience rather than his faith (1 Macc. 2:52; Sir. 44:19–21). In later Jewish theology, this accounting as righteous is "represented as a credit entry in heaven for a humanly merited earning."[34] Paul turns this around by arguing that Abraham was justified on the basis of his trust/faith in God even before the covenant requirement of circumcision. His trust was accounted to him as righteousness. Paul will go on to show that, in the same way, the Galatians' faith is counted as righteousness.

3:7 *Know therefore that the ones who are by faith, these are Abraham's children.*

Having established the basis on which Abraham was declared righteous, Paul begins to settle the issue of identity. He begins with another inferential conjunction, "therefore" (*ara*). The title "Abraham's children" was normally used to refer to the Jewish people but occasionally referred to those who excelled in righteousness. Notably, it was never applied to gentiles.[35] Scholars debate what "the ones who are by faith" (*hoi ek pisteōs*; see also Gal. 3:9) means. In the Greek it can refer to either "those who have faith [in Christ]" or "those who are faithful." In this context, Paul clearly means the former. Moreover, as seen above, Galatians 3:6 clearly places emphasis on Abraham's believing and not on his faithfulness. The conclusion is that because faith takes center stage in Abraham's righteousness, one can become a child of Abraham by putting their faith in Christ.

30. Schreiner, *Galatians*, 189.
31. Schreiner, *Galatians*, 189.
32. Keener, *Bible Background*, 529.
33. Moo, *Galatians*, 192.
34. Ridderbos, *Galatians*, 118
35. Keener, *Bible Background*, 529.

Paul therefore redefines the identity of "Abraham's children." Because it is no longer based on ancestry or circumcision but on faith in Christ, it is applied to gentile believers who are now the spiritual children of Abraham through adoption (cf. Gal. 4:5). The various ethnic groups in Kenya have specific traditions and practices that reinforce their sense of identity within the group and show whose descendants they are. This ethnic identity is so strong that the "other" is often regarded in dehumanizing terms resulting in negative ethnicity. This verse reminds us that ethnic identity must never overshadow our Christian identity as spiritual children of Abraham.

3:8 *And the Scriptures, having foreseen that God justifies [would justify] the gentiles by faith, preached the gospel beforehand to Abraham that "all the nations will be blessed in you."*

In the Old Testament, God promises Abraham that he will be a universal blessing to the nations. Paul's skill as a Jewish expositor comes to the fore here as he proves his inference from Genesis 12:3 by appealing to Genesis 18:18.[36] For Paul, the promise to Abraham already had the gospel embedded in it even though it would not have been evident to Abraham at the time. Paul interprets the phrase "will be blessed" as a predictive future that looks forward to the work of Christ on the cross.

What does it mean for the nations to be blessed in Abraham? There are two major interpretations. The first is that it is based on the faithfulness of Abraham; the second, on his believing. However, since Galatians 3:6 clearly talks about Abraham's believing and not his faithfulness, and later on 3:9 refutes any idea that gentiles are blessed on the basis of Abraham's faithfulness, the second option is preferred. This is both a theological and a sociological issue. Theologically the inclusion of gentiles is by faith, and, sociologically, they do not have to nationalize to be included.[37]

3:9 *So then, those who are of faith have been blessed with the believing Abraham.*

Having made his argument from Scripture, Paul once again begins with an inferential conjunction, "so then" (*hōste*), in order to draw a conclusion from Galatians 3:8 (see 3:7, which is parallel). In the previous verse, Paul argued that believers are blessed "in" Abraham. In this verse, he argues that they are blessed "with" (*syn*) Abraham. This intentional repetition puts emphasis on faith as the necessary factor for belonging to Abraham's family and being a participant in his blessings.[38] Kenyans believe that an elder's curse or bless-

36. Keener, *Bible Background*, 529.
37. McKnight, *Galatians*, 158.
38. Schreiner, *Galatians*, 195.

ing can be stopped only by divine intervention. The implication, then, is that because Abraham is our elder in matters of faith, we are blessed just as he is.[39] If we read beyond this text to 3:16, Paul's redefinition of "seed" confirms that this blessing extends beyond Jewish national boundaries. As Keener points out, "Christ was the ultimate seed through whom gentiles were being blessed (Gal. 3:8), as is evident in the fruit of Paul's gentile mission in obedience to Christ (cf. Rom. 1:5–6; 15:8–12)."[40]

Galatians 3:10–14: True Righteousness

Paul concludes this section with several warnings from Scripture about trying to attain righteousness by "works of the law." Such attempts result in a curse, which can be removed only by the cross of Christ.

3:10 *For as many as are of works of the law are under a curse; for it is written that "cursed is everyone who does not abide by all that is written in the book of the law, to perform them."*

As Paul wraps up this section, he makes three assertions that show that law and faith are incompatible. To connect the two sections tightly together, he begins with the conjunction "for" (*gar*). This conjunction is functioning in a causal sense. To further demonstrate that faith is the only means of getting into a right relationship with God, Paul provides reasons why even those who "are of works of the law" are under a curse. This is counterintuitive reasoning to his readers because, in the Jewish mind, it is gentiles who are cursed because they do not have the law.

In traditional Kenya, curses were frequently pronounced on members of the community who had offended the spiritual realm or the physical community. The language of curse is still evident in modern Kenya. It is not unusual to hear someone explain that a misfortune in their life is due to a curse. Curses are believed to have both spiritual and physical consequences. Curses go deeper than a mere utterance, as this proverb from the Akamba of Kenya demonstrates: "Kiumo ti, 'Wookw'wa'" (A curse is not simply telling someone, "May you die").[41] At the same time, not all curses are effective.[42] It is believed that only divine intervention can stop a curse from taking place.

---

39. Samuel Ngewa, *Galatians*, ABCS (Nairobi, Kenya: HippoBooks, 2010), 106.
40. Craig S. Keener, *Galatians: A Commentary* (Grand Rapids: Baker Academic, 2019), 269.
41. Nathan Nzyoka Joshua, "A Christian Response to Curses in Africa," in *Christianity and Suffering: African Perspectives*, ed. Rodney L. Reed, ASET (Carlisle, UK: Langham Global Library, 2017), 148.
42. Joshua, "Christian Response," 148.

The idea of curses was also familiar in the ancient world, as can be seen in the Greek magical papyri from Greco-Roman Egypt (second century BC to fifth century AD). Curses were central to ancient magic for offensive or defensive reasons. Indeed, Jewish sources recognized that curses could be effective as well as dangerous.[43] In his first assertion, Paul quotes Deuteronomy 27:26. Most likely the Judaizers had used this as a decisive passage in their teaching. Paul, however, argues that a reliance on works of the law to obtain a right standing with God can only lead to a curse (cf. Gal. 1:8, 9). A curse is inevitable because no one can obey every aspect of the law perfectly. God's curse implies final destruction and condemnation, the eschatological punishment administered by God himself.[44] Commentators note that to emphasize his point regarding perfect and total obedience to the law, Paul selectively uses the Septuagint and avoids quoting the Masoretic Text, which does not include the word "all." The problem with the law was that atonement was no longer possible through the Old Testament sacrificial system. Christ's death on the cross made this system obsolete. If one insisted on living under the law, one therefore had to obey it perfectly.

3:11 *And that no one is justified in the law before God is evident, because the righteous will live by faith.*

To further demonstrate that obedience to the law can never be enough, Paul makes his second assertion. The word "justified" is a forensic term that denotes a right standing before God, the judge.[45] Paul cites yet another Old Testament Scripture, Habakkuk 2:4. The Septuagint version places the emphasis on God and not the believer. Because Paul wants to emphasize the believer's faith or trust in God, he uses the Masoretic Text.[46]

There are two main problems in interpreting this text. The first has to do with word order. Should this phrase read "the righteous *by faith* shall live" or "the righteous shall live *by faith*"? Both are possible, and the difference in meaning is not significant. The second is whether Habakkuk should be interpreted to reflect human faith or divine faithfulness. It is likely that Paul applies this text to those who have put their faith in Christ and are consequently considered righteous.[47] It is faith, and not the law, that is at the heart of justification.

3:12 *For the law is not by faith, but "the one who does them [the commandments] will live by them."*

43. Craig S. Keener, *Galatians: A Commentary* (Grand Rapids: Baker Academic, 2019), 209.
44. Longenecker, *Galatians*, 17.
45. Schreiner, *Galatians*, 207.
46. Schreiner, *Galatians*, 208.
47. Keener, *Bible Background*, 530.

Paul then makes his conclusion as to why the law can never justify. The two parts of this statement are connected by a strong adversative conjunction, "but" (*alla*), which makes the argument even stronger. He cites another Old Testament text, Leviticus 18:5. Every Jew would agree that the law is concerned with "doing." There is no need for Paul to prove it. What Paul is pointing out is that Mosaic Judaism has become a thoroughly "natural" system, whatever its original aim and object. It has evolved to resemble every system of natural religion that depends on doing.[48] Once again, Paul chooses his Old Testament texts carefully. Most likely, the Judaizers argued from this text that faith is not enough, and so Paul turns it around as an example of the works approach.[49]

This verse reiterates what Paul stated so strongly in Galatians 3:10. Circumcision of the gentile Galatians can never be enough because the law "requires perfect obedience and human performance whereas faith looks to what God has done in Christ for salvation."[50] Paul's position contrasts sharply with the transactional African traditional religions. Christianity says, "*Because* I am accepted, I do good works." African traditional religions teach, "I must do good works *so that* I can be accepted."

3:13 *Christ redeemed us from the curse of the law by becoming a curse for us, for it is written, "Cursed is everyone who hangs on a tree . . ."*

What, then, is the solution to this predicament? Quoting from Deuteronomy 21:23, Paul explains that Christ redeemed us by becoming a curse for us through his crucifixion. Such a death was the outward sign in Israel of being cursed by God. While the verb "redeem" (*exagorazō*) literally means "to release by means of paying a price," Paul means this metaphorically. We are the beneficiaries and not God. As Friedrich Büchsel affirms, "In this liberation from the curse of the Law, the essential point is that it confers both an actual and also a legally established freedom ensuring against any renewal of slavery."[51]

Paradoxically, it is by Christ himself taking on the curse on our behalf that this redemption is achieved. One might argue that, since the gentile Galatians were never under the law, they are exempt from this curse. However, with the pronoun "us," Paul argues that all are condemned.[52]

---

48. R. A. Cole, *Galatians: An Introduction and Commentary*, 2nd ed., TNTC 9 (Downers Grove, IL: InterVarsity, 1989), 142.
49. Keener, *Galatians*, 248.
50. Schreiner, *Galatians*, 210.
51. Friedrich Büchsel, "ἐξαγοράζω," *TDNT* 1:126.
52. Schreiner, *Galatians*, 215.

It is difficult to comprehend how one who is cursed can be our redemption. However, it is even harder to understand how one who has been redeemed from this curse would willingly put themselves under it again by going back to traditional religious practices. This crisis of identity comes from an inadequate Christology. Like many Africans on the rest of the continent, Kenyan Christians have an image of Christ who is irrelevant and passive, remote and unconcerned with the situations of suffering. However, when we understand that Christ is our liberator and curse bearer, this becomes the grid through which we redefine our identity.[53]

3:14... *in order that the blessing of Abraham might come in Christ Jesus to the gentiles, so that we might receive the promise of the Spirit through faith.*

Paul now gets to the main purpose of this section. There are two purpose clauses in this verse, both identified by *hina* ("in order that," "so that"). Christ's redemptive activity was for the purpose of concretizing the blessing promised to Abraham. Circumcision, or any other aspect of the law that the Judaizers were promoting (cf. Gal. 4:10), was never intended as *the* avenue to fulfill this promise. Paul begins this section with the Spirit and faith, and he ends it the same way. Some commentators argue that the blessing of Abraham is in fact the reception of the Spirit.[54] Others propose that the promise of the Spirit is a related but separate gift of the new covenant.[55] Regardless of one's position, the point is that the law no longer applies, and circumcision is useless to make one acceptable before God. Paul has come full circle: the cross means that the markers of a genuine Christian identity—namely, faith and the Spirit—have superseded all Jewish markers of identity.

Conclusion

The people of Kenya have a Kiswahili proverb that states, "Mwacha mila ni mtumwa" (One who abandons his culture becomes a slave). Galatians 3:1–14 challenges this proverb and leads to the inevitable conclusion that an indiscriminate embrace of the past is, in fact, a rejection of the liberation achieved for us in Christ and a return to slavery. Our Christian identity must be redefined in alignment with Christ and what he has done for us. As Paul emphasizes to his original readers, faith and the Spirit, rather than

53. Elizabeth W. Mburu, "Exploring the Multidimensional Nature of Christology in Galatians through the Lens of an African Hermeneutic," in *Who Do You Say That I Am? Christology in Africa*, ed. Rodney L. Reed and David K. Ngaruiya, ASET Series (Carlisle, UK: Langham Global Library, 2021), 57–76.

54. Schreiner, *Galatians*, 219.

55. Moo, *Galatians*, 216.

circumcision and the law, are the markers of a genuine Christian identity. This text is a reminder that we must learn how to hold our past and our present in tension as we learn to navigate continuity and discontinuity in our religious and cultural identities. Not everything from our past is wrong—in fact, some of it has proven to be useful in developing contextual language. Nevertheless, our identity markers are not to be imposed upon us by our past, be it African traditional religions, culture, or even worldview.

10

Galatians as the Basis for Resisting American Evangelicalism's "Works of the Law"

A Word for Ethnic Minorities

MIGUEL G. ECHEVARRÍA

Paul is at his most polemical in his epistle to the Galatians. In this letter, he combats the influence of a group of Jews pressuring gentiles to adopt "works of the law."[1] We can sense Paul's raw emotion when he calls the Galatians "foolish" (Gal. 3:1)[2] and the Jews "troublemakers" and "agitators" (1:6–7; 5:12, AT).[3] He even wishes that the latter would emasculate themselves (5:12). Since the Jewish group in Galatia "came from James," a pillar and head of the Jerusalem church, we assume that they were followers of the Messiah

---

1. For helpful studies on Paul's opponents in Galatia, see Craig S. Keener, *Galatians: A Commentary* (Grand Rapids: Baker Academic, 2019), 27–36; James D. G. Dunn, *The Theology of Paul's Letter to the Galatians*, NTT (Cambridge: Cambridge University Press, 2004), 8–12.

2. Scripture quotations are from the ESV unless otherwise indicated.

3. The Epistle to the Galatians does not support anti-Semitism. First, Paul himself was a Jew whose desire was to see his fellow kinsmen come to faith in the Messiah (Rom. 9–11). Second, Paul was addressing a particular group of Jews who were enforcing works of the law on gentile converts in Galatia. His comments are therefore not universal—they were directed at a specific group of Jews.

enforcing works of the law on gentile converts (2:12).[4] James gave Paul "the right hand of fellowship," so the two were not at odds (2:9). The friction was between Paul and the Jerusalem group.

Traditionally, at least from the Reformation to the end of World War II, Protestant Christians have interpreted "works of the law" in Galatians in view of Paul's emphasis on faith in Christ over and against a Jewish emphasis on keeping all the requirements of the torah. This reading envisions Paul's opponents as legalists. Whether they were successful in persuading the Galatians remains a matter of contention. The point is that Paul warns his readers about the dangers of succumbing to Jewish legalism.

At the conclusion of World War II, when the world finally witnessed the unchecked effects of anti-Semitism, many scholars showed a renewed interest in studying Judaism on its own terms (e.g., Second Temple Jewish writings) and moving away from centuries-old caricatures. Scholars such as W. D. Davies began to chip away at a legalistic understanding of Judaism.[5] Yet, it was not until E. P. Sanders's *Paul and Palestinian Judaism* that large cracks began to appear in the facade. Sanders argued that first-century Judaism was not legalistic; it was a religion of grace.[6] Jews believed that God had graciously elected his people and given them the Mosaic law. Since God had already chosen and delivered his people from Egypt, keeping the law was how Israelites maintained their covenant status. Sanders called this "covenantal nomism."

New Perspective proponents such as James D. G. Dunn and N. T. Wright accepted Sanders's thesis but qualified some of his arguments. With relevance to this essay, they narrowed "works of the law" to Jewish boundary markers, such as Sabbath, circumcision, and food laws, which distinguished Jewish "insiders" from gentile "outsiders."[7] This reading has direct implications for understanding Paul's opponents in Galatia. Paul was not combating legalists;

---

4. Whether Paul wrote to ethnic Galatians in the northern Galatian province or to the churches he evangelized in Acts 13–14 is a matter of debate. This short essay is not the place to solve this dilemma. Taking either the northern or the southern Galatian view does not change that the original recipients of the letter were gentiles. We will assume, then, that the "churches of Galatia" to whom Paul writes were composed of believing gentiles, without specifying further about their ethnic makeup (Gal. 1:2). For the north Galatian view, see J. B. Lightfoot, *The Epistle of Paul to the Galatians with Introductions, Notes and Dissertations* (repr., Grand Rapids: Zondervan, 1957), 4, 12–14. For the south Galatian view, see Thomas R. Schreiner, *Galatians*, ZECNT (Grand Rapids: Zondervan, 2010), 26–29.

5. See, for instance, W. D. Davies, *Paul and Rabbinic Judaism: Some Elements of Pauline Theology*, 4th ed. (Minneapolis: Fortress, 1980).

6. E. P. Sanders, *Paul and Palestinian Judaism: A Comparison of Patterns of Religion* (Minneapolis: Fortress, 1977).

7. See the discussion in N. T. Wright, *Paul and the Faithfulness of God*, book 1, parts 1–2 (Minneapolis: Fortress, 2013), 90–107.

he was opposing Jewish believers who were trying to enforce ethnic boundary markers—primarily circumcision—on gentile believers, which would visibly distinguish them as members of the covenant community.

My argument in this essay will follow this shift in understanding first-century Judaism. The traditional reading's emphasis on seeing legalism as the problem in Galatians (keeping all the works of the law) has the tendency to overshadow the main issue Paul addresses: that Jewish ethnic requirements were being enforced on gentile converts.[8] If we follow the traditional reading, we may overlook how Paul's Letter to the Galatians still speaks to people who face pressure to conform to the distinctives of the influential ethnic group. This often happens in American evangelicalism, where believers from ethnic minority groups are expected to adopt the values of the Anglo majority group to be considered members of God's people. If they refuse, they can expect to be relegated to the outer courts of the temple, so to speak, where they can carry out their own worship services and mercy ministries, often in their own languages, so as not to infringe on the comfort of genuine covenant members. This happens despite what Paul preaches, that "there is neither Jew nor Greek, there is neither slave nor free, there is no male nor female, for we are all one in Messiah Jesus" (Gal. 3:28 ESV alt.). That is, there are no ethnic, social, or gender distinctives required to be considered equal members of the Messiah's community.

As a Cuban American, I resonate with the pressures that ethnic minority groups—particularly Latinos/as—face in American evangelicalism. The problem is analogous to the demands that the Galatians were facing at the hands of Jewish believers, who were the dominant group among first-century Messiah followers. Like the Galatians, minorities do not have to adopt the distinctives associated with American evangelicalism to be considered "one of them"—they can refuse, just like Paul (Gal. 2:5). With that in mind, this essay will argue that Paul's Letter to the Galatians gives ethnic minorities the scriptural basis for resisting conformity to the majority group's works of the law. We will see this in four movements: first, a reminder of Paul's gospel (1:1–2:21); second, Paul's analysis of the problem in Galatia (3:1–4:31); third, a short pause from Galatians to consider the analogous problem for ethnic minorities in American evangelicalism; and fourth, Paul's solution to the pressure to adopt "works of the law" (5:1–6:18).

My hope is that this essay will offer a reading of Galatians that, while faithful to its message, will encourage minority groups to resist conformity

---

8. See the helpful discussion in Brad R. Braxton, "Galatians," in *True to Our Native Land: An African American New Testament Commentary*, ed. Brian Blount (Minneapolis: Fortress, 2007), 334–35.

to the majority group's boundary markers—those matters that define who is "in" and who is "out"—knowing they have believed the gospel that liberates them from burdensome expectations. While I acknowledge the importance of defining genuine membership in the community of believers, our boundaries should be the same as those for which Paul would have contended. His Letter to the Galatians shows that the single, distinguishing mark of who was "in" the community was faithfulness to Jesus the Messiah. This is all that was needed to become a recipient of the Spirit and an heir of the promises.

A Reminder of Paul's Gospel (Gal. 1:1–2:21)

Before reminding the Galatians of his gospel, Paul expresses bewilderment at how the Galatians have turned to "a different gospel" (Gal. 1:6). Since he refers to their message as "gospel," we should assume that many of the Jewish Christians who had entered the Galatian churches were claiming to preach the good news of the Messiah.[9] Despite the familiar terminology, Paul stresses that their message is different from what the Galatians originally heard (1:6). He is so upset with the Jewish believers that he (twice!) wishes they would be "accursed" (1:8–9), an emotive way of wishing that they would be cut off from membership in the covenant community, devoting them to eschatological destruction.[10]

To differentiate his message from that of the Jewish believers, Paul contends that he received his gospel directly from Jesus the Messiah (Gal. 1:12; cf. Acts 9:1–9). After his encounter with Jesus, his life was radically transformed, as he was no longer seeking to advance beyond his ethnic kin in the scrupulous observances of Judaism and in persecuting the church but had turned his focus to preaching the gospel to the gentiles (Gal. 1:13–17). He did so without the initial approval of the apostles in Jerusalem, going to the gentile regions of Arabia and Damascus (1:17). Only three years later did he go to Jerusalem to visit Peter and James (1:18–19). Shortly thereafter, he returned to gentile lands—this time to Syria and Cilicia (1:21–24).

When he returned to Jerusalem fourteen years later, the pillars of the church—Peter, James, and John—approved his gospel to the gentiles and Peter's to ethnic Jews ("the circumcised," Gal. 2:1–10). This occurred despite a group who attempted to impose Jewish boundary markers, such as circumcision, on him

9. James D. G. Dunn, *The Epistle to the Galatians*, BNTC (repr., Peabody, MA: Hendrickson, 2002), 43.

10. Commentaries usually focus on Paul's desire for the troublemakers to be devoted to destruction (e.g., Schreiner, *Galatians*, 88). Since this destiny is for those who violate the covenant, I have noted eternal destruction is a result of being cut off from the community. There is an allusion to the covenantal curses of Deut. 27–30. See also 1 Cor. 16:22.

and Titus (2:3–4). Not yielding for a moment to their pressure, Paul and Titus preserved the truth of the gospel, which is free of such ethnic distinctives (2:5).

Unlike Paul, Peter had succumbed to the pressure of the Jerusalem group (Gal. 2:12). Fearing their disapproval, he no longer ate with gentiles, even leading others to follow in the hypocrisy of again observing Jewish food laws (2:12–13). That meant no more *lechón*, only vegetables and grass-fed, antibiotic-free, hormone-free beef, the kind the elites from Jerusalem would approve of. Paul wastes no time in confronting Peter's duplicity (2:14). After all, covenant membership does not depend on keeping Jewish works of the law, such as food laws, but relies only on faith in Christ (2:16–17).[11]

If the Galatians had forgotten, and perhaps some had, 1:1–2:21 reminds them of the heavenly origin of Paul's gospel, which he proclaimed in gentile lands, setting his message apart from what Jewish believers were preaching to the Galatians. He even sets himself apart from Peter, who succumbed to the pressures and separated from gentiles, who undoubtedly enjoyed a little *mojo* with their *lechón* (2:4–5). And who is to say that Peter did not? At least, of course, until his status as one of the faithful was threatened; then he went back to vegetables and grass-fed, antibiotic-free, hormone-free beef.

While the historical context of the letter speaks to first-century Galatian churches, it also speaks a word to minorities who are expected to conform to the boundary markers of American evangelicalism. I will note specific examples later. For now, I will affirm that, like the Galatians, all Christians have heard the gospel that liberates them from the burden of succumbing to any group's ethnic distinctives, no matter how great the influence or insistent the pressure.

Paul's Analysis of the Problem in Galatia (Gal. 3:1–4:31)

Paul now turns his attention to his readers, calling them "foolish Galatians!" (Gal. 3:1). If that did not startle them, Paul follows with a series of rhetorical questions intended to show the Galatians the stupidity of succumbing to works of the law. As I have argued, the phrase "works of the law" refers to ethnic boundary markers such as circumcision and food laws, external indicators of a person's covenant membership. But what made the Galatians full participants in the covenant community was not adherence to Jewish

11. The *dik-* word group (*dikaioō, dikaiosynē, dikaios*), often associated with translations such as "righteousness" and "justice," usually appears in covenantal contexts in the LXX and other Second Temple literature (e.g., Dan. 9:15–19; 1QS IV, 23; CD III, 20; 1QH XVII, 15). When Abraham is first "declared righteous" in Gen. 15, for instance, a text to which Paul alludes in Gal. 3:6–9, it is certainly in connection with the covenant God makes with him. Paul's use of *dik-* words in Galatians follows this covenantal understanding of "righteousness" (e.g., Gal. 3:6–9, 15–18).

distinctives—it was the Spirit, whom the Galatians received through faith (3:1–4).[12] As a result, they were to resist the imposition of ethnic standards that have no bearing on their standing in the new covenant community.

The troublemakers were likely using the example of Abraham to argue that true covenant members had to adopt the ethnic distinctives of the old covenant, making circumcision an uncompromisable requirement (Gal. 3:6–9).[13] Paul reads the Abraham story differently. He alludes to Genesis 15 to argue that Abraham believed in the God who promised that he would be the father of innumerable descendants and that his offspring would receive an eternal land inheritance (Gal. 3:6–9; cf. Gen. 12). Abraham simply believed God and was declared righteous—no incision was required (Gal. 3:6).[14] For the sake of clarity, being righteous is more than being in a right relationship with God. While the notion of righteousness certainly includes this, there is an acute emphasis on covenant membership. This means that, when Abraham was declared righteous, he became a participant of the covenant, placing him in a right relationship with God.

In keeping with the nature of the Abrahamic covenant, Paul argues that those who exhibit the same faith as Abraham become his spiritual offspring and receive the promised land inheritance (Gal. 3:7, 18, 29). Since Galatians never unpacks the nature of the inheritance, we should recall that the exile from Canaan brought about a recontextualization of the promise. Later Old Testament texts, such as Psalm 2 and Isaiah 65–66, and Second Temple texts, such as 4 Ezra 7 and Sirach 44, expand the promise of inheritance beyond the original borders of Canaan to include the entire earth. Paul follows this developed understanding of the inheritance in Romans 4:13, saying that Abraham and his offspring are the heirs of the world. All this fulfills the promises to Abraham of a family of innumerable nations who would experience the blessings of the covenant. This family would be brought together in the same way that their forefather Abraham was brought into the covenant: through faith (Gal. 3:8–9; cf. Gen. 12:3; 18:18).

---

12. The genitive phrase *akoēs pisteōs* (Gal. 3:2, 5) may be rendered in a number of different ways: "faithful hearing" (attributive genitive); "hearing that produces faith" (genitive of product); "message about faith" (genitive of content); "the message that is the faith" (genitive of apposition); "message of trust" (genitive of association). One's choice should be reflective of Paul's immediate argument: the Galatians received the Spirit by faith, not by keeping works of the law.

13. N. T. Wright, *Paul for Everyone: Galatians and Thessalonians* (Louisville: Westminster John Knox, 2004), 30–31. See also David A. deSilva, *The Letter to the Galatians*, NICNT (Grand Rapids: Eerdmans, 2018), 279–80.

14. Circumcision did not become a marker of covenant membership until the later arrival of the Mosaic covenant (Exod. 19).

With that in mind, Paul wants those who desire to observe works of the law for the sake of covenantal status to realize the ramifications of their pursuit (Gal. 3:10). Appealing primarily to Deuteronomy 27:26, he argues that such people are obligated to go beyond boundary markers such as circumcision and food laws. They must keep all the requirements of the law, lest they experience the curse of eternal exile from the promised inheritance (Gal. 3:10; cf. Deut. 28:58; 30:10). Since it is impossible for any person to keep all the law's requirements, those who choose to live according to works of the law must bear the weight of the curse (Gal. 3:12). As he does throughout the letter, Paul argues that covenant membership is only through faith in the Messiah—who took the penalty of the curse, the exile of death, so that the gentiles would also become beneficiaries of the promised blessing of the Spirit (Gal. 3:12–14; cf. Isa. 44:3). Though the Genesis narrative does not define the promise of blessing, Paul envisions the blessing of Abraham fulfilled in the arrival of the Spirit, who brings both Jews and gentiles into the same covenant family, while still allowing the latter to enjoy *lechón* and avoid unnecessary, painful incisions (Gal. 3:13–14; 4:6–7; cf. Isa. 44:3).[15]

Since the troublemakers were likely appealing to the Mosaic covenant as the basis for their imposition of Jewish distinctives, Paul shows the foolishness of such an argument, contending that the later Mosaic covenant does not nullify the earlier Abrahamic covenant, which is based on faith (Gal. 3:15–18).[16] Thus, it is only by trusting in the true descendant of Abraham, Jesus the Messiah, that people become fellow members of Abraham's family and beneficiaries of the cosmic inheritance (3:16–18, 26, 29). Adopting ethnic boundary markers, placing one under obligation to the entire law, means the gentiles would forfeit the promise. But this is not the message Paul received and preached among the gentiles. That is why he goes to great lengths to remind the Galatians of what they would forfeit by yielding to the pressures of Jewish believers.

Thus far in the letter, Paul has clarified that he received his gospel directly from Messiah Jesus (Gal. 1:11–12). This is the very message he preached in gentile lands, and the pillar apostles endorsed, which was free from any Jewish boundary markers such as circumcision (1:17–2:10). Paul was so convinced about the truth of his gospel that he confronted Peter with the hypocrisy of succumbing to the expectation that Jews should not eat with unclean gentiles, forsaking those whom he had previously accepted as equal members of the covenant community (2:11–15). That means he no longer partook of *noche buena*,

---

15. See Miguel G. Echevarría Jr., *The Future Inheritance of Land in the Pauline Epistles* (Eugene, OR: Pickwick, 2019), 105–6.

16. Mika Heitanen makes the argument that in rabbinic circles "priority equals superiority." Mika Heitanen, *Paul's Argument in Galatians: A Pragmatic-Dialectical Analysis*, ed. Michael Labahn (London: T&T Clark, 2007), 123.

where he would have been expected to eat some *lechón asado*. Consequently, the Galatians would be foolish to even consider adopting Jewish distinctives—for that would be contrary to the message they first believed, which made them recipients of the Spirit and members of the covenant community (3:1–5).

Contrary to what the Jewish troublemakers were arguing, faith is all Abraham exhibited to become a recipient of the covenant (Gal. 3:6–9). If they choose to go beyond Paul's gospel and the faith of Abraham, being persuaded to adopt Jewish boundary markers, the Galatians would be obligated to keep the entire law, which leads only to the exile of death (3:10–12). It would be foolish to adopt the very markers of Jewish ethnicity that lead to the eternal penalty for which the Messiah has already died to make gentiles beneficiaries of the Abrahamic promises (3:13–4:7).

All in all, Paul tailors his argument to persuade the Galatians to resist the pressure to adopt ethnic boundary markers so as to be considered members of the covenant community. Paul would expect the same from ethnic minority Christians in American evangelicalism.

The Analogous Problem for Ethnic Minority Groups

The pressure to adopt the distinctives of the powerful group is analogous to what ethnic minorities experience in American evangelicalism, where outsiders are expected to adopt the values of the majority to be considered one of the faithful. Although we are not being asked to take a knife to our flesh, the expectations are no less painful. I will now identify three boundary markers commonly associated with American evangelicalism. While I will address the way they have impacted Latino/a Christians, my assumption is that these boundary markers have also negatively impacted other ethnic minority groups.

The first boundary marker is allegiance to the Republican party.[17] Since the election of Ronald Reagan, Republican politicians have consistently campaigned on traditional marriage, pro-life policies, and conservative Supreme Court nominees. In return, many evangelical leaders have promoted the Republican party as the only political choice for evangelicals, even if it means ignoring moral inconsistencies in candidates. In the 2020 election, several prominent evangelicals argued that, for Christians, the only legitimate choice for president was Republican incumbent Donald Trump, because of his staunch support for the pro-life agenda and traditional marriage. While many evangelicals rightly support these ethical positions, Trump's vitriolic rhetoric

---

17. I have narrowed my critique on the Republican party because this is the dominant political group in American evangelicalism. My critique should not be taken as an endorsement of the Democratic party.

against Latinos, calling them rapists and thugs, and his anti-immigrant policies, such as his attempt to revoke DACA (Deferred Action for Childhood Arrivals) benefits, made many Latinos/as petrified of voting for a man who threatened and devalued their very existence. So, while Trump may promote the values of many evangelicals, he shows little concern for the lives of Latino/a people, the majority of whom are not bad *hombres* but people who have come to America to provide a better life for their families. We should not be surprised, then, that many Latino/a Christians are not beholden to a party that makes them feel like strangers in their own country.

The second boundary marker is indifference to societal injustice. American evangelicalism broadly (though, of course, not all evangelicals) has a history of neglecting injustices, exhorting its adherents to "just preach the gospel." This was the case during the days of slavery, segregation, civil rights, and recent strife over racial equality. With specific regard to Latinos/as, we saw this in the American Southwest, where people like Catholic activist Cesar Chávez fought for the fair treatment of migrant farm workers, despite churchgoers, some of whom were landowners, who ignored the cries of the exploited. James speaks to this hypocrisy: "Behold, the wages of the laborers who mowed your fields, which you kept back by fraud, are crying out against you, and the cries of the harvesters have reached the ears of the Lord of hosts" (5:4). For many Latino/a people, to heed the call to "just preach the gospel," despite the cries of their *hermanos y hermanas*, is to ignore the very *buenas nuevas* that Jesus preached:

> The Spirit of the Lord is upon me,
>   because he has anointed me
>   to proclaim good news to the poor.
> He has sent me to proclaim liberty to the captive
>   and recovering of sight to the blind,
>   to set free the oppressed,
> to proclaim the year of the Lord's favor. (Luke 4:18–19; cf. Isa. 61:1–2)

The third boundary marker is Christian nationalism. That America's founding fathers established a country based on biblical principles is a myth that a sizable percentage of evangelicals has adopted as orthodoxy.[18] Even if it were true (and it is not), the way Latino/a people have been treated makes it difficult for them to believe that America is a Christian nation. The ideology of manifest destiny, for instance, led Americans to goad Mexicans into a war

---

18. Drew Straight, "Let's Talk about 'Christian Nationalism,'" *Christianity Today*, August 26, 2020, https://www.christianitytoday.com/scot-mcknight/2020/august/lets-talk-about-christian-nationalism.html.

whose main purpose was to allow America to swallow up California, New Mexico, Nevada, and portions of Colorado, Arizona, Utah, and even Oklahoma.[19] The God of the Bible should not be hijacked to sanction a nation to kill native Americans and Mexicans, claim their lands, and impose their version of Christianity on "inferior peoples."[20] Nor should he be used to sanction the segregation of "unclean" Latino/a students from Anglo students in southwestern states, practices that the courts overturned in the 1940s and 1950s, in cases such as Méndez versus Westminster School District in California and similar ones in Texas and Arizona. Nor should he be used to sanction any of the other government injustices against Latino/a people.[21] So, while stories of America's Christian roots are more myth than fact, the way Latinos/as have been treated is what makes Christian nationalism an unadoptable boundary marker for people with surnames like Pérez, González, and Castillo.

Expecting Latinos/as, and by extension other minority groups, to adopt the boundary markers of the majority group in American evangelicalism would be nothing short of expecting them to excise the foreskin of their souls. The blessings of Abraham, however, are far better than the curse that weighs down those who adopt such "works of the law." But since the pressure is unrelenting, just as it was in Galatia, Paul provides a solution for resisting the burden to conform to the values of the dominant group.

The Solution to the Burden of Submitting to "Works of the Law" (Gal. 5:1–6:18)

Paul's solution to the problem the Galatians—and many ethnic minorities—face is fairly straightforward: stand firm in the freedom of the gospel (Gal. 5:1). Christ has already delivered believers from the bondage of upholding the Jewish distinctives of the law. As a result, Christians from ethnic minority groups are to stand firm in the gospel that frees them from the burden of adopting any group's boundary markers of inclusion.

19. Robert Chao Romero, *Brown Church: Five Centuries of Latina/o Social Justice, Theology, and Identity* (Downers Grove, IL: IVP Academic, 2020), 99–119.

20. Romero cites the following text, which provides insight into the mentality of those who believed that claiming the territories of Mexico was their righteous duty: "The old Saxon blood must stride the continent, must command all its northern shores, must here press the grape and the olive, here eat the orange and the fig, and in their own unaided might, erect the alter of civil and religious freedom on the plains of the Californias." Romero (*Brown Church*, 101), quoted in Robert H. Heizer and Alan J. Almquist, *The Other Californians: Prejudice and Discrimination under Spain, Mexico, and the United States to 1920* (Berkeley: University of California Press, 1971), 140; and in Thomas J. Farnham, *Travels in the Californias, and Scenes in the Pacific Ocean* (New York: Saxton & Miles, 1844), 413.

21. Examples abound in Romero's *Brown Church*. See especially pp. 99–141.

Paul reminds the Galatians that adopting the boundary marker of circumcision in order to be members of the covenant ("righteous") means they are obligated to keep the entire law (Gal. 5:2–4). This in turn results in being separated from the one who makes them true heirs of Abraham—Messiah Jesus (5:4; cf. 3:15–29). For those in Christ, circumcision has no bearing on their covenant status (5:6). Paul practices what he preaches, being willing to suffer persecution for no longer enforcing the legal requirement of circumcision (5:11). Since the gospel has freed believers from the obligation to maintain the markers of the old covenant, there is no reason to adopt any group's ethnic distinctives.

At the heart of why Jewish Christians were enforcing the ethnic distinctive of circumcision on the Galatians was "to make a good showing in the flesh" (Gal. 6:12). That is to say, they were enforcing circumcision on gentiles to make themselves "look good" before those they highly esteemed, non-Christian Jews. The goal was that their ethnic kin would be comfortable joining a movement that retained the distinctives of Judaism—mainly circumcision—and required gentiles to do the same.[22] Their concern, then, was not for those who followed the same Messiah but came from different ethnic backgrounds, but to appease their brothers and sisters according to the flesh.

When we consider how many evangelicals have melded their faith with Republican politics and traditional American positions, zealously expecting adherence from minority groups, it seems that many would rather appease politically conservative Americans than brothers and sisters who follow the same Messiah but come from different cultural and ethnic backgrounds. If Americans who follow an elephant—but have no concern for a Middle Eastern Messiah—feel as comfortable in evangelical churches as they do at political conventions or patriotic rallies, then many evangelicals have succeeded in "making a good showing in the flesh." I imagine Paul would say to such people, "Why stop with the foreskin? Why not go all the way with the knife?" (cf. Gal. 5:12).

The apostle Paul would urge believers of all backgrounds to stand firm in the gospel that liberates people from bondage to the values of the dominant group (Gal. 5:1). This gospel is sourced in the crucified Messiah, who makes all believers participants in a new creation where circumcision—or any other ethnic identity marker—has no bearing on our covenant status (6:15). That is why Paul will boast in the only incision that matters: the crucified flesh of the Messiah (6:14). While minority groups may be outsiders to many segments of American evangelicalism, their adherence to the gospel of Messiah Jesus is what shows that they are indeed genuine heirs of the covenant promises to Abraham and his offspring.

22. DeSilva, *Galatians*, 505.

Conclusion

The influence of Sanders and the New Perspective enables us to envision how Galatians addresses the problem of imposing Jewish boundary markers on gentiles. The gospel Paul received, the very one the Galatians believed, frees them from such demands—all that is required for covenant membership is faith in the Messiah. Read in this light, Paul's Letter to the Galatians becomes the scriptural basis from which ethnic minorities can resist the imposition of boundary markers associated with American evangelicalism—those distinctives that define who is "in" and who is "out"—like support for the Republican party, indifference to societal injustice, and Christian nationalism.

Though refusal to "accept the knife" means ethnic minorities are outsiders to the promises of American evangelicalism, we should remember that being free sons and daughters of Abraham has a far greater reward: the promise of a cosmic inheritance, a new creation, where we will be accepted solely based on our faithfulness to the Messiah (Gal. 3–4; cf. Rom. 4; 8). Those who will inherit the coming world are Messiah followers from different nations and backgrounds who will not be compelled to conform to any one group's works of the law (Rev. 7:9; 15:3–4; 21:24). So, no matter how persistent the pressure, or how blind others may be to recognize what they are doing, ethnic minority groups should resist the pressure to conform to the majority group's boundary markers and hold fast to the gospel that makes them recipients of all that Abraham (who, at the time of receiving the covenant, was neither circumcised nor forbidden from eating *lechón*) received through faith. This is a far better inheritance than the temporary power and prosperity that American evangelicalism promises to its adherents.

11

Grace at Work

Reading Ephesians 2:11–22 with the Filipino Diaspora

GABRIEL J. CATANUS

In *A Good Provider Is One Who Leaves*,[1] author Jason DeParle seeks to understand the hidden realities of global poverty by taking up residence among the Philippine poor, embedding himself for eight months in the daily lives of Tita and Emet Comodas and their five children. Emet, Tita's husband, is an overseas foreign worker (OFW) on repeated two-year contracts in Saudi Arabia. Cleaning swimming pools overseas enables Emet to earn ten times more than he could by doing the same job in the Philippines, so he accepts this opportunity as an answered prayer. With his earnings, Emet is able to send money to Tita and the children, making their survival possible while he lives and works eight thousand kilometers away, coming home only occasionally.

DeParle's friendship with the Comodas family continues long after his short stay in their home, and in the succeeding decades he learns that Emet's earnings enable their children to attend school and eventually move abroad as OFWs like their father. One of the daughters, Rosalie, is especially fortunate, as she is able to graduate from nursing school and find work as a registered

---

1. Jason DeParle, *A Good Provider Is One Who Leaves: One Family and Migration in the 21st Century* (New York: Penguin, 2019).

nurse in Saudi Arabia. By God's grace and through her family's sacrifices, seven years later Rosalie finds a nursing job in the United States, where her children can grow up differently, alongside their parents in the suburbs of Houston, Texas.

To his surprise, DeParle's initial research on poverty develops into a weightier lesson on the complexities of global migration. As this essay will show, the problems faced by the Comodas family and millions like them must be understood in light of Philippine history, colonialism, poverty, and government policy. Out of necessity, "no country does more to promote migration than the Philippines."[2] The Filipino diaspora now exceeds ten million people spread across two hundred countries, mostly due to labor migration.[3]

Similarly, diasporic Filipino Christianity cannot be understood apart from these complexities. Given the colonial relationship between the two countries, the US remains the primary destination for Filipino migrants. There are presently 4.5 million people of Filipino ancestry living in the United States.[4] Rooted in "Asia's Christian nation," Filipino Americans are more likely to identify as Christian than US Latinos[5] or all other Asian Americans.[6] DeParle also observes that wherever Filipinos go, they bring with them an active, tested faith.[7] This faith has revitalized existing churches and led to the planting of countless Filipino American congregations.

In recent years, however, the percentage of Filipino Americans who identify as Christian has decreased significantly, from 89 percent in 2012[8] to 74 percent in 2023,[9] raising important questions for pastors and parents alike concerning the future of churches throughout the Filipino diaspora. What are the biggest factors causing this disaffiliation from Christianity? If the decrease is primarily

2. "Global Migration: 'The World's Greatest Anti-Poverty Program,'" Institute for Policy Research, March 19, 2020, https://www.ipr.northwestern.edu/news/2020/deparle-greatest-anti-poverty-story.html.

3. Romulo V. Arugay, press release, Commission on Filipinos Overseas (website), accessed May 30, 2024, https://cfo.gov.ph/.

4. Caitlin Davis and Jeanne Batalova, "Filipino Immigrants in the United States," Migration Policy Institute, August 8, 2023, https://www.migrationpolicy.org/article/filipino-immigrants-united-states#pathways-naturalization.

5. "Among U.S. Latinos, Catholicism Continues to Decline but Is Still the Largest Faith," Pew Research Center, April 13, 2023, https://www.pewresearch.org/religion/2023/04/13/among-u-s-latinos-catholicism-continues-to-decline-but-is-still-the-largest-faith/.

6. "Christianity among Asian Americans," Pew Research Center, October 11, 2023, https://www.pewresearch.org/religion/2023/10/11/christianity-among-asian-americans/.

7. Jason DeParle, "The Religious Resilience of Global Migrants," *Faith and Leadership*, January 21, 2020, https://faithandleadership.com/jason-deparle-religious-resilience-global-migrants.

8. "Asian Americans: A Mosaic of Faiths," Pew Research Center, July 19, 2012, https://www.pewresearch.org/religion/2012/07/19/asian-americans-a-mosaic-of-faiths-overview/.

9. "Christianity among Asian Americans."

among younger people or the second generation as some reports suggest,[10] what might this mean for the churches their parents once planted as new arrivals? How can Filipino American families and churches more effectively reach newcomers and disciple the next generation in light of diasporic realities?

Although very little research on these contexts and questions has been published, my pastoral work and scholarship have focused on them for more than two decades. A few years ago, I supported a research team exploring these questions across diverse ethnic backgrounds, and I was pained to see that intergenerational conflict remains a leading cause of unhealth and division for immigrant churches.[11] As the director of the only Filipino American–focused entity at any theological or religious institution, I currently spend countless hours supporting seminarians and young ministry leaders who either have left their parents' Filipino immigrant churches or are struggling to remain in them.

In this chapter, I respond pastorally and theologically from within the Filipino American church. I show how Ephesians 2:11–22 helps us to understand the intergenerational conflicts that characterize many Filipino immigrant churches. Along the way, I also draw hope from these verses for Filipino churches in the US and throughout the diaspora.[12]

Worlds Apart

Before proceeding, we must acknowledge that contemporary applications of texts like Ephesians 2:11–22 are to be made with caution. Paul's focus in this and other letters is on relations between Christians from Jewish and gentile backgrounds in light of God's unfolding plan through Israel (1:11–14; 2:12). Paul also articulates God's plan in a specific way, for a developing community with whom he is personally connected (Acts 20:17–21). Keeping this in mind enables us to move wisely from the world of the text to our own world, prioritizing spiritual health and guarding against abuses.

Perhaps counterintuitively, the fact that God's love is demonstrated within human history and ethnic particularity is good news for Filipinos. Our churches

---

10. Agnes Constante, "Filipino American Culture and Catholicism Are Interconnected," *LA Times*, October 20, 2022, https://www.latimes.com/lifestyle/story/2022-10-20/filipino-american-mental-health-catholicism-story.

11. In 2021, I served as associate director of the Thriving Immigrant Congregations Initiative (TICI), a study funded by the Lilly Foundation and led by the Paul G. Hiebert Center for World Christianity and Global Theology at Trinity Evangelical Divinity School, which served twenty-four intergenerational immigrant churches from Asian, African, and Hispanic communities.

12. Given my research and ministry context, much of this discussion focuses on Filipino Protestants in the US. However, similar dynamics exist in places like Canada and Australia, though more research is needed on diasporic churches in other settings.

can celebrate God's faithfulness in Jesus Christ to biblical, diasporized Israel and thus appreciate even more the Holy Spirit's embrace of gentiles *as gentiles* into the body of Christ. Because the gospel brings believers from Jewish and gentile backgrounds (Eph. 2:14), Scripture can be trusted to bear good news for diasporic Filipino churches struggling with intergenerational conflict.

Saved by Grace

The Letter to the Ephesians holds a special place among Filipino evangelicals due in part to Paul's emphatic statements about God's saving grace in Ephesians 2:1–10. Reacting against the popular Catholicism practiced around them by more than 80 percent of the country[13]—with its perceived clericalism, ritual, and "works righteousness"—many evangelicals cite Ephesians 2:8–9 as a proof text against Catholic teachings about salvation. Of course, these perceptions are often simplistic and unfair, and they point to the ongoing, global influence of the American fundamentalist-modernist controversy from the 1920s. When the US colonized the Philippines, the term "Christian" meant "Protestant," in opposition to Catholicism.[14]

Ironically, many evangelicals also de-emphasize or omit Ephesians 2:10 ("For we are God's handiwork, created in Christ Jesus to do good works"), even while criticizing Catholics for being unbiblical.[15] Rightly understood, Paul's teaching in 2:11–22 builds on his celebration of God's grace in verses 1–10, as Paul shows us the kind of "good works" (*ergois agathois*) that characterize the reconciled body of believers. Three themes from 2:11–22 are especially relevant to diasporic Filipino churches struggling through intergenerational conflict: shared memory, new community, and powerful testimony. God's grace works in each of these areas, and I elaborate on their significance here.

Shared Memory (Eph. 2:11–12)

The command to remember (*mnēmoneuete*) is given at the start of Ephesians 2:11, in response to Paul's lesson on grace in the previous section. Even though the command is given just once in Greek, the NIV uses the word twice so that the force of the command is not lost in the midst of Paul's

13. Xave Gregorio, "Philippines Still Overwhelmingly Catholic," *PhilStar Global*, February 22, 2023, https://www.philstar.com/headlines/2023/02/22/2246855/philippines-still-overwhelmingly-catholic.

14. Susan K. Harris, *God's Arbiters: Americans and the Philippines 1898-1902*, vol. 6 (Oxford: Oxford University Press, 2011), 15.

15. All Scripture quotations are from the NIV translation.

many clauses. And yet, when considering the traumatic poverty, hardship, and family separation that many migrants like Emet and his family have suffered, a certain level of amnesia is understandable, even necessary for the sake of survival. OFW families cannot be blamed for wanting to forget many of their experiences. Still, the call to remember remains.

Notably, Paul is not calling the gentile believers in Ephesus to remember that they were once materially poor and have now become middle or upper class. This is a common and fraught refrain among grateful immigrants, similar to the message preached by boxer-turned-politician Manny Pacquiao: "I used to sleep on the streets, starving, hungry. I could not have imagined that the Lord has raised and put me in this position. . . . God can raise nothing into something. Jesus is the name of the Lord."[16] Of course, God is just and concerned for the poor, and every provision comes from God by grace. The twenty-five million Philippine poor who will likely never be rich or famous are eternally loved, blessed, chosen, and redeemed (Eph. 1:3–10) by faith in Jesus Christ. They are already "something," and survival should not require what families like the Comodas have endured.

Paul, however, has more in mind than what Pacquiao preaches. In Acts 19, the dramatic work of the Holy Spirit actually threatens Ephesus's spiritual and economic idols. In context, Paul is calling the gentile Christians to remember that they were once far from God, dead in transgressions and sins (Eph. 2:1, 5) regardless of their financial or social status. As John Stott comments on 2:12 (quoting William Hendriksen), before the gentiles knew Jesus Christ, they were "Christless, stateless, friendless, hopeless, and Godless."[17] They had no chance of experiencing the life-giving power of God without divine intervention.

Many North American–born Filipinos do not have their own memory or firsthand experience of being raised from "nothing into something" as Pacquiao describes. This is especially true for those whose parents migrated as professionals. The daily lives of Tita and Emet Comodas are dramatically different from those of their daughter and grandchildren in Texas. What the later generations experience and remember of God's grace might be less tied to material or geographic change and more tied to relational and social change. More will be said about this in the next section.

What is clear is that these different generation of Filipino Americans lack a shared memory or story. As George Erasmus famously said, "Where common

16. Leocciano Callao, "How Christianity Fueled Manny Pacquiao's Rise from Poverty to Presidential Candidate," *Religion Unplugged*, September 30, 2021, https://religionunplugged.com/news/2021/9/23/0asa38kk7iydi6cvq56o4shjtlfuxz.

17. John Stott, *The Message of Ephesians* (Downers Grove, IL: InterVarsity, 1979), 96.

memory is lacking, where people do not share in the same past, there can be no real community. Where community is to be formed, common memory must be created."[18] It is no wonder, then, that the book of Deuteronomy, more frequently than any other book in the Bible, repeatedly calls Israel to remember God's past faithfulness.

Deuteronomy 8:18 holds together the socioeconomic and spiritual dimensions of God's gracious intervention in an instructive sequence: "But remember the LORD your God, for it is he who gives you the ability to produce wealth, and so confirms his covenant, which he swore to your ancestors, as it is today." The God who accompanies migrant laborers and provides for them is the same God who keeps promises to ancestors and includes gentiles in Christ. Filipino American churches must bear witness to God's gracious intervention and new life in Christ ("But now . . . ," Eph. 2:13) in ways that all generations can remember and celebrate as their own.

New Community (Eph. 2:13–18)

As alluded to above, for first-generation Filipino Americans and Filipino Canadians, immigrant churches served as community centers where cultural and spiritual needs could be simultaneously met. Filipinos migrated to both countries centuries ago, but the largest waves arrived after pro-immigration legislation—to the US after 1965 and to Canada after 1976.[19] In these churches, the new arrivals were welcomed and supported as they adjusted to life in new, distant lands. Immigrants who were discriminated against in other contexts could lead with dignity and freedom in these spaces, connecting with God and each other in safety, in their own languages and around tables of their own food. Immigrant churches like those my parents planted were vital communities of belonging.[20]

The children of these pioneers have increasingly expressed different needs, however. Growing up away from their parents' home country has left many longing for connections to Filipino culture and ancestry. Especially for those

18. Quoted in Mark Charles, "We Don't Talk about That," *Comment Magazine*, December 1, 2015, https://comment.org/we-dont-talk-about-that/.

19. Jie Zong and Jeanne Batalova, "Filipino Immigrants in the United States," Migration Policy Institute, March 14, 2018, https://www.migrationpolicy.org/article/filipino-immigrants-united-states-2016; Gerald E. Dirks, "Immigration Policy in Canada," *The Canadian Encyclopedia*, February 7, 2006, https://www.thecanadianencyclopedia.ca/en/article/immigration-policy.

20. From 1978 to 2009, my parents planted Filipino immigrant churches throughout North America, including the First Filipino Baptist Church of Toronto (1978) and the Northwest Filipino Baptist Church (1987) near Chicago. The former was the first Filipino Baptist church in Canada and the latter was the largest Filipino American evangelical church in the US Midwest. Both congregations have since planted several additional churches serving similar communities.

educated in Western universities, Christianity's connection to colonialism has raised pressing questions about the merits of Christian belief altogether. Because of this, InterVarsity Christian Fellowship has developed campus ministries across the US since 1994 that intentionally integrate Christian faith and Filipino American identity.[21]

In recent years, racial unrest tied to the Black Lives Matter movement, widespread support for Donald Trump and his policies among evangelicals, and anti-Asian violence during the COVID-19 pandemic all reinvigorated this search for ethnic identity, as many children of the diaspora felt that they could not find belonging in the US. As they sought to express Christian faith by responding to these events, many in the second generation were in turn alienated (*apēllotriōmenoi*, Eph. 2:12) from their churches because they spoke out on social media or participated in racial-justice demonstrations. They were called "liberals," "woke," and "cultural Marxists" by their more conservative parents and elders—those in the community who had received God's promises first. The second generation could not reconcile their inherited faith and practices with support for far-right politicians and policies. As a result, many left their home churches, never to return.

On the other hand, first-generation parents and leaders were unable to understand the second generation's pain and anger. Pastors who planted these churches and once baptized their young people suddenly felt threatened by the intensity of the second generation's responses. Most of the first generation who arrived in their twenties and thirties were focused on surviving in and adjusting to a new culture. They experienced racism and oppression directly, but they lacked the time and freedom to respond to them as young people do today. A hostility (*echthran*, Eph. 2:14, 16) has grown between the first and second generations that has yet to be resolved.

In a culture that highly values family and respect for elders,[22] often to a fault, a close reading of Ephesians 2:11–22 speaks prophetically to intergenerational conflict. In verse 11, Paul makes a critical, if not sarcastic, parenthetical statement to the gentiles about the emptiness of the pejorative label ("uncircumcised") put on them by believers from Jewish backgrounds (who proudly labeled themselves "the circumcision"). In light of verse 9, Paul wants to make clear for the gentiles that the Jewish believers are also saved by grace. Grace makes null any notion of "first in time, first in right."

21. "A Brief History of Kapwa," Kapwa IVCF, UC Berkeley, accessed June 8, 2024, https://www.ocf.berkeley.edu/~kapwa/history.html.

22. Myrna Tordillo, "What Every Vocation Director Should Know about Filipino Families," *Horizon* (Fall 2015), https://www.usccb.org/issues-and-action/cultural-diversity/asian-pacific-islander/resources/upload/What-every-Vocation-Director-should-know-about-Filipino-families-MT.pdf.

Building on this, Paul points out that both groups in the Ephesian Christian community are guilty of being "hostile" toward each other. Many commentators believe that the "dividing wall of hostility" (Eph. 2:14) refers to the partition that stood between the Jewish and gentile areas of the temple. Josephus describes the wall as strong and beautiful, standing three cubits high (about four and a half feet tall), with a clear warning to gentiles that they are not to enter the Jewish area, upon punishment of death.[23]

To Paul's point, Thomas Slater describes the mutual hostility produced by the wall and all that goes with it: "The Jews saw themselves as a chosen, pure race and the only civilized people because Yahweh gave them alone the Torah. In contrast, they saw their neighbors as impure pagans. However, those 'impure' neighbors were often more prominent and more powerful in society. Such social realities wrought unrequited Jewish aspirations on the one hand and gentile resentment and bigotry toward Jews on the other."[24] The dividing wall works both ways, and the hostility emanating from it is shared. This is demonstrated by the NIV translation "*their* hostility" (Eph. 2:16), meaning that hostility belonged to both groups. Because of this, the major groups in conflict—Jews *and* gentiles, first *and* second generation, and so on—need peace embodied (2:14) and preached (2:17) for them. Among Filipino immigrants, hostility between generations is often rooted in intergenerational trauma, passed on to children and surfacing in times of high stress. In other words, their intergenerational church conflicts are not merely ecclesial; they are also familial.

In response, Ephesians 2:14 presents good news. Jesus himself is "our peace," and his peace is present in a reconciled body through the cross, where hostility also died (2:16). Most striking here is that the single body replacing the two groups is "one new humanity" (*hena kainon anthrōpon*, 2:15). Andrew Lincoln points out that the new humanity formed by the Spirit is a totally new community, incomparable with anything beforehand and different from what any predominantly Jewish or gentile Christian community would be.[25] Slater comments, "The result is 'one new person,' a new ethnicity called Christians."[26]

This is good and challenging news for diasporic churches facing intergenerational conflict. By the Holy Spirit, the church is reconciled in Jesus Christ,

---

23. Robert G. Bratcher and Eugene Albert Nida, *A Handbook on Paul's Letter to the Ephesians*, UBSHS (New York: United Bible Societies, 1993), 55.

24. Thomas B. Slater, *Ephesians*, ed. R. Alan Culpepper, SHBC (Macon, GA: Smyth & Helwys, 2012), 71.

25. Andrew T. Lincoln, *Ephesians*, WBC 42 (Dallas: Word, 1990), 135.

26. Slater, *Ephesians*, 71.

and he has absorbed into his own body the hostilities of each group, in order to raise them up together into a new community beyond what either group envisions the church to be. The grace that saves both Jews and gentiles also saves first-generation immigrants and their descendants. This grace creates a new kind of community that is not owned or controlled by either group. The new community is not a first-generation church with second-generation members; nor is it a second-generation church with first-generation members. It is something different altogether, always new and creative.

Moving beyond the above binaries, all groups and generations are invited into Christ's body to receive God's grace and to give it to others, to be empowered and to empower others, to relinquish control and to honor others. This is even more challenging for people from traditional cultures: by grace, parents of any age become children of the Father (Eph. 2:18) and at the same time spiritual siblings with their believing children. This is neither easy nor simple, but upon this countercultural theological foundation real peace is possible.

Powerful Testimony (Eph. 2:19–22)

Through a series of images, Ephesians 2:19–22 illustrates how the grace of God changes the community of believers from a set of groups into a new kind of community. First, the reconciled church is transformed from (1) a collection of foreigners and strangers (*zenoi kai paroikoi*, 2:19) with no status to (2) fellow citizens (*sympolitai*, 2:19) who have rights within a state or nation. Filipino Americans and their families understand both sides of this process well. As many as 370,000 or 8.2 percent of US Filipinos remain undocumented, without legal status.[27] Specifically, the gentile Christians in these verses are by grace included among God's people, with citizenship in the kingdom and the full benefits therein.

Receiving "every spiritual blessing" (Eph. 1:3) that comes with citizenship and inclusion in Christ (1:13) is a cause for celebration, in the same way that Filipino immigrants in the US, Canada, Australia, and Europe hold parties to celebrate naturalization. For vulnerable immigrants, gaining the rights and responsibilities of citizenship under a more stable government is empowering, and it calls forth agency in new ways. These new citizens can travel with a passport, receive government benefits, vote, and plan for the future. They also gain full participation in the political process.

Of course, citizenship in God's kingdom is also upside down when compared with worldly citizenship. Understood in light of the new humanity,

27. Davis and Batalova, "Filipino Immigrants in the United States."

belonging to God as Ephesians 2:19–22 depicts is empowering because of the intimacy it creates. As Willie Jennings writes, the work of the Holy Spirit at Pentecost is a "revolution of the intimate."[28] Jewish and gentile believers alike are members of God's household/family (*oikeioi*, 2:19). They belong to God and to each other. Together with the apostles and prophets and Jesus himself, the reconciled church is being "joined together" (2:21) and "built together" (2:22) into a temple (*naon*, 2:21) where the Spirit dwells through their communion.

For Filipinos dealing with intergenerational conflict, this good news should be readily received. The first generation's desire for family closeness is affirmed, even as the spiritual family is expanded to include non-Filipinos and others who belong to God. They are not second-class citizens in the shadow of the US empire but have full access to God as part of God's family (Eph. 2:18).

For the second generation and those after them who are living in diaspora, this vision of community overlaps significantly with the precolonial Filipino concept of *kapwa*, which means "identity with others" or "mutual belonging." According to Virgilio Enriquez, the founder of the movement to recover indigenous Filipino psychology (*Sikolohiyang Pilipino*), "*Kapwa* is a recognition of shared identity, an inner self shared with others."[29] This recognition is what makes a Filipino a Filipino.[30]

Enriquez's influence on second-generation Filipino Americans cannot be overstated because he has given scholars and diasporic Filipinos a window into an ethnic identity that many argue precedes and transcends Christianity. While the two concepts—the new humanity in Christ and *kapwa*—are not quite the same, to practice or live out the principle of *kapwa* among Christians is to do as Ephesians 2:11–22 prescribes: to recognize the church as a community marked by Jesus's reconciling power. The Ephesian Christian community would fail to be the church if it excluded either the Jews or the gentiles. For either generation of diasporic Filipino Christians to abandon or alienate the other has proven to be a loss of *kapwa*, painful for families and entire churches. Neither generation can simply move on to a new church without losing a part of themselves.

In response, the image of the reconciled body as a holy temple is rich with meaning. As the US church continues to struggle through divisions related to

---

28. Willie J. Jennings, *Acts: A Theological Commentary on the Bible* (Louisville: Westminster John Knox, 2017), 18.

29. Virgilio Enriquez, *From Colonial to Liberation Psychology: The Philippine Experience* (Manila, Philippines: De La Salle University Press, 2004), 5.

30. E. J. R. David, *Brown Skin, White Minds: Filipino-/American Postcolonial Psychology* (Charlotte, NC: Information Age, 2013), 113.

politics, race, sexuality, and immigration status, Paul's vision is revolution-ary. While it goes beyond the scope of this chapter to adequately develop a biblical theology of the temple, Psalm 84 reminds us that God's dwelling place is lovely, a place where deep human longings are satisfied and a source of blessing for all who seek God there. By the Holy Spirit, God dwells with us in these ways as we receive grace, reconcile, and make peace.

Jesus spoke of his own body as a temple, which he raised up as promised (John 2:19). After all, in his arrival "the Word became flesh and made his dwell-ing among us. We have seen his glory, the glory of the one and only Son, who came from the Father, full of grace and truth" (1:14). For Paul, using temple imagery in Ephesians 2:21–22 communicates a similar, revelatory idea: just as Jesus reveals the Father, the reconciled body of believers reveals Jesus Christ. In both cases, God gives grace to diasporic people whose families and identities are not tied to a single place. Paul also spoke of individual believers' bodies as temples of the Holy Spirit (1 Cor. 6:19) in a text that ties the Christian's body to the body of Christ. For the church in our day, reading these texts in canonical order loads Ephesians 2:21–22 with even more significance.

Conclusion

In an era of polarization, during which the US church has fared no better than the rest of its surrounding society, Paul invites us to bear witness to God's grace and power by participating in a kind of healing and peace that are beyond human ability. This is the empowerment that Paul later prays for in Ephesians 3:16–19, and our churches would be helped by each generation praying for others in this way:

> I pray that out of his glorious riches he may strengthen you with power through his Spirit in your inner being, so that Christ may dwell in your hearts through faith. And I pray that you, being rooted and established in love, may have power, together with all the Lord's holy people, to grasp how wide and long and high and deep is the love of Christ, and to know this love that surpasses knowledge—that you may be filled to the measure of all the fullness of God.

God has grace for the church that works more powerfully than we can imag-ine, and the same power that strengthened the Ephesian Christians works within us. "To him be glory in the church and in Christ Jesus throughout all generations, for ever and ever! Amen" (3:21).

12

Philippians and a Spirituality of Joy

A Colombian Reading

DAVINSON KEVIN BOHORQUEZ

In recent decades there has been a keen interest in *lament* in Christian academic and ecclesiastical circles. Biblical scholars as well as theologians have commented on how lament, an ancient biblical expression of faith articulated first in the Old Testament, is essential for a believer's spiritual health in times of excruciating suffering and long-lasting trauma.[1] The rediscovery of lament as an essential aspect of Christian spirituality, in my opinion, is an indispensable gift that the Spirit has brought to his wounded people.

As I reflect on the emphasis placed on lament in Christian spirituality, I cannot help but wonder how the Letter to the Philippians, an epistle highly marked by references to suffering for the sake of Christ, can speak into the development of this spiritual practice. And personally, how my own cultural and personal rereading of this letter as a *Colombian* can give a particular shape to what Paul says about enduring affliction faithfully.

---

1. For a recent volume on this topic that captures the intersection of theological, biblical, and psychological reflection, see Diane Leclerc and Brent Peterson, *The Back Side of the Cross: An Atonement Theology for the Abused and Abandoned* (Eugene, OR: Wipf & Stock, 2022).

In this chapter I will focus on what I see as the essential resource that this short letter "to the Philippians" has for developing a spirituality in response to suffering—namely, joy. First, via a discourse analysis of the letter, I will demonstrate the thematic crux that this concept of "joy" (*chara*, *chairō*) has in the epistle, especially highlighting its relation to suffering. Second, I will attempt to summarize Paul's spirituality of joy as found in Philippians. Then I will conclude by outlining some ways in which the Colombian experience of suffering and faith, that I perceive and have experienced, can be tethered to Paul's spirituality of joy.

Is It Really about Joy?

The Letter to the Philippians is considered, even by the most skeptical of readers, to be among Paul's "authentic" letters. Throughout the history of interpretation, there have been several—at times conflicting—views on what its occasion was and what Paul intended to accomplish with it. It is reasonable to conclude that the purpose of the letter is simply pastoral in nature; as Gordon Fee puts it, "He is altogether concerned for his friends in Philippi and their ongoing relationship to Christ."[2]

When it comes to specifically identifying the theological core of the letter, there is greater debate. A traditional way of naming the theological core of a biblical document has been by identifying the author's use of specific and recurring language, although this can be difficult with Paul's letters since they are extremely intricate. When one approaches his Letter to the Philippians, one encounters this same difficulty, since there are several candidates that could be seen as Paul's thematic vocabulary.[3] And yet, because of its short length, there is still benefit from employing this method to see whether Paul is marking his discourse with a predominant theme by recurrent vocabulary.

In his masterful analysis of Philippians, Fee concludes, "The singular and most frequent word group in the letter is 'joy,' which comes as often by way of imperative—and this is full of theological import—as of experience."[4] I will build on this insight from Fee by outlining exactly where and how this language of "joy" appears in the letter and its relationship to references to suffering. The implementation of *discourse analysis* will aid us in this endeavor.[5]

---

2. Gordon Fee, *Paul's Letter to the Philippians*, NICNT (Grand Rapids: Eerdmans, 1995), 14.

3. For a list of Paul's vocabulary and a discussion on the significance of it in Philippians, see Fee, *Philippians*, 18–21.

4. Fee, *Philippians*, 20–21.

5. Discourse analysis refers to the interpretive strategy that focuses on examining a passage's linguistic characteristics in order to better understand its structure, meaning, and function in its overall literary context—the examination of language above the level of the sentence. As

In the Letter to the Philippians, the theme of joy is unmistakably pronounced. The noun form *chara* appears in five instances (1:4, 25; 2:2, 29; 4:1), the verbal form *chairō* nine times (1:18 [×2]; 2:17–18, 28; 3:1; 4:4 [×2], 10), and the compound form *synchairō* twice (2:17–18).[6] Apart from its numerical presence, a brief glance shows that these terms are well spread throughout the letter and at crucial junctures in Paul's discourse.

The first occurrence of this concept appears at the outset of the letter, where Paul outlines his pastoral heart for the church in Philippi. The gist of his opening (Phil. 1:3–11) is that Paul continues to be an apostolic presence for the church in Philippi even during detainment (*desmois mou*, 1:7).[7] The primary apostolic action he exalts is his *constant* prayerfulness (1:3, 9). The main clause of this section is 1:3a: "I thank my God . . ."[8] (*Eucharistō tō theō mou*), which in turn is immediately modified by a series of dependent clauses, one of them being 1:4b, "I always pray with joy" (*meta charas tēn deēsin poioumenos*). Syntactically, our first encounter with "joy" is not the most prominent element in Paul's discourse, and yet it is significant, as it sets the tone for its recurring appearance throughout the letter.

First, notice that *chara*/joy is the only qualifier of his constant apostolic thanksgiving and intercession that highlights emotion. We hear about when he prays (Phil. 1:3b) and how often (1:4a), but it is only with his use of the prepositional phrase "with joy" (*meta charas*) that Paul invites his hearers to see into his emotional posture. As Stephen Voorwinde notes, "Paul's joy is not a fleeting feeling, but a settled or at least recurring emotion. Whenever he

---

J. P. Louw notes, "Discourse Analysis is . . . a demonstration, a displaying, a showing, first of all to oneself, how the text is being read, then giving account to others how the text is read and used to eventually come to an understanding of the text. In short, it is revealed reading; it charts the course of the reading process" ("Reading a Text as Discourse," in *Linguistics and New Testament Interpretation: Essays on Discourse Analysis*, ed. David Alan Black, Katharine Barnwell, and Stephen Levinsohn [Nashville: Broadman, 1992], 18). For more information on this exegetical approach, see the introduction to *Discourse Analysis of the New Testament Writings*, ed. Todd Scacewater (Dallas: Fontes, 2020).

6. Johannes P. Louw and Eugene A. Nida list χαρά/χαίρω under the section titled "Attitudes and Emotions," and more specifically within the semantic domain of "Happy, Glad, Joyful." They suggest that this word group connotes ideas relating to "a state of joy and gladness" (*Greek-English Lexicon: Based on Semantic Domains* [New York: United Bible Societies, 1988], sections 25.116–34, p. 302). For the verbal form, BDAG suggests it to mean "to be in a state of happiness and well-being, rejoice, be glad," and that in some specific contexts its verbal form could be used simply as a greeting (pp. 1074–75).

7. David Creech insists that a less anachronistic translation of the word *desmos* is "under watch," since "the more common practice [in the empire during the first and second centuries] was temporary detainment until the decision about punishment was made." David A. Creech, "Criminal Christianities," WW 38, no. 4 (2018): 356.

8. The NIV is used for the English translation throughout.

prays for the Philippians, it is with joy."[9] Second, we are told that Paul's basis for his joyful thanksgiving is the Philippians' partnership in the gospel (1:5a).[10] And third, Paul introduces affliction immediately in the letter by referencing his detainment (lit., "chains"). Interestingly, then, our first image of Paul's emotional status during his time of detainment is joy.

The apparent relationship between joy and affliction is made clear and expounded on in the following passage, where Paul reflects on his current detainment (Phil. 1:12–30). Here the verbal form "rejoicing" (*chairō*) appears twice (1:18) and the noun "joy" (*chara*) once (1:25). Paul chooses his words carefully. He sets the tone of his report by stating his ultimate intent: "Now I want you to know, brothers and sisters, that what has happened to me has actually served to advance the gospel" (1:12). Paul then reflects on how his detainment has advanced the gospel, since unbelievers are becoming aware of his apostolic mission and believers are being encouraged by his tenacity (1:13–14). This brief report is followed by an unsettling detail—that is, among those preaching the gospel there are some who are doing it because of "selfish ambition" against Paul himself (1:17).

It is apparent from other letters that this sort of aggrievance from so-called believers hurt Paul deeply (e.g., 2 Cor. 11:26). It is not surprising, then, that after reporting on the ill intentions of these so-called preachers, Paul pauses to ask a rhetorical question, an invitation for both himself and his hearers to respond to this issue: "But what does it matter?" (Phil. 1:18a). His response is clear: although these envious fellows are aiming their preaching against Paul, "just as Paul does not look to himself, he does not look to these preachers. He only focuses on the result 'Christ is being proclaimed'" (see 1:18b).[11]

Of interest to our study is that this crucial juncture in Paul's discourse is followed by a reference to his emotional response: "And because of this I rejoice" (*kai en toutō chairō*, Phil. 1:18c). In this short clause, we are introduced to Paul's source for his emotional and spiritual standing. Paul's reframing of his adversaries' ill intentions in light of the exaltation of Christ results in him choosing joy.[12]

---

9. Stephen Voorwinde, "Paul's Joy in Philippians," *RTR* 76, no. 3 (December 2017): 146.

10. Some commentators read this partnership to be primarily financial; e.g., see Julien M. Ogereau, *Paul's Koinōnia with the Philippians: A Socio-Historical Investigation of a Pauline Economic Partnership* (Tübingen: Mohr Siebeck, 2014).

11. Eduardo de la Serna, "El kerigma de Pablo: Una mirada al ministerio paulino," *TX* 61, no. 172 (2011): 509–36, here 517. Translation mine.

12. Paul had at his disposal other vocabulary to describe his existential positioning; for instance, in 2 Corinthians we hear in similar contexts about Paul experiencing "comfort" (*paraklēsis*, 1:7), "encouragement" (*tharrheō*, 5:6, 8), or even "boasting" (*kauchaomai*, 11:16). In this instance, Paul chooses to rejoice.

As an experienced speaker, Paul anticipates the confusion of his hearers, adding a clause that clarifies that indeed he has chosen to rejoice and will remain in this posture in the midst of detainment and opposition: "Yes, and I will continue to rejoice" (*alla kai charēsomai*, Phil. 1:18d).[13] Usually, *alla* "follow[s] a negative clause to introduce a positive alternative,"[14] but it is unclear what exactly is the "negative" that the clause introduced by *alla* is standing against. F. Blass and A. Debrunner conclude that *alla* here is "used to introduce an additional point in an emphatic way."[15] And yet, I would also suggest that Paul could have in mind an implicit negative response that was a genuine possibility in his situation but that he chooses to reject.[16] In my reading, this negative possibility is shame, which Paul explicitly rejects by reassuring himself and his readers that his hope is set on a future deliverance (1:25).[17]

The noun *chara* reappears in Philippians 1:25. Paul suggests that the single reason he would choose to live instead of going on to be with Christ (1:23), a possibility that he is confident would be the case, is that he desires to continue to serve the Philippians in helping them in their "progress and joy in the faith" (*prokopēn kai charan tēs pisteōs*, 1:25c). And once again, Paul's choice of "joy" is not random; this is Paul's first reference to joy with respect to the Philippians. And why at this point? In verses 27–30, Paul acknowledges that they too are experiencing their own hardships for the sake of the gospel; hence, they need help reframing their afflictions within joy.

The next reference to joy appears in Philippians 2:2a in its noun form as the direct object of the second imperative of the letter, "make my joy complete" (*plērōsate mou tēn charan*). The first imperative appears a few verses back in 1:27, where Paul exhorts the Philippians to "conduct yourselves in a manner worthy of the gospel of Christ." The imperative to "make" Paul's "joy

13. I agree with the NIV's choice here to translate the future indicative *charēsomai* as durative rather than punctiliar as suggested by C. F. D. Moule, *An Idiom Book of New Testament Greek*, 2nd ed. (Cambridge: Cambridge University Press, 1960), 10. Although the future tense is mostly perfective in aspect, the future verb here is affected by the imperfective aspect of the previous verb, *chairō*.

14. Steven E. Runge, *Discourse Grammar of the Greek New Testament: A Practical Introduction for Teaching and Exegesis*, LBRS (Peabody, MA: Hendrickson, 2010), 56.

15. F. Blass and A. Debrunner, *A Greek Grammar of the New Testament and Other Early Christian Literature*, trans. and rev. R. W. Funk (Chicago: University of Chicago Press, 1961), §448, T 300.

16. Hence the addition of *kai* after *alla*, most likely to underscore the continuation of his joyful attitude; so comments Joseph H. Hellerman, *Philippians*, EGGNT (Nashville: B&H, 2015), 57.

17. Notice the contrast conceptually between rejoicing and being ashamed, but also their grammatical relationship since both are indicative verbs in the future tense in the same paragraph. This contrast is further unpacked with a lengthy discussion on Paul's internal turmoil regarding the possibility of deliverance from imprisonment or death.

complete" stands in direct relation to this first imperative, as the *hina* clause right after indicates: "by being like-minded" (*hina to auto phronēte*, 2:2). In other words, Paul describes his joy as being rooted in the fact that his life serves the exaltation of Christ by advancing the gospel, despite the sufferings or oppositions brought against him. And Paul has also added that his joy can expand to a fuller degree by his knowing that the Philippians themselves too are experiencing the fullness of fellowship with Christ *in their sufferings*. In this reading, the Christ hymn functions as the theological grounds for adopting this pattern of faithful living (2:6–11). The concept of joy is contextualized within an apostolic, and even a christological, framing of suffering.

Paul continues to draw out further implications from the previous imperatives in Philippians 2:12–18. Here he again references joy by way of its verbal form. Paul warns the Philippians concerning false appearances (2:12) and futile grumbling (2:14), saying instead that they should honor Paul's "labor" on their behalf (2:16) by "working" out their salvation (2:12). Interestingly for our study, Paul shifts gears at the end of this passage by referring back to the possibility of what he calls "being poured out like a drink offering" (2:17), which likely refers to punishment, if not martyrdom itself. And again, Paul reframes his potential suffering/death as an event that would be for the encouragement of their faith, and so it should be experienced within the context of joy: "I am glad and rejoice with all of you. So you too should be glad and rejoice with me" (*chairō kai synchairō pasin hymin; to de auto kai hymeis chairete kai synchairete moi*, 2:17b–18).

Paul culminates this lengthy segment (Phil. 1:12–2:18) by reiterating that his posture toward affliction and opposition is joy—joy rooted in his suffering for Christ's sake and in his hope for deliverance. Hence, in his iconic writing style, Paul captures the progression of his discourse with the compound form *synchairō*, which appears only here in the entire letter. Paul's choice of this vocabulary summarizes his intent throughout the discourse so far: apostolic joy should also be ecclesiastical joy since it is a christological gift.

The following section (Phil. 2:19–30) illustrates this partnership in joy from a different perspective—namely, caring for two individuals who are also living for Christ. In these verses, Paul discusses his plans for Timothy and Epaphroditus. Paul reveals the illness that Epaphroditus experienced and how he almost ended up dead (2:27). Such was his deteriorating condition that Paul was greatly grieved, so much so that he attributes Epaphroditus's healing to divine intervention (2:27b)—a miracle that overflowed as mercy toward Paul in the midst of his already grievous situation (2:27c). Paul goes on to say that he will send Epaphroditus to the Philippians "so that when you see him again you may be glad" (*hina idontes auton palin charēte*, 2:28). In return,

Paul asks them to "welcome him in the Lord with great joy, and honor people like him" (*prosdechesthe oun auton en kyriō meta pasēs charas*, 2:29). Paul makes explicit in verse 30 what is assumed throughout, that Epaphroditus is worth celebrating because of his willingness to partner in the sufferings for Christ's sake. The pattern at this point is self-evident: suffering for the sake of Christ must be contextualized within the experience of joy in community.

This leads us then to chapter 3, which begins with a transitional phrase curiously centered on the imperative "to rejoice": "Further, my brothers and sisters, rejoice in the Lord!" (*To loipon, adelphoi mou, chairete en kyriō*, 3:1). While *chairō* could be taken as a farewell, I take it as an imperative. Stanley Porter has shown how *loipon* has "a connective sense" and not merely a concluding sense;[18] thus Joseph Hellerman is right when he argues that "it is unlikely, moreover, that [*chairō*]—'rejoice' elsewhere in Philippians . . . should suddenly acquire a new meaning at this point in the letter."[19] It makes more sense to read this imperative as a rhetorical framing for Paul's commentary on the opposition facing the Philippians in 3:2–4:1. Hence, it is not surprising that Paul ends this lengthy discourse by referring back to the concept of joy in 4:1: "my brothers and sisters, you whom I love and long for, my joy and crown [*chara kai stephanos mou*]."

We arrive now at the last couple of references to joy, in the culminating section of the letter. The first of these references is perhaps its most iconic: "Rejoice in the Lord always. I will say it again: Rejoice!" (*Chairete en kyriō pantote; palin erō, chairete*, Phil. 4:4). By way of two consecutive imperatives of *chairō*, Paul brings his apostolic teaching full circle. He began back in chapter 1 commenting on his thanksgiving and prayerfulness for the Philippians *with joy*. Now, Paul invites the Philippians to embrace this same spirituality of joy and prayerfulness in search of God's peace that passes understanding (4:4–7).

This "rejoicing" is embodied once again by Paul himself in his concluding remarks to the Philippians with respect to their gift (Phil. 4:10–20). Not surprisingly, Paul begins his acknowledgment of the Philippians' gift with reference to joy: "I rejoiced greatly in the Lord [*Echarēn de en kyriō megalōs*] that at last you renewed your concern for me" (4:10). Paul recalls his reception of the gift as a greatly joyful experience "in the Lord." This acknowledgment of joy is also an opportunity for the apostle to confess his posture in the midst of affliction. Hence, before concluding his letter, Paul once more comments on

18. Stanley E. Porter, *Idioms of the Greek New Testament*, 2nd ed. (Sheffield: Sheffield Academic Press, 1994), 122.

19. Hellerman, *Philippians*, 168.

the correct attitude a believer should have in the midst of the hardships that might come when one follows Christ (4:11–13).

Paul's Spirituality of Joy

For Paul, joy is an all-encompassing experience. And yet this experience of joy does not shelter him from experiencing other emotions that often tend to be held in conflict with joy, emotions like feeling hard-pressed (Phil. 1:23), experiencing grief (2:27), feeling anxious (2:28), or lamenting with tears (3:18). But for Paul, joy is seen as a resource to help the believer stand against shame (1:20), from feeling frightened by opponents (1:28), from taking a selfish posture in life (2:3), and from unwarranted grumbling (2:14). To embrace a spirituality of joy is to frame one's life in the Lord; hence, Paul's joy is *in the Lord* (4:4). Although throughout the letter several factors are listed as reasons for Paul's joy, ultimately the basis for his joy is Christ and his gospel.

Through joy's prominence as an imperative throughout the letter, Paul argues that it needs to be sought by believers. Paul demonstrates that this begins in prayer, especially intercessory prayer (Phil. 1:4; 4:4–7). It is in his *constant* posture before the Lord that Paul's joy is centered in Christ, in the advancement of the gospel, and in the persevering of believers, and away from any other earthly comfort or reward that he is currently lacking.

This description of joy also leads us to reconsider joy as a communal experience; hence, the imperatives are all plural (Phil. 2:18; 3:1; 4:4 [×2]).[20] As argued above, with the repetition of *chairō* and the double reference to *synchairō*, 2:17–18 stands as the crux for the theme of joy in the letter: "I am *glad* and *rejoice* with all of you. So you too should be *glad* and *rejoice* with me." Paul was unable to be present with the Philippians due to his detainment; nevertheless, both the apostle and his friends in Philippi took meaningful steps toward experiencing joy in communion.

These insights in turn lead us to see joy as a divine possibility in unjust and harsh circumstances (Phil. 1:18). Although the idea of experiencing joy in the midst of trials and opposition is a prominent theme throughout the New Testament (e.g., James 1:3; 1 Pet. 4:13), in Philippians it takes new dimensions. Unlike in any other New Testament text, it is only in Philippians that we see biographical details and deep psychological ponderings woven into a spirituality of joy. For Paul, joy is not merely an emotion that springs up naturally; it is a spiritual experience that is both given by Christ and sought out by believers together *in the midst of suffering*. This kind of joy proves

---

20. Perhaps a helpful translation for *chairō* should be something akin to "celebrating" since words of this type could invoke "rejoicing" as a communal act.

to be life-giving in life-threatening circumstances. Paul's spirituality of joy is indeed "a walking in freedom according to the Spirit of love and life."[21]

In summary, joy is presented as an all-encompassing emotion derived from communion with Christ, cultivated in prayerfulness, experienced in community, and serving as a defense against discouragement or shame in unjust suffering or opposition. Paul presents joy as worthy of being exalted among other emotions in the context of suffering hardships for the sake of Christ and his gospel. To choose joy is to choose a spirituality fit for following Christ until he returns, in a world where enemies of the cross need to be endured and citizens of heaven need to be encouraged.

A Colombian Spirituality of Joy

Sociopolitically and culturally, first-century Philippi is far different from contemporary Colombia.[22] The most obvious difference is that Christians in Philippi had to follow Christ in an overly non-Christian society, while Christians in Colombia live in what even up to this day is still considered predominantly a Christian country. At one point Colombia was considered to be "the most Catholic nation in Latin America."[23] Although in recent times Colombia has not been spared from the secularization that has swept South America, its Christian heritage still holds true to a large extent, especially with the growth of Protestant churches in Colombia. Being a Christian in Colombia is not an anomaly, especially among the poorest.[24]

The point of commonality between the Christian experience of many in Colombia and the one outlined in the Epistle to the Philippians is that both happen within the context of suffering *unjust* hardships. Colombia is marked by gut-wrenching affliction. A long and complicated history of political corruption; armed conflict between the state, guerrillas, and other paramilitary groups; violence financed by organized crime; high levels of displaced

21. Gustavo Gutiérrez, *We Drink from Our Own Wells: A Spiritual Journey of a People*, 20th anniv. ed. (New York: Orbis Books, 2003), 35.

22. My intent in this section is simply to tether the faith experience I witness among faithful Colombian brothers and sisters who follow Christ through paths filled with injustices, unnecessary sufferings, and poverty with what I understand to be Paul's spirituality of joy. In what follows, I do not claim to speak for all Christians in Colombia, but hopefully this brief reflection can be profitable, at least by way of exploring what I call a spirituality of joy.

23. Luis Carlos Mantilla Ruiz, "Between Progress and Dissatisfaction: The Last 50 Years of History of the Church in Colombia (1965–2015)," *Anuario de Historia de la iglesia* 25 (2016): 60, translation mine.

24. It has been my experience that Protestants in Colombia prefer to refer to themselves as "Christian" and Roman Catholics as "Catholics." In this essay, when I use "Christian" I am referring to both.

minorities; unemployment; and all sorts of manifestations of poverty and many other problems have marked Colombia for decades up to the present.[25] It is in this context that Colombian Christians follow Christ.

At first glance it might seem that many of these problems afflicting Christians in Colombia are not immediately caused *because of* their faith, since these affect all Colombians. Nevertheless, many of these problems are targeted at those who desire to do good, many of whom, if not the majority, are Christians doing what is good because of Christ. This is especially highlighted by the high levels of murders of social leaders, many of whom are Christian. In 2023 alone, Colombia's Ombudsman Office reported that 181 murders of this kind took place.[26]

In this threatening context for following Christ, it feels warranted that *lament* would rise as the resource to help believers navigate through this. And yet, I am not aware of a meaningful resurgence of lament among Colombian Christians. Instead, time after time I have witnessed what Gustavo Gutiérrez proclaimed about the Latin American church's response to unjust suffering to be true among Colombian Christians: "The Latin American situation is characterized by profound suffering out of which *comes a new, paschal experience of joy that flows from the gift of life.*"[27] Joy has been an integral part of the Christian spirituality among many Colombians following Christ through the harshest of circumstances.

Perhaps this insight might not come as a surprise to many, since a common characteristic of the Colombian identity is that we are cheerful people regardless of the circumstance.[28] However, the huge Colombian diaspora in

25. By way of example, Colombia's level of violence in its urban centers is captured by realities like *La Escombrera* in Medellín, which was described as potentially the largest urban mass grave in the world, where it is believed three hundred disappeared are buried; see Giraldo Moreno, "La escombrera, la fosa común urbana más grande del mundo (Medellín-Colombia)," *Kavilando* 7, no. 1 (2015): 47–52. Ironically, in a country that prides itself on its agricultural diversity, 30 percent of the Colombian population is food insecure, which means that 15.5 million people do not have sufficient access to food and face difficulties covering their basic needs. See World Food Programme, "2023 Food Security Assessment of Colombian Population—Executive Summary," March 3, 2023, https://www.wfp.org/publications/2023-food-security-assessment -colombian-population-executive-summary.

26. "Durante el 2023, en Colombia fueron asesinados 181 líderes sociales y defensores de derechos humanos," Defensoría del Pueblo, March 9, 2024, https://www.defensoria.gov.co /web/guest/-/durante-el-2023-en-colombia-fueron-asesinados-181-l%C3%ADderes-sociales -y-defensores-de-derechos-humanos?p_l_back_url=%2Fweb%2Fguest%2Fsearch%3Fq%3 Dasesinados%2Blideres%2Bsociales%2B2023.

27. Gutiérrez, *We Drink from Our Own Wells*, 93 (emphasis added).

28. Most recently Colombian culture has been characterized by Disney in the movie *Encanto* (2021), which, in my opinion, did a fantastic job capturing our lively and cheerful approach to life.

the US and the turning to violence among Christians are signs that just being *berracos* and *echados pa'lante* is not enough to follow Christ in challenging places like Colombia.[29] These two Colombian slang terms can roughly be translated to mean "tough/enduring" and "pushed forward," and they are among the many valuable expressions in Colombian culture to express what we see as our unique ability to be hopeful and hardworking through sufferings and injustices. But neither lament nor a traditional let's-push-through-it attitude has been the dominant Colombian spiritual response to following Christ in the midst of unjust hardships. Instead, it has been a spirituality of joy.

Lament is the appropriate response when the loving presence of God is not felt in unjust suffering, while joy is the appropriate response when the life-giving presence of Christ is the truest reality despite times of unjust suffering. Christ is in Colombia, especially among the least of his brothers and sisters who, although facing all sorts of threats and challenges, continue to opt to do good in their land.

It is difficult to provide examples of how this spirituality of joy takes place among Colombian Christians. I would do a disservice to simply list things like the charismatic and colorful worship style among Colombian churches as evidence of this spirituality of joy, although I see this as a sign of it. Joy is much deeper than that. As with Paul, it is a joy cultivated and expressed first in prayerfulness. As with Paul, they are joyful since they are free *even if it does not seem so.* Freedom is found in "acts of gratitude and hope in the Lord."[30] Gratefulness is a prominent posture of Colombian spirituality. Also, many Colombian Christians live out their vocations to serve Christ by serving the poor even against evildoers who with *real* (threats of) violence try to halt their work. Eduardo de la Serna summarizes Paul's spirituality as narrowed down to these two things: "Christ and the community is what counts, and this is what gives Paul freedom."[31] Many Colombian Christians have freedom to be joyful since they understand that serving Christ and their community is possible regardless of danger.

I believe that a Colombian spirituality of joy has much to offer Western Christianity. James K. A. Smith, commenting on lament, notes that "sometimes in this fallen world the best thing we can do is teach our children how

---

29. The most famous example of Christians turning to weapons is the revolutionary priest Camilo Torres Restrepo. For an analysis of his life, see Dario Martinez Morales, "Camilo Torres Restrepo: Cristianismo y Violencia," *TX* 61, no. 171 (2011): 131–68. For a history and analysis of liberation theology in Colombia, see Antonio José Echeverry P., *Teología de la Liberación en Colombia* (Cali, Colombia: Programa Editorial Universidad del Valle, 2007).

30. Gutiérrez, *We Drink from Our Own Wells*, 22.

31. Serna, "El kerigma de Pablo," 528. Translation mine.

to be sad."[32] I would add that the next thing to do is to teach our children how to be joyful when the things that make us sad remain.

The other side to the spirituality of joy is that it creates a unique way of bridging protest with resignation in a spiritually healthy way, in a time when the obstacles and evils hindering our walk with Christ show no sign of leaving. Choosing joy is a form of healthy protest, a way of throwing a wrench into the vicious wheel of sin, early death, and despair, since these have power only when Christ is felt as absent. Joy is the celebration of the loving presence of Christ in the face of the enemies of the cross. Choosing joy is a form of healthy resignation, as Gutiérrez puts it: "There is a kind of paradoxical 'resignation' to joy that is nothing else than *the recognition of the strengthening presence of God and the community*—a recognition in which our fears, doubts, and discouragement . . . are routed by the power of the Lord's love."[33] Joy in the Lord propels Christians who are not able to alter their circumstances to nevertheless do what is possible to advance the gospel with acts of love and with words of truth. We protest evil by celebrating the presence of Christ, and we exercise resignation by focusing on doing what only we can do through Christ, who gives us strength.

Conclusion: Mi Mamá

I said above that the power behind how the spirituality of joy is presented in the Epistle to the Philippians is in part due to how it weaves its theological theme with Paul's biography. I will conclude by doing the same. As I wrote this chapter, I had several Colombian Christians in mind, Catholics as well as Protestants, but one person stood out the most: my mom.

As portrayed in the film *Encanto*, culturally the Colombian family revolves around the mother figure, and usually she is the towering figure when it comes to matters of faith. Like Euodia and Syntyche (Phil. 4:2), my mom led the way in our home, showing what faithfulness to Christ looks like. She is perhaps the most Colombian person I know, she is the most joyful person I know, and unfortunately she is one of the persons I know who has suffered the most. A practicing Catholic, she raised ten children by herself, since the men in her life left her. For the majority of her life, she was very poor, making her vulnerable to all sorts of abuse and sufferings. Among the hardest of her afflictions, she has shared, was suffering the loss of her children. While still young herself, she lost a child at age four due to a lack

---

32. James K. A. Smith, *You Are What You Love: The Spiritual Power of Habit* (Grand Rapids: Brazos, 2016), 133.

33. Gutiérrez, *We Drink from Our Own Wells*, 119 (emphasis added).

of access to proper medical attention. As an adult, she suffered the loss of two of her older boys as a result of the war in our country. Both of my older brothers were kidnapped by paramilitary groups and forced to join their forces. One of my older brothers, Sebastian, was murdered, and we never found his grave. My other brother, Francisco, returned home, but he was never the same. After falling into drug abuse, he was found murdered a few years later outside a slum in downtown Bogotá. We have not experienced justice for these tragedies.

Through all of this, my mom learned how to be sad, and she also learned how to find her joy in the Lord. She is not a theologian; her faith is simple and practical. I asked her where she finds the strength to have such an encouraging and joyful approach to life even though she has suffered so much. She responded, "*Mijo*, because Jesus is with us, he has never abandoned us, he has forgiven our sins, and he has been so good to us." Even as she still carries pain and grief, my mom has been able to set her life heavenward (*echada pa'l cielo*) since in her sufferings she found out that Christ was there for her. Stories like these abound throughout Colombia, and so does joy in the Lord because, like no other, Christ understands our sufferings and shares in our sufferings, and unlike anything or anyone else, he only is our hope throughout our sufferings (Phil. 1:29).

13

Colossians and Philemon

An Egyptian Coptic Perspective

FADY MEKHAEL

The normal objective of biblical interpretation in the Western world, especially in Protestant circles, is to uncover the original meaning of a given author. Usually, Western scholars employ different methodologies to deconstruct the textual elements to discover the original meaning of the text. These methodologies traditionally include source criticism, redactional criticism, historical criticism, and other forms of interpretive enterprises that seek to go back in time and understand the *Sitz im Leben* of the text. That is not the case in other parts of the world, including the modern Coptic community.

Historical Introduction

The modern Coptic community is a minority religious Christian community in Egypt that constitutes 10–15 percent of the population of Egypt today.[1]

1. The exact percentage of Christians in Egypt remains unclear. Official government figures consistently place the Coptic Christian population at 6 percent of the country's total. However, some church and community leaders claim much higher estimates, with 10 percent being frequently cited in media reports about Egypt. Despite this, the absence of concrete demographic data makes these figures uncertain (for more on this, see Conrad Hackett, "How Many Christians Are There in Egypt?," Pew Research Center, February 16, 2011, https://www.pewresearch.org/2011/02/16/how-many-christians-are-there-in-egypt/). Egypt's fourteenth national census,

The term "Coptic" etymologically means "Egyptian." Aziz Atiya argues, "In all simplicity, this term is equivalent to the word 'Egyptian.' It is derived from the Greek *Aigyptos*, which in turn is a corruption of the ancient Egyptian *Hak-ka-Ptah*—the house of the temple of the spirit of Ptah, a most highly revered deity in Egyptian mythology; this was the name of Memphis, the oldest capital of the unified Upper and Lower Egypt."[2] Culturally speaking, the term today denotes Egyptian Christians, especially those who belong to the Coptic Orthodox Church. Historically, Coptic is the script development of the ancient Egyptian language that took place after the disappearance of the Demotic script, employing Greek letters for its script.[3] This development took place when Egypt became mostly Christian, and the Coptic language and script became the characteristic features of Egyptian Christian literature, especially in liturgical worship, biblical translations, and religious writings. Using the Coptic language became (and still is) one of the most significant identity markers of the Egyptian Christian community during the Islamic conquest of Egypt (AD 639),[4] and the Bible became one of the most instrumental tools in drawing the lines between the Coptic community and Islam.[5] Egypt underwent a national identity crisis with the arrival of the Arabs, who brought a new culture, a new language, and most significantly a new religion: Islam. Egyptian Christians went through new challenges in terms of their

---

conducted by the Central Agency for Public Mobilization and Statistics and released in September 2017, did not disclose specific religious statistics (see "Infographic: Facts and Figures from CAPMAS' 2017 Census," Mada Masr, October 1, 2017, https://madamasr.com/en/2017/10/01/news/u/infographic-facts-and-figures-from-capmas-2017-census/).

2. Aziz S. Atiya, *The Coptic Contribution to Christian Civilisation* (Surrey, BC: St. George Coptic Orthodox Church, n.d.), 4. See also Atiya, *The Copts and Christian Civilization* (Salt Lake: University of Utah Press, 1979).

3. For a survey of the reasons behind the disappearance of Demotic and the rise of Coptic, see Jean-Luc Fournet, *The Rise of Coptic: Egyptian versus Greek in Late Antiquity* (Princeton: Princeton University Press, 2020), 1–5. For a helpful overview of the history of scholarship on Coptic dialects, see A. Shisha-Halevy, *Topics in Coptic Syntax: Structural Studies in the Bohairic Dialect*, OLA 160 (Leuven: Peeters, 2007), 12–19. For the significance of using the Coptic language in the practices and rituals of the contemporary Coptic Orthodox Church, see Hiroko Miyokawa, "The Revival of the Coptic Language and the Formation of Coptic Ethnoreligious Identity in Modern Egypt," in *Copts in Context: Negotiating Identity, Tradition and Modernity*, ed. Nelly van Doorn-Harder (Columbia: University of South Carolina Press, 2017), 151–57.

4. For an overview of the Coptic conditions during the Arab conquest, see Otto F. A. Meinardus, *Two Thousand Years of Coptic Christianity* (Cairo: American University in Cairo Press, 2002), 64–65; see also Meinardus, "The Attitudes of the Orthodox Copts towards the Islamic State from the 7th to the 12th Century," *OS* 13 (1964): 153–70.

5. The instrumentality of the Bible in shaping the Christian identity in the world of Islam has been the case in the whole Arab region, not only within the Coptic community in Egypt. See Alexander Treiger, "From Theodore Abū Qurra to Abed Azrié: The Arabic Bible in Context," in *Senses of Scripture, Treasures of Tradition: The Bible in Arabic among Jews, Christians and Muslims*, ed. Miriam Lindgren Hjälm, BibAr 5 (Leiden: Brill, 2017), 28.

relationships with the new ruling culture, and the Arabs treated the Coptic community in different ways throughout history, ranging from tolerance to open persecution.[6] However, one thing became clear to the Coptic community century after century: they were becoming the religious minority.[7] My goal behind this historical introduction is to contextualize what the modern Coptic community has to offer to Western Christianity in terms of reading the New Testament: reading the New Testament while being a Christian minority, sometimes persecuted, is a different experience than in the West. Admittedly, Copts today enjoy privileges under the leadership of President Abd El-Fattah El-Sissi, as observers witness that religious freedom is taken seriously and churches are built in Egypt as never before. However, this has not been the case during the history of modern Egypt, especially under the rule of the Muslim Brotherhood and Mubarak.[8]

I attempt here to offer a fresh answer to the following questions: What does it mean to read the New Testament from a minority Christian perspective? What does it mean to read the New Testament in churches that could be bombed at any time? How may context alter the theological/hermeneutical conclusions that readers arrive at? In short, when you do not have the leisure of life, you do not turn to the text looking for its sources, editors, compilers, and historical developments. *The Coptic community turned to Scripture to find resources for living with religious differences, awareness of cultural and religious uniqueness, and, sometimes, religious violence.* These resources usually were found through theological and ethical interpretations of biblical books. Applying these questions to Colossians and Philemon, I seek to show what it means to read Colossians and Philemon when life is not always safe. I belong to the Coptic community, and even though I received

6. Herald Suermann, "Coptic and the Islam of the Seventh Century," in *The Encounter of Eastern Christianity with Early Islam*, ed. Emmanouela Grypeou, Mark Swanson, and David Thomas, HCMR 5 (Leiden: Brill, 2006), 95–110.

7. Sidney Griffith comments on the numbers of Christians under Islam: "The history of Christians under Muslim rule is a history of continuous, if gradual, diminishment; over the centuries the numbers declined from a substantial majority of the population in many places in the conquered territories in the times before the Crusades, to significant minorities in most of the Islamic world by Ottoman times." Sidney H. Griffith, *The Church in the Shadow of the Mosque: Christians and Muslims in the World of Islam* (Princeton: Princeton University Press, 2008), 14.

8. Cf. Vivian Ibrahim, *The Copts of Egypt: The Challenges of Modernisation and Identity*, Library of Modern Middle East Studies 99 (London: Tauris Academic Studies, 2011); Sebastian Elsässer, *The Coptic Question in the Mubarak Era* (Oxford: Oxford University Press, 2014). Additionally, Mariz Tadros offers a careful analysis of the sectarian violence incidents that the Copts endured during the period of 2008–11, which led to their active participation in the 2011 uprisings. See Mariz Tadros, *Copts at the Crossroads: The Challenges of Building Inclusive Democracy in Egypt* (Cairo: American University in Cairo Press, 2013), 45–60.

most of my training in biblical studies in North American universities (Duke and McMaster), I still know that these texts were lifesaving resources for my ancestors. To begin with, let me explain the current mosaic of the Coptic community and one basic pillar of its biblical culture: orality.

The Biblical Oral Culture in Modern Egypt

The vast majority of the contemporary Coptic community belongs to the Coptic Orthodox Church, the largest Christian church in the Middle East, an Oriental Orthodox church headed by the See of Alexandria, the Pope of Alexandria on the Holy Apostolic See of Saint Mark, who is currently Pope Tawadros II.[9] The Coptic community also includes the second-largest church in the Middle East, the Protestant Church of Egypt (which consists of eighteen denominations, chief among them the Presbyterian Church of Egypt), headed by Dr. Rev. Andrea Zaki, which represents 2–3 percent of the population in Egypt.[10] Finally, the Catholic Coptic Church is the regional Catholic church in Egypt, currently headed by the Catholic patriarch Ibrahim Isaac Sidrak, and the members of this church are less than 1 percent of the Egyptian population.[11] Putting these numbers together, the Christian Coptic community in Egypt is still a religious minority, and the Coptic population is today numerically even smaller than a few centuries ago.

During its long history of living in the world of Islam, the Coptic Church became culturally assimilated to Islam in different ways. One of these major assimilations is the borrowing of orality into the practices of the Coptic Orthodox Church, especially in preaching using biblical passages. Generally speaking, Middle Eastern cultures have depended more on oral traditions than written resources, especially when it comes to religious matters. It does not trouble Arabs to admit the fact that the average person only spends six minutes a year reading, according to a recent UNESCO report.[12] The Arabic culture that shapes the modern Coptic community perceives orality as a much better (and more secure!) way to preserve the most treasured cultural components, especially religious elements (e.g., the Qur'an).

Febe Armanios shows that oral sermons were the weapon of the Coptic Orthodox clerical preachers in encountering the Catholic missions in Egypt

9. Stephen J. Davis, *The Early Coptic Papacy: The Egyptian Church and Its Leadership in Late Antiquity* (Cairo: American University in Cairo Press, 2004), ix.

10. Hackett, "How Many Christians Are There in Egypt?"

11. Hackett, "How Many Christians Are There in Egypt?"

12. "Arab Reading Challenge," Policy Monitoring Platforms Reports, UNESCO, accessed March 22, 2022, https://en.unesco.org/creativity/policy-monitoring-platform/arab-reading-challenge.

during the Ottoman era.[13] Armanios concludes her study by saying, "The clergy were particularly conscious of what constituted appropriate behavior for Copts within a predominantly Muslim society. . . . Through preaching, higher clergymen offered a rigorous moral program that protected church traditions on marriage, fasting, and prayer and that attempted to revamp the priesthood."[14] The pulpit has always been the place where Coptic clergy articulated and defended their identity. These sermons were later textualized to survive after the death of their preachers. Any observer of the contemporary community and church life of the Copts in Egypt today would immediately recognize that the Coptic biblical culture and knowledge are shaped through weekly clerical preaching during the Mass. The Coptic Mass, in all its versions, includes readings from different sections of biblical books, including the Psalms, the Gospels, Paul's letters, and the Catholic Letters, with the reading from the Gospel at the center of the whole Mass, highlighted with a special reading tone and lighting of candles. Traditionally, the Gospel reading is the text on which the priest builds his sermon, connecting the other readings from the New and Old Testaments to the Gospel reading. Over time, this centralization of the Gospels led to building more knowledge of the Gospels and Jesus's life than the rest of the Bible. Ironically, most of the Coptic Protestant preaching in Egypt today is based on Paul's letters. It is well known that if you know the Gospels better, then you are a Coptic Orthodox, while if you know Paul better, then you are a Protestant.

Oral biblical culture persists in modern Egypt. Muslims pride themselves on preserving the Qur'an through memorization, which has guided the Copts to highlight the value of oral teaching and memorization. Additionally, the Egyptian illiteracy rate is considerably high. In 1976, the illiteracy rate was 61.8 percent, while in 2017 it was 29.9 percent of the population.[15] This meant the church needed to communicate with its flock in a way other than writing. Consequently, clergy resorted to their traditional weapon: the pulpit.

Adopting the oral culture in engaging the New and Old Testaments means there are very few sophisticated or critical studies of the biblical texts. Rather, the biblical texts are memorized and used to defend the faith and edify the flock in ways sensible to their Muslim context. In a sense, the Coptic community still engages Scripture in a pre-Enlightenment way. Moreover, the Coptic Orthodox Church is aware of being a minority, with

13. Febe Armanios, *Coptic Christianity in Ottoman Egypt* (Oxford: Oxford University Press, 2011), 117–45.

14. Armanios, *Coptic Christianity*, 145.

15. "Egypt Literacy Rate 1976–2022," Macrotrends, accessed March 22, 2022, https://www.macrotrends.net/countries/EGY/egypt/literacy-rate.

a long history of bloody persecution; thus the emphasis on persecution texts (e.g., Matt. 5:10–12; 10:28) recurs in the Coptic pulpit preaching to shape the Christian imagination of the flock. Clergy expound biblical passages to offer fuel for daily life, create patience, and dogmatically prepare the community to keep the faith in a mostly Muslim society. Furthermore, the Coptic Orthodox Church is a traditional church that prides itself on a long line of papal ancestry that goes back to Mark the Evangelist.[16] The church established its biblical engagement on its traditions, church fathers' homiletics, and liturgical use. Fr. Tadros Y. Malaty is the most popular and influential priest in the Coptic Orthodox Church today and the author of the most influential commentaries on biblical books. Malaty explains how the New Testament is a part of the church's tradition: "The Holy Scriptures in fact are a part of the Church tradition. The tradition in its essence is declaring the word of God by various methods, for tradition concentrated on the apostolic teaching. The appearance of the books of the New Testament did not cancel the tradition, but these books command us to preserve the tradition."[17] This approach means that biblical books are already interpreted in church traditions. We only need to rediscover these interpretations. For this reason, Malaty bases his commentary series on patristic writings, filling it with many quotations for each verse he comments on.[18] The traditional interpretation of Scripture also contributed to the oral biblical culture in the Coptic community. If the fathers of the church already interpreted the biblical books, and there is no need for ongoing engagement with Scripture, then the only thing we need is to have access to these patristic interpretations and preach from them.[19]

Having explained the effects of orality on the Coptic biblical culture, I now turn to the few published commentaries on the New Testament in the Coptic community. Looking into Coptic commentaries on the New Testament, all written in Arabic, gives the observer a major impression: *Coptic engagement*

---

16. See Davis, *Early Coptic Papacy*; Mark N. Swanson, *The Coptic Papacy in Islamic Egypt 641–1517* (Cairo: American University in Cairo Press, 2010).

17. Tadros Y. Malaty, *Introduction to the Coptic Orthodox Church* (Alexandria, Egypt: St. George Coptic Orthodox Church, 1993), 324. All Coptic Christian authors write in Arabic today, and all translations from Arabic resources in this chapter are mine. Few exceptional works have been translated into English to serve the globally increasing Coptic diaspora. This quotation comes from one of these translated works into English, and it is the only one that is used from a Coptic English resource in this article. The rest that follow later in the article are translated from Arabic.

18. This series is similar to Thomas Oden's series titled Ancient Christian Commentary on Scripture (Downers Grove, IL: InterVarsity, 2001–).

19. Hence, the second half of the twentieth century witnessed a wide movement to translate patristic writings into Arabic in the Coptic Orthodox Church.

with Scripture is focused on theological interpretation and ethical practices of Scripture as a guiding resource for daily life decisions in a mostly Muslim society. I will present two examples from Colossians and Philemon to show the features of this hermeneutical strategy.

Western Vis-à-Vis Coptic Take on Colossians

Western scholarship on Colossians has spilled much ink on the question of authorship in an effort to ascertain whether Paul or someone else wrote the letter. Additionally, scholars have been occupied with reconstructing what was going on in the nascent Christian community in the city of Colossae.[20] Colossae was a city in the province of Phrygia, located at an approximate distance from the cities of Laodicea and Hierapolis, in Asia Minor.[21] The author emphasizes that the churches in these cities were founded by Epaphras, but Paul is still somehow connected to these local communities (Col. 4:12–13). The heresy that appeared in Colossae prompted Paul to write the letter to protect the emerging local Christian community. While Paul starts with strong language to the church in Galatia, he addresses the members of the church of Colossae in calm and pleasant language (see especially 1:1–9), as if it is an innocent local church that the false teachers are attempting to deceive (cf. 2:4).

Western scholarship also tends to focus on the religious syncretistic nature in the province of Phrygia to reconstruct the heretical teachings that spread in Colossae (see especially Col. 2:8–23). It likely involved the mixing of beliefs and practices from different religious traditions in Phrygia, including philosophical ideas associated with arrogance and human (emphatically, not divine or heavenly) traditions, and was connected to "the elemental spirits of the universe" (*stoicheia tou kosmou*, 2:8).[22] The Western reconstruction, broadly speaking, views the heresy as an invitation to interact with the divine based on a specific philosophy (way of life) that depends on the religiously perceived spirits of the universe, not on Christ's life, death, and resurrection.[23] In his response, the author identifies Christ as the head of all powers and authorities (2:10, 15). As N. T. Wright puts it, "Christ is the ruler of all nations, and of any powers or authorities that may stand behind them in the shadowy world

---

20. For an overview of the scholarly reconstructions of the Colossian heresy, see Mark Allan Powell, *Introducing the New Testament: A Historical, Literary, and Theological Survey* (Grand Rapids: Baker Academic, 2009), 360–61.

21. Powell, *Introducing the New Testament*, 359.

22. Unless otherwise indicated, all Bible translations in this chapter are from the NRSV.

23. Powell, *Introducing the New Testament*, 378–87.

of superstition and mythology."[24] The author becomes more direct in verse 18 when he explicitly condemns the false teachers' invitation to worship angels.

Seemingly, Epaphras needed help to confront these heretical claims, so Paul wrote the letter to assist him. Building on the mentioned elements of the heresy, Paul argues with the Colossian church members: "If with Christ you died to the elemental spirits of the universe, why do you live as if you still belonged to the world? Why do you submit to regulations, 'Do not handle, Do not taste, Do not touch'? All these regulations refer to things that perish with use; they are simply human commands and teachings" (Col. 2:20–22). Christ's supremacy is diminished in the Colossian community's beliefs and practices, to the extent that Paul has to argue for the divinity of Christ in the christological hymn (1:15–20), an argument that has shaped Coptic hermeneutics of the Bible for centuries. Christ's centrality has been marginalized in the Colossian church, and so the author writes (or quotes) the hymn that puts Christ in a unique place above all things.

One of the phrases that the modern Coptic community focuses on is the clause "firstborn of all creation" (Col. 1:15). Does this clause mean that Christ is created? Does it mean that Christ is not the Son of God or, in a sense, God? Is Jesus privileged over other creatures only by being the first one? These questions have been raised in Western scholarship,[25] but the problem has its own sensibilities for the Coptic community living in the Middle East. Since Coptic Christians are surrounded by a Sunni Muslim majority, polemics against the deity of Christ have been one of the main features of Coptic-Muslim dialogues over the centuries. In Islam, Jesus is only a created human prophet, and Muslim polemics use biblical passages that might support Islamic views. The Coptic community must explain to their neighbors that they worship not a created man but God incarnate. Some of the Islamic polemics against the Coptic community are based on Western scholarship on Colossians 1:15b, especially those pieces that argue for the verse as including Christ in creation.

Probably the most famous commentary in the Coptic Orthodox Church is one written by Fr. Malaty, priest of St. George Church, Alexandria, Egypt.

---

24. N. T. Wright, *Colossians and Philemon: An Introduction and Commentary*, TNTC 12 (Grand Rapids: Eerdmans, 1986), 107.

25. Cf. Eduard Lohse, *Colossians and Philemon: A Commentary on the Epistles to the Colossians and to Philemon*, Hermeneia (Philadelphia: Fortress, 1971), 48–49. Interestingly, for Lohse, *prōtotokos pasēs ktiseōs* denotes not a temporal sense but the cosmic status of Christ. However, according to James Dunn, "We should note the ambiguity attaching to the imagery, since 'firstborn' can mean first created being and/or that which has precedence over creation" (*The Epistles to the Colossians and to Philemon: A Commentary on the Greek Text*, NIGTC [Grand Rapids: Eerdmans, 1996], 90). Muslim polemics would quote Dunn only to show the possibility that Jesus is, according to Col. 1:15b, the first created human being.

The commentary series is based on the commentaries and homiletics of the early church fathers and is the main biblical reference for ten to fifteen million Coptic Orthodox Christians. In his comments on Colossians 1:15–20, Malaty says, "Apostle Paul quotes this hymn about the Lord Christ, the author of our salvation, chanting Christ's centrality through which Christ offers us his divine potentials. Whether Paul quoted the hymn in its original form, authored it himself, or even put his theological and exegetical touches on the hymn, what matters is that this is one of the most significant passages in the New Testament concerning the person of Christ."[26] Malaty reflects what matters for the Coptic interpreter: not the tradition that stands behind the text or how it was circulated before Paul quotes it but the person of Christ. This interpretive direction reflects the theological hermeneutics with which the Coptic community engages Scripture.

Malaty spends quite a good deal of time defending the appropriate interpretation of Colossians 1:15b: "Calling Christ 'the firstborn of creation' or its head does not mean that he is just one of the exalted creatures, but that he incarnated and, willingly, he became a brother of humanity, to take her back to the bosom of his father. He is the only one who is able, by his blood, to complete the reconciliation between the Father and humanity."[27] Malaty defends this interpretation further, building on Athanasius of Alexandria: "Pope Athanasius the Apostolic says that the Bible never calls Christ as a 'firstborn from God' or 'created by God' but the Bible calls Christ as the unique Son, the Word, the Wisdom, and all these attributions describe the relationship between the second person of the Trinity and the first. When Paul says about Christ that he is 'firstborn of all creation' he speaks of Christ's descendance and excelling for creation."[28] For Malaty, Christ is not one among creation, nor even an exalted member of humanity, and, from the Coptic perspective, this is the first comment a reader of Colossians should make. Furthermore, Malaty does not base his conclusions on linguistic or grammatical analysis, nor does he consider the possible echoes of Paul's language with Israel as the firstborn in Exodus. Malaty goes directly to the heart of the matter: Christ is no less than God—because this is the most significant fact for the Christian community surrounded by a Muslim majority that denies that Christ is anything more than a human prophet. He argues, "If all creation is created through him, and he himself is before all creation, then he is not a created being but the creator of creation. Consequently, he is called the firstborn, not

26. Tadros Y. Malaty, *Paul's Epistle to the Colossians: A Commentary from the Early Church Fathers* [in Arabic] (Alexandria, Egypt: St. George Sporting Press, 2003), 35.

27. Malaty, *Colossians*, 35.

28. Malaty, *Colossians*, 40.

because he is created by the Father, but because all creation came into existence through him, and he did not cease to be the unique Son of the Father."[29]

There is another significant nuance concerning Malaty's use of Athanasius of Alexandria, the celebrated champion saint of the Church of Alexandria in the fourth century. Athanasius was the one who heavily responded to Arius's heresy that Christ is a created being, an exalted and semi-godly creature. Paul's clause might have been interpreted in ways that supported Arianism,[30] and Malaty is aware of this possibility. The Coptic Orthodox Church is a traditional church that cherishes its heritage and prides itself on how much blood has been shed through the centuries to keep the right doctrines, chief among them the deity of Christ. This emphatic language engages with polemics against Coptic Christians that they worship a created God, and in some cases, that they turned a created human into God. In commenting on the clause "the God and father of our Lord"[31] in Colossians 1:3, Antonious Fikry says, "Using 'and' in this context does not mean that we have two different gods, God, and the Father, but these are two descriptions for God, who is the Father of Jesus Christ. . . . God is the God of Jesus Christ for the second person of the trinity incarnated, so God is the God of Jesus Christ in relation to his humanity, and the Father of Jesus Christ in relation to his divinity, for the sonship of Jesus Christ to the Father is eternal."[32] These comments are theological and tend to reflect later theological developments in church history on the biblical text. The assumption is that these later developments originated in the biblical text. However, as has been shown, these comments are apologetic in nature. They defend Coptic Christianity against the Islamic polemic that Copts worship three gods.

Another well-respected commentary on the Bible comes from the evangelical church. Mennis Abd El-Nour was the pastor of the largest and most influential evangelical church in the Middle East. He authored one of the most widely used apologetic commentaries in Egypt and the Middle East, which could be translated into English as "Fake Suspicions about the Bible." In this volume, Abd El-Nour engages with Muslim polemics concerning biblical credibility verse by verse through the sixty-six books of the Protestant canon. In

29. Malaty, *Colossians*, 40.

30. Again, interestingly, Dunn (*Epistles*, 90) refers to this possibility: "The former sense, first created being, gave scope to subsequent Arian christology (the Son as created by God . . .). But we should recognize that the categories at this stage were not at all so precise." It is not clear to me how Dunn can know that the categories at this time were not precise.

31. This is my translation into English, which best represents how the clause appears in the Arabic version (Smyth-VanDyck's version).

32. Antonius Fikry, *Commentary on Paul's Letter to the Colossians* [in Arabic] (Cairo: Maktbet El-Mahaba, 2000), 20.

his comment on Colossians 1:15b, Abd El-Nour quotes the Muslim polemic explicitly and engages with it:

> Colossians 1:15–16 speaks of Christ as "the firstborn of all creation, through him all are created, everything in heavens and on earth." From these verses, it becomes clear the reason behind calling Christ "the firstborn of creation," not because he is the first person God created as the objector says, but because all creation came to existence through him. And the word "firstborn" should not be understood in its literal sense, but in its metaphorical sense, which, applied here, denotes the headship or priority. The same word came in the Bible meaning "head" or "first" because Moses's law gives the headship to the firstborn son. Also, God said of David: "I will make him the firstborn, the highest of the kings of the earth" (Ps. 89:27), even though David was the eighth son for his father, and was not the first to rule over Israel, and he was even a younger king compared to other kings. Additionally, Jesus is called "firstborn" in other places, including Romans 8:29. . . . For these reasons, it is not strange to call Christ "the firstborn of all creation" because he is the head and lord of creation, as the one who brought it into existence.[33]

Abd El-Nour's comments use biblical allusions to explain the difficulty associated with the firstborn clause in Colossians 1:15. This broadly reflects the Protestant way of reading biblical passages. However, Abd El-Nour, as most of Protestant leaders tend to be, is more explicit toward the polemics with Islam, giving the obscure title "objector" to his interlocutor. This objector could be a famous Muslim imam, or sheikh, who highlighted Colossians 1:15 on satellite or radio to discredit Christianity.

Donald Hagner argues that the core point of Paul in Colossians is that "a proper view of Christ is fundamental to knowledge and ethics, and points to the salvation from the powers announced in the gospel."[34] For Coptic readers, this is the gist of interpreting Colossians: a theological basis for ethical exhortation. Malaty shows the significance of this theological-ethical interpretation, saying, "This letter astonishingly reveals the majesty of Christ, but only those who live in Jesus Christ can glimpse this majesty. They will know the treasures of his grace, find real satisfaction in him. Thus, Colossians is a doctrinal-practical letter."[35] For the Coptic community, Colossians as a witness for Christ's divinity is a resource from which readers get the wisdom to live for Christ's divinity each day.

---

33. Mennis Abd El-Nour, *Shobhat Wahmiya Hawl Al-Kitab Al-Mokkadas* [in Arabic] (Cairo: Kasr El-Dobara Evangelical Church, 1982), 403.

34. Donald A. Hagner, *The New Testament: A Historical and Theological Introduction* (Grand Rapids: Baker Academic, 2012), 563.

35. Malaty, *Colossians*, 15.

Western Vis-à-Vis Coptic Take on Philemon

The modern Coptic approach to Philemon is an ecclesiological one. Paul is pictured as a priest who taught Onesimus the faith; thus he speaks using his priestly authority: "I would rather appeal to you on the basis of love—and I, Paul, do this as an old man [*presbytēs*], and now also as a prisoner of Christ Jesus. I am appealing to you for my child, Onesimus, whose father I have become [*hon egennēsa en tois desmois*] during my imprisonment" (Philem. 1:9–10). The Arabic translation used in the Coptic community translates *presbytēs* literally as "elder" and *hon egennēsa en tois desmois* as "whom I gave birth to." Malaty comments, "The word 'elder' here has the force of fatherly priestly authority. Paul as an elderly father spent his life serving the Lord, enduring sufferings for the preaching of the gospel, and he is now captive in the Lord. Thus he speaks with priestly love full of experience. This father cannot stay silent when there is an opportunity for a pastor or layman to seek goodness."[36] In Malaty's interpretation, *presbytēs* is a technical term here that refers to the priesthood; thus Paul uses his apostolic authority as he speaks to Onesimus. This conclusion is further confirmed by the clause *hon egennēsa en tois desmois*, which denotes that Paul became a father (a priestly father) to Onesimus. However, Paul's priestly authority finds its roots in love. Malaty reflects his views of Coptic priesthood in his explanation of Paul's priesthood. As in the relationship between the Coptic priest and his flock, Paul's priestly authority could be effective only in love.

While the theological interpretation is the dominant approach to Colossians in the Coptic community, in Philemon the ethical interpretation predominates. Malaty explains, "Although it is a short letter, it reflects the apostolic spirit that is full of love in each letter, that it is a model for the practical side of Christian values."[37] Western scholarship has focused on the images of slavery in the ancient Mediterranean that Philemon offers.[38] This may reflect the historical struggle related to slavery in North America, a struggle we know little about in the Middle East. Instead, there are other concerns behind the ethical interpretation of Scripture. Simply put, in a social context that did not encourage religious freedom for many decades in modern Egypt, the only way Coptic Christians could witness for their faith was through their behaviors. Thus, emphasis on individual ethics was at the core of biblical interpretations in the Coptic community because it was a communicative approach. Reaching

---

36. Tadros Y. Malaty, *Paul's Epistle to Philemon: A Commentary from the Early Church Fathers* [in Arabic] (Alexandria, Egypt: St. George Sporting Press, 1979), 9.

37. Malaty, *Philemon*, 4.

38. See Norman R. Petersen, *Rediscovering Paul: Philemon and the Sociology of Paul's Narrative World* (Eugene, OR: Wipf & Stock, 2008).

out to Muslims with Christian ethics was, and still is, the main approach to practicing local missions in the Egyptian and Arabic society.

Another aspect of Coptic interpretation of Scripture is allegorical interpretation. Christians in Egypt inherited this methodology from the Jews for, unsurprisingly, similar reasons. Coptic Christians live in a society where they need to offer a justified explanation of their faith. Thus, allegorical interpretation is mostly employed to explain odd expressions and notions in the Bible. But these are not the only cases, since it is possible to allegorize for theological purposes. For instance, Pope Tawadros II, the current pope of the Coptic Orthodox Church, comments on Paul's reconciliatory work in his Letter to Philemon, saying, "Paul explained to the fleeing slave what Christ did for us, so Paul reconciled between the master Philemon and the slave Onesimus, as Christ reconciled us to God when we were slaves in sin, and as Paul was the one who guaranteed Onesimus salvation, so Christ is the one who guaranteed our salvation. . . . Let's go back to God our Lord with our repentance, confession, ministry, and love."[39] The allegorization aims at exploring possible theological connections between Paul's ministry and Christ's saving work.

Conclusion

We all come to the biblical text with questions, and our interpretive direction is determined by the kind of questions we bring to the biblical text. However, these questions are also shaped by the social, economic, and political context we experience. Members of the modern Coptic community have to live as a religious minority in a mostly Muslim society, so they come to the biblical text with the questions they hear. Living as a minority in the Arabic culture impacted the Coptic biblical engagement in that it is mostly oral, and, historically, the Coptic pulpit has always been the tool by which clergy expressed and defended their Christian understanding of the biblical text.

Living in such a situation meant that the Coptic experience of the biblical text focused on theological and ethical interpretation. That does not mean that historical-critical approaches are not significant. However, this might explain the increasing interest in the theological interpretation of Scripture recently. From a theological perspective, the modern Coptic approach to the biblical text reminds us not to forget the core message of the biblical text. No one can underestimate the significance of working on

39. Pope Tawadros II, *The Key to the New Testament*, 2 vols. [in Arabic] (Cairo: Coptic Orthodox Patriarchate, 2013), 2:168.

authorship, sources, redactional layers, similarities with literature from cognate cultures, and so many other reading strategies. However, let's never forget to listen to what the text really wants to say at the end of the day. These messages were the fuel that helped the Coptic community survive through the centuries.

14

Paul's *Dokimazō* in 1 Thessalonians 2:4 in Light of Ancient Greece *Dokimasia* of Orators

Implications for Ministers of the Gospel in the Twenty-First Century

GIFT MTUKWA

In April 2023, pastor Paul Nthenge Mackenzie of Good News International Ministries led his parishioners to the Shakahola forest in Kilifi, Kenya. He taught them that they should fast to death so as to "meet Jesus." When the police visited the forest after a tip-off from one of the relatives, they found emaciated people and fresh mass graves of those who had died and were buried, a reported 427 people.[1] This number included children (forced to drop out of school) and people from all socioeconomic levels. In some cases, an entire family was buried in the same grave. Several were found alive in some

---

1. "Number of Bodies Exhumed from Suspected Kenyan Cult Graves Jumps to 47," *Hindustan Times*, April 23, 2023, https://www.hindustantimes.com/world-news/number-of-bodies-exhumed-from-suspected-kenyan-cult-graves-jumps-to-47-101682280821087.html.

of the mass graves. It is reported that Mackenzie told his followers that "the fast would count only if they gathered together, and offered them his farm as a fasting venue. They were not to mingle with anyone from the 'outside' world if they wanted to go to heaven, and were to destroy all documents given by the government, including national IDs and birth certificates."[2]

As the police investigated further, it became clear that those who might have wished to change their minds were murdered with crude weapons. One body recovered from a mass grave was that of a "healthy-looking person, whose body was not emaciated." Dr. William Samoei Ruto, president of the Republic of Kenya, observed, "What is being witnessed in Shakahola is akin to terrorism." The question of Amason Kingi, senator of Kilifi, is pertinent: "How [did] such a heinous crime, organised and executed over a considerable period of time, escape the radar of our intelligence system? How did evil of such an astounding magnitude take place without being detected? How did this 'pastor' gather so many people, indoctrinate, brainwash and starve them to death in the name of fasting and then bury them in a forest without being detected?"[3] However, the more pertinent question for the church is how did such a pastor get licensed to be a preacher? What might we learn about Paul and how he understood himself as a minister of the gospel?

This chapter will look at the use of *dokimasia* of ancient Greece to shed light on Paul's usage of *dokimazō* (test, approve) in 1 Thessalonians 2:4. We will particularly consider the *dokimasia* of *orators* in the Greek assembly and contrast that with how Paul uses *dokimazō*. Next, we will consider how this verse has been translated in various Shona translations of the Bible and make some recommendations. Finally, we will draw implications for how gospel ministers should view their calling and ministry in light of God's approval.

The Meaning of *Dokimazō*

Various Bible translations translate the word *dokimazō* with words like "to be approved" (NASB, RSV), "to be judged worthy" (GNT), and "to be allowed" (KJV). These translations demonstrate the semantic range of this word. *Dokimazō* has several meanings and usages—it was mostly used in a political context and at times in religious spheres as well. *Dokimazō* means "an examination for genuineness, *testing, examination.*"[4] The word

2. Immaculate Akello, "Why Did 73 Kenyan Cult Members Starve to Death?," *Aljazeera*, April 25, 2023, https://www.aljazeera.com/news/2023/4/25/why-did-73-kenya-cult-members -starve-to-death.

3. Akello, "Why Did 73 Kenyan Cult Members Starve to Death?"

4. BDAG, 256.

is used for the idea of refining precious metals. Paul Zell has noted, "In such instances the verb itself gives no hint as to whether the results of the trial are positive or negative. Instead it focuses on the fiery process that must take place."[5]

In the New Testament, the word changed to include not only "putting to test" but also the "thought that the test has been successfully surmounted (Rom. 1:28, 2:18, 14:22)."[6] Walter Grundmann believes that it is in the New Testament where the entire word group attains religious connotation, and this has its roots in the Old Testament.[7] He states, "This [testing] is determined by received salvation on the one side and impending judgment on the other. The resultant conduct is a striving for attestation, i.e., for the attestation of the salvation already received and for attestation in the test of judgment."[8]

Greco-Roman Usage of *Dokimazō*

This section will explore the various usages of the word *dokimazō* in the Greco-Roman context to provide a background and a contrast for how Paul uses this word in his writings and 1 Thessalonians 2:4 in particular. Plato "speaks of the appointment of state officials and envisages [*dokimazesthai*] for those nominated to office."[9] In ancient Greece, it was common practice for candidates who aspired to public office to be "tested as to antecedents and character."[10] Since religion and politics were intertwined, initially the election of public officials had a religious element to it. As Rajendra Avasthi has observed, the early Greek "lived in constant intercourse with his gods; for every work he performed and every decision he made he looked to them for advice and guidance. . . . [People] were guided by dreams, omens, portents and oracles in private and public life alike."[11] However, with time, the religious aspect was neglected, and the *demos* (the people) took its place.[12]

---

5. Paul E. Zell, "Exegetical Brief: Ephesians 5:10 and 1 Peter 1:7—'Tested and Approved,'" *WLQ* 105, no. 1 (2008): 52.

6. George Milligan, *St. Paul's Epistles to the Thessalonians: The Greek Text, with Introduction and Notes* (London: Macmillan, 1908), 18.

7. Walter Grundmann, "Δοκιμάζω," *TDNT* 2:256.

8. Grundmann, *TDNT* 2:257.

9. Grundmann, *TDNT* 2:256.

10. Maurice Jones, "I and II Thessalonians," in *A New Commentary on Holy Scripture, Including the Apocrypha*, ed. Charles Gore, Henry Leighton Goudge, and Alfred Guillaume (New York: Macmillan, 1942), 1370.

11. Rajendra Avasthi, "Elections and Electioneering in Ancient Greece," *IJPS* 19, no. 3 (1958): 276.

12. Avasthi, "Elections and Electioneering," 276.

The choice of individuals for public office morphed to focus primarily on one's ability to perform and one's character,[13] whether one was "fit for election to a public office."[14] For instance, Lysias writes concerning Alcibiades, "I do not believe, gentlemen of the jury, that you desire to hear any excuse for the action of those who have resolved to accuse Alcibiades: for from the outset he has shown himself so unworthy of the citizenship that it is the duty of anyone, even in the absence of a personal wrong suffered at his hands, to regard him none the less as an enemy because of the general tenor of his life."[15] Lysias considered Alcibiades unfit for citizenship but also for public service. Magistrates were able to enter office only having undergone what they called a *dokimasia*, or "the test."[16] In Athenian procedures, the *dokimasia*, which is often translated as "vetting," entailed scrutinizing if a candidate had the requisite qualifications for the office they desired to enter, followed by witnesses and counterwitnesses, and finally a vote.[17] Avasthi states, "This was deemed good since it kept back the unworthy—undutiful sons, bad soldiers, bad tax-payers and the enemies of democracy."[18] The conclusion of the vetting was then followed by what we might call today the swearing in.[19]

The Athenians did not envision a dichotomy between one's private life and one's public life. A failure in one's private life was considered detrimental to their public life, since "these activities were considered to be signs that a man had weak judgement or a poor moral character, so that any advice which he gave to his fellow-citizens was likely to be unreliable or immoral."[20] Douglas Macdowell states, "They were simply thinking that men who conducted their personal affairs badly, in certain ways, were not fit to tell the Athenians how to conduct their public affairs."[21] For our purposes, it should be noted that even though "the demos sought the sanction and approval of the god, . . . the god was debarred from undertaking any initiative except at the express invitation of the demos."[22]

---

13. Avasthi, "Elections and Electioneering," 277.

14. Milligan, *Thessalonians*, 18; cf. Plato, *Leg.* 6.765C–D.

15. Lysias, *Or.* 14.1 (W. R. M. Lamb, trans., *Lysias*, LCL 244 [Cambridge, MA: Harvard University Press, 1930], 339).

16. Avasthi, "Elections and Electioneering," 279.

17. Douglas M. Macdowell, "The Athenian Procedure of *Dokimasia* of Orators," in *Symposion 2001: Papers on Greek and Hellenistic Legal History (Evanston, Illinois, September 5–8, 2001)*, ed. R. W. Wallace and M. Gagarin (Vienna: Verlag der Österreichischen Akademie der Wissenschaften, 2005), 79. See Aristotle, *Ath. pol.* 55.

18. Avasthi, "Elections and Electioneering," 280.

19. See Aristotle, *Ath. pol.* 55.

20. Macdowell, "Athenian Procedure," 81.

21. Macdowell, "Athenian Procedure," 87.

22. R. S. J. Garland, "Religious Authority in Archaic and Classical Athens," *ABSA* 79 (1984): 120.

We can see here the difference between what Paul envisioned in his own *dokimasia* vis-à-vis that of ancient Greece. Whereas in ancient Greece, "the principle was that the 'demos' must govern,"[23] in Paul's perspective, God was to govern in matters of who was to represent him. Beyond public officials who entered public service, the closest parallel for our case is the priesthood. Robert Garland states concerning the priesthood, "No qualifications seem to have been necessary for the office of priest, other than those of a purely external nature, though the conferment of office upon those entering democratic priesthoods was probably subject to their undergoing a satisfactory *dokimasia*."[24]

The common crimes that would disqualify a *dokimasia* include maltreatment of parents, failure to perform military duty, the charge of prostitution, or being reckless with one's inheritance.[25] It is these crimes that an accuser would bring before the assembly as evidence of poor judgment and could bar one from assuming public office.

Ancient Greece provides us with a background for the word *dokimazō*. The use of the *dokimasia* ensures that only worthy candidates rise up the ranks to occupy public office. Although the use of the *dokimasia* started off with a religious connotation, the *dokimasia* became one that was conducted by the *demos* with very limited participation of the gods. We will see that this is a critical difference from what we see in Paul. He moves his *dokimasia* from the human realm back to the divine realm, where it belongs.

Tested and Approved by God

First Thessalonians 2:4 is part of 1 Thessalonians 2:1–16, which has as its focus the "motives and conduct of Paul and his co-workers during their past visit" (vv. 1–12) and also "the response of the Thessalonian Christians to that visit" (vv. 13–16).[26] Verses 3 and 4, where Paul uses "antithetical statements (not *x* but *y*),"[27] are related. Paul states, "For our appeal does not spring from deceit or impure motives or trickery" (2:3 NRSV). This statement is followed by "but" (*alla*) in verse 4, which contrasts what Paul and his coworkers did. Paul speaks about how he and his coworkers have been "approved [*dedokimasmetha*] by God to be entrusted with the message of the gospel, even so we speak, not to please mortals, but to please God who tests [*dokimazonti*] our hearts" (2:4 NRSV). Both *dedokimasmetha* and *dokimazonti* are derived from the same

23. Avasthi, "Elections and Electioneering," 280.
24. Garland, "Religious Authority," 119.
25. Macdowell, "Athenian Procedure," 86.
26. Jeffrey A. D. Weima, *1–2 Thessalonians*, BECNT (Grand Rapids: Baker Academic, 2014), 126.
27. Weima, *1–2 Thessalonians*, 126.

root word *dokimazō*, which Paul's audience would have recognized, given its use in the city assemblies.

Jeffrey Weima notes that elsewhere (except 1 Tim. 3:10) *dokimazō* is used in the active voice with persons or people being the subject doing the examining.[28] This usage is consistent with what we have seen in ancient Greece with the *dokimasia* of orators. In this passage, however, it is in the passive voice, and God is the agent who examines Paul and his colleagues.[29] *Dedokimasmetha* is in the perfect tense, as Leon Morris notes: "The verb *approved* means first 'to test' and then to approve as a result of the test, and the perfect tense used here conveys the meaning that the approval continues."[30]

God is the one doing the approving or the examining of the candidates. Gary Shogren states, "All that pertains to salvation, including its proclamation, begins and ends with divine intervention. God tests and approves those true envoys who aid its spread around the world."[31] God is the one who deemed them worthy to be proclaimers of the gospel, and he is the one who continues "to judge their words, their actions, and their very hearts."[32] Unlike public officials or philosophers who were examined by the boule to determine their fitness to enter public life or engage in philosophy, God is the subject, testing and approving Paul and his coworkers.[33]

Entrusted with the Gospel

The reason for the testing is that the preachers could be "entrusted with . . . the gospel" (*pisteuthēnai to euangelion*, 1 Thess. 2:4 NRSV).[34] Even though *pisteuō* has the meaning of "to believe," BDAG notes that it can also have the sense of "to entrust."[35] The prerequisite for being entrusted with the gospel has to do with the conduct of the messengers. I have argued elsewhere that

---

28. Weima, *1–2 Thessalonians*, 136.

29. Weima, *1–2 Thessalonians*, 136.

30. Leon L. Morris, *1 and 2 Thessalonians: An Introduction and Commentary*, TNTC 13 (Downers Grove, IL: InterVarsity, 2015), 54. See also G. K. Beale, *1–2 Thessalonians*, IVPNTC (Downers Grove, IL: InterVarsity, 2003), 67; Paul Ellingworth and Eugene A. Nida, *A Translator's Handbook on the Letter to the Hebrews*, HFTS (New York: United Bible Societies, 1983), 25–26; Gene L. Green, *The Letters to the Thessalonians*, PNTC (Grand Rapids: Eerdmans, 2002), 121.

31. Gary S. Shogren, *1 and 2 Thessalonians*, ZECNT (Grand Rapids: Zondervan, 2013), 93.

32. D. Michael Martin, *1, 2 Thessalonians*, NAC 33 (Nashville: Broadman & Holman, 1995), 73.

33. Abraham J. Malherbe, *The Letters to the Thessalonians: A New Translation with Introduction and Commentary*, AB 32B (New York: Doubleday, 2000), 141.

34. Charles A. Wanamaker, *The Epistles to the Thessalonians: A Commentary on the Greek Text*, NIGTC (Grand Rapids: Eerdmans, 1990), 95.

35. BDAG, 818.

Paul's and his coworkers' conduct was cruciform.[36] God entrusts his gospel only to those whom "he has examined and found worthy."[37] The gospel messengers need to embody the gospel they proclaim. Charles Wanamaker states, "He [Paul, along with his coworkers] spoke (and acted) as one approved by God for his task."[38] Related to the conduct of the messengers is their moral authority to offer moral instructions. Based on God's examination, which entailed their integrity and purity of motive, Paul and his coworkers were able to present themselves as models for the Thessalonians.[39]

The issue of integrity connects verses 3 and 4. It is the vices that are castigated in verse 3 that the ministers of the gospel should not entertain.[40] Seyoon Kim eloquently states that the "message, the gospel, stands or falls with the integrity of its preacher. . . . *Therefore* it is absolutely necessary for him to defend his integrity."[41] Yet Paul was aware that ultimately the gospel rests on not his conduct but "God's evaluation of his ministry."[42] The source of the gospel is divine; therefore, those who proclaim it cannot call themselves. God has to choose them and tests them prior to entrusting them with the gospel.[43] John Chrysostom paraphrases what Paul is saying in verse 4 thus: "It is a proof of our virtue, that we are entrusted with the Gospel; if there had been anything bad in us, God would not have approved us."[44] F. F. Bruce notes that the gospel "could be neutralized by conduct on the preachers' part which was inconsistent with its character or unworthy of the God whose gospel it was."[45] Psalm 26:1–7 makes a connection between walking in integrity and declaring God's wondrous deeds, as well as being tested and vindicated by God. The connection between holy living and proclamation of God's wonderful deeds is undeniable.[46]

Paul further states that their proclamation of the gospel is predicated on the fact that they have been tested, approved, and entrusted with the gospel. In his comment *houtōs laloumen* ("even so we speak," NRSV), the verb is a present tense, signifying that the ongoing proclamation of

---

36. Gift Mtukwa, "Paul's Cruciform Mission in Thessalonica: The Shape of Incarnational Ministry," *Didache* 17, no. 2 (2018): 1–14.

37. Weima, *1–2 Thessalonians*, 136–37.

38. Wanamaker, *Thessalonians*, 96.

39. Wanamaker, *Thessalonians*, 95–96.

40. Malherbe, *Thessalonians*, 140–41.

41. Seyoon Kim, "Paul's Entry (Εισοδος) and the Thessalonians' Faith (1 Thessalonians 1–3)," *NTS* 51, no. 4 (2005): 540.

42. Shogren, *1 and 2 Thessalonians*, 95.

43. Morris, *1 and 2 Thessalonians*, 63.

44. John Chrysostom, *Hom. 1 Thess.* 2.3–4 (*NPNF*[1] 13:329).

45. F. F. Bruce, *1 & 2 Thessalonians*, WBC 45 (Waco: Word, 1982), 28.

46. Shogren, *1 and 2 Thessalonians*, 95.

the gospel is based not on the qualifications of the ministers but on their approval as messengers of God. The verb "we speak" (*laloumen*) "refers to their evangelistic proclamation (as in 1:8; 2:2, 16). In the Greek text this declaration is placed after the statement about God's approval and commission. The heralds had carried out the mission for which God had commissioned them."[47]

Paul has the law of the *dokimasia* of orators in mind as he speaks about the proclamation of the good news. In ancient Greece, one who made a speech at the assembly (*ekklēsia*) was challenged by another citizen, and until a *dokimasia* was conducted, he stood forbidden from addressing the assembly.[48] Paul counters that his approval to speak has divine sanction. However, unlike the law of the *dokimasia* of orators, which focused on past behavior,[49] Paul's *dokimasia* includes his present conduct as well. For Paul, this is not a way to avoid human scrutiny since, even when a real *dokimasia* is conducted on him, he will still be blameless. He talks about this fact later in this passage when he says, "You are witnesses, and God also, how pure, upright, and blameless our conduct was toward you believers" (1 Thess. 2:10 NRSV). Paul demonstrates that he is familiar with how a *dokimasia* works and that he has passed.

Pleasing God, Not People

Paul references the manner in which he went about speaking the gospel—he did not desire to please people but aimed to please God. The participle *areskontes* comes from *areskō*, which conveys "the action of trying to please" someone.[50] Speech that pleases others often "originates from deceit, impure motive, or trickery (2:3) and that in a self-serving manner is interested only in winning the favor of others."[51] Abraham Malherbe informs us: "Genuine philosophers insistently claimed that they did not seek to please people, particularly the crowds, in order to gain reputation or glory (*doxa*) from them. . . . To do so, they claimed, would be to behave like flatterers, the very antithesis to the frank speaker."[52] Paul tried to distinguish himself from the charlatans who went around teaching their philosophical ideas for money. Such philosophers ran away at the first sign of trouble, which some might see in his flight from Thessalonica.

---

47. Green, *Thessalonians*, 120.
48. Macdowell, "Athenian Procedure," 82.
49. Macdowell, "Athenian Procedure," 82.
50. Werner Foerster, "Ἀρέσκω," *TDNT* 10:455.
51. Weima, *1–2 Thessalonians*, 137.
52. Malherbe, *Thessalonians*, 141.

Paul's policy had social and economic ramifications.[53] The temptation to make the message inoffensive to patrons was real. Philosophers had to find ways of meeting their daily needs, and the easiest was to be a household philosopher and get support from a patron. Paul's insistence on manual work provides evidence that he did not want to be a household philosopher.[54] As Shogren observes, "An apostle with the prudence not to cause offense might have attracted patronage, prestige for his message, a pleasant hall in which to teach it, and a well-earned respite from manual labor."[55] One would never teach anything that would be offensive to the patron who pays one's upkeep.

When not referencing speech, the idea of "pleasing" (*areskō*) describes well-to-do citizens who, through their public service, have received honor from the city.[56] Yet for Paul it was clear that "the fundamental motivation in their ministry was to please God rather than people" (cf. Gal. 1:10).[57] For Paul, "those who endeavor to obtain human favor are not influenced by an upright conscience and do nothing from the heart."[58] As Malherbe has noted, "With the goal of doing everything for God's glory (*doxa*), not his own, he can nevertheless say that he attempts to please all people, seeking their advantage (*symphoron*), not his own (1 Cor. 10:31–33; cf. 9:19–23)."[59]

God the Heart Examiner

Toward the end of 1 Thessalonians 2:4, Paul speaks about God, who "tests" or "examines" (*dokimazonti*) the heart. Thus, "it is a probing which is done with the full expectation that whatever is under scrutiny will be approved."[60] Even though the testing is mentioned after the approval, for Paul the approval comes after the scrutiny or the test. Nijay Gupta states, "They were thoroughly inspected by the God who knows and sees all and they were found responsible as trustees of the truth."[61]

53. Shogren, *1 and 2 Thessalonians*, 94.

54. Gift Mtukwa, *Work and Community in the Thessalonian Correspondence: An African Communal Reading of Paul's Work Exhortations* (Carlisle, UK: Langham Creative Projects, 2021), 134–200.

55. Shogren, *1 and 2 Thessalonians*, 94.

56. Paul Ellingworth and Eugene Albert Nida, *A Handbook on Paul's Letters to the Thessalonians*, UBSHS (New York: United Bible Societies, 1976), 26.

57. Green, *Thessalonians*, 121.

58. Jean Calvin, *1, 2 Thessalonians*, ed. Alister McGrath and J. I. Parker (Wheaton: Crossway, 1999), 26.

59. Malherbe, *Thessalonians*, 141.

60. Knute Larson and Max E. Anders, *I & II Thessalonians, I & II Timothy, Titus, Philemon*, HNTC (Nashville: Broadman & Holman, 2000), 23.

61. Nijay K. Gupta, *1–2 Thessalonians: A New Covenant Commentary*, NCCS (Cambridge: Lutterworth, 2017), 53.

Translation Issues for 1 Thessalonians 2:4 in the Shona Bible

Shona is a language spoken predominantly in Zimbabwe. In Shona, three words are used by different translations to translate the Greek words *dedoki-masmetha/dokimazonti*. These words are *kutendiwa* ("to be believed," Shona Bible 1949/2002), *ketenderwa* ("approval," Bhaibheri Dvene MuChiShona Chanhasi [BDSC]), and *kuonekwa* ("to be seen," Bhaibhiri Idzva MuChi-Shona [SCLB]). The word *kutendiwa* does not adequately convey the aspect of testing and approval. In earlier periods, this word may have communicated this; however, in the modern era, it is not commonly used. *Ketenderwa*, on the other hand, has the connotation of approval to do something, including the aspect of being tested to see if one is the right person for the job. The Greek participle *dokimazonti* is always translated with the Shona word *anoedza* (tempt). The word *anoedza* or *kuedzwa* (tempt) is the same one that is used to translate the Greek *peirasmos* (temptation). A more positive Shona word would be *bvunzo* (test), rather than *kuedzwa* (tempt), which is negative in its orientation.

The Greek word "entrusted" (*pisteuthēnai*) is rendered with the Shona word *kukodzera*, which has the connotation of being "worthy" or "appro-priate." This translation is suitable in the sense that the entrusting is not being done indiscriminately but occurs after an investigation to see if one is worthy to be entrusted with the word of God. "The gospel" (Grk: *to euange-lion*) is translated with two phrases: *Vhangeri* (Shona Bible 1949) and *Shoko rakanaka* (SCLB). *Vhangeri* transliterates the Greek *euangelion* and, given Christian usage of this word through the years, is now understood as the word that expresses the "good news." In contrast, *Shoko rakanaka* literally translates as "good words," as in "good advice," but loses the aspect of the "good news."

The Shona Bibles clearly convey the fact that it is God who does the *kutenderwa* (entrusting). The genitive phrase "by God" (*hypo tou theou*) is captured by the Shona *naMwari* (by God). The Shona Bible of 1949, which was revised in 2002 (SNA2002), translates "thus / so we speak" (*houtōs laloumen*) with the phrase *ndizvo zvatinotaura*. The problem with the phrase is that it translates as "that is what we say" rather than "so we speak." Paul is reporting not *what* they say but *that they speak* because they have been entrusted with the gospel. The SCLB, on the other hand, accurately translates the same phrase with *naizvozvo tinotaura* (so we speak). "Not as" (*ouch hōs*) is translated as *tisingaiti kuti* ("not trying to," Shona Bible 1949), *kwete kuti* ("not to," SCLB), and *hatisi* ("we are not," BDSC). All translations do justice to the negative particle. However, the BDSC adds *kuedza*, "trying," which adds something not in the Greek. The apostles were not *trying* not to please people; rather, they were *not* pleasing people.

Nearly all translate the last Greek phrase, "not to please people but God" (*ouch hōs anthrōpois areskontes alla theō*) the same way: *kuti tifadze vanhu, asi kuti tifadze Mwari*. The variation comes with the last phrase, "who tests our hearts" (*tō dokimazonti tas kardias hēmōn*), which is translated *anoedza mwoyo yedu* in the Shona Bible 1949 and BDSC, while the SCLB says *anoongorora zvatiri* (who inspects what we are [in the inside]). The first two have gone with a literal translation, whereas the SCLB opts for dynamic equivalence, which captures the essence of *tas kardias*.

In summary, how the message is translated influences whether or not it is clearly understood. Using words that are not close to the concept being conveyed by the biblical words results in confusion. When a word has various nuances, those need to be adequately conveyed so that the meaning does not get lost. I therefore propose that 1 Thessalonians 2:4 be translated as follows: *Asi sezvatakatenderwa naMwari kuti takakodzera kuti tipihwe Vhangeri, naizvozvo tinotaura kwete kuti tifadze vanhu as kuti tifadze Mwari anoongorora zvatiri* ("Just as we were approved by God to be entrusted with the gospel of God, so we speak not to please people but to please God, who inspects our hearts"). This, then, has further implications.

Implications for Ministers of the Gospel

We began by examining what has come to be known in Kenya as the Shakahola massacre. A number of such massacres have been committed around the world by people who claimed to be representatives of God. First Thessalonians 2:4 has much to offer in terms of how ministers should be approved by God and the church. The issue of integrity is a critical test of whether someone is "tested and approved by God." God's focus in testing is on the heart and not the minister's performance.[62] In a world in which ministers are often judged by how talented they are, this is a stark contrast where the focus is on who someone *is* rather than what they *do*. Just because a preacher is gifted does not necessarily mean that God approves him or her. The church needs to go beyond what people see to what cannot be seen.

Ministers are ultimately accountable to God; as a result, Christian ministry should be God centered.[63] John R. W. Stott has observed, "To be accountable

---

62. Warren Woolsey, *1 & 2 Thessalonians: A Bible Commentary in the Wesleyan Tradition* (Indianapolis: Wesleyan Publishing House, 1997), 37.

63. John R. W. Stott, *The Message of 1 & 2 Thessalonians: The Gospel and the End of Time*, ed. J. A. Motyer and Derek Tidball (Leicester, UK: Inter-Varsity, 1991), 50.

to him is to be delivered from the tyranny of human criticism."[64] The implication for the church is that it should desist from calling people to ministry. The call to ministry must first of all come from God. The first approval needs to be that of God, and the church needs to approve candidates upon determining that God has already approved them and entrusted them with his gospel. We should be able to say what Grundmann says of Paul in reference to 1 Thessalonians 2:4: "The counsel of God, which sifts the hearts, has found them fit for the evangelical office. Their apostolate is grounded in the sifting counsel of God, and in their discharge of it they know [they] are under His searching eye."[65] Unless we can say this, we should not be too quick to recruit ministers.

Not only should ministers not be called by the church, but they should also not call themselves. In Acts, God is known as the "heart-knower" (*kardiognōsta*, Acts 1:24) and as such he inspects each person to see if he or she is the right candidate for the assignment.[66] "Paul did not choose his work; God selected him for the high calling of proclaiming the gospel."[67] In 1 Thessalonians 2:1–12, Paul categorically denies the charge of making the gospel suit its hearers. Those who are not called by God become flatterers who are interested only in what they can get. As a result, "Paul's standard goes far beyond being true to oneself; he must remain true to God, or else he could cast away the hope for God's power in his work."[68]

In a world in which people are interested in new ideas, we should note that Paul did not formulate the gospel; it was entrusted to him.[69] Paul's task was to hand it over the same way it had been handed to him. Consequently, "Paul was a steward of the message that had been entrusted to him by Jesus Christ, so he was constrained to preach it faithfully,"[70] D. Michael Martin is right to note that "a person obligated to speak for one who can judge the heart would be foolish to change the message in order to please the hearers."[71] Paul was capable of tailoring his message to the audience he was speaking to, as he says in 1 Corinthians 9:22: "I have become all things to all people, that I might by all means save some" (NRSV). Yet this was not unqualified. Paul follows this statement with "I do it all for the sake of the gospel, so that I may

64. Stott, *Message of 1 & 2 Thessalonians*, 50–51.

65. Grundmann, *TDNT* 2:257.

66. David Ewert, "1–2 Thessalonians," in *Evangelical Commentary on the Bible*, vol. 3 of *Baker Reference Library* (Grand Rapids: Baker, 1995), 1073.

67. Thomas L. Constable, J. F. Walvoord, and R. B. Zuck, "1 Thessalonians," in *The Bible Knowledge Commentary: An Exposition of the Scriptures* (Wheaton: Victor Books, 1985), 2:694.

68. Shogren, *1 and 2 Thessalonians*, 94.

69. Ewert, "1–2 Thessalonians," 1072.

70. Richard D. Phillips, *1 and 2 Thessalonians* (Phillipsburg, NJ: P&R, 2015), 192.

71. Martin, *1, 2 Thessalonians*, 73.

share in its blessings" (9:23 NRSV). As Weima has noted, "This concern for others, however, was motivated only out of a genuine desire that unbelievers would be saved, and it in no way came at the expense of compromising the truth of the gospel."[72]

Conclusion

We set out to understand Paul's use of *dokimazō* and its cognates, and we suggested that Paul was familiar with how it was used in the Greco-Roman world. However, instead of focusing on qualifications, Paul focuses on integrity. Rather than people approving his right to speak as in the *dokimazō* of orators, Paul invokes God as the one who has tested and approved him. The *dokimazō* Paul has gone through can be verified by Paul's audience; therefore, Paul is not under public scrutiny. In fact, he raises the bar by invoking God since God is able to test hearts, something that no *dokimazō* can do, and is thereby familiar with people's motives. First Thessalonians 2:4 has much to offer in terms of ensuring that only women and men called by God can assume the role of minister of the gospel. This will reduce abuses that we have witnessed like the recent Shakahola massacre in Kenya.

72. Weima, *1–2 Thessalonians*, 137; see also Bruce, *1 & 2 Thessalonians*, 28.

15

The Pastoral Epistles and Training the Younger Generation on Ancient Crete

LYN M. KIDSON

Crete was renowned for its cities—it is described in the *Iliad* as "a land of a hundred cities" (*Krētēn hekatompolin*).[1] The writer of the Letter to Titus, identified as Paul, reminds Titus that he was left in Crete to put things in order and "appoint elders in every town [*kata polin*]" (Titus 1:5).[2] In this chapter we are exploring the theme of "household" in the Pastoral Epistles through the lens of Titus 2:2–6. In these verses we will consider the role of the older men and older women, and their relationship with the younger women and the younger men "in the church" on Crete. However, we must bear in mind that the word "church" (*ekklēsia*) does not appear in Titus, as it does in 1 Timothy, where it is closely connected to the "household of God" (1 Tim. 3:15). What we have is not a meeting but a multigenerational extended family, "a people of [God's] own" (Titus 2:14), spread across the island and coming

The author wishes to thank Aboriginal Christian leader Brooke Prentis for her assistance and advice in writing the conclusion of this chapter.

1. Paula Perlman, "One Hundred-Citied Crete and the 'Cretan ΠΟΛΙΤΕΙΑ,'" *CP* 87, no. 3 (1992): 193–205. See Homer, *The Iliad*, 2.649.

2. All Scripture quotations in this chapter, unless otherwise indicated, are from the NRSV.

together in many households in many "towns."[3] The population of Crete was, and still is, an ancient people that can trace its lineage into the Neolithic era, complemented by successive waves of migrants. In some ways Crete is like Australia: the home of one of the most ancient living cultures in the world. So we will be taking a long historical perspective in interpreting Titus. After this we will then consider how these instructions relate to contemporary Australian society, and in turn how Australia's own indigenous culture can shed light on the reading of Titus.

Authorship of the Pastoral Epistles

When writing on the Pastoral Epistles the inevitable question about authorship comes into view. The obvious answer is that Paul, the apostle, is the letter writer, writing to Timothy and Titus. However, since the nineteenth century biblical scholars have raised doubts over the Pauline authorship of these letters. F. C. Baur (1835) and H. J. Holtzmann (1880) noted the similarities in vocabulary and themes between 1 Timothy, 2 Timothy, and Titus, so they made the case that all three letters were written by the same author but were written pseudonymously. They identified the author as a second-generation Christian pastor.[4] Many imagine that if the Pastoral Epistles were written by a pseudonymous author then this means that the writer was being deceptive.[5] Now, authors write with a pseudonym for all kinds of reasons.[6] Indeed, there was a great tradition of writing in character for educational and "religious" reasons.[7] Both Greeks and Jews practiced this fictive form of writing, so we cannot rule out this possibility.[8] Given this, it is best to take the author as someone writing in the first or second century who is standing in a Pauline

---

3. Similarly, 1 Pet. 2:9–10; 2 Pet. 1:10–11.

4. F. C. Baur, *Die sogenannten Pastoralbriefe des Apostels Paulus aufs neue kritisch unteruscht* (Tübingen: Stuttgart, 1835); H. J. Holtzmann, *Die Pastoralbriefe, kritisch und exegetisch behandelt* (Leipzig: Engelmann, 1880). For more detail, see Lyn M. Kidson, "Pastoral Epistles," in *Dictionary of Paul and His Letters*, 2nd ed., ed. Scot McKnight, Lynn Cohick, and Nijay Gupta (Downers Grove, IL: InterVarsity, 2023), 755–96.

5. Terry L. Wilder, *Pseudonymity, the New Testament and Deception: An Inquiry into Intention and Reception* (Lanham, MD: University Press of America, 2004), 296–335; Bart D. Ehrman, *The New Testament: A Historical Introduction to the Early Christian Writings*, 6th ed. (New York: Oxford University Press, 2016), 443–44, 453–56.

6. Patricia A. Rosenmeyer, *Ancient Epistolary Fictions: The Letter in Greek Literature* (Cambridge: Cambridge University Press, 2001), passim.

7. Rosenmeyer, *Ancient Epistolary Fictions*, 196–99.

8. Abraham J. Malherbe, ed., *The Cynic Epistles: A Study Edition*, SBLSBS (Missoula, MT: Scholars Press, 1977), passim; James H. Charlesworth, "Introduction for the General Reader," in *The Old Testament Pseudepigrapha*, ed. James H. Charlesworth (Peabody, MA: Hendrickson, 1983), xxi–xxxiv.

tradition. This doesn't rule out Paul as the author, but it allows us to consider the historical evidence beyond the middle of the first century.[9]

Place and Audience of the Pastoral Epistles

Positing a pseudonymous author does not rule out the possibility that the audience of Titus is actually on Crete. This is because the Cretan setting for Titus is quite perplexing. It is central to the dramatic story of Paul's shipwreck in Acts that Paul's ship sails to the south of the island but is unable to make landfall (Acts 27:1–15). Instead, it is blown by a violent storm and wrecked on the island of Malta (28:1). If the Letter to Titus were entirely fictional, then Malta would seem a more logical location, or a church in Macedonia, which was more closely associated with Titus (2 Cor. 2:13; 7:6). Therefore, what we could surmise regarding the audience of the Pastoral Epistles is that Timothy is in Ephesus and Titus is on Crete.

Purpose of the Pastoral Epistles

In my research I found that 1 Timothy acts more like an occasional letter, addressing a specific set of conditions facing the church in question.[10] Many scholars consider the letter a church order manual, setting out general instructions for how to run a church.[11] I do not think this is the case. I have argued in numerous places that the letter's primary function is to deal with the false teachers and their ascetic program.[12] All the instructions belonging to the sound, good educational program (1 Tim. 1:10; 4:13, 16; 5:17; Titus 1:9; 2:1, 7) are in response to this other, ascetic program.[13] For instance, the false teachers are prohibiting marriage (1 Tim. 4:3), whereas in the Pauline program the leaders are to be married and bear children (1 Tim. 2:15; 3:1–13; 5:9–10; Titus 1:5–6; 2:1–5). I would like to suggest that this ascetic program in Timothy is the same program troubling the church on Crete.[14] The short letter of Titus may act as a cover letter for 1 Timothy, introducing and making

9. Lyn M. Kidson, *Persuading Shipwrecked Men: Rhetorical Strategies of 1 Timothy 1*, WUNT 526 (Tübingen: Mohr Siebeck, 2020), 37–54.

10. Lyn Kidson, "1 Timothy: An Administrative Letter," *EC* 5, no. 1 (2014): 97–116.

11. Martin Dibelius and Hans Conzelmann, *The Pastoral Epistles*, trans. Philip Buttolph and Adela Yarbro, Hermeneia (Philadelphia: Fortress, 1972), 5.

12. Kidson, *Persuading*, 103–38, 232–34; Kidson, "Naming 1 Timothy 3.16b: A 'Hymn' by Another Name?," *NTS* 69 (2023): 43–56; Kidson, "Pastoral Epistles"; Kidson, "Fasting, Bodily Care, and the Widows of 1 Timothy 5:3–15," *EC* 11, no. 2 (2020): 191–205.

13. Kidson, *Persuading*, 232–34 and 269–73.

14. Philip H. Towner, *The Letters to Timothy and Titus*, NICNT (Grand Rapids: Eerdmans, 2006), 41–47.

available to the church on Crete the educational program set out in 1 Timothy.[15] Thus Titus needs to be read in conjunction with 1 Timothy, but since it is contextualized to Crete, the interpreter must read it against the local Cretan conditions.

A Short History of Crete and Its Housing

The island of Crete encapsulates the very ancient history of the Mediterranean basin. Crete has had continual human occupation since Neolithic times.[16] The Bronze Age saw the rise of the indigenous Minoan civilization, followed by the Greek-speaking Mycenaean colonizers.[17] These civilizations used a written script in their economic and administrative activities known as Linear A (ca. fifteenth century BC, Minoan) and Linear B (1400–1200 BC, Mycenaean).[18] At present we are unable to read Linear A, but in the frescos from buildings described as palaces, we see depictions of large corporate activities out of doors. In these, groups of women are depicted actively engaged in ritual activity while large crowds of men look on in the background.[19] There are intense scholarly debates over whether Minoan culture was matriarchal or if the Mycenaean society was ruled by a king.[20] Some scholars have utilized the literature from Classical Greece to argue that Cretan society was similar to Sparta, which was more an oligarchy.[21]

General housing in the Minoan-Mycenaean period tended to have a large central room with a column, with other rooms radiating off this. Privacy did not seem to be a priority.[22] Evidence from the Classical and Hellenistic

15. Jerome D. Quinn, *The Letter to Titus*, AB 35 (New York: Doubleday, 1990), 19–20.

16. Tristan Carter et al., "The Cretan Mesolithic in Context: New Data from Livari Skiadi (Se Crete)," *DocPraeh* 43 (2016): 87–102.

17. John Bintliff, *The Complete Archaeology of Greece: From Hunter-Gatherers to the 20th Century A.D.* (Chichester, UK: Wiley, 2012), 49–50, 123–54.

18. Barbara A. Olsen, *Women in Mycenaean Greece: The Linear B Tablets from Pylos and Knossos* (London: Taylor & Francis, 2014), 32–33.

19. Jan Driessen, "Chercher la femme: Identifying Minoan Gender Relations in the Built Environment," in *Minoan Realities: Approaches to Images, Architecture, and Society in the Aegean Bronze Age*, ed. Diamantis Panagiotopoulos and Ute Günkel-Maschek (Louvain-la-Neuve: Presses universitaires de Louvain, 2012), 141–64.

20. Joan M. Cichon, "Matriarchy in Minoan Crete: A Perspective from Archaeomythology and Modern Matriarchal Studies" (PhD diss., California Institute of Integral Studies, 2013), 52–63.

21. Ruth Westgate, "House and Society in Classical and Hellenistic Crete: A Case Study in Regional Variation," *AJA* 111, no. 3 (2007): 450; Perlman, "One Hundred-Citied Crete," 200.

22. Louise A. Hitchcock, "Fluid and Flexible: Revisiting the Vernacular Tradition on Bronze Age Crete, Thera, and Cyprus," in Στεγα: *The Archaeology of Houses and Households in Ancient Crete*, ed. Kevin T. Glowacki and Natalia Vogeikoff-Brogan (Princeton: American School of Classical Studies at Athens, 2011), 233–54.

periods suggests that the men and women lived relatively separate lives; the men ate regularly in an *andreion*, a "men's club," and women controlled the household activities.[23] Unlike in Greek cities, Cretan domestic housing did not have separate women's quarters or a men's *andreion* at the front of the house.[24] Hellenistic Cretan housing tended to be on a simple linear pattern, with the main cooking and living quarters at the front of the house.[25] Domestic duties were carried out in the front room, as suggested by the archaeological finds, including fixed grinding stones, cooking hearths, fragments of pottery, and loom weights.[26] In a Greek house, these tasks were normally performed in the courtyard at the back of the house, out of sight from anyone in the street.[27] The overall impression is that women in Cretan society tended to live far more in the public eye than their Greek counterparts.[28]

Although there are some examples of Greek housing on Crete, the housing type stays consistently linear into the Roman era.[29] The Romans conquered Crete in 69 BC.[30] Some cities, like ancient Knossos, resisted, whereas Gortyn supported the Romans and for this reason became their administrative capital.[31] Roman Crete saw a surge in economic activity with the development of ports and roads across the island.[32] The island became an exporter of wine, along with other agricultural goods, and cemented its place as a transit port in the grain trade from North Africa.[33]

We can assume that Cretan housing built in the Hellenistic period continued to be occupied in the Roman era.[34] However, once the Roman administration became established, Roman-style housing began to be built in various

23. Bintliff, *Complete Archaeology*, 301; Westgate, "House," 451.

24. Westgate, "House," 426–27.

25. Westgate, "House," 434, 446, 452.

26. Westgate, "House," 447.

27. Westgate, "House," 426–32.

28. Westgate, "House," 439, 441, 447.

29. Westgate, "House," 446, 450.

30. I. F. Sanders, *Roman Crete: An Archaeological Survey and Gazetteer of Late Hellenistic, Roman and Early Byzantine Crete* (Warminster, UK: Aris & Phillips, 1982), 1.

31. Jane Francis and George W. M. Harrison, "Gortyn: First City of Roman Crete," *AJA* 107, no. 3 (2003): 487.

32. Rebecca J. Sweetman, "Domus, Villa, and Farmstead: The Globalization of Crete," in Glowacki and Vogeikoff-Brogan, Στέγα, 441–50; Scott C. Gallimore, "An Island Economy: Ierapetra and Crete in the Roman Empire" (PhD diss., State University of New York, 2011), 74–75, 109.

33. Sanders, *Roman Crete*, 32–35; Angelos Chaniotis, "Inscribed Instrumenta Domestica and the Economy of Hellenistic and Roman Crete," in *Making, Moving, and Managing: The New World of Ancient Economies*, ed. Z. Archibald, J. K. Davies, and V. Gabrielsen (Oxford: Oxbow, 2005), 101–2; Scott C. Gallimore, "Food Surplus and Archaeological Proxies: A Case Study from Roman Crete," *WA* 49 (2017): 138–50.

34. Westgate, "House," 446; Sweetman, "Domus," 446–47.

centers across the island.[35] This housing, both urban and rural villas, was for the more well-to-do and was more lavishly decorated than the traditional Cretan house.[36] Yet there was a certain continuity between the older style of Cretan housing and the Roman house. The doors of a Roman house were always open to the public, who could wait in the atrium to see the patriarch (or matriarch, if her husband was not available).[37] The inside of the house was designed to be seen into, and for this reason Roman women also lived in the public eye.[38] Smaller rooms off the atrium provided some private space to discuss business.[39] Formal dinners were given in the triclinium, a separate dining room, but not all meals were eaten there.[40] If nothing else, the ideal Roman house was flexible. The Roman house reflected the dignity of the man who owned and lived in it; it was a monument to his *dignitas*.[41] Furthermore, the installment of baths in many Cretan cities suggests that a Roman lifestyle, at least superficially, became very fashionable.[42] Conformity to Roman values was expected by the more well-to-do citizenry, as it was across the Roman Empire.[43] However, one suspects that aspects of ancient cultural life remained deeply rooted in Roman Cretan society.[44] For this reason, a multicultural perspective must be borne in mind when considering Titus.

Themes in the Pastoral Epistles

First Timothy and Titus share many similarities. Both are styled as administrative letters: they are playing a role in the management of a collective of churches. This administrative subgenre aligns neatly with the overarching metaphor of these letters: God as king in his household.[45] In 1 Timothy believers are instructed in "how one ought to behave in the household of God [*en*

35. Sweetman, "Domus," 441–50; Andrew Wallace-Hadrill, "The Social Structure of the Roman House," *Papers of the British School at Rome* 56 (1988): 43–97.

36. Sweetman, "Domus," 450; Westgate, "House," 448.

37. Wallace-Hadrill, "Social Structure," 46, 55–56, 81–83.

38. Wallace-Hadrill, "Social Structure," 50–52, 82–84.

39. Wallace-Hadrill, "Social Structure," 85.

40. Wallace-Hadrill, "Social Structure," 64, 92.

41. Andrew Bell, *Spectacular Power in the Greek and Roman City* (Oxford: Oxford University Press, 2004), 183.

42. Andreas N. Angelakis, Yannis Christodoulakos, and Vasileios A. Tzanakakis, "Roman Aqueducts in Crete, Greece: Learning from the Past," *Water* 13, no. 8 (2021), https://doi.org/10.3390/w13081069.

43. Sweetman, "Domus," 442.

44. Suggestive is the work of Martin P. Nilsson, *The Minoan-Mycenaean Religion and Its Survival in Greek Religion*, 2nd ed. (New York: Biblo & Tannen, 1970), passim.

45. Korinna Zamfir, "Is the Ekklēsia a Household (of God)? Reassessing the Notion of Οἶκος Θεοῦ in 1 Tim 3.15," *NTS* 60, no. 4 (2014): 511–28.

oikō theou]" (3:15). For any Greek reader in the East, this has connotations of the royal household of a god, and this impression is further enhanced in the closing doxology, which says, "[God,] who is the blessed and only Sovereign, the King of kings [*ho basileus tōn basileuontōn*] and Lord of lords" (6:15).[46] The royal "house" (*oikos*) refers not to a building but to the lineage and family of the king (Herodotus, *Hist.* 5.31; 6.9), his household staff, and his courtiers or "friends," who assist him in the management of his kingdom.[47] This could be summed up as the king's "whole house" (*holōn . . . tou oikou*).[48] As Korinna Zamfir argues, "The image of the sacred community as household appears very clearly in the conception of the universe as *oikos* and *polis* of God."[49] Zamfir goes on to make the case that "the paradigm ekklēsia [*oikos theou* of 1 Tim. 3:16] defines the community of Christ-believers as a public, sacred and cosmic space."[50] I would argue that Titus sets up this complex *polis*–royal *oikos* metaphor by introducing believers as God's "own people" (Titus 2:14), who, while they wait for the appearance of their "great God and Savior, Jesus Christ" (2:13), are to live lives imbued with the most idealized virtues of Greco-Roman citizenship (2:1–14).[51]

Overview of Titus as a Letter

Titus is a short letter in comparison to the other Pauline letters but is more in keeping with everyday letters written by ordinary people that survive (mostly in Egypt).[52] It opens with the expected salutation and prayer and closes by sending greetings, final instructions, and prayer, which are all conventional features of contemporary letters.[53] However, there are some extraordinary features, including the extended appellation of Paul. Normally in administrative letters, the appellation signals the writer's status and social position relative to the recipient.[54] Paul also uses this appellation of "an apostle . . . by the will of God" in the Corinthian correspondence, and this is repeated in Ephesians, Colossians, and 2 Timothy (with a slight extension). In 1 Timothy,

---

46. Zamfir, "Is the Ekklēsia a Household?," 524–26.
47. Charles B. Welles, *Royal Correspondence in the Hellenistic Period: A Study in Greek Epigraphy* (New Haven: Yale University Press, 1934), 106 (letter 22, lines 9 and 13).
48. Welles, *Royal Correspondence*, 265 (letter 65, line 18).
49. Zamfir, "Is the Ekklēsia a Household?," 524.
50. Zamfir, "Is the Ekklēsia a Household?," 527.
51. T. Christopher Hoklotubbe, *Civilized Piety: The Rhetoric of Pietas in the Pastoral Epistles and the Roman Empire* (Waco: Baylor University Press, 2017), 100–102.
52. E. Randolph Richards, *Paul and First-Century Letter Writing: Secretaries, Composition, and Collection* (Downers Grove, IL: InterVarsity, 2004), 122–33.
53. Richards, *Paul*, 127–39; Kidson, "1 Timothy," 105–7.
54. Kidson, *Persuading*, 70, 83–89.

this is modified by using "by the command," a phrase commonly used in Asia Minor when inscribing an epiphany of a god or gods.[55] In Titus the extended appellation is built on this phrase: "by the command of God our Savior" (Titus 1:3). An extended appellation occurs in Galatians (1:1), and this reinforces Paul's status as an apostle, which is under question in the churches in Galatia.[56] It reinforces Paul's response made in the body of the letter. Thus it is proposed here that the appellation in Titus is in response to the opponents addressed in the body of the letter.

There are four aspects to this appellation, which I suggest is a response to the "many rebellious people . . . teaching . . . what it is not right to teach" (Titus 1:10–11). Such people need to be silenced (1:11). It follows that Paul is "a slave" and "an apostle" in four aspects, beginning with "for the sake of the faith of God's elect" (1:1) and followed by the second aspect, "the knowledge of the truth" (1:1), the third, "in the hope of eternal life that God" (1:2), and the fourth, "in due time he revealed his word" (1:3).[57] In Titus it is difficult to grasp the content of the teaching, but 1:1–3 gives the reader some indication that it involves disputes about who is God's elect, what is knowledge of the truth, what is the hope of eternal life promised by God before the ages began, and the due time. The opponents are either Jews (1:10) or influenced by Jewish literature and commandments (1:14).[58] The opponents cause divisions (3:10) through "controversies, genealogies, dissensions, and quarrels about the law" (3:9). This reflects a similar pattern of factionalism and disputes about genealogies and the law in 1 Timothy (1:4, 6–7; 6:4–5). But these things are more the effect; the real nub of the problem seems to be with opponents who are arrogant, who are insistent that their instruction on how to live the Christ life is godly and pure (Titus 1:15) and that their knowledge is correct (1:16).[59] Philip Towner observes, "At the center of the false teachers' gnosis was the belief that the resurrection had already occurred" (1 Tim. 6:20–21; 2 Tim. 2:15–18).[60] This overrealized eschatology is met by the writer of the Pastoral Epistles with a sober response directing the sound instruction of Paul to life in this present age.[61] Though Towner demurs that the situation is less clear on Crete, there is certainly an emphasis on this "present age" situated

55. Kidson, *Persuading*, 89–97.

56. Kidson, *Persuading*, 86–87.

57. Cf. Towner, *Timothy and Titus*, 664.

58. Towner, *Timothy and Titus*, 705.

59. As with the opponents in 1 Timothy; see Kidson, *Persuading*, 218–20.

60. Philip H. Towner, "Gnosis and Realized Eschatology in Ephesus (of the Pastoral Epistles) and the Corinthian Enthusiasm," *JSNT* 10, no. 31 (1987): 104.

61. P. H. Towner, "The Present Age in the Eschatology of the Pastoral Epistles," *NTS* 32, no. 3 (1986): 444.

in "the salvation plan of God" (see Titus 2:11–13).[62] Yet for the writer of the Pastoral Epistles, the nature of salvation is unfinished, which draws him into the realm of ethics, since this "present age," as Towner describes it, is "the age in which a new manner of life is required. That is, in the author's opinion, how one will fare at the eschaton is integrally related to how one lives here and now; he implores a specific manner of conduct for the present by pointing to the second coming (. . . Titus 2. 1–13)."[63] Thus when we come to the "sound [instruction]" of Titus 2:1, we need to see the instructions about ethics from the perspective of this present age looking toward the parousia (3:4–7).[64] We are not to see these ethical instructions rooted in the Jewish teaching of the opponents (1:10, 14), since in terms of the Pastoral Epistles, continuing to argue on the terms of the opponents would continue to contribute to the quarreling and the dysfunction among the believers (3:2–3; 1 Tim. 1:6–7).

Focus on Titus 2:1–6

Titus 2 forms a unit opening with "but as for you, [tell]" (2:1) and closing with "[tell] these things" (2:15).[65] "These things" are consistent with "the sound [instruction]" (2:1, AT), which relates to instruction in the art of living rather than doctrine.[66] The adjective "sound" refers to that which is healthy, so what is being urged is healthy living between the community members rather than the sickness of factionalism and disputes.[67] "You tell" (2:1) begins a long, loosely connected series, which unpacks "things which suit the healthy instructions" (AT).[68] Those addressed are "older men" (2:2), "older women" (2:3), "young women" (2:4–5), "younger men" (2:6), and "slaves" (2:9–10). The instructions to slaves seem parenthetical to the first four groups, coming after a reminder to Titus to be a model "of good works in the instruction" (2:7, AT). Some scholars refer to these instructions as a household code, but the language is more reminiscent of the *polis* (the city).[69] Rather than addressing husbands and wives (cf. Eph. 5), the writer focuses on old men and young

---

62. Towner, "Present Age," 443–44.

63. Towner, "Present Age," 444.

64. Towner, "Present Age," 444; cf. *didaskalia* as "instruction," Kidson, *Persuading*, 112–20, 124.

65. Towner, *Timothy and Titus*, 717.

66. Cf. Kidson, *Persuading*, 120.

67. Abraham J. Malherbe, "Medical Imagery in the Pastoral Epistles," in *Light from the Gentiles: Hellenistic Philosophy and Early Christianity; Collected Essays, 1959–2012*, ed. Carl R. Holladay et al., NovTSup 150 (Boston: Brill, 2014), 117–34.

68. Cf. I. Howard Marshall, *The Pastoral Epistles*, with Philip H. Towner, ICC (London: T&T Clark, 1999), 237–38.

69. Martin Dibelius and Hans Conzelmann, *The Pastoral Epistles*, trans. P. Buttolph and A. Yarbro, Hermeneia (Philadelphia: Fortress, 1972), 139; Robert W. Wall, *1 & 2 Timothy and*

men. Their relationship forms a frame (Titus 2:2, 6) in which the older and younger women sit (2:3–5).

The audience of Titus would have a clear idea at which age the men became "older" and were no longer "younger." City constitutions usually assigned older men (fifty years or older) a place in a council (a *gerousia*).[70] In the Hellenistic period, these men would become generals in times of war, but usually they were advisers and the repositories of knowledge of the law and custom.[71] Plutarch, in *Whether an Old Man Should Engage in Public Affairs*, saw great advantage in the older men continuing to participate in civic affairs. He did not think it fitting for them to retire to the domestic sphere. "They possess [an advantage] in their caution and prudence and in the fact that they do not . . . dash headlong upon public affairs, dragging the mob along with them in confusion like the storm-tossed sea, but manage gently and moderately the matters which arise. And that is why States when they are in difficulties or in fear yearn for the rule of the elder men [*presbyterōn*]" (788C).[72] The older man, says Plutarch, is free from "love of contention, love of fame, the desire to be first and greatest, which is a disease most prolific of envy, jealousy, and discord" (788E).[73] Similarly in Titus, "the older men [are] to be temperate, serious, prudent [*sōphronas*], and sound in faith, in love, and in endurance" (2:2).[74] A man could be considered "young" from the age of eighteen until the age of forty.[75] Plutarch, on the other hand, thought that younger men needed training and were not to rush into civic affairs.[76] Plutarch advises the young, aspiring statesman to find an older mentor, who could act as a model.[77] We thus have standardized advice that the older man sets a pattern for the younger man, which is introduced by "likewise" (2:6). However, the "likewise" does not directly relate to the older man but is mediated by the "older women" and the

---

Titus, THNTC (Grand Rapids: Eerdmans, 2012), 346–67. On virtues of the *polis*, see Hoklotubbe, *Civilized Piety*, 111–25.

70. Colin Bailey, "The Gerousia of Ephesus" (PhD thesis, University of British Columbia, 2006), 2; some thought the age began at sixty: Chris De Wet, "Grumpy Old Men? Gender, Gerontology, and the Geriatrics of Soul in John Chrysostom," *JECS* 24, no. 4 (2016): 494.

71. See, e.g., Michel M. Austin, "Ptolemy I and Cyrene (322/1)," in *The Hellenistic World from Alexander to the Roman Conquest: A Selection of Ancient Sources in Translation*, 2nd ed. (Cambridge: Cambridge University Press, 2006), 69–71.

72. H. N. Fowler, trans., *Plutarch: Moralia*, vol. 10, LCL 321 (Cambridge, MA: Harvard University Press, 1936), 103, 105.

73. Fowler, *Plutarch*, 107.

74. A similar list appears in Dio Chrysostom, *The Wise Man Is Happy* (Or. 23.6).

75. Kidson, *Persuading*, 142–46.

76. Plutarch, *Praec. ger. rei publ.* 798A–C; in the constitution of Ptolemy I, men over the age of thirty could take on a substantive role in the city, but not as an elder (*gerōn*); Austin, "Ptolemy I and Cyrene (322/1)," line 12.

77. Plutarch, *Praec. ger. rei publ.* 805E–806B.

"younger women." The young men are to be "self-controlled" (*sōphronein*), as are the young women (2:5–6), which is the quintessential virtue of youth.[78] This key virtue is "self-restraint" (*sōphrosynē*).[79]

Sōphrosynē, *sōphrōn*, and *sōphroneō*, and their related lexemes, refer to one of the Greek cardinal virtues. It is a concept that sprawls across Greek literature from Homer to the Greek church fathers.[80] *Sōphrosynē* is basically "soundness of mind" and relates to self-knowledge that is prudent and modest.[81] *Sōphrosynē* acts to restrain "*hybris*, the arrogant violation of limits set by the gods or by human society."[82] So indelible in Greek culture was this concept that these words did not even need to be used to evoke an association. In classical works it was *the* "virtue of the polis" rather than the ethics of the individual in one's private life.[83] This applies to both men and women. This is its aspect in Titus, whose instructions are directed to believers living in "every town" on Crete (1:5). And as we have described, men and women appear to have lived very public lives in these cities.

Not only is the "older man" in Titus to be a "man of restraint" (*sōphrōn*), but he is to possess two other closely related virtues, "sobriety" and "dignity" (Titus 2:2, AT).[84] These three virtues are closely tied to civic life—the "man of restraint" who has dignity is the best fit to lead.[85] The "older women" are "likewise" to attend to their publicly observed virtues (cf. 1 Tim. 3:11).

The women's virtues parallel the men's virtues. They are to be reverent in their behavior (*en katastēmati hieroprepeis*, Titus 2:3), as the men are to be serious (*semnous*, 2:2); both *hieroprepēs* and *semnos* have the connotation to be reverent (BDAG). The women are not to be liars, like those who are rebellious (1:10–12) and paying attention to "Jewish myths" (1:14). In contrast, it would seem they are to be sound (*hygiainōsin*) in the faith (1:13), as the

---

78. Helen F. North, "The Mare, the Vixen, and the Bee: 'Sophrosyne' as the Virtue of Women in Antiquity," *ICS* 2 (1977): 37.

79. Titus 2:5–6 NRSV = "self-controlled"; translated "self-restraint" by Helen North, *Sophrosyne: Self-Knowledge and Self-Restraint in Greek Literature* (Ithaca: Cornell University Press, 1966), 38–40; William D. Mounce, *Pastoral Epistles*, WBC 46 (Nashville: Nelson, 2000), 407.

80. North, *Sophrosyne*, passim.

81. North, *Sophrosyne*, 4–5.

82. North, *Sophrosyne*, 6.

83. North, *Sophrosyne*, 23, 44–45.

84. This is the definition of *sōphrōn* in North, *Sophrosyne*, 2; for sobriety as restraint, see 21, 76. The NRSV has "temperate" (*nēphalios*) and "serious" (*semnos*) in Titus 2:2. For "sobriety" and "dignity," see Marshall, *Pastoral Epistles*, 186–89; see also Euripides, *Hipp.* 1364; Plutarch, *Pyth. orac.* 401D; Dio Chrysostom, *Or.* 40.35; cf. *moderatio* and *dignitate*, Cicero, *Fin.* 2.47 (14).

85. North, *Sophrosyne*, 73. In Roman terms, *dignitas* "was to be registered through . . . practical manifestations" in view and judgment of the crowd. Bell, *Spectacular Power*, 17.

men are sound (*hygiainontas*) also in faith, in love, and in endurance (2:2). As the men are to be "temperate" (2:2; or "sober"), the women are not to be "slaves to [much wine]" (2:3).[86] In traditional Roman society women did not drink wine—a husband could inflict the death penalty for this indulgence.[87] However, in a Christian community that celebrated the Lord's Supper, women would be drinking wine (1 Cor. 11:25–26), hence perhaps the warning not to be enslaved.

Then the writer breaks away from the pattern of the men to tell older women they are to be either "teach[ers of] what is good" or "good teachers" (Titus 2:3).[88] Since a conditional clause follows, it is perhaps best to take it as "good teachers," who are in a position to train the younger women. The virtues that follow are, on first blush, the standard virtues of Greco-Roman wives; for example, Valeria was "kind, affectionate, dignified, blameless; she loved her husband and her children" (*SEG* 1536).[89] While the virtues of the young women are domestic virtues that every Roman woman was expected to have, they are in no way "private."[90] That such virtues accompany a good reputation and are praised on tombstones speaks of the public visibility of wives. As we discussed above, "a manager of the household" implies observation by the neighbors as a wife went about her duties. Wives were expected to be at home and not out at dinner parties with their friends (cf. 1 Tim. 5:13).[91]

Where the writer departs from the "common virtues" is in the expectation that the young wives will be trained by the older women to be "submissive to their [own] husbands" (Titus 2:5). This is a surprising twist to the usual Roman expectation that wives were to be obedient to their husbands. In the laudatory praise given by the Roman husband for his dead wife, he lists one of her domestic virtues as "obedience" (*opsequi*).[92] Traditionally, the young

---

86. Adapted from Quinn, *Titus*, 119.

87. Sarah Pomeroy, *Goddesses, Whores, Wives, and Slaves: Women in Classical Antiquity* (New York: Shocken Books, 2011), 153.

88. Annette Bourland Huizenga, *Moral Education for Women in the Pastoral and Pythagorean Letters: Philosophers of the Household* (Boston: Brill, 2013), 276; "good woman" as philosophical *topos*, 201–13.

89. G. H. R. Horsley, *New Documents Illustrating Early Christianity*, vol. 3 (Grand Rapids: Eerdmans, 1983), No. 11 (40–43); cf. No. 14 (47–48); also see in the same volume, No. 8 (33–36), a virtuous matron: "as for your domestic virtues, loyalty . . . obedience, courteousness, easy good-nature, your assiduous wool-working, reverence for the gods without superstition . . . modest refinement." For a Jewish example, see *JIWE* 2:103 in Christopher R. Hutson, *First and Second Timothy and Titus*, Paideia (Grand Rapids: Baker Academic, 2019), 230.

90. Kristina Milnor, *Gender, Domesticity, and the Age of Augustus: Inventing Private Life* (Oxford: Oxford University Press, 2005), 27–34.

91. Milnor, *Gender*, 30.

92. Horsley, *New Documents*, No. 8 (33–36).

wife was trained to be obedient by her husband: "As Hesiod instructs, 'to teach her congenial habits.' If he is going to teach her, he will give her orders; and if he is going to give his wife orders, he will bring her as close as he can to his own character, as superior leading inferior."[93] Here in Titus a different educational scheme is set in place. Conventionally, the older man would train the younger man.[94] Yet the focus here is on the training of the younger women. This is somewhat out of the ordinary.[95] The younger men are urged, like the younger women, to be "self-restrained" (*sōphronein*, Titus 2:6).[96] In the Christian community, the older train the younger in this one overarching virtue. As E. A. Judge has pointed out, the Christ community was a scholastic community.[97] While looking respectable, these older men and women are participating in a subversive social experiment: the husband is no longer a "guide, philosopher, and teacher" in his own home, as this role belongs to a woman outside the house.[98] This advice reshapes the marital relationship so that it brings the couple onto a more equal footing, yet all the while they are in full view of the neighbors. The true master of the household is no longer the husband but God the King (1 Tim. 6:15; Titus 2:14).

Relating Titus 2:1–6 to Modern Australia

Australia is a nation occupying an island continent. Yet our population clings to the coast.[99] Our lifestyle is undergoing dramatic changes as the housing pressure in our great cities is increasing. We're moving to a population of apartment dwellers rather than families in stand-alone houses.[100] Also, with the advent of the internet, more of us are working from home rather than

93. Aelius Aristides, *A Reply to Plato* (*Or.* 2.129) (Michael Trapp, ed. and trans., *Aelius Aristides: Orations*, vol. 1, LCL 533 [Cambridge, MA: Harvard University Press, 2017], 427–28); cf. Plutarch, *Cat. Ma.* 347; *Conj. praec.* 145C.

94. Plutarch, *Cat. Min.* 2.760.5; *Lib. ed.*, passim.

95. In the Neopythagorean literature, older women advise younger women (Huizenga, *Moral Education*, 77–127); however, the letters offer a "complete curriculum" for women and are not advising older women to actually train younger women as Titus 2:3 is doing.

96. The object of the educational system was to train young men to be obedient (*eupeithesteroi*), respectful, and temperate citizens; see Xenophon, *Lac.* 2.14; Kidson, *Persuading*, 139–77.

97. E. A. Judge, "The Early Christians as a Scholastic Community," *JRH* 1 (1960/61): 4–15, 125–37.

98. Plutarch, *Conj. praec.* 145C.

99. "Profile of Australia's Population," Australian Institute of Health and Welfare, April 18, 2024, https://www.aihw.gov.au/reports/australias-health/profile-of-australias-population.

100. Elias Visontay, "Living with Density: Will Australia's Housing Crisis Finally Change the Way Its Cities Work?," *The Guardian*, April 16, 2023, https://www.theguardian.com/australia-news/2023/apr/16/living-with-density-will-australias-housing-crisis-finally-change-the-way-its-cities-work.

commuting to an office. This change has been hastened by changes in the workplace caused by the COVID-19 pandemic.[101] However, some things have not changed. Australians love to be outdoors; holidays are dominated by beach going, camping, hiking, picnicking, and the like.[102] We also love our sports, and many of us play sports, while vast numbers of us attend sporting events.[103] While there has been a shift away from entertaining guests in our homes, we are still "catching up," but in places such as coffee shops, pubs, and clubs.[104] We live our lives in a casual and relaxed fashion, with little distinctions between private and public in our manner of dress and address. Rarely would we address our social superiors with anything but their first name. We still have faith in our cultural myth that we are an egalitarian nation.[105] The greatest cultural shift has been the place of women; in the past married women tended to stay at home, while now most women participate in the workforce.[106]

This open public lifestyle seems reminiscent of the lifestyle of Roman Crete, where women lived and worked in the public eye. The emphasis on the decorum of all categories addressed in Titus—older men, older women,

101. Chantelle Al-Khouri, "Working from Home Has Become Normal in Australia. But Is That a Good Thing?," Australian Broadcasting Commission News, August 8, 2024, https://www .abc.net.au/news/2024-08-09/working-from-home-australia-good-thing/104202068; "Changing Patterns of Work," Australian Institute of Health and Welfare, September 7, 2023, https://www .aihw.gov.au/reports/australias-welfare/changing-patterns-of-work.

102. Jade Toomey, "Australian Institute of Sport Data Shows COVID Sped up Grassroots Exercise Activities like Parkrun," Australian Broadcasting Commission News, November 2, 2022, https://www.abc.net.au/news/2022-11-02/australian-institute-of-sport-data-covid-increased -exercise/101604122.

103. "Australia, the Sporting Nation," McCrindle Research, 2019, https://mccrindle.com.au /article/blog/australia-the-sporting-nation-2/; D. Crawford, *The Future of Sport in Australia* (Canberra: Commonwealth of Australia, 2009); J. Currie, "The Relationship between Sport and Children's Mental Health," *Education Connect* 14 (2009): 14–15.

104. Brodie Lancaster, "The Dinner Party Is Dead, but We Can't Let Go of the Dream," Australian Broadcasting Commission News, December 1, 2018, https://www.abc.net.au /everyday/why-the-dinner-party-is-dead/10558990; "Australia's Coffee Trends," McCrindle Research, accessed August 20, 2024, https://mccrindle.com.au/article/australias-coffee-trends/; "11 Million Australians Visit Pubs—Mostly for a Good Feed," Roy Morgan, July 7, 2020, https://www.roymorgan.com/findings/11-million-australians-visit-pubs-mostly-for-a-good -feed; "Pubs, Bars and Nightclubs in Australia—Industry Market Research Report Now Updated by IBISWorld," PRWeb, November 5, 2013, https://www.prweb.com/releases/pubs_bars _and_nightclubs_in_australia_industry_market_research_report_now_updated_by_ibisworld /prweb11298046.htm.

105. Ross Gittins, "Egalitarianism in Australia Is Just a Façade: We Call Each Other Mates but the Widening Gap between Rich and Poor Tells the Real Story," *Sydney Morning Herald*, July 17, 2013, https://www.smh.com.au/opinion/egalitarianism-in-australia-is-just-a-facade -20130716-2q25k.html.

106. "Changing Female Employment over Time," Australian Bureau of Statistics, March 18, 2021, https://www.abs.gov.au/articles/changing-female-employment-over-time.

younger women, and younger men—reflects a life lived in view of their neighbors. The writer of Titus seems to be aware of the more open lifestyle of the Cretans, especially for the women, whom he urges to be "reverent in the way they live" (Titus 2:3 NIV). He also seems to be aware of a drinking culture on Crete in which men and women liberally partake. The overseer is "not [to be] given to drunkenness" (1:7 NIV), and neither is the older woman (2:3). Australians too have a relaxed attitude toward drinking alcohol, and many Christian believers drink as it is a part of our culture.[107] While the writer of Titus does not urge complete sobriety, the stress he places on believers living their lives in the public eye should remind us Australian believers that self-restraint, conduct worthy of respect, self-control, and soundness in faith, love, and endurance (2:2) are valued even in laid-back Australia.[108]

Furthermore, there has been an awakening to Australia's long indigenous past. Very recently, in 2023, Australia held a referendum about changing our constitution to recognize the indigenous peoples of Australia and give them a permanent voice in the parliament. The question that the Australian people were asked to vote on was whether they agreed "to alter the Constitution to recognise the First Peoples of Australia by establishing an Aboriginal and Torres Strait Islander Voice."[109] The referendum failed, but that this question was even a possibility seems astonishing to me as someone who grew up in Australia in the 1970s. Over the course of the last twenty-five to thirty years, the vast majority of Australians have been awakened to the long and continuous history of Australia before British settlement.[110] Australia was

---

107. "Australians' Attitudes towards Their Health, Consuming Alcohol and Taking a Break from Alcohol: Survey Highlights," VicHealth, December 2014, https://www.vichealth.vic.gov .au/sites/default/files/VicHealth-Febfast-factsheet.pdf; "Alcohol Consumption Increases during COVID-19 Crisis," Australian National University, June 10, 2020, https://reporter.anu.edu.au /all-stories/alcohol-consumption-increases-during-covid-19-crisis.

108. Importance of self-confidence and trustworthiness: Ashley Fell, "The Top Trends of 2023," McCrindle Research, 2023, https://mccrindle.com.au/article/the-top-trends-of-2023/, no. 3. Competency and empathy valued in leaders: "Top Leadership Styles: Today's Ideal Leader," McCrindle Research, 2022, https://mccrindle.com.au/article/top-leadership-styles -todays-ideal-leader/. Top Australian values include "respect for the freedom and dignity of the individual," "commitment to the rule of law," and "freedom of religion." "Australian Values," Department of Home Affairs, last updated February 29, 2024, https://www.homeaffairs.gov.au /about-us/our-portfolios/social-cohesion/australian-values.

109. "Culture and Empowering Communities," National Indigenous Australians Agency, accessed August 20, 2024, https://www.niaa.gov.au/our-work/culture-and-empowering-communities.

110. Aboriginal occupation of the Australian continent has been estimated at about sixty-five thousand years ("Evidence of First Peoples," National Museum of Australia, updated October 27, 2022, https://www.nma.gov.au/defining-moments/resources/evidence-of-first-peoples). The High Court ruling in 1992 that Australia was not "terra nullius," or a land belonging to no one, awakened many Australians to the idea of multiple indigenous nations. This High Court ruling is now known as the Mabo decision ("The Mabo Case," Australian Institute of Aboriginal and

originally a multitude of nations, each with its own language, culture, and traditions. Aboriginal Christian leader Brooke Prentis has a nice phrase to describe this: "the Aboriginal peoples of these lands now called Australia."[111] In a theological chapter on the stewardship and sustainability of Aboriginal cultural practices to care for the country and the land as the household of God, Prentis calls on non-Aboriginal peoples to "reframe their knowledge of Aboriginal peoples."[112]

Graham Paulson and Mark Brett, in their article "Five Smooth Stones: Reading the Bible through Aboriginal Eyes," describe how Aboriginal peoples can shed an informative light on reading the Bible in its original social and historical context.[113] Paulson and Brett's paper focuses on the culture of Israel in the Old Testament, but a parallel exists for ethnic groups in the Roman Empire. Aboriginal peoples can reveal how a long and continuing culture can still exist under the hegemony of a colonizing power. While we might see the writer of Titus urging believers to blend into Roman culture for the sake of survival, he is still mindful of the Cretan traditions.[114] Crete, it would seem, had a tradition that men and women maintained separate spheres, and this seems in some respects to parallel traditional Aboriginal society, in which there is "men's business" and "women's business."[115] And this particularly stands out in Titus, as the Roman tradition that husbands trained their wives

Torres Strait Islander Studies, updated July 13, 2023, https://aiatsis.gov.au/explore/mabo-case; see also "Map of Indigenous Australia," AIATSIS, updated May 14, 2024, https://aiatsis.gov.au/explore/map-indigenous-australia; "Changing Policies Towards Aboriginal People," Australian Law Reform Commission, August 18, 2010, https://www.alrc.gov.au/publication/recognition-of-aboriginal-customary-laws-alrc-report-31/3-aboriginal-societies-the-experience-of-contact/changing-policies-towards-aboriginal-people/; "Voice to Parliament," Reconciliation Australia, 2023, https://www.reconciliation.org.au/reconciliation/support-a-voice-to-parliament/). Further, the publication of these works seems instrumental in awakening the general Australian population to the voices of Aboriginal and Torres Strait islanders. See Henry Reynolds, *Why Weren't We Told? A Personal Search for the Truth about Our History* (North Sydney: Penguin, 2000); Anne Pattel-Gray, *The Great White Flood: Racism in Australia; Critically Appraised from an Aboriginal Historico-Theological Viewpoint* (Atlanta: Scholars Press, 1998); Rosalind Kidd, *The Way We Civilise: Aboriginal Affairs, the Untold Story* (Brisbane: University of Queensland Press, 1997).

111. Brooke Prentis, "What Can the Birds of the Land Tell Us?," in *Grounded in the Body, in Time and Place, in Scripture: Papers by Australian Women Scholars in the Evangelical Tradition*, ed. Jill Firth and Denise Cooper-Clarke (Eugene, OR: Wipf & Stock, 2021), 19–30.

112. Prentis, "What Can the Birds of the Land Tell Us?," 29.

113. Graham Paulson and Mark Brett, "Five Smooth Stones: Reading the Bible through Aboriginal Eyes," *Colloq* 45, no. 2 (2013): 199–214.

114. This is not to imply that any unwanted or forced assimilation has a biblical warrant.

115. On what this is in Australian indigenous cultures, see "Men's and Women's Business," Deadly Story, accessed August 20, 2024, https://deadlystory.com/page/culture/Life_Lore/Ceremony/Men_s_and_Women_s_Business.

is set aside for a tradition in which older women trained younger women in "women's business" (Titus 2:4). In particular, the deep respect Aboriginal peoples have for their elders, both female and male, should be an attitude borne in mind when reading Titus.[116] There is a tendency to read Titus (and the Pastoral Epistles) through a colonizing and hierarchical lens when Titus 2:1–6 might be evidence of a society organized along lines more analogous to Australian Aboriginal society.[117]

Final Thoughts on Titus

In this chapter I have argued that the Letter to Titus was written to a Christian community on the island of Crete in order to shore up what the writer believes is the Pauline tradition. The lifestyle of the Cretans plays a large role in the commands given to the men and women in the letter, which must be taken into account in its interpretation. An appreciation of the long and multicultural aspects of Cretan society allows us to draw connections with a modern society like Australia that is grappling with reconciling itself with its colonial past and the impact on the ancient indigenous nations present at colonization. Australia is a very open and free society, and Australians tend to spend a lot of our lives in public spaces, which believers need to consider as we conduct ourselves as disciples of Christ, much as the Cretan believers had to do in the first and second centuries.

116. See Paulson and Brett's discussion on "Law," "Ceremony," and "Family" in "Five Smooth Stones," 199–214; cf. "Aboriginal and Torres Strait Islander Culture and History: Aboriginal and Torres Strait Islander People Have a Shared History of Colonisation and Forced Removal of Their Children," Victorian Public Sector Commission, June 28, 2022, https://vpsc.vic.gov.au/workforce-programs/aboriginal-cultural-capability-toolkit/aboriginal-culture-and-history/.
117. Paulson and Brett, "Five Smooth Stones," 199.

Part 3

HEBREWS THROUGH REVELATION

16

Christ Intercedes or Judges?

An Examination of the Ethiopian Orthodox Tewahido *Church's Rendering and Interpretation of* Entynchanō *in Hebrews 7:25*

ABENEAZER G. URGA

The introduction of Christianity to Ethiopia has been associated with various figures: the Ethiopian eunuch,[1] the apostle Matthew, nameless individual Christian merchants who conducted trade around the Red Sea, and Frumentius (Abba Selama).[2] However, when King Ezana embraced Christianity in AD 341, Ethiopia accepted Christianity as an organized religion. The Ethiopian Orthodox *Tewahido* Church (EOTC) traces its history and theology to the fourth century AD and to the Syrian tradition that was promulgated by the "Nine Saints" who sought a safe haven in Ethiopia from their Roman Christian persecutors because of their non-Chalcedonian

---

Parts of this paper were presented at the Society of Biblical Literature Hebrews section in San Antonio, Texas, on November 22, 2021.

1. Jacques A. Blocher and Jacques Blandenier, *The Evangelization of the World: A History of Christian Mission*, trans. Michael Parker (Pasadena: William Carey Library, 2013), 49; Steven Kaplan, *The Monastic Holy Man and the Christianization of Early Solomonic Ethiopia* (Wiesbaden: Steiner, 1984), 15.

2. Tibebe Eshete, *The Evangelical Movement in Ethiopia: Resistance and Resilience* (Waco: Baylor University Press, 2009), 16.

theology.[3] This means the EOTC has one of the longest continuous histories in the world.

Christ's heavenly intercession has been a contentious biblical and theological motif in the Ethiopian milieu. Although the traditions of the EOTC are replete with the notion of intercession, divine intercession is downplayed or vehemently rejected. Since 2007, the EOTC has taken this rejection to another level by translating *entynchanō* in the Amharic version as "judge" (*yemiferdew*) instead of "intercede" (*yimalidal*) in Romans 8:34 and as "reconcile" (*yastarqachewal*) in Hebrews 7:25. Steve Strauss brings to light the issue of Christ's intercession in his study of Christ's nature in the EOTC.[4] His approach, however, is descriptive rather than dealing with lexical changes, as he showcases through interviewing various EOTC members. Tewodros Demelash very briefly highlights the alteration, but only in Romans 8:34.[5] In this chapter, I will interact with the Ethiopic, Greek, and Amharic versions of the texts and explore the meaning of *entynchanō* to argue that the biblical texts warrant Christ's intercession. I will provide a detailed exegesis of Hebrews 7:25 by situating the passage in the author's overall argument of Jesus's heavenly ministry. Finally, I will argue that the EOTC's translation and interpretation of *entynchanō* is based on traditional/theological grounds, as the term challenges some long-held theological traditions of the church.

The Meaning of Intercession

The most controversial topic between the EOTC and Ethiopian Protestants has been Christ's intercession on behalf of his people. The EOTC has recently made a strident effort to counter the Protestants' claim that Christ is an intercessor (*amalaj*), using various platforms. While the EOTC's rejection of Christ's intercessory ministry through various writings has always been present, in 2007 the alteration of biblical passages that explicitly state Christ's intercessory task revealed the EOTC's aversion to divine intercession.[6]

The term "intercession" conveys the idea of prayer carried out by a mediator "seeking divine intervention on behalf of a person or people who are in

---

3. Eshete, *Evangelical Movement in Ethiopia*, 16.
4. Stephen J. Strauss, *Perspectives on the Nature of Christ in the Ethiopian Orthodox Church: A Case Study in Contextualized Theology*, EMS Dissertation Series (Pasadena: William Carey International University Press, 2014).
5. Tewodros Demelash, *Jesus: True Intercessor, Just Judge* [in Amharic], 3rd ed. (Addis Ababa: Solar Printing Press, 2021).
6. Demelash, *Jesus*, 13.

danger of God's wrath, military invasion, or sickness."[7] Since this essay is concerned with Hebrews 7:25, the discussion of intercession is limited to a single Greek term: *entynchanō.*

The usage of *entynchanō* can be divided into two categories. First, *entynchanō* can mean "to make an earnest request through contact with the person(s) approached."[8] In this major category, "approach" or "appeal" and "pray" are listed as two subcategories. The second major category is "encountering" or "reading."[9]

Otto Bauernfeind notes that in the New Testament, the term is used in two ways: "to complain against" (*entynchanō kata,* Rom. 11:2; Acts 25:24[10]) or "to intercede for" (*entynchanō hyper,* Rom. 8:34; Heb. 7:25).[11] In Romans 8:34 and Hebrews 7:25, *entynchanō hyper* is used in the sense of appeal or prayer.[12] Hence, the term *entynchanō* in no way conveys the idea of judging someone, as the EOTC claims. In Hebrews 7:25, the term relays the notion of Christ's mediatorial prayer on behalf of his people who are in the already-but-not-yet state of their faith journey.

The Ethiopian Orthodox *Tewahido* Church's Rendering of *Entynchanō*

The verb *entynchanō* appears six times in the Greek New Testament. In Acts 25:24, *entynchanō* reveals the Jewish people's petition against Paul. The pre-2007 edition of the EOTC's Amharic version renders the phrase *enetychon* as *yelemenugn* ("they petitioned me"), as does the 2007 edition.

In Romans 8:26, Paul writes, "For we do not know what to pray for as we ought, but the Spirit himself intercedes for us with groanings too deep for words."[13] The pre-2007 edition (the EOTC Amharic) captures the Spirit's intercession (*to pneuma hyperentynchanei*) by rendering it as "the Spirit himself intercedes for us." However, the 2007 edition alters the meaning of *hyperentynchanei* to "judges" ("the Spirit himself judges for us").

---

7. Abeneazer G. Urga, "Suffering and Intercession: Pauline Missionary Methods as a Paradigm for the Future of Evangelical Mission," *JEMS* 1, no. 2 (2021): 48; cf. Urga, *Intercession of Jesus in Hebrews: The Background and Nature of Jesus' Heavenly Intercession in the Epistle to the Hebrews,* WUNT 2/585 (Tübingen: Mohr Siebeck, 2023), 33–36.

8. BDAG, 341.

9. BDAG, 341.

10. Acts 25:24 has the notion of "complaining against" even though the preposition *kata* does not appear in the Greek text.

11. Otto Bauernfeind, "ἐντυγχάνω," *TDNT* 8:243.

12. Johannes P. Louw and Eugene A. Nida, *Greek-English Lexicon of the New Testament: Based on Semantic Domains,* 2nd ed. (New York: United Bible Societies, 1989), 408.

13. Unless otherwise indicated, all English Bible quotations in this chapter are from the ESV.

Similarly, in Romans 8:27, Paul asserts that "the Spirit intercedes for the saints." The verb "intercedes" (*entynchanei*) is rendered as *yimalidilinal* in the pre-2007 edition in a similar sense as the English and the Greek. Nonetheless, the 2007 Amharic edition renders the Spirit's intercession as "He [the Spirit] judges for the saints before God."

Romans 8:34 declares, "Christ Jesus is . . . interceding for us" (*Christos Iēsous . . . estin . . . entynchanei hyper hēmōn*). The standard meaning of this passage is rendered in the pre-2007 edition of the Amharic version as "Christ Jesus is . . . interceding for us." But the 2007 edition again shows a lexical alteration. It reads, "Christ Jesus is judging for us." There is a remark on the word *yehmiferdew* ("is judging") in the footnote of the recent Amharic version. It states, "The Greek says 'is interceding.'" The *Andəmta* commentary[14] explains the Ethiopic phrase *entynchanei hyper hēmōn* as "he argues for us" rather than "he judges for us."[15] But then in a self-contradictory manner, the commentary proceeds to assert that "there is no arguing on our behalf because of his mission on Friday because we will receive the perfect wage."[16]

In Romans 11:2, Paul reminds the audience that Elijah "appeals to God against Israel" (*entynchanei tō theō kata tou Israēl*). Notice here that *entynchanō* is utilized along with *kata*, conveying the notion of verbal complaint against Israel. The term *entynchanō* here relays the idea of accusation. Both the pre-2007 and the 2007 editions correctly capture the meaning of *entynchanō*. Nonetheless, notice also that the 2007 edition does not say "judge against Israel" but says "appeal against" or "accuse" Israel.

Last, in Hebrews 7:25, the author announces that Jesus "always lives to make intercession for them" (*pantote zōn eis to entynchanein hyper autōn*). Here, the term "intercession" is used in a positive sense, because *entynchanō* is followed by the preposition *hyper* to denote that Jesus appeals or intercedes for his people. Whereas the pre-2007 edition renders *entynchanein hyper* as "intercedes for them," the 2007 edition renders it as "he reconciles them." The commentary explains that the term *entynchanō* depicts Christ's intercession

---

14. The *Andəmta* commentary is an Ethiopian commentary tradition that was originally in an oral format in the tenth century BC, and later, it was written down in AD 1682. The commentary employs the Ge'ez Bible, various Greek versions, Syrian, Coptic, and Arabic commentaries and exegetical works, rabbinic sources, patristic writings, and hagiographies. See Keon-Sang An, *An Ethiopian Reading of the Bible: Biblical Interpretation of the Ethiopian* Tewahido *Church*, ASM 25 (Eugene, OR: Pickwick, 2015), 121; Ralph Lee, "The Ethiopic 'Andemta' Commentary on Ethiopic Enoch 2 (1 Enoch 6–9)," *JSP* 23, no. 3 (2014): 181.

15. Tewodros Demelash, *Weighing the 81 Books of the Bible of the Ethiopian Church* [in Amharic], 4th ed. (Addis Ababa: n.p., 2020), 177.

16. My translation from the *Andəmta* commentary.

in Romans 8:34, even though *entynchanō* is rendered with another semantic domain here in Hebrews 7:25. The *Andəmta* tradition recognizes Christ's intercessory task on behalf of believers but sees that task as concluded on Friday (at the time of Jesus's crucifixion) and effectual until the parousia. The pre-2007 edition gets the literal meaning of *entynchanō*, whereas the 2007 edition indicates Jesus's general mediatorial task but waters down the intercessory nature of Jesus's mediation.

The above passages make clear that the 2007 edition of the EOTC's Bible rejects divine intercession. This is evident in the fact that where the term *entynchanō* appears with the Spirit or Jesus, the rendering is altered to "judge" or "reconcile." But the meaning of the term *entynchanō* in other places—for instance, in Romans 11:2—is kept intact. The pre-2007 edition of the EOTC's Bible is faithful to the original meaning of *entynchanō*. However, the recent edition betrays theological motives behind the alteration of the rendering and interpretation of *entynchanō*.

In the following section, I will exegete Hebrews 7:25, showing that *entynchanō* conveys Jesus's active, real, and verbal intercession for us and countering the alteration done by the EOTC.

Exegesis of Hebrews 7:25

Jesus the Melchizedekian High Priest

Hebrews 7:1–28 discusses the high priesthood of Melchizedek, already noted in 5:6, 10.[17] Melchizedek is mentioned only in two places in the Old Testament: Genesis 14:18–20 and Psalm 110:4. The name Melchizedek comes from the combination of two Hebrew terms, *malki-tsedeq*, which are rendered together as "king of righteousness." Melchizedek is also identified as "king of peace" (*ho . . . basileus eirēnēs*, Heb. 7:2), a translation from the Hebrew counterpart *melek shalem* (Gen. 14:18). Melchizedek is a king-priest to whom Abraham and his descendants "gave . . . a tenth of everything" (14:20). Outside of the Old Testament, he is mentioned in the Dead Sea Scrolls (e.g., 11Q13) as "the heavenly deliverer."[18]

Hebrews 7:1–10 details who Melchizedek is. The author of Hebrews directly quotes from Genesis 14:18, "Melchizedek, king of Salem, priest of the most high God" (*Melchisedek, basileus Salēm, hiereus tou theou tou hypistou*, Heb. 7:1), and further asserts one essential point: "He is without father or

---

17. The section under the heading "Exegesis of Hebrews 7:25" originally appeared in my *Intercession of Jesus in Hebrews*. Used by permission from Mohr Siebeck.
18. Geza Vermes, *The Complete Dead Sea Scrolls in English*, rev. ed. (London: Penguin Books, 2011), 532.

mother or genealogy, having neither beginning of days nor end of life" (7:3). This statement has garnered various speculations as to the real identity of the Melchizedek figure. Some have taken this to mean that Melchizedek, in line with 11QMelchizedek, is an angelic being. Others have suggested that Melchizedek is the preincarnate Christ.[19]

With Mary Healy, I contend that verse 3 "does not mean that Hebrews views him as a certain supernatural being. Rather, the fact that Genesis, a book full of genealogies, says nothing about his parentage is striking. It means he lacks the essential qualification for priesthood according to the law of Moses: priestly lineage."[20] In other words, the Melchizedekian priestly order deviates from the Levitical priestly order and reveals the ephemeral nature of the Aaronic priesthood.[21]

The subsequent pericope (Heb. 7:11–28) traces Jesus's priesthood back to that of Melchizedek. The prepositional phrase *kata tēn taxin Melchisedek* is a direct quote from Psalm 109:4 (LXX) and repeatedly appears in the epistle (Heb. 5:6, 10; 6:20; 7:11, 17). Here the notion of succession is not in view. Nonetheless, the similarity between Melchizedek and Jesus's priesthood is drawn, for Hebrews 7:15 conveys a similar idea by substituting *kata tēn taxin Melchisedek* with *kata tēn homoiotēta Melchisedek*.[22] It is vital to note here that the author is not comparing and contrasting Jesus and Melchizedek, as he does with Jesus versus the Old Testament, angels, Moses, or Aaron. Rather, the utilization of Melchizedek in the author's discourse undergirds the fact that the Aaronic/Levitical order is inferior, whereas Jesus's priesthood—which is similar to that of Melchizedek—is superior and effective.[23]

This superiority is unique in that Jesus is installed as a high priest by God's oath, as opposed to the Aaronic priests, who lack such an oath (Heb. 7:20; cf. 6:13–20).[24] The oath enables Jesus to become "the guarantor of a better covenant" (7:22). As the term "guarantor" (*engyos*) makes clear, Jesus provides a definitive assurance and security of salvation.[25]

---

19. See David L. Allen, *Hebrews*, NAC 35 (Nashville: B&H, 2010), 408–10.
20. Mary Healy, *Hebrews*, CCSS (Grand Rapids: Baker Academic, 2016), 133.
21. Jean Massonnet, *L'épître aux Hébreux*, CBNT 19 (Paris: Cerf, 2016), 169–70.
22. See Healy, *Hebrews*, 133; Alan C. Mitchell, *Hebrews*, SP 13 (Collegeville, MN: Liturgical Press, 2007), 110.
23. Massonnet, *L'épître aux Hébreux*, 184; Mathias Rissi, *Die Theologie des Hebräerbriefs: Ihre Verankerung in der Situation des Verfassers und seiner Leser*, WUNT 41 (Tübingen: Mohr Siebeck, 1987), 83.
24. F. F. Bruce, *The Epistle to the Hebrews*, NICNT (Grand Rapids: Eerdmans, 1990), 170; Harold W. Attridge, *The Epistle to the Hebrews*, Hermeneia (Philadelphia: Fortress, 1989), 207–8.
25. BDAG, 271.

Engyos is a New Testament *hapax legomenon* that accents the security of future salvation with Jesus as the intermediary.[26] The term has a conceptual affinity with *ankyra* ("anchor") in Hebrews 6:19, where believers are promised stability and security. Jesus provides such a sure-footed guarantee, "at the cost of his life, that God's covenant with us will remain forever."[27] Time and again, the author accents Jesus's unique priesthood.[28] Whereas the Aaronic priests were overcome by death and disabled from continual priesthood (Heb. 7:8, 23), Jesus overcame death and continued to hold his priestly office (7:16, 24; cf. 2:14–15).[29] The language in Hebrews 7:24 cements Jesus's permanent and continual priesthood, reminiscent of 7:3 and 7:16. While verse 3 states that Melchizedek "continues [as] a priest forever" (*menei hiereus eis to diēnekes*), verse 16 asserts that Jesus is a priest *kata dynamin zōēs akatalytou* ("according to the power of an indestructible life" ESV alt.). The big idea put forth by these expressions is that Jesus's priesthood is permanent (*aparabatos*, 7:24)[30] and endless (*akatalytos*, 7:16).[31]

Jesus's Perpetual Intercession in Heaven

One of the surpassing features of Jesus's superior high priesthood is indicated in Hebrews 7:25, focusing more explicitly on Jesus's perpetual heavenly intercession. In the preceding passages, the author has asserted the enduring nature of Jesus's priesthood (7:17, 22–24).

The text in Hebrews 7:25 begins with the inferential coordinate conjunction *hothen* ("consequently") to link Jesus's permanent, eternal, and perpetual priesthood mentioned earlier and his continual priestly intercession in heaven that brings about effectual salvation.[32] The author declares *sōzein eis to panteles* ("to save completely / for all time"; see the ESV note). The infinitive *sōzein* is fronted to accentuate that Jesus's priestly task is providing salvation from the consequence of sin, which is God's judgment.[33] Unlike the

---

26. Paul Ellingworth, *The Epistle to the Hebrews*, NIGTC (Grand Rapids: Eerdmans, 1993), 388–89; James W. Thompson, *Hebrews*, Paideia (Grand Rapids: Baker Academic, 2008), 160; H. Preisker, "ἔγγυος," *TDNT* 2:329.

27. Healy, *Hebrews*, 144; cf. William L. Lane, *Hebrews 1–8*, WBC 47A (Grand Rapids: Zondervan, 1991), 188.

28. See Rissi, *Die Theologie*, 83.

29. Nicholas J. Moore, "Sacrifice, Session and Intercession: The End of Christ's Offering in Hebrews," *JSNT* 42, no. 4 (2020): 529.

30. J. Schneider, "ἀπαράβατος," *TDNT* 5:742–43.

31. Friedrich Büchsel, "ἀκατάλυτος," *TDNT* 4:338–39; BDAG, 35.

32. Erich Grässer, *An die Hebräer (Hebr 7,1–10,18)*, 3 vols., EKKNT 17 (Zürich: Benziger, 1993), 2:61.

33. Craig R. Koester, *Hebrews: A New Translation with Introduction and Commentary*, AB 36 (New York: Doubleday, 2001), 365.

mediators of the past and the Levitical priests, Jesus is capable of providing a secure, stable, and sure-footed salvation "because His priesthood is absolute 'and final."[34] Scholars understand the prepositional phrase *eis to panteles* to be expressing either time ("forever") or extent ("completely").[35] Nonetheless, the dichotomy should be resisted, as both the temporal and the comprehensive sense of the expression are possible. Erich Grässer avers, "The one who saves *forever* is also the one who saves completely."[36] Jesus is able to save completely and perpetually; hence, this is an encouragement to the audience—which is tempted to fall away—to persevere in the faith, for Jesus provides guaranteed salvation.

The author stresses that perpetual and absolute salvation is available not to those who slip away or leave the faith but to "those who draw near to God through him" (*tous proserchomenous di' autou tō theō*, Heb. 7:25). The responsibility of the audience to approach God and worship and pray is already mentioned in the epistle. In Hebrews 4:16, the author exhorts, "Let us then with confidence draw near to the throne of grace." Again, in 7:19, believers' ability to "draw near to God" (*di' hēs engizomen tō theō*) is mentioned.

The language of drawing near to God is conveyed with the Greek terms *engizō* and *proserchomai* (cf. Heb. 10:1; 11:6; 12:18, 22). When directed to the audience, these terms encourage those who are on the brink of apostasy to approach God and receive either assistance or forgiveness to enable them to maintain their course in the ups and downs of the faith journey. Note here in Hebrews 7:25 that for believers to access God's presence, Jesus's intermediary function is accented. The prepositional phrase *di' autou* denotes that believers' continual approach to God's throne or presence is predicated on Jesus's perpetual agency or mediation. As Craig Koester rightly points out, "For a person to approach God 'through' Jesus means he or she lodges a request with Jesus, trusting that he will bring it before God for a favorable response."[37] Christians have direct access to God's ears through the superior high priest and Son of God. Like the angels, the prophets, Levitical priests, and mediators of the Old Testament and Second Temple literature, Jesus prays and brings our requests before the Father. Nevertheless, in contrast to other mediators, his priesthood is eternal, and

---

34. Brooke F. Westcott, *The Epistle to the Hebrews: The Greek Text with Notes and Essays* (Grand Rapids: Eerdmans, 1984), 190; see also Samuel Bénétreau, *L'Épître aux Hébreux*, 2 vols. (Vaux-sur-Seine: Édifac, 1990), 2:44.

35. Dana M. Harris, *Hebrews*, EGGNT (Nashville: B&H, 2019), 183; Koester, *Hebrews*, 365.

36. Grässer, *An die Hebräer*, 2:62; see also Philip E. Hughes, *A Commentary on Hebrews* (Grand Rapids: Eerdmans, 1977), 269n35; Thomas R. Schreiner, *A Commentary on Hebrews*, BTCP (Nashville: B&H, 2015), 233.

37. Koester, *Hebrews*, 365.

his proximity is unparalleled.[38] The fact that Jesus brings our requests before the Father and prays on our behalf reveals that Christians both have access and do not have access to the Father. In other words, Christians are in the already-but-not-yet state, needing a perpetual intercessor in the presence of God as they struggle with sin, temptation, and Satan.

The purpose of Jesus's eternal priesthood is *eis to entynchanein hyper autōn* (Heb. 7:25). The infinitive clause not only reveals Jesus's perpetual mediatorial intercession for believers but also mirrors the audience's continual struggle in the face of temptation and possible apostasy.[39] The *terminus technicus* for intercession is *entynchanō*. The term appears once in the Old Testament (Dan. 6:13 LXX [6:12 ET]) and numerous times in the Second Temple literature (e.g., 1 Macc. 10:61; 2 Macc. 4:36). We have already seen that *entynchanō* is utilized to accuse someone to a superior figure. In the Maccabean tradition, for instance, *entynchanō* is usually accompanied by the preposition *kata* (1 Macc. 10:61, 63, 64; 11:25). However, here in Hebrews 7:25, as in Romans 8:34, *entynchanō* is followed by the preposition *hyper*. The term could mean "read," "encounter," or "appeal."[40] What is germane to our study is the meaning of "appeal." The appeal or intercession could be—as shown above—for or against someone. The author of Hebrews employs the term in 7:25 to communicate the idea that Jesus's intercession is for his people (*hyper autōn*). The heavenly high priest who is continually advocating for the people he represents will assist those who draw near to God (*proserchomai*) and make their need for help or forgiveness known.[41] The author has repeatedly shown that Jesus prays, advocates for, and represents God's people. In other words, intercession is at the heart of Jesus's heavenly ministry.

As a result, David Hay's argument that Jesus's intercession is "a passing remark" is not convincing.[42] There is nothing "foreign" about Jesus's heavenly intercession for his people. Instead, Jesus's intercession is the natural task of the high priest in his priestly office. While on earth, Jesus interceded, but after the ultimate sacrificial offering on earth, Jesus's perpetual intercession resumed in heaven.[43] In heaven, Jesus's sacrifice on earth functions as a

---

38. Koester, *Hebrews*, 365–66.
39. Thompson, *Hebrews*, 161.
40. BDAG, 341; Bauernfeind, *TDNT* 8:238–45.
41. See William R. G. Loader, *Sohn und Hoherpriester: Eine traditionsgeschichtliche Untersuchung zur Christologie des Hebräerbriefes*, WMANT 53 (Neukirchen-Vluyn: Neukirchener Verlag, 1981), 139.
42. David M. Hay, *Glory at the Right Hand: Psalm 110 in Early Christianity*, SBLMS 18 (Nashville: Abingdon, 1973), 150.
43. Rissi, *Die Theologie*, 68–69.

background for his perpetual intercession, assisting believers in the face of danger so that they may persevere to the end (Heb. 7:26–28).[44]

By highlighting Jesus's eternal high priesthood and effectual intercession, the author may be putting other mediators in their rightful place—like angels, Moses, and the Levitical priests—who are competing for the audience's attention. Philip Hughes aptly comments, "To rely upon angels or saints or any other finite beings for their intercessions is not only futile; it also betrays a failure of confidence in the adequacy of Christ as our intercessor, and it is to honor the creature rather than him who is our Creator and Redeemer (cf. Rom. 1:25)."[45] Many scholars argue that *entynchanō* refers merely to Jesus's appearance before God rather than verbal intercession on behalf of believers.[46] For instance, Celsus Spicq understands *entynchanō* as a presence rather than as verbal intercession for the people he represents. Although Spicq appears not to deny verbal intercession, his statement that intercession is "a living intercession" indicates that he perceives intercession to be nonverbal.[47]

Usually, scholars provide Exodus 28:29 as proof for rendering *entynchanō* as a mere mediatorial presence before God.[48] However, the concept of intercession—as we have seen thus far—encapsulates both drawing near to God and uttering words for or against someone. Mere physical presence before God is not sufficient to be considered intercession. William Loader is correct to identify *entynchanō* in Hebrews 7:25 as a prayer when he writes, "Jesus speaks for us who are tempted. Thus, our salvation is assured."[49]

David Moffitt claims that it is Jesus's risen body presented in heaven, not his death on the cross, that procures atonement. He views Jesus's death as

---

44. Schreiner, *Hebrews*, 234.

45. Hughes, *Hebrews*, 270.

46. In addition to Hughes (*Hebrews*, 270), see Aelred Cody, *Heavenly Sanctuary and Liturgy in the Epistle to the Hebrews: The Achievement of Salvation in the Epistle's Perspective* (St. Meinrad, IN: Grail, 1960), 198–99, cf. 200–202; see also David Peterson, *Hebrews and Perfection: An Examination of the Concept of Perfection in the Epistle to the Hebrews*, SNTSMS 47 (Cambridge: Cambridge University Press, 1982), 115, 249n75; however, Alexander Nairne, *The Epistle of Priesthood* (Edinburgh: T&T Clark, 1913), 201, rightly argues that Jesus pleads his sacrifices before the Father.

47. Celsus Spicq, *L'Épître aux Hébreux*, 2 vols. (Paris: Gabalda, 1953), 2:198. Howard Griffith, "Priest in Heaven: The Intercession of the Exalted Christ in Reformed Theology, Analysis and Critique" (PhD diss., Westminster Theological Seminary, 2004), 185, also notes Spicq's mistaken understanding of *entynchanō* in Heb. 7:25. Christian Rose, *Der Hebräerbrief*, BNT (Göttingen: Vandenhoeck & Ruprecht, 2019), 119, also takes the same position as Spicq by taking intercession as mere appearance. See also, Westcott, *Hebrews*, 230; Wilfrid Stott, "The Conception of 'Offering' in the Epistle to the Hebrews," *NTS* 9 (1962): 67.

48. See Massonnet, *L'épître aux Hébreux*, 192.

49. Loader, *Sohn und Hoherpriester*, 111, my translation.

more of the preparation for the heavenly offering of his sacrifices.[50] Such a reading of Hebrews is a result of applying a strict "hermeneutical corollary"[51] between the Levitical sacrificial system and Hebrews' delineation of Jesus's high priesthood and sacrifice.[52]

Jesus's suffering since his incarnation ultimately ended on the cross. Put differently, Jesus's repeated offering on earth culminated in his crucifixion on the cross. This finality then was ratified by his sitting at God's right hand.[53] The offering was done once for all at Jesus's expiration on the cross (cf. John 19:30).[54] However, his intercession will continue. The problem with Moffitt's position is that he conflates Jesus's sacrificial offering and his continual intercession in heaven.[55] For Moffitt, continual intercession is a signal for an "ongoing atonement."[56]

Moffitt contends that in heaven, Jesus's intercession and his perpetual presentation of offering are continuous. In so doing, Moffitt rehearses William Milligan, who asserts that Jesus "is not simply interceding on the strength of a past gift or sacrifice. He is presenting an offering on which his intercession is based, and in which it is involved. The idea of offering . . . cannot be separated from the action of our Lord after His Ascension, unless we also separate the thought of offering from what was done by the high-priest of Israel in the innermost sanctuary of his people. Such a separation the ceremonial of the law does not permit."[57] Milligan's argument poses

50. See David M. Moffitt, *Atonement and the Logic of Resurrection in the Epistle to the Hebrews*, NovTSup 141 (Leiden: Brill, 2011), 220, 294. Moffitt insists that sacrifice does not occur during slaughter or death. He repeatedly argues that Jesus's death on the cross should not be taken as the moment that atoning sacrifice took place. Rather, Jesus's presentation of himself after his bodily resurrection and entrance into the heavenly sanctuary is when atonement happened and is happening. See also Moffitt, "Wilderness Identity and Pentateuchal Narrative: Distinguishing between Jesus' Inauguration and Maintenance of the New Covenant in Hebrews," in *Muted Voices of the New Testament: Readings in the Catholic Epistles and Hebrews*, ed. Katherine M. Hockey, Madison N. Pierce, and Francis Watson, LNTS 565 (London: Bloomsbury T&T Clark, 2017), 153–71.

51. David M. Moffitt, "It Is Not Finished: Jesus's Perpetual Atoning Work as the Heavenly High Priest in Hebrews," in *So Great a Salvation: A Dialogue of the Atonement in Hebrews*, ed. Jon C. Laansma, George H. Guthrie, and Cynthia Long Westfall, LNTS 516 (London: Bloomsbury T&T Clark, 2019), 163, cf. 159.

52. See William Loader, "Revisiting High Priesthood Christology in Hebrews," *ZNW* 109 (2018): 238–42.

53. Contra Moffitt, "It Is Not Finished," 158.

54. Contra Walter E. Brooks, "Perpetuity of Christ's Sacrifice in the Epistle to the Hebrews," *JBL* 89, no. 2 (1970): 205–14, who argues for a postresurrection priesthood and sacrificial offering.

55. For a similar observation of Moffitt's assertion, see Moore, "Sacrifice, Session and Intercession," 524.

56. Moffitt, "It Is Not Finished," 168.

57. William Milligan, *The Ascension and Heavenly Priesthood of Our Lord* (London: Macmillan, 1892), 122, quoted in Moffitt, "It Is Not Finished," 168n32.

a significant hermeneutical and theological problem. Similar to Moffitt's works, Milligan's approach suffers from a hermeneutical blind spot. That is, his reading attempts to impose the Aaronic/Levitical system, especially Yom Kippur, on Hebrews, denying the reapplication or recontextualization of the previous sacrificial system used by the author of Hebrews. The theological problem with Milligan's and Moffitt's reading of Hebrews is their attempt to strictly align it with the old system and place Jesus's priesthood *kata tēn taxin Aarōn* instead of *kata tēn taxin Melchisedek* (see Heb. 7:11). The point here is that one should not expect a complete correspondence between Jesus's priesthood and the Aaronic priesthood.[58] One area in which the two systems are at variance is the offering of sacrifices. Jesus does not offer any sacrifice in heaven when he intercedes for God's people.[59] Rather, he intercedes by appealing to his atoning earthly suffering, which culminated in his death on the cross.[60]

On the other hand, Nicholas Moore does not find intercession in the inner sanctum during the Day of Atonement (Lev. 16); correspondingly, he believes that the Day of Atonement does not inform Moffitt's proposal that sacrifice and intercession are coextensive. In Moore's estimation, the *tamid* is the background for Jesus's intercession in heaven.[61] Moore is correct that sacrifice and intercession do not occur at the same time in heaven, where Jesus is sitting at God's right hand. Nonetheless, Moore is mistaken in contending that there is no intercession in the holy place during Yom Kippur and that Yom Kippur does not inform Hebrews' explication of Jesus's heavenly intercession.[62] The term *entynchanō* possibly has *ydh* (Hb.) / *exagoreuō* (Grk.) as its background. In other words, in addition to other Old Testament mediators, Leviticus 16:21—the intercession on the Day of Atonement—is the background for Jesus's heavenly intercession. However, the offering of sacrifice in the case of Jesus is already done on the cross; thus, there is no sacrificial offering occurring in heaven.

58. David M. Moffitt, "Jesus as Interceding High Priest and Sacrifice in Hebrews: A Response to Nicholas Moore," *JSNT* 42, no. 4 (2020): 546, claims that the author of Hebrews "does not work with a rigid one-to-one correspondence between Jesus' atoning work and that of the earthly high priest." However, Moffitt displays the contrary in his approach.

59. Jesus's physical appearance is the reason for Moffitt's assertion that Jesus is offering sacrifices perpetually in being simply present before the Father; see Moffitt, "It Is Not Finished," 175; Moffitt, "Wilderness Identity," 163.

60. Moore, "Sacrifice, Session and Intercession," 529, aptly states, "Mention of intercession comes in a context which foregrounds continuity, and mention of sacrifice in a context which foregrounds completion; these two aspects are summed up in 8:1 under the dual heads of Jesus' priesthood and his session, respectively."

61. Moore, "Sacrifice, Session and Intercession," 534.

62. Moore, "Sacrifice, Session and Intercession," 535, 537.

Moore also contends that intercession in Hebrews is solely to assist believers to persevere.[63] However, intercession—in the Old Testament, Second Temple literature, and the New Testament outside of Hebrews—is done in the context of doubt, sin, possibly apostasy, and the danger of God's judgment. Hence, confining intercession merely to help is too limited.[64] Besides, the already-but-not-yet state of God's people inhibits us theologically from concurring that they do not need the forgiveness of sin, in the sense of needing sanctification (cf. 1 John 1:8–2:2). Grässer's cogent argument that the wandering people of God always struggle between faith and sin, obedience and disobedience, because they are surrounded by sin is noteworthy (Heb. 12:1).[65] Put in a different way, intercession in Hebrews—as in other parts of the Scriptures—is concerned with both help to persevere and addressing the issue of sin by appealing to the sacrifice offered once for all through the death of Jesus on the cross and his subsequent victorious resurrection.

It is important to observe here that the intercession of the high priest in the inner sanctum on the Day of Atonement informs Jesus's intercessory ministry. Jesus's intercession on earth and later in heaven is also highly informed by other Old Testament mediators, like the prophets or even angels. His intercession, however, surpasses that of all the other intercessors, since Jesus's intercession brings about effectual salvation to those who need help to persevere or who need forgiveness for their sins.

Conclusion: Theological Motives

In the foregoing section, we saw in detail that *entynchanō* denotes Jesus's mediatorial task in the heavenly temple on behalf of God's people. His mediatorial prayer is in line with his high-priestly task based on his atoning death on the altar of the cross. However, the EOTC rejects Jesus's intercessory ministry in heaven. Why? There are several theological reasons why many in the EOTC resist the fact that Jesus is an intercessor (*amalaj*). The two main theological motives for denying Christ's intercessory ministry are Christ's divinity and the place of other intercessors in the teachings of the church.

Christ's Divinity

The EOTC argues that Christ is divine, and as such he cannot intercede to himself. Strauss's ethnographic research reveals that most of his Ethiopian

---

63. Moore, "Sacrifice, Session and Intercession," 536.
64. Massonnet, *L'épître aux Hébreux*, 188.
65. Grässer, *An die Hebräer*, 2:64.

Orthodox interviewees assert Christ cannot intercede on behalf of his people because "He Himself is God."[66] In other words, to insist that Christ is an intercessor or *amalaj* diminishes the divinity of Christ.[67] Rather, his interviewees claim that Christ is *temalaj*, which means "one who receives intercession or mediation."[68] In the same vein, Tewodros Demelash denotes that some members of the EOTC posit that "intercession is the function of a created being, and because he [Christ] is not a created being but divine to whom does he petition?"[69] Some members of the EOTC contend that Jesus Christ was an *amalaj* (intercessor-mediator) while on earth, but now that function has ceased for two reasons.[70] First, he finished the work of mediation on earth. Second, Christ "is no longer a man, [and] he could no longer be an *amalaj*."[71] Thus, the motivation for changing the term *entynchanō* from *yimalidal* to *yemiferdew* ("judges") in Romans 8:34 and to *yastarqachewal* ("reconcile") in Hebrews 7:25 is because the EOTC believes that intercession disparages the divinity of Christ.

To the contrary, Alemayehu Moges Dereso correctly argues that Christ's petition and crucifixion definitively dealt with sin, but he continually intercedes and advocates for humanity at God's right hand. Alemayehu insists that Christ's intercessory ministry in heaven does not make him unequal with God the Father.[72]

The Place of Other Intercessors

Because of the EOTC's high Christology and because of the church's rejection of Christ's perpetual intercession, the church has made room for other substitute intercessors. Again, Strauss's research is helpful in this regard. He writes, "Subjects frequently answered the question about whether or not Christ was an *amalaj* by mentioning others they considered to be *amalajoch*. The Virgin Mary was the most common *amalaj* mentioned. The angels Gabriel and Michael and St. George were also mentioned frequently."[73] Human and angelic intercessors (*amalajoch*) offer intercession to the triune God,

66. Strauss, *Perspectives*, 155.

67. Paulos Fekadu Tessema, *The Son of God* [in Amharic] (Addis Ababa: Paul's Pulpit, 2021), 359.

68. Strauss, *Perspectives*, 156n39.

69. Demelash, *Jesus*, 87, cf. 103.

70. Tessema, *Son of God*, 359–60.

71. Strauss, *Perspectives*, 157; cf. Demelash, *Jesus*, 52.

72. Alemayehu Moges Dereso, *Let Everyone Know Everything* [in Amharic] (Addis Ababa: Bole Printing Press, 1994), 47–48.

73. Strauss, *Perspectives*, 158; cf. Demelash, *Jesus*, 15–16.

including Christ the Creator, on behalf of God's people. These *amalajoch* (intercessors) take the supplications of the saints and bring them before God.[74] Accepting Christ's high-priestly intercessory task would put these intercessors out of their place. Nonetheless, the EOTC has taught and defended the intercessory function of the *amalajoch* to the exclusion of Christ's intercession for a long time. And this theological tradition has now motivated the church to alter explicit passages that evince Christ's intercessory function. In doing so, the new version of the EOTC Bible has undermined Christ's unique intercessory ministry on behalf of his people.

74. Cf. Strauss, *Perspectives*, 160.

17

Patience in the Light of the Lord's Coming (James 5:7–11)

A Latin American Reading

NELSON MORALES

Is patience resignation? How does the way we understand patience lead us to face situations with people and circumstances?

Beginning on October 18, 2019, many Chileans went out to the streets to protest because of social inequalities. The protests continued for more than ninety days. A rise of 30 pesos (4 US cents) in the metro system triggered the riots. The people said, "It is not about 30 pesos but about 30 years of inequality." Christian leaders have had different reactions to those issues. Some called for believers to be submissive to the authorities appointed by God: do not protest, since what the government does is right because it is appointed by God. Other pastors and priests identified themselves with the people and supported and advised people in their dialogue with the authorities. What does patience mean? How should we speak about patience in the light of significant inequality throughout the Latin American context?

One of the latest reports of the Economic Commission for Latin America and the Caribbean (ECLAC; also La Comisión Económica para América Latina, CEPAL) gives account that around 30.8 percent of the Latin American population lives under the poverty line, and 11.5 percent lives in extreme poverty.[1] This situation of poverty is more dramatic if one takes into account a measurement of the income inequality, the Gini coefficient. The average Gini coefficient for the region was 0.465 in 2018.[2] By way of comparison, the average Gini coefficient for the countries in the Organization for Economic Co-operation and Development (OECD) was 0.320 in 2014.[3] This financial inequality is concurrent with a lack of access to the judicial, health, and educational systems. This is the context in which Christians live and serve the kingdom of God. Christianity represents around 79 percent of the population (60 percent Catholics, 19 percent evangelicals/Protestants).[4] Interestingly, secularism is increasing vis-à-vis a systematic decrease in Catholicism. In fact, 17 percent of the population identifies as atheists/agnostics/nonreligious.[5] In Guatemala, where I serve as professor at the Central American Theological Seminary, around 43 percent of the population is Catholic, 41 percent evangelical/Protestant, and 13 percent atheist/agnostic/nonreligious.[6]

Again, how should we speak about patience in light of such levels of inequality throughout such a seemingly Christian Latin American context? Many times, pastors, priests, and counselors in Latin America quote James 5:7–11 as a basis for an attitude of resignation, not only in these situations of inequality but also in circumstances of abuse and exploitation. Is James promoting resignation and tolerance of violence and inequality?

James builds his ethic from the Old Testament and Jesus's teachings. He frames it with an eschatological tone. He deals with various topics, from trials and temptation to wealth and poverty, law, control of speech, discrimination, and planning. One thread in this tapestry of themes is patience. He addresses patience in the context of trials (James 1:2–3, 12) and temptation (1:12–14).

1. *Panorama social de América Latina* (Santiago: CEPAL, 2019), 17.

2. *Panorama social*, 21.

3. Celine Thévenot, "Inequality in OECD Countries," *SJPH* 45, no. 18 (2017): 10.

4. *El papa Francisco y la religión en Chile y América Latina: Latinobarómetro 1995–2017*, Latinobarómetro, January 2018, https://sxpolitics.org/es/wp-content/uploads/sites/3/2020/01/F00006494-RELIGION_CHILE-AMERICA_LATINA_2017-1.pdf, p. 15. The religious situation has not changed significantly in these last years, as the Latinobarómetro web page gives account in its last study in 2023 (www.latinobarometro.org).

5. *El papa Francisco*, 15.

6. *El papa Francisco*, 15. In other research, Catholics represent 45 percent of the population, evangelicals 43 percent, and almost 3 percent of the population practices Mayan religions. Geovanni Contreras Corzantes, "Católicos superan por poco a evangélicos," *Prensa Libre*, May 31, 2015, https://www.prensalibre.com/guatemala/comunitario/catolicos-evangelicos-cifras-encuesta. In the last publication of Latinobarómetro (*Latinobarómetro 2023: Guatemala*), 42.4 percent of the population is Catholic, 45.7 percent evangelical, and 11 percent has no religious affiliation (www.latinobarometro.org).

Additionally, he associates patience with faith (1:2–3), wisdom (1:4–5), and suffering (5:7–11).

This chapter seeks to demonstrate that, for James, patience is not a passive trait to be exercised alone but rather an active trait that is experienced in community. This chapter will explore this understanding of patience in James along the following lines. First, the context of the passage and its literary structure is presented. Second, two common interpretations of patience are discussed. Third, the concept of militant patience is introduced. Fourth comes a reflection on patience in community. Finally, a reading of James 5:7–11 is provided from a Latin American perspective.

Context and Structure of the Passage

James presents an important criticism to those who have economic resources. He makes this criticism on two fronts, both of which are introduced with "come now" (*age nyn*, James 4:13; 5:1). First, he corrects the arrogance of some Christian merchants who do not consider God in their lives and businesses (4:13–17). Second, he criticizes and condemns some landlords for the exploitation of their laborers, their luxurious and indulgent life (5:1–5), and their legal attacks against the righteous (5:6). Immediately after this prophetic denunciation, he comforts his audience with eschatological hope (5:7–11).

Several words and phrases give internal coherence to James 5:7–11. James connects this paragraph with the former by the inferential particle *oun* (5:7). Internally, he builds a thematic *inclusio* revolving around the concept of patient endurance in 5:7–11. The center is highlighted by using aorist imperatives in the extreme of the structure (*makrothymēsate*, 5:7, 8; *stērixate*, 5:8; *labete*, 5:10), and at the center, a present imperative (*mē stenazete*, 5:9).[7] He gives cohesion to the paragraph by using two semantically related word groups for "patience/endurance": *makrothymia/makrothymeō* (5:7–8, 10) and *hypomonē/hypomenō* (5:11). He also unites the paragraph by repeating key words such as the noun *kyrios* ("Lord," 5:7, 8, 10, 11 [2×])[8] and through the use of discourse markers such as *idou* ("behold," 5:7, 9, 11) and *adelphoi* ("brothers

---

7. See a recent discussion on the use of the imperative mood in Joseph D. Fantin, "May the Force Be with You: Volition, Direction, and Force; A Communicative Approach to the Imperative Mood," *BAGL* 7 (2018): 173–99; Stanley E. Porter, "Aspect and Imperative Once More," *BAGL* 7 (2018): 141–72.

8. *Ho kritēs* (James 5:9) has the same referent as *ho kyrios*. It is not clear in this passage if it refers to Jesus or the Father. It could be either. Or James even could be intentionally ambiguous in order to evoke the Old Testament prophetic image of God's coming in judgment and vindication.

and sisters," 5:7, 9, 10).[9] Also, the eschatological hope is emphasized by the imminence of the Lord's coming (*hē parousia tou kyriou*, 5:7, 8), the nearness of the judge (*ho kritēs pro tōn thyrōn hestēken*, 5:9), and the Lord's mercy and compassion (5:11).

James uses one metaphor and two examples in order to encourage his readers/hearers to develop patient endurance in the light of the Lord's coming. The metaphor of the small farmer (James 5:7) and the exemplar of the prophets (5:10) and Job (5:11) define what he understands by patient endurance. In the midst of this exhortation, James encourages his addressees to eradicate groaning against each other (5:9).

Recurrent Western Interpretations

Through the centuries, different authors have given their interpretation of this passage, and in particular what it means to be patient. The interpretation of Western authors has been very influential. They typically conceive of patience as a passive attitude of hope. In many cases, this passivity leads to inaction, even resignation. The explanation given about the prophets focuses on their endurance, but even then, the example of Job causes difficulties because he is viewed as imperfectly patient.[10] Ralph Martin, for example, understands patience as waiting without doing anything regarding the actual situation. Regarding Job's example, he says, "It is not clear why Job is chosen to exemplify patience in suffering. He was anything but an example of a godly person who was patient in the midst of adversity. The character Job in the canonical Scriptures was not a silent party to his suffering; rather, he was one who complained bitterly to God because of his dire circumstances."[11] Luke Timothy Johnson adds, "The portrayal of Job in the canonical book is scarcely that of the 'patient Job' presumed here."[12]

The view of patience in James as passive forbearance is not limited to Western interpreters. Some Asian, African, African American, and Latin American interpreters follow the same train of thought. For example, Luke Cheung

9. This vocative, *adelphoi*, introduces the imperatives with a pastoral tone. James uses the same vocative with some variants throughout the letter (1:2, 16, 19; 2:1, 5, 14; 3:1, 10, 12; 5:12, 19).

10. Cf. John Calvin, *Commentaries on the Catholic Epistles*, trans. John Owen (Bellingham, WA: Logos Bible Software, 2010), 351; Matthew Henry, *Matthew Henry's Commentary on the Whole Bible: Complete and Unabridged in One Volume* (Peabody, MA: Hendrickson, 1994), 2418; Peter H. Davids, *The Epistle of James: A Commentary on the Greek Text*, NIGTC (Grand Rapids: Eerdmans, 1982), 181, 187; Douglas J. Moo, *The Letter of James*, PNTC (Grand Rapids: Eerdmans, 2000), 222.

11. Ralph P. Martin, *James*, WBC 48 (Waco: Word, 1988), 194.

12. Luke Timothy Johnson, *The Letter of James: A New Translation with Introduction and Commentary*, AB 37A (New Haven: Yale University Press, 1995), 319.

highlights this passivity, saying that "those who love God with all their life, as exemplified particularly in the concrete example of Job (as portrayed in traditions like that in *T. Job*), will look to the future and endure to the end, even unto death as martyrs."[13] In the same vein, Solomon Andria highlights the patience that the farmers, prophets, and Job express: every one of them waits patiently until the end, in the midst of suffering.[14] Evis Carballosa understands patience as a passive attitude toward trials and tribunals, which leads Christians to act with a spirit of hope and trust.[15]

Many other authors see a more active meaning in the concept of patient endurance. For example, François Vouga sees *makrothymia* as resistance, not as a passive attitude. For that reason, he points out, "Our author does not engage with a simple expectation or submission, but with an active faithfulness, a dissidence and an endurance."[16] Scot McKnight likewise refuses to adopt a "complacent theory of patience." On the contrary, he points out, "Any reading of Job reveals a character who stuck it out, who trusted in God, and who did so fully aware of the fundamental injustice he had experienced. Maybe, then, Job is the perfect example for the oppressed poor. Patience here need not be understood as quietude or passivity; perhaps genuine patience involves realities like protesting to God, yet without surrendering one's integrity or one's faith in God or losing the path of following Jesus."[17] These last two examples reveal a more robust approach to the theme. It will be apparent in the next sections why this understanding of patient endurance better fits the passage.

Militant Patience

Many Christians in Guatemala live in rural areas. A high percentage of them are farmers. There are many regions in the country that depend, just as in Palestine, exclusively on rain for the irrigation of crops. Thus, they understand well James's illustration of the patience of farmers. In this context, a farmer is far from being passive. Farmers prepare the soil and plant the seed before the rain comes. But after planting and during the season of rain, there is more work to do until the precious fruit becomes ready for harvest. As Craig Blomberg and Mariam Kamell point out, "Farmers . . . hardly sat idle in between, but rather worked hard in weeding, hoeing, fertilizing, and doing

---

13. Luke L. Cheung, *The Genre, Composition and Hermeneutics of the Epistle of James* (Eugene, OR: Wipf & Stock, 2006), 269.

14. Solomon Andria, "James," in *Africa Bible Commentary*, ed. Tokunboh Adeyemo (Grand Rapids: Zondervan, 2006), 1541.

15. Evis L. Carballosa, *Santiago, Una fe en acción* (Grand Rapids: Portavoz, 1986), 232.

16. François Vouga, *L'Épître de saint Jacques*, CNT 13a (Geneva: Labor et Fides, 1984), 133.

17. Scot McKnight, *The Letter of James*, NICNT (Grand Rapids: Eerdmans, 2011), 420.

whatever they could to bring their crops to full fruition."[18] It is true that the farmer can do nothing to control weather and the time when rain comes. In that sense, farmers do their job with the total hope that in due time rain will come. In the same way, James encourages his readers/hearers to be patient until the coming of the Lord (5:7–8). Instead of being resigned in the midst of their situation, they should strengthen their hearts because the coming of the Lord is near (5:8).

This active waiting of the farmer leads Elsa Támez to define patience as militant.[19] For her, to be patient means "to persevere, to resist, to be constant, unbreakable, immovable."[20] In that sense, it is "a question of doing everything possible not to despair in spite of the desperate situation, relying on the future that will put an end to the sufferings."[21] In the case of James's readers, it is a militant patience "that arises from the roots of oppression; it is an active, working patience."[22] The hope of Jesus's coming permits his addressees to focus on the present situation with the correct attitude and, in community, to live their lives with integrity and genuine prayer.[23]

In the third block of the *inclusio* (James 5:10–11), James reinforces the concept of active patience in the context of the Lord's coming with two examples from the Old Testament. The first is a call to imitate the prophets as models of suffering and patient endurance. It is noteworthy that James describes these prophets as those who spoke in the name of the Lord.

Reflecting on the prophetic ministry, Samuel Escobar and Eduardo Delás reinforce the idea of patience as opposite to resignation. They harmonize with Támez's concept of militant patience. Escobar and Delás present two aspects of this patience: patience/waiting and patience/strength. They point out that patience "describes perseverance, resolve and resistance of someone who has a vision that goes beyond the present situation. It has nothing to do with resignation, nor with indifference or fatalism."[24] When people are faced with the prospect of living in an unjust, painful, or otherwise difficult situation, a patient person looks forward, as the prophets did, to the coming of a

18. Craig L. Blomberg and Mariam J. Kamell, *James*, ZECNT 16 (Grand Rapids: Zondervan, 2008), 227.

19. In his commentary, when talking about Job's patience, Dale Allison rejects Elsa Támez's concept but does not give any argument for his decision: Dale C. Allison Jr., *A Critical and Exegetical Commentary on the Epistle of James*, ICC (New York: Bloomsbury, 2013), 716n186.

20. Elsa Támez, *The Scandalous Message of James: Faith without Works Is Dead*, rev. ed. (New York: Crossroad, 2002), 44.

21. Támez, *Scandalous Message*, 46.

22. Támez, *Scandalous Message*, 44.

23. Támez, *Scandalous Message*, 46–59.

24. Samuel Escobar and Eduardo Delás, *Santiago: La fe viva que impulsa a la misión* (Bogotá: Ediciones Puma, 2012), 70, my translation.

new world and seeks to live the values of the kingdom of God in the midst of the present condition.[25] Strength is the characteristic of prophetic endurance. As Escobar and Delás say, "Even in the midst of pain and in circumstances in which all they could do was to clench their teeth, the prophets stood up, they were not silent, they denounced the corruption of such a socioeconomic reality that intended to perpetuate and legitimate wealth, privileges and power of a few, before poverty."[26] This is precisely the type of prophetic denunciation that James employs in 5:1–6.

James encourages his addressees to consider the prophets as exemplars of suffering and patience, but he also describes them as those who spoke in the name of the Lord (5:10). The Old Testament prophets both denounced sin and proclaimed God's will. This announcement, as David Suazo Jiménez points out, revolves around three elements:[27] (1) God's imminent judgment,[28] (2) the restoration of the people of God, and (3) a new eschatological reality, the kingdom of God. Not only has a prophetic tone been discerned in James's style, but these three aspects of the prophetic announcement are also present in his letter. James begins his letter by appealing to the eschatological reversal of both the poor and the rich (1:9–11). He faces his readers/hearers with their lack of loyalty to God and calls them "adulteresses" (*moichalides*, 4:4). He confronts the rich landlords due to their exploitation of their laborers (5:1–5). At the same time, he encourages his readers to be patient because they will receive a crown of life (1:12), the Lord's coming is near (5:7, 8), and God is full of compassion and mercy (5:11). He also mentions the presence of the kingdom of God in the context of confronting discrimination (2:6). Thus, James not only encourages his readers to imitate the prophets but also is an example of how to do it.[29] Additionally, as a result of their ministry, prophets experienced suffering, but in the midst of it they faithfully proclaimed God's word. James does not exhort the community to avoid hostility and suffering;[30] instead, he corrects their focus and gives them hope in Jesus's imminent coming.

25. Escobar and Delás, *Santiago*, 70.

26. Escobar and Delás, *Santiago*, 70.

27. David Suazo Jiménez, *La función profética de la educación teológica evangélica en América Latina* (Barcelona: Clie, 2012), 13–14.

28. This announcement of judgment is threefold in that it includes a judgment of (1) the people of God, (2) the enemies of the people of God, and (3) the world in general.

29. In the same vein, Craig Blomberg says that in these verses, James, as Jesus did before him, chooses a "prophetic option" and discards both the violent revolt of the Zealots and the quiet separatism of the Essenes. Craig L. Blomberg, "Las posesiones materiales en el cristianismo primitivo," *Kairós* 25 (1999): 26.

30. It is possible that the just who cannot resist the oppressive rich in James 5:6 could have been denouncing the habits of those rich landlords (5:1–5).

James also uses Job as an example of patience. As mentioned above, Job's life is a test case for the concept of patience that various authors have. Some authors see incongruence between the biblical Job and their concept of patience. Some of them resolve this perceived tension by connecting James's interpretation with the Testament of Job. In that book, Job seems to fit that passive framework better. However, it is not necessary to make this connection. First, it is not clear when that work was written. Also, the canonical Job fits with what has been argued so far regarding a militant patience.[31] From Job 3 onward, Job argues with his friends and defends his innocence and righteousness. He vehemently asks God about his situation. As Gustavo Gutiérrez says, "That cry cannot be quiet. The one who unjustly suffers has the right of groaning and protesting. In it, the person expresses [to God] his/her perplexity and at the same time his/her faith."[32] At the end of the book, God vindicates Job, even though he never explained to Job what happened in the spiritual realm (Job 42:7–9). In James's terms, the end of Job's story presents God as compassionate and merciful (James 5:11). The same compassion and mercy are at the disposal of James's addressees. God not only is willing to give his wisdom to face trials (1:5) but also is ready to help and concretely express his love to his people under oppression.

Patience in Community

Farmers do not do their job isolated from their community. Small farming in the first century was a communitarian activity. The farmer's family was fully involved in the whole process. Thus, the farmer's patience was not an individualistic patience but one lived in community. James reinforces the importance of community by warning his addressees of the danger that complaining and groaning represent for the group, in particular in the context of suffering. They have been witnesses to the oppression and hostility of some landlords and wealthy oppressors. In the midst of this situation, they are tempted to complain and groan against one another. That attitude reflects a cracking of the unity of the community. If they are not united, they will not be able to face hostility and adversity, and their patience will weaken. The force of

31. McKnight (*James*, 421) clearly highlights this unnecessary connection between Job in James and Job of the Testament of Job. He says, "But we should not fall for this generality about patience so easily. Indeed, Job is cast in the Testament of Job in altogether patient terms, but that is not James's point. He has more in mind the poor oppressed who cry out to God (like Job), who are not to resort to violence, and who will retain their faith and integrity without always falling from their commitments."

32. Gustavo Gutiérrez, *Hablar de Dios desde el sufrimiento del inocente: Una reflexión sobre el libro de Job* (Salamanca: Sígueme, 1988), 182, my translation.

the community lies with their commitment to and protection of one another (James 5:19–20). Grumbling against one another requires repentance (5:9).

James emphasizes the role of the community throughout his letter. For example, when describing the true religion, he points out the centrality of taking care of widows and orphans in the midst of their affliction (James 1:27). He mentions that a real faith is manifested by supporting the extreme poor; otherwise, that faith is empty (2:14–17). It is very important that the sick are not left alone. When they are experiencing illness, community prayer is fundamental (5:14–16). Finally, James expresses that it is a blessing to bring back the wandering sinner (5:19–20). Without a doubt, patient endurance is strengthened when the community is free from groaning, when the individual finds support in the community. As a community, they face trials with hope in the imminent coming of the Lord, which brings vindication and blessing. In the midst of trials, their faith increases, and their patience is strengthened (1:2–3). In fact, the one who endures under trials receives a crown of life (1:12). However, people should not experience trials isolated from their community; they should find refuge in their community. For those who slander and complain, destroying their community, the judge is at the gates ready to judge them (5:9; cf. 4:12).

Patience in the Light of Suffering and Violence in Latin America

Today, the Christian community is broader than in James's times. Many issues may divide us, but we need to follow James's exhortations. Jesus's coming is nearer than in James's days. Not just the cry of laborers has reached the ears of the Lord of Hosts but also the cry of women and children. What should we say to them?

In the Guatemalan context, about 46 percent of the population is evangelical.[33] At the same time, about 60 percent of the population lives below the poverty line, and 50 percent of the population lives in rural areas.[34] Most evangelicals are poor and in rural areas. There are businesspersons, politicians, and professionals, but most are workers and peasants. Thus, James's letter is still a letter close to our Christian reality.

Beginning in 2018, caravans of Honduran migrants traversed over a thousand miles from their country, crossing Guatemala and Mexico in order to

---

33. I use the concept "evangelical" in the broader sense of non-Catholic Christians. As I mention in the introduction, Catholics represent 43 percent of the population, and almost 3 percent of the population practices Mayan religions.

34. Intituto Nacional de Estadísticas, *Encuesta nacional de condiciones de vida 2014* (Guatemala City: INE, 2016); Banco de Guatemala, *Guatemala en cifras 2018* (Guatemala City: Banguat, 2018).

enter the United States. I do not know the motivation of the promoters of the caravans, but many of the participants are motivated by the extreme desperation they feel. Many of them are also Christians. Violence, labor exploitation, extortion, and lack of work push them to look for better opportunities. How can we speak about a passive patience to them?

Additionally, political turmoil has characterized several countries in the region. Venezuela, Nicaragua, Argentina, Brazil, Peru, and Guatemala, just to name a few, have experienced significant political problems, such as corruption, new forms of dictatorships, and coups d'état. This political instability causes or stimulates unemployment or abuse by business owners. In Guatemala, many of those politicians and business owners are also Christians. What role should the church have in the midst of these challenges?

James calls believers to be patient like the farmer until the Lord's coming. But he also presents the prophets and Job as exemplars. Through them we can understand what he means by patience. He presents a militant patience, which is the vehicle to face adversity and affliction. This militant patience is lived in community and strengthened by the hope of the imminent coming of our Lord.

For many years, the church in Latin America understood patience in the sense of resignation. From Catholic and evangelical pulpits, the message was almost the same: Christians should be quiet and bow their heads during difficult situations.[35] However, this attitude has been changing in the last decade. Two contemporary Latin American examples demonstrate how a militant patience can help the church to face trials with a strong hope in Jesus's coming.

First, Claudia Dary has done important research on churches, both Catholic and evangelical, located in extremely violent neighborhoods in Guatemala City.[36] These churches are deeply committed to their communities. Their parish priests and pastors have created small groups among gang members in order to rescue them from the gangs. They also have developed multidisciplinary support groups in order to help them stop consuming drugs, committing violence, and so on. There are also some organizations, such as the Christian Movement against Violence toward Children, known by the Spanish acronym MOCVIN, that are working to end the abuse of women

---

35. Liberation theologians have understood patience in different ways through the years. In the 1960s, some actively promoted changing the status quo by any means, including armed violence. However, today, ideas such as Elsa Támez's concept of militant patience used in this chapter are the norm.

36. Claudia Dary, *Cristianos en un país violento: Respuestas de las iglesias frente a la violencia en dos colonias del área metropolitana de Guatemala* (Guatemala: Universidad de San Carlos de Guatemala, 2016).

and children.[37] Thus, besides the regular services on Sundays, churches have crossed the bridge between the sacred and the secular world and have begun to preach a more holistic gospel. Pastors are not just preaching patience in the midst of violence; they have shown concrete ways to face that violence. Some of them have experienced persecution as a result; however, they are prepared to assume that cost. Like the prophets, they speak the word of God and are also examples of patience amid suffering.

Second, following Walter Brueggemann's concept of prophetic imagination and Daniel Carroll Rodas's application of that concept to Amos, Suazo Jiménez challenges the status quo of evangelical theological education in Latin America.[38] He says, "When people speak about the phenomenal growing of the evangelical church in Latin America, people really think of the growing of the evangelical religious activities. There are more church buildings, more 'worship services,' more Christian concerts, more people attending these religious activities; at the end of the day, there are more ministries. Sadly, one could say that the growing of the evangelical church in Latin America is not the same as the growing of the kingdom of God, namely, of the divine values which the prophets proclaimed by their imagination."[39] Suazo Jiménez proposes that the prophetic imagination expands beyond a limited conception of being Christian. It permits believers to go beyond the borders of traditional religious activities into all the spheres of human life and activity. Prophets not only denounce individual and social sins, as well as issue a call to repentance of those sins, but also describe the future, in both individual and community terms. In that way, the reach of the prophetic imagination challenges the imagination of the church today. The task of teachers in seminaries is not simply to "promote a dialogue between the reality of the biblical context and the current reality; it goes beyond that. It is about looking for patterns of action based upon universal, abstract and eternal principles that can be applied

37. MOCVIN is El Movimiento Cristiano Contra la Violencia Hacia la Niñez. Important and influential churches in the capital and five other big cities support this organization, among them Iglesia Fraternidad Cristiana de Guatemala, Iglesia Nazareth Sur, Iglesia Casa de Pan y Alabanza, Iglesia Vida Real, Iglesia de Dios del Evangelio Completo, and Iglesia Central del Príncipe de Paz. Organizations that are also part of this initiative include World Vision, International Justice Mission, GBN-Guatemala, Compassion International, I58, and Buckner Guatemala. See Dary, *Cristianos en un país violento*, 108–10.

38. Suazo Jiménez, *La función profética*. Suazo Jiménez builds his thought on Walter Brueggemann, *The Prophetic Imagination*, 2nd ed. (Minneapolis: Fortress, 2001); M. Daniel Carroll R., "La ética social de los profetas y su relevancia para América Latina hoy: La opción por la ética profética," *Kairós* 32 (2003): 7–25.

39. Suazo Jiménez, *La función profética*, 38. This and the following quotations are my own translation.

to the current situation."[40] Furthermore, "teachers should dream with a new church, a new society, and should invite his/her students to dream with him/her, transmitting to them with passion his/her dreams, as the Old Testament prophets did . . . and commit to those dreams and stimulate his/her students' commitment."[41]

Many of us, as Suazo Jiménez's disciples, have pursued this same theological thinking. Throughout Latin American, presidents, deans, and faculty members have embraced a transformative theological education that challenges the church and society. In this way, little by little, the worldview of pastors and local church leaders in our context is changing. All of us wait for the coming of our Lord, not with passivity but with a strong commitment of giving hope to the hopeless and new ways to face injustice.[42]

Christian communities stand firm amid suffering through the persistent work of their members, in particular their leaders. Pastors and professors should take seriously James's exhortations. They are called to teach and lead communities of believers who face violence and desperation. Dary's study reveals that this is possible, but it involves high risks. Suazo Jiménez's proposal gives a theological basis on which to build that labor. As Job modeled, Christian communities should be patient and express to God all their afflictions with a deep faith. God is still full of mercy and compassionate. His ears are ready to hear their cry, and his hands are always acting in their favor.

As in James's times, so still today, we need to stop grumbling against one another. Fights and criticism within and between denominations and the disconnect between many seminaries and the church are sins of which we need to repent. When churches learn to work together and stop complaining against one another, they will strengthen their patience and be in better condition to face difficulties together.

Conclusion

The understanding of patience advocated by this chapter reveals that even though the idea of a passive patience is broad and still popular, it is not adequate to explain James's illustrations in 5:7–11. His illustrations of the small farmer, the prophets, and Job point toward a more active concept of patience. Támez defines this patience as militant: an active patience that arises from

40. Suazo Jiménez, *La función profética*, 41.
41. Suazo Jiménez, *La función profética*, 42–43.
42. Other important theologians, such as Elsa Támez, Irene Foulkes, Emilio A. Núñez, Samuel Escobar, René Padilla, and Juan Stam, have inspired the same concerns and attitude.

oppression. It is a patience that finds its strength in faith in Jesus and develops its hope in the certain and imminent coming of Jesus.

This militant patience characterizes the life and ministry of the prophets and Job. Denunciation and proclamation of the reality of the kingdom of God are essential components of the words of the prophets. Through his letter, James guides his audience to deal with suffering. He does not exhort them to avoid hostility and suffering but corrects their focus and gives them hope and purpose in the light of the Lord's imminent coming. Likewise, Job exemplifies one who deeply knows in whom he has believed. He expresses, from a profound faith, his affliction and perplexity to God, just like the laborers cry for their salary.

As we have seen, believers express their patience fully integrated in their community. For that reason, there is no room for groaning and complaining against one another. These sins break up the cohesion of the community and weaken the strength to face suffering. Patience is strengthened in a united community. Members of the community care for one another and support one another amid their afflictions as an expression of a pure and unblemished religion before God the Father.

Dary and Suazo Jiménez have proposed examples of what patience looks like in Latin America today, in practice and in transformative theological education. These examples illustrate that a militant patience moves the church of Christ toward a better world while suffering in the light of the imminent coming of Jesus Christ.

18

Reading 1 Peter among the Elect Resident Aliens in Sri Lanka

DAVID A. DESILVA

This chapter represents the principal fruits of my conversations about 1 Peter with the students and faculty of Colombo Theological Seminary, whose mission is to provide theological education and ministry training especially to evangelical Protestant Christians throughout the island of Sri Lanka. The author of 1 Peter returns repeatedly to his addressees' experience of socially imposed shame (1 Pet. 1:6; 2:12, 19; 3:14, 16; 4:4, 12–16, 19), suggesting that this is indeed an important feature of the situation that he is addressing.[1] It is

---

1. Throughout this chapter I will simply refer to the "author" without engaging the question whether or not this involved the historical Peter. Readers may review discussions of authorship in critical commentaries. These positions and supporting literature are briefly surveyed in D. A. deSilva, *An Introduction to the New Testament: Contexts, Methods and Ministry Formation*, 2nd ed. (Downers Grove, IL: InterVarsity, 2018), 748–51. On the challenges to his addressees' honor foregrounded by the author of 1 Peter and the strategies he promotes in order to help them overcome those challenges while remaining loyal to the Christian movement, see John H. Elliott, "Disgraced yet Graced: The Gospel according to 1 Peter in the Key of Honor and Shame," *BTB* 25 (1995): 166–74; deSilva, *Introduction to the New Testament*, 744–48, 751–65; deSilva, "Turning Shame into Honor: The Pastoral Strategy of 1 Peter," in *The Shame Factor: How Shame Shapes Society*, ed. Robert Jewett, Wayne Alloway Jr., and John G. Lacey (Eugene, OR: Wipf & Stock, 2010), 159–86.

this facet of the text and of the situation it addresses with which Sri Lankan Christians identify most readily and, indeed, which drew them to desire to study this text in the first place.

Context

Slightly more than 70 percent of Sri Lankans identify themselves as Buddhist. Hinduism is a distant second at 12.6 percent.[2] There is a great deal of practical overlap between popular Buddhism and Hindu practice, since the Hindu pantheon has long been part of lay Buddhist culture on the island.[3] The demographics of the two, however, are quite different. Almost all Buddhists are Sinhalese, and almost all Hindus are Tamil. The ethnic strife between these two groups has been well known, resulting in nearly thirty years of civil war that ended only by a successful, though excessively violent, stratagem in 2009. Approximately 9.7 percent of the population subscribes to Islam and 7.6 percent to Christianity. Of the latter, about four out of five are Roman Catholic Christians, and the remainder are one or another variety of Protestant.[4] These figures add up to almost 100 percent. Sri Lanka is very much more akin to the first-century Mediterranean than the twenty-first-century Western context insofar as almost everyone on the island would claim a particular religious affiliation. While the Sri Lankan constitution protects freedom of religion and the freedom to *change* religious affiliation, Buddhism is formally awarded "foremost place" among the country's religions and is afforded more explicit protections than minority religions.[5]

The non-Christian dominant and majority cultures of Sri Lanka respond to the Christian presence there much as did the non-Christian dominant and majority cultures of Roman Anatolia in the regions addressed by 1 Peter. Despite the legal right to freedom of religion, there exists significant prejudice against Christianity in Sri Lanka, often manifesting itself in harassment, intimidation, and even violent hostility. A principal cause for this is the fact that the Christian gospel is seen—quite rightly—as a foreign import into Sri Lankan territory. Indeed, although there was a small Christian presence in Sri Lanka prior

---

2. Data from "Census of Population and Housing 2012: Key Findings," Department of Census and Statistics, Colombo, Sri Lanka, https://srilanka.unfpa.org/sites/default/files/pub-pdf/Census-2012.pdf.

3. G. P. V. Somaratna, *The Foreignness of the Christian Church in Sri Lanka* (Kohuwela, Sri Lanka: CTS Publishing, 2006), 4.

4. These figures are taken from "Census of Population and Housing 2012," 21.

5. Bureau of Democracy, Human Rights, and Labor, "International Religious Freedom Report for 2017: Executive Summary," US Department of State, accessed January 12, 2024, https://www.state.gov/reports/2017-report-on-international-religious-freedom/sri-lanka/.

to the colonization of the island by European powers,[6] "the Christianity which is found in Sri Lanka today owes its origins to the colonial rule of the past."[7] Christianity had been an accoutrement, even an instrument, of colonization for almost three centuries and, since Sri Lankan independence in 1947, has continued to be viewed as an instrument of Westernization. Colonial rule was often brutal. Under Portuguese domination, the colonizers confiscated sacred sites, burned the temples, and erected Roman Catholic churches in their place, sometimes slaughtering the Buddhist clergy who resisted.[8] During Dutch rule, the Dutch Reformed Church suppressed Sri Lankan Catholics while seeking to win converts from among the very poor with material support (whence the pejorative expression "rice Christians" originates). The Dutch did not allow new buildings to be constructed for the worship of any other religion.[9] Under the British Raj, Christians, especially Anglicans, enjoyed significant privilege. Since political independence, many have promoted the view that Buddhism is the religion most proper to Sri Lanka and, indeed, central to its postcolonial recovery of indigenous Sri Lankan identity. As this impetus gained ground, local toleration for other religions decreased, especially for overtly and energetically proselytizing Christian groups, which local Buddhist leaders regard as a corrosive and antipatriotic influence.

Christians in Sri Lanka are no strangers to the social dynamics reflected in 1 Peter. Sculpted images and their veneration continue to play a prominent, even central, role in Sri Lankan Buddhism and Hinduism. The tendency of a great many Christians to avoid the religious ceremonies valued by their non-Christian neighbors, which involve the invocation of other gods and some ritual presence of idols, is a constant reminder of the lack of unity and solidarity within a family or a community. This is all the more problematic insofar as the religious convictions of Buddhists and Hindus allow them to participate readily in the religious ceremonies of their Christian family members and friends. The latter's refusal to reciprocate exacerbates the tensions between them. This is again very much akin to the first-century setting—polytheists can accommodate the rites of monotheists, but the reverse is highly problematic for the monotheist. The non-Christian families and neighbors are indeed "surprised," "estranged," and even "alienated" (*xenizontai*) by the antisocial behavior of former friends, associates, and

---

6. See Prabo Mihindukulasuriya, *The "Nestorian" Cross and the Persian Christians of the Anuradhapura Period* (Kohuwela, Sri Lanka: CTS Publishing, 2012).

7. Somaratna, *Foreignness*, 7.

8. Somaratna, *Foreignness*, 32–34.

9. Somaratna, *Foreignness*, 34. During these centuries almost no attention was given to developing either indigenous forms or indigenous leaders (p. 9).

otherwise reliable citizens (1 Pet. 4:3–4). Non-Christian family members often view converts as betraying the family—"forsaking father and mother" is a common idiom in this regard.

Outside of pressure within a family, the most significant and overt hostility tends to surface against evangelical Christian groups, particularly outside of the major urban centers. According to the National Christian Evangelical Alliance of Sri Lanka, there were ninety-seven "incidents of attacks on churches, intimidation, violence against pastors and their congregations, and obstruction of worship services" in 2017, an increase from eighty-nine recorded incidents in 2016.[10] Local Buddhist monks will often be found in the forefront of a mob that gathers to confront a local Christian pastor or assembly. These mobs, which have been known to turn violent, have numbered from dozens to as high as two thousand on one occasion in the southern village of Devinuwara.[11] Local police and other authorities are often seen to be slow to respond or even to side with those harassing or threatening Christian leaders and their assemblies, advising against filing complaints and even urging acquiescence to the demands of non-Christian protesters for the sake of preserving the peace or the local Christians' safety.

First Peter and Responses to Harassment and Hostility

Passages like 1 Peter 3:13–17 and 4:12–16 speak with a keen immediacy to the situation of thousands of Sri Lankan Christians. Many of my conversation partners sympathized quite personally with the challenges facing the audience of 1 Peter—either succumb to the social forces pressing for "rehabilitation" or come to grips with the experience of shame and hostility in such a way that these do not become debilitating.

10. "2017 Report on International Religious Freedom: Sri Lanka," Bureau of Democracy, Human Rights, and Labor, US Department of State, accessed November 3, 2018, https://www.state.gov/reports/2017-report-on-international-religious-freedom/sri-lanka/ (pp. 1, 9 in the pdf). A perusal of other reports from the US Department of State on Sri Lanka indicates a pervasive pattern of harassment, vandalism, and assault island-wide. The 2009 report includes the murder of a Protestant pastor and his two sons, a Jesuit relief coordinator, and (likely) a Seventh Day Adventist pastor ("2009 Report on International Religious Freedom: Sri Lanka," Bureau of Democracy, Human Rights, and Labor, US Department of State, accessed November 9, 2018, http://www.state.gov/j/drl/rls/irf/2009/127371.htm). The 2011 report shows a slight decrease in physical violence and greater responsiveness on the part of local police ("2011 Report on International Religious Freedom: Sri Lanka," Bureau of Democracy, Human Rights, and Labor, US Department of State, accessed November 9, 2018, https://2009-2017.state.gov/j/drl/rls/irf/2011/sca/192935.htm). It is important to note that Muslim leaders, congregations, places of worship, citizens, and places of business experience the same kinds and degrees of harassment, for generally all the same reasons.

11. "2017 Report on International Religious Freedom," 10.

An interesting development in our conversations was the recognition of the importance of thinking critically about both antagonism and rapprochement in the Sri Lankan context. How much of the former is *essential* if one is to maintain one's Christian identity and practice intact? How much of the rapprochement can be effectively pursued without sacrificing that Christian identity, and with what hope for changed relationships? The author of 1 Peter himself seems concerned that any experience of being slandered or otherwise shamed by non-Christians be rooted in their fidelity to the call and example of Christ, and not in any behavior to which non-Christians might *legitimately* object. The principal unavoidable offenses would be those inherent in "turning to God from idols" (to borrow a phrase from 1 Thess. 1:9) and transferring their allegiance to this God and the kingdom of God's Son—not the avoidable offenses of, for example, disturbing a neighborhood with excessively loud, Western-style worship bands or choosing to visit a sacred archaeological site while failing to remove one's shoes out of respect. My conversation partners also latched onto the ways in which 1 Peter suggests avenues toward rapprochement, particularly through foregrounding the embodiment of shared ethical ideals.

Shared Ethical Ideals

The author of 1 Peter exploits the substantial areas of overlap between what the Christian community and the non-Christian majority culture affirm as noble and avoid as vicious. He calls the hearers to counter the feelings of shame evoked by their neighbors' hostility and reproach by developing a healthy self-respect based on the embodiment of ideals and virtues they *know* to be held in esteem within both the Christian subculture and the majority culture, the culture of their primary upbringing. He expresses the hope that the consonance of Christian conduct with celebrated ideals will eventually lead to acceptance of this alternative way of life, thereby "silencing the ignorant slander of foolish people" (1 Pet. 2:13–15).[12] If the outsiders continue to degrade and reject the Christians, however, the latter will be in a position to consider this a reflection of their neighbors' ignorance—their failure to *recognize* virtue—and so nullify the social pressure of shame rather than inclining them to internalize and act on it.

The author draws prominently on the ethical topic of mastering one's desires and cravings, rather than being mastered by the same, so that one could live a consistently virtuous life: "I exhort you to abstain from the fleshly desires

12. Unless otherwise indicated, all translations from 1 Peter in this chapter are my own.

that wage war against your soul, keeping your conduct among the Gentiles honorable" (1 Pet. 2:11–12); "don't continue to conform yourselves to the desires of your former ignorance" (1:14).[13] The topic of "mastery of the passions" as an ideal of philosophical ethics is widely attested in Greco-Roman and Hellenistic Jewish literature; it is also central to the Buddhist ideal.[14] The Buddha identified desire—"the entangling and embroiling craving"—as the principal problem at the core of human existence most diligently to be eliminated (*Dhammapada* 180, 359). "Just as the rain does not break through a well-thatched house, even so passion never penetrates a well-developed mind" (*Dhammapada* 14).[15]

Another prominently shared value is cultivating and acting on the desire to bring benefit to others. The author of 1 Peter urges his readers to remain steadfast in their love and hospitality toward one another (1:22; 4:8–9); other New Testament voices are more specific about the doing of good to *all* people beyond the household of faith (while ensuring that they have not overlooked the needs of the household of faith). This resonates with the Buddhist ideal of *mettā*, "loving-kindness through all bodily, verbal, and mental activities," or "that which 'promotes welfare.'"[16] This is indeed an area in which many Christian bodies in Sri Lanka have distinguished themselves, very dramatically in the aftermath of the 2004 tsunami, less dramatically but quite consistently through ongoing investment in coming alongside and helping the refugee, the homeless, and the displaced throughout the island.

The remaining ethical teachings that run throughout 1 Peter continue to resonate significantly with the teachings of the Buddha. Compare, for example, 1 Peter's recitation from Psalm 34 enjoining the devotee to "turn away from evil and do good" (1 Pet. 3:11) with the Buddha's injunction to "hasten

---

13. See Plato, *Resp.* 431A; *Gorg.* 491; *Phaed.* 93–94; Cicero, *Tusc.* 2.22; 3.22; 4.10–11; Plutarch, *Virt. mor.* 1–4 (*Mor.* 440D–443D); Let. Aris. 222; 4 Maccabees. This was an ideal that the Christian movement was quite intent on fulfilling (see, e.g., Gal. 5:13–25).

14. This connection also emerged forcefully among my conversation partners in a previous visit to conduct a seminar on Galatians at Colombo Theological Seminary. The fruits of that particular discussion can be found in D. A. deSilva, *Global Readings: A Sri Lankan Commentary on Paul's Letter to the Galatians* (Eugene, OR: Cascade Books, 2011), 281–83.

15. Consider also the following quotations: "Just as a storm throws down a weak tree, so does Mara overpower one who lives for the pursuit of pleasures, who is uncontrolled in his senses, immoderate in eating, indolent and dissipated" (*Dhammapada* 7); "The wise control themselves" (*Dhammapada* 80); "For a person tormented by evil thoughts, who is passion-dominated and given to the pursuit of pleasure, his craving steadily grows. He makes the fetter strong indeed" (*Dhammapada* 349). Translations from the *Dhammapada* are taken from *The Dhammapada: The Buddha's Path of Wisdom*, trans. Buddharakkhita Thera, 2nd ed. (Kandy, Sri Lanka: Buddhist Publication Society, 1996).

16. Acharya Buddharakkhita, *Mettā: The Philosophy and Practice of Universal Love* (Kandy, Sri Lanka: Buddhist Publication Society, 1989), 13, 22.

to do good and restrain your mind from evil" (*Dhammapada* 116). Similarly, the Buddha affirms that "to avoid all evil, to cultivate good, and to cleanse one's own mind—this is the teaching of the Buddhas" (*Dhammapada* 183). The Buddha identifies anger, pride, jealousy, selfishness, deceit, hatred, lust, and hypocrisy as "fetters" from which to seek to free oneself (*Dhammapada* 7, 221, 262–63, 399–400, 407) and truthfulness, virtue, inoffensiveness, restraint, patience, and self-mastery as qualities to be cultivated (*Dhammapada* 10, 261, 399–400). There is a great deal of overlap with the author of 1 Peter's censure of wickedness, guile, hypocrisy, envy, and slander, and promotion of harmony, sympathy, mutual love, compassion, and humility. All of these came to be seen by my conversation partners as bridges by means of which Christ followers could affirm the Buddha's ethical insights, offering honor to him and, thereby, to their Buddhist neighbors, and, to the extent that they invested themselves in the realization of these ideals, quite plausibly raise the stature of Christian teaching in their neighbors' eyes.

It is in this context that the author of 1 Peter's directions concerning how Christians should respond to their harassers became particularly important. Christians confronted with such attacks on their honor as verbal challenges, reproachful speech, or even physical affronts might be sorely tempted to respond in kind, playing out the challenge-riposte game before the onlookers.[17] Beginning with Jesus, however, Christian leaders sought to cultivate a specifically Christian riposte: "When he was reviled, he did not riposte with more reviling in kind" but instead "committed himself to the One who judges justly"—that is, to God (1 Pet. 2:22–23). The author calls *all* Christians, therefore, not to respond in kind to harassment and abuse but rather to follow Christ's example, "not returning injury for injury or insult for insult, but, on the contrary, extending blessing—for to this you were called, in order that you might inherit a blessing" (3:9).[18]

---

17. On the "challenge-riposte" interaction in both ancient and modern Mediterranean societies, see Julian Pitt-Rivers, "Honour and Social Status," in *Honour and Shame: The Values of Mediterranean Society*, ed. John G. Peristiany (London: Weidenfeld & Nicolson, 1965), 21–77 (esp. 27); Bruce J. Malina and Jerome H. Neyrey, "Honor and Shame in Luke-Acts: Pivotal Values of the Mediterranean World," in *The Social World of Luke-Acts*, ed. J. H. Neyrey (Peabody, MA: Hendrickson, 1991), 25–66 (esp. 30). For an analysis of several instances of the interaction in the Gospels, see D. A. deSilva, *Honor, Patronage, Kinship and Purity: Unlocking New Testament Culture* (Downers Grove, IL: InterVarsity, 2000), 29–31.

18. Elliott helpfully compares 1 Peter's advice to the similar course promoted by Plutarch: "'How shall I defend myself against my enemy?' 'By proving yourself good and honorable'" (*Inim. util.* 4 [*Mor.* 88B]; Elliott, "Disgraced yet Graced," 171). It will distress the enemy more than being insulted, Plutarch writes, to see you bear yourself with self-control, justice, and kindness toward those with whom you come in contact. The insulted person must use the insult as an occasion to examine his life and rid himself of any semblance of that vice (*Inim. util.* 6 [*Mor.* 89D–E]).

This response resonates especially closely with Buddhist ideals concerning the sage's conduct in the midst of hostility: "Hatred is never appeased by hatred in this world; by non-hatred alone is hatred appeased" (*Dhammapada* 5); "overcome the angry by non-anger; overcome the wicked by goodness" (*Dhammapada* 223).[19] The Christian who remains committed to 1 Peter's advice would be in a position to declare, along with the Buddha, "Happy indeed we live, friendly amid the hostile! Amid hostile people we dwell free from hatred" (*Dhammapada* 197).

Rather than *either* yield to the feelings of shame *or* riposte in a manner that would antagonize, the author of 1 Peter calls Christians to be ready to give a gentle but committed verbal defense (an *apologia*, 3:15) for their new commitments and practices. In the Sri Lankan context, this defense would plausibly include the affirmation that "without Christ, I could not be a Buddhist"[20]—namely, without Christ's model and the Spirit's empowerment, it is impossible to fulfill the Buddhist ideals.

Avoiding Unnecessary Offensiveness: Westernization as **Skandalon**

While it seemed fairly self-evident that my conversation partners would not, in fact, suffer "as murderers or thieves or evildoers or busybodies" (1 Pet. 4:15), the author's concerns that the host society not find legitimate cause for complaint against the members of the Christian movement promoted a good deal of constructive, critical reflection on their part concerning the practices of their churches and congregations. Their attention focused on the need to reassess the degree of Westernization present in Sri Lankan Christianity in every area, since the adoption and ongoing importation of Western Christian music, theologies, worship practices, strategies for congregational growth and development, and even Bible translations used in worship and related settings present an unnecessary obstacle to the acceptance of Christianity as a naturalized religion.[21]

Is a more indigenous expression of Christianity possible, such that Buddhist nationalists, for example, would be less inclined to see Christianity as a force for (or, at least, a vestige of) Western imperialism? My conversation partners acknowledged this call. They have sought to develop ways of singing

19. See also *Dhammapada* 389: "One should not strike a holy man, nor should a holy man, when struck, give way to anger. Shame on him who strikes a holy man, and more shame on him [that is, on the holy man] who gives way to anger."

20. Prabo Mihindakulasuriya, "Without Christ I Could Not Be a Buddhist: An Evangelical Response to Christian Self-Understanding in a Buddhist Context," CD 51 (2011): 73–87.

21. The presence of KJV-only-ism among some Christian groups in Sri Lanka is a singular triumph for colonialism!

the psalms and writing new hymns that could be sung to tunes and with instrumentation more closely representative of indigenous musical practice. They look to continue to formulate a Christian theology that, while firmly grounded in Scripture and the global church's heritage, places the pressing issues of Sri Lankan existence at the center of concern to that emerging theology. They also are seeking to pay greater attention to the values inherent in Sri Lankan culture (e.g., community and relationship) and develop congregational life around those values rather than pattern congregations after Western patterns (which tend to be more "program-centered" than "people-centered" and which tend to think in terms of marketing the church, hence in more "commercial" than "community" terms).[22]

Further Observations

There are several other places in which the text of 1 Peter can serve to inspire conversations regarding this challenge of cultural rapprochement without compromising the essentials of Christian faith.

For example, the author's injunctions to respect authority (1 Pet. 2:13–17) occasioned conversations about how to offer honor even to those impeding one's legal access to religious freedoms and rights—honor being an important value in Sri Lankan culture—while still rigorously pursuing those freedoms and rights.

The author's words to Christian wives and Christian husbands (1 Pet. 3:1–7) occasioned a great deal of discussion concerning gender issues in Sri Lanka, particularly the more traditional roles assigned to and expected of women in the less urbanized areas, and the importance of addressing domestic violence, particularly where this is fueled by patriarchal expectations.[23]

The author's attention throughout to nurturing Christian identity as "an elect race, a holy nation," the formation of a people where formerly there was not a "people" (1 Pet. 2:9–10), invited reflections on the ongoing tensions of race and nation(alism) in Sri Lanka, especially between the Sinhalese majority and the Tamil minority, and the invitation to transcend these tensions *and* the categories that sustain them.[24]

My conversation partners were attentive to the author's program of nurturing inner-church solidarity, urging his hearers to show one another "an unfeigned brotherly and sisterly love . . . constantly from the heart" (1 Pet.

22. A number of recommendations for building bridges between Christian worship and major elements of worship already familiar to Sri Lankan Buddhists can be found in G. P. V. Somaratna, *Sinhala Christian Worship* (Kohuwela, Sri Lanka: CTS Publishing, 2006).

23. This was also a focus of an earlier group of students' critical examination of the Sri Lankan context in connection with their study of Galatians (see deSilva, *Global Readings*, 192–95).

24. See also deSilva, *Global Readings*, 144–45, 193–94.

1:22; see also 3:8), shaping their relationships within the church according to the ethical ideal of family at its best.[25] Internal harmony and unity (3:8), ungrudging mutual support and hospitality (4:8–11), and bearing oneself with that gentle humility that nurtures solidarity and harmony (5:3, 6) were affirmed as much-to-be-desired qualities in the midst of a hostile environment.

This further stimulated reflection on the ills of denominationalism, division, and the erosion of witness in the Sri Lankan context—in a number of ways a direct result of the manner of Christianity's introduction under a series of colonial powers, each with its own brand of Christianity, and ongoingly the result of Western denominations staking their claim in Sri Lanka through their independent missions.[26]

Despite their limited resources and local needs, my conversation partners were sensitive to the fact that, as the author of 1 Peter puts it, their "sisters and brothers throughout the world are facing the same kinds of sufferings" (5:9). They were stimulated to think of ways in which they could put themselves in contact with those who face even more stringent pressures because of their commitment to the faith, extending honor to them in their experience of being shamed and making the reality of the church universal as a social matrix for perseverance felt more keenly through prayer, personal support, and material assistance.

Why Should Western Readers of 1 Peter Care?

I would answer the question "Why should Western readers of 1 Peter care?" from my own location for those teaching in similar locations—theological schools with a commitment to the Christian tradition and ministry. Some of our commonly shared Scriptures speak much more directly to other bodies within the global church than to our own. While we are still interested in these texts' message "to us," we will become both more globally aware and less self-centered in our engagement with Scripture as we are ourselves attentive to, and teach our students to attend to, those Christian contexts to which these texts speak more immediately. This, in turn, puts those other parts of the global church more forthrightly on our radar. We may come to see that *their* challenges and needs should take priority *for us* over our own as we seek to discern our own response to "the word."[27]

---

25. See further deSilva, *Honor, Patronage, Kinship and Purity*, 165–73, 212–26, and the literature cited therein. An especially important primary text is Plutarch's essay *On Fraternal [and Sororal] Affection*.

26. See also deSilva, *Global Readings*, 136–40.

27. The Association of Theological Schools has made such investigation a matter of priority by including "global awareness and engagement" as a focal point within its "General Institutional Standards" regarding theological scholarship and the curriculum (The Commission

At the same time, reading 1 Peter with Sri Lankan Christians cautions well-resourced and marketing-savvy Christians in the West concerning their relationship with the church in the non-Western world. Is it in the interests of the Sri Lankan church (for example) for every one of our Western denominations to establish its own franchise and brand in their land, or do we need to radically rethink our missiological practice if we are not to continue to replicate the problems of former missiological practices? Is it in their interests for us to continue to package our music, our programs, our church-growth strategies as ecclesiastical solutions for the world and not acknowledge them more forthrightly as culture-bound and location-bound expressions that should not simply become products to export?[28] It seems that by listening well to Sri Lankan Christians, we in the West may find ourselves called to be more creative in training and preparing indigenous leadership to reach their culture rather than exporting more of our materials as the solution to their need for "church growth."

I also find that reading 1 Peter and other texts with Sri Lankan Christians in their contexts assists me in the exegetical task of entering into the ancient texts themselves in their ancient contexts. The social dynamics surrounding Sri Lankan Christians resemble those of 1 Peter's audience much more closely than any reference points in my Western experience. Reading 1 Peter with those who face shame, alienation, and even persecution for aligning with the Christian faith brings us much closer to the original audience than most of us in the West will ever experience.

---

on Accrediting, "Standards of Accreditation: General Institutional Standards," Association of Theological Schools, June 13, 2020, https://www.ats.edu/uploads/accrediting/documents/standards-of-accreditation-161130.pdf, 8–9 [§3.3.4]).

28. See also deSilva, *Global Readings*, 238–41.

19

1 Peter and African American Experience

DENNIS R. EDWARDS

I was serving as the senior pastor of a church in Minneapolis when Philando Castile was shot by a police officer near St. Paul, Minnesota, after a routine traffic stop. After that incident, as well as after other high-profile shootings of African Americans by police officers, Americans became increasingly aware of "the talk." "The talk" is shorthand for a phenomenon that has long been part of many African American families. It consists of instructing younger members of the family—most often the males—of the necessity of being especially deferential to those in authority, such as police officers. Such deference, or submission, is a strategy for survival. The author of 1 Peter offers a similar strategy for survival in 2:18–20.[1]

African Americans, being diaspora people, live in a tension in which conformity is pitted against resistance and in which the stakes may be life and death. Such was the case for 1 Peter's initial audience. Their diaspora status meant shame and alienation. First Peter resonates well with the experience of many African American Christians because the letter acknowledges the

---

1. I am aware of the debates surrounding the authorship of 1 Peter and discuss some of them in my commentary. For simplicity, I refer to the author of the letter as "Peter" throughout this essay. See Dennis R. Edwards, *1 Peter*, SGBC 17 (Grand Rapids: Zondervan, 2017), 18–20.

shame of diaspora life. The letter also extends encouragement while providing teaching that serves to strengthen community life and offer protection against hostile leaders and neighbors. The author of the letter offers hope to the readers based on their faith while giving practical instruction designed to preserve life under oppressive conditions. Presuming that the original audience of 1 Peter attempted to put the teachings of the letter into practice, those Christians become examples for subsequent generations of Christians. Indeed, diaspora Christians, such as African American followers of Jesus, are perhaps the best teachers of what it means to imitate Christ.

Shame as Characteristic of Diaspora Life

African Americans are diaspora people. Several years ago, when I used to subscribe to *Christianity Today*, I was annoyed by the ads for Christians to submit a last name and find their family crest. The ad bothered me on a few levels. I understand that those who provided such a service knew that there would be a market among evangelicals for such a thing, to connect them to their European roots. But it was frustrating for me. I have this last name of Edwards, which I am sure is an English name, but how I got that name I will likely never know. I cannot accurately trace my roots to any country in Africa. It will have to suffice to name an entire continent: I'm "African American." Diaspora implies alienation. Shively Smith, after tracing the meaning of "diaspora" from its earliest usage with regard to Israel, points out that "social and cultural intellectual circles broadened the meaning of diaspora to encompass the migration and dispersal patterns of contemporary migrating populations (e.g., Africans, Armenians, Hispanics, Turks), not just Jews."[2] Smith goes on to list nine features that are considered by many experts to be typical of diaspora existence:

1. Dispersal from an original homeland, often traumatically, to two or more foreign regions
2. Alternatively, the expansion from a homeland in search of work, in pursuit of trade, or to further colonial ambitions
3. A collective memory and myth about the homeland, including its location history and achievements
4. An idealization of the putative ancestral home and a collective commitment to its maintenance, restoration, safety, and prosperity, even to its creation

---

2. Shively T. J. Smith, *Strangers to Family: Diaspora and 1 Peter's Invention of God's Household* (Waco: Baylor University Press, 2016), 7.

5. The development of a return movement that gains collective approbation

6. A strong ethnic group consciousness sustained over a long time and based on a sense of distinctiveness, a common history, and the belief in a common fate

7. A troubled relationship with host societies, suggesting a lack of acceptance at the least or the possibility that another calamity might befall the group

8. A sense of empathy and solidarity with coethnic members in other countries of settlement

9. The possibility of a distinctive yet creative and enriching life in host countries with a tolerance for pluralism[3]

These features may not apply exactly to the situation of 1 Peter's readers, but they do highlight the vulnerable condition of diaspora people throughout time. Diaspora is a liminal condition, fraught with the tensions of being among but not part of a dominant group.

There is no shortage of studies or debate surrounding the terms 1 Peter uses in describing the readers, particularly "elect" (*eklektos*, 1:1; 2:9), "sojourners" (*parepidēmos*, 1:1; 2:11), "diaspora" (*diaspora*, 1:1), and "foreigners" (*paroikia*, 1:17). All the commentaries—including my own—discuss these terms, including whether the descriptors *parepidēmos*, *diaspora*, and *paroikia* should be taken literally or metaphorically.[4] Steven Bechtler avers that the terms "are figures of speech, metaphors, by which a situation of social alienness is characterized."[5] Smith agrees, concluding, "In 1 Peter the notion of diaspora is central to properly understanding the letter's purpose and impact. Diverging from more traditional Hellenistic scriptural notions concerning diaspora, 1 Peter does not define it as a geographic dislocation from physical and human place of origin."[6] Even if geographic displacement is not an issue, "diaspora" is an apt description of the condition of those who are out of place for their faith, as in the case of 1 Peter's audience. Smith adds that 1 Peter "considers suffering as an unavoidable feature of diaspora life."[7]

---

3. Smith, *Strangers to Family*, 10. Smith observes that "while these features are insightful and necessary categories from which to study and theorize diaspora, this schema is too rigid to be particularly helpful in describing the diaspora constructions outlined by Second Temple Jewish and early Christian writers" (10–11).

4. Edwards, *1 Peter*, 29–31, 100.

5. Steven Richard Bechtler, *Following in His Steps: Suffering, Community, and Christology in 1 Peter*, SBLDS 162 (Atlanta: Scholars Press, 1998), 81.

6. Smith, *Strangers to Family*, 42.

7. Smith, *Strangers to Family*, 42.

Furthermore, Betsy Bauman-Martin points out the vulnerability of the Christian community addressed in 1 Peter under the Roman Empire:

> 1 Peter was written in a time of, and for an audience that experienced, imperialism (an ideology that upholds the legitimacy of the economic and military control of one country by another), and colonialism (a practice which results from imperialism, specifically the settlement of groups from the more dominant country in the country of the conquered, often for means of control). Asia Minor, the site of the audience for 1 Peter, had experienced imperialism since the time of Alexander the Great and colonialism in the form of taxation and new religious demands, extraction of resources, including human ones, less autonomy for governors, and overall imperial supervision.[8]

The addressees of 1 Peter, because of their faith, confronted the negative aspects of living under imperialism even if that did not involve resettlement. Willie Jennings poignantly describes what diaspora can mean with regard to imperial rule:

> Diaspora means scattering and fragmentation, exile and loss. It means being displaced and in search of a place that could be made home. . . . Danger and threat surround diaspora life. Diaspora life is crowded with self-questioning and questions for God concerning the anger, hatred, and violence visited upon a people. We must never confuse voluntary migration with diaspora, because diaspora is a geographic and social world not chosen and a psychic state inescapable. The peoples who inhabit diaspora live with animus and violence filling the air they breathe. They live always on the verge of being classified enemy, always in evaluation of their productivity to the empire, always having an acceptance on loan, ready to be taken away at the first sign of sedition. They live with fear, as an ever-present partner in their lives, the fear of being turned into a *them, a dangerous other, those people* among *us.* They also remember loss—of land and place, of life and hope, and even for some of faith. Yet diaspora is also power, the power of a conviction to survive and the power of a confession to never yield to the forces that would destroy them. Diaspora is life by any means necessary. The condition of diaspora is often bound up with life under empire. . . . Faith is always caught between diaspora and empire. It is always caught between those on the one side focused on survival and fixated on securing a future for their people and on the other side those intoxicated with the power and possibilities of empire and of building a world ordered by

---

8. Betsy Bauman-Martin, "Speaking Jewish: Postcolonial Aliens and Strangers in First Peter," in *Reading First Peter with New Eyes: Methodological Reassessments of the Letter of First Peter*, ed. Robert L. Webb and Betsy Bauman-Martin, LNTS 364 (London: T&T Clark, 2007), 157.

its financial, social and political logics that claim to be the best possible way to bring stability and lasting peace.[9]

Diaspora signifies shame. Diaspora people have a compromised social status, which was true of the first readers of 1 Peter. Honor, of supreme value in the first century, was reckoned by the currency of one's good name, fame, esteem from others, and also social ranking.[10]

Historian Mary Beard asserts, "[Roman] citizenship brought with it all kinds of specific rights under Roman law, covering a wide range of topics, from contracts to punishments. The simple reason that, in the 60s AD, Saint Peter was crucified while Saint Paul enjoyed the privilege of being beheaded was that Paul was a Roman citizen."[11] When considering that citizenship held privileges, I was not imagining a quick death versus a slow one, but the point is that citizenship meant advantage! Model citizens were those who gained honor, at times through their beneficence. "The pivotal value in first-century Mediterranean society is honor. . . . Honor is a claim to worth and the social acknowledgement publicly that her/his actions conform to social obligations."[12]

African Americans, as diaspora people, have long been objects of shame. However, like the recipients of 1 Peter, African American Christians came to believe that despite their shameful status in the world, they were esteemed in God's eyes. As John Elliott concludes, in 1 Peter "honor ultimately is ascribed not according to blood and birth, as convention would dictate, nor is it achieved by one heroic act of valor and *andreia* ('manliness,' 'courage'). Instead it is conferred by an act of divine grace, by the favor of a God who gives grace to the lowly (5:5); a divine patron who raises slaves to the status of sons and daughters (2:18–25) and wives to the status of coheirs of the grace of life (3:1–7)."[13]

Turning Words of Shame into Badges of Honor

Acknowledging God's favor is one way that the recipients of 1 Peter erased—or at least reframed—the stigma of diaspora. Rather than looking for honor in

9. Willie James Jennings, *Acts: A Theological Commentary on the Bible*, Belief (Louisville: Westminster John Knox, 2017), 6 (emphasis original).

10. See John H. Elliott, "Disgraced yet Graced: The Gospel according to 1 Peter in the Key of Honor and Shame," *BTB* 25 (1995): 166–78.

11. Mary Beard, *SPQR: A History of Ancient Rome* (New York: Liveright, 2015), 521.

12. Barth L. Campbell, *Honor, Shame, and the Rhetoric of 1 Peter*, SBLDS 160 (Atlanta: Scholars Press, 1998), 12.

13. John H. Elliott, *1 Peter: A New Translation with Introduction and Commentary*, AB 37B (New York: Anchor Bible, 2001), 117.

the eyes of their pagan neighbors, the followers of Jesus were to trust that God valued them. In addition to the aforementioned verses cited by Elliott, 1 Peter's allusions to Exodus 19:5–6 and Hosea 2:23 (i.e., 1 Pet. 2:9–10) also communicate that God's people have honor in God's sight. During slavery, African American Christians similarly sought to see their value in the eyes of God despite the treatment from slave masters. The spirituals, which have become an art form, serve as examples of how African Americans creatively expressed their dignity before God. Theologian Arthur Sutherland notes that "the spirituals emerged not just because of slavery, but because the slaves were working people surrounded by the preaching and teaching of the gospel."[14] Many spirituals have an otherworldly perspective, as slaves fully expected God's deliverance—if not in the present life, then in the life to come.[15] And the life to come would be one where they would be welcomed into the Lord's presence as honored members of the family.

The spirituals grew out of the dynamic tension of living with faith in God, who promises deliverance, while simultaneously experiencing the slave master's whip. Although the spirituals were fundamentally work songs that provided some measure of relief from backbreaking labor, they also served to help build a measure of community.[16] The spirituals helped the slaves to affirm that they were not defined by their work; their identity was rooted in a spiritual reality that transcended their present circumstances. African American slaves could retrieve at least a shred of their dignity through singing to and about a God who delivers, who would give them shoes and a robe—items of privilege and honor—when they arrived in heaven. Similarly, the readers of 1 Peter could erase their shame by recalling—perhaps even singing—the words of Scripture that affirmed their status as God's beloved and God's special possession.

The contemporary chant of "Black lives matter" is an attempt to affirm the dignity of African Americans (and other dark-skinned people). There is evidence that Black lives are viewed as threatening and deserving of deadly

14. Arthur Sutherland, *I Was a Stranger: A Christian Theology of Hospitality* (Nashville: Abingdon, 2006), 5.

15. E. Franklin Frazier and C. Eric Lincoln, *The Negro Church in America / The Black Church Since Frazier*, Sourcebooks in Negro History (New York: Schocken, 1974), 19–23.

16. Community among diaspora people is an important topic that goes beyond the scope of this paper. However, Smith, *Strangers to Family*, is especially helpful in this regard. She acknowledges, "The image of diaspora expresses a core belief that no body constitutes merely a group of isolated strangers striving to make it on their own in a world known for responding with great cruelty, disregard, and violence for the unrecognizable 'other.' Diaspora in 1 Peter reminds readers they are members of a diverse and vast kinship requiring only acknowledgment and embrace" (19).

force—by police as well as by private citizens, as in the case of George Floyd's murder by a Minneapolis police officer in 2020 or of George Zimmerman's shooting of young Travon Martin in 2012. To exclaim that "Black lives matter" is a small way to acknowledge that what may appear dishonorable (i.e., Black skin) should at least be worthy of respect. Many years before #BlackLivesMatter morphed into a movement, purveyors of Black pride had many of us saying, "Black is beautiful." James Brown's song "Say It Loud, I'm Black and I'm Proud" served as an anthem for many of us. The slogan and the song were attempts to bring honor to what had long been viewed as shameful—that is, Black skin, Black hair, and Black bodies in general. Such effort to turn something shameful into a badge of honor may also be happening in 1 Peter. In 4:16, Peter admonishes the audience not to be ashamed if they suffer for bearing the name Christian. *Christianos* is rare in the New Testament (elsewhere only in Acts 11:26; 26:28), and most likely the word was initially an epithet, coined by outsiders.[17] But Peter attempts to turn an insult into a title of honor. David Horrell observes, "The label [*Christianos*] is a stigmatizing label associated not with a facet of personal identity—such as disability or disfigurement—but with a feature of social identity deriving from group membership. In relation to the term [*Christianos*], one thing that is interesting is that it is outsiders who heighten the salience of this label not only by coining it in the first place but also by making it, in judicial settings, *the* crucial identifier that determines whether a person is or is not a social deviant, whether they can be permitted to remain in society or not."[18] Horrell considers the work of social science and suggests that the use of *Christianos* in 1 Peter 4:16 is an example of "the strategy of changing the values assigned to the attributes of the group, so that comparisons which were previously negative are now perceived as positive. . . . In other words terms and designators with a negative social-identity value are retained, but reclaimed and reinterpreted, with what we may perhaps call polemical pride, as positive ones." A derogatory term is converted into a badge of honor. Smith applies similar reasoning, suggesting, "The cosmology of 1 Peter functions as a narrative of knowledge in which diaspora is transformed from a punitive and embarrassing situation to a condition of being the legitimate people of God. Instead of titles such as 'foreigner' and 'Christian' being

---

17. J. Ramsey Michaels, *1 Peter*, WBC 49 (Waco: Word, 1988), 268–69. Michaels points out that the formation "Christian" is analogous to "Herodian," indicating "partisans of Christ" (268). But see Elias J. Bickerman, "The Name of Christians," *HTR* 42 (1949): 109–24, who argues that the Antiochene Christians coined the term themselves.

18. David G. Horrell, "The Label Χριστιανός: 1 Peter 4:16 and the Formation of Christian Identity," *JBL* 126 (2007): 377 (emphasis original).

pejorative and limiting, the letter tells them to embrace these as markers of the diaspora-Christian situation."[19]

For diaspora people, honor may be found in co-opting the language of oppression and reframing it to signify specialness. Additionally, 1 Peter declares that honor comes through participating with Jesus. Participation means following the Lord's example and also sharing in his suffering (e.g., 1 Pet. 2:18–25; 4:12–19). Suffering, in 1 Peter, entails enduring injustice without retaliation, as 2:23 stresses: "When they hurled their insults at him, he did not retaliate; when he suffered, he made no threats. Instead, he entrusted himself to him who judges justly" (NIV). For African Americans, much of the civil rights movement exemplifies honor through suffering without retaliation.

Imitating Christ through Nonviolent Resistance and Model Citizenship

In my 1 Peter commentary, I point out, "One of the things that made the Civil Rights Movement effective was the abuse taken by innocent protesters who did not retaliate. Dr. Martin Luther King, Jr., through his studies of theology and of Mohandas Gandhi, embraced and propagated the notion of non-violent protest. And although there were some who disagreed with his approach, many look back on history and note that his philosophy, which was at the heart of the movement, drove the changes that gradually moved through the United States of America."[20] Many people consider Dr. Martin Luther King Jr. to be a martyr because he died practicing his faith. That faith propelled him to nonviolent resistance to unjust laws. In my commentary, I go on to discuss Rep. John Lewis's recounting of Bloody Sunday, when peaceful demonstrators in Selma, Alabama, were brutalized by law enforcement officers.[21] Lewis notes in his memoir, *Walking with the Wind*, that Bloody Sunday provoked positive action from President Lyndon Johnson.[22] The positive action was a result of ordinary citizens being able to view the brutality of Bloody Sunday on television in the comfort of their own homes. Selma pricked the consciences of many Americans and perhaps served to "silence the ignorance of the foolish" (1 Pet. 2:15 NRSV).

Despite the contempt that some Romans had for Christians, 1 Peter alleges that the Christian's good conduct—conduct of a sort uncommon among the pagans—might find approval among unbelievers. It turns out that within

19. Smith, *Strangers to Family*, 42.
20. Edwards, *1 Peter*, 109.
21. Edwards, *1 Peter*, 109–10.
22. John Lewis and Michael D'Orso, *Walking with the Wind: A Memoir of the Movement* (New York: Simon & Schuster, 1998), 344–45.

the decadent ancient Greco-Roman society, some gentiles demonstrated an understanding of what might be considered upright behavior. Stephen Barton writes, "The moral rigor that attracted pagans to Christianity and Judaism was not without parallel in Greco-Roman society beyond the church and synagogue. It needs to be recognized more widely that many pagans converted to Christianity because they found in the Christian groups moral standards that they recognized already as profoundly important for human welfare."[23] Apparently, some among the pagans found aspects of Christian life inviting.

In 1 Peter 2:16, the "aliens" and "strangers" of 1 Peter are given the paradoxical encouragement to live as free slaves. Directly following that admonition are the author's instructions for "household servants" (*oiketai*, AT). Slaves who follow Jesus become models for all Christians. "Regardless of one's social status, Christians are to consider themselves to be slaves to God, and so the actual slave who is obedient to his master exemplifies that role for the entire Christian community."[24] Slaves had minimal social status in ancient Rome, being "defined as chattel who, lacking citizenship, lacked the essential qualification of humanity."[25] In 1 Peter 2:18, the author addresses household slaves with the command to submit to their masters "in all fear" (AT).[26] The same attitude that the entire community should have toward God (1:17; 2:17) must be expressly evident among slaves toward their masters. Godly slaves must submit to their masters no matter how kind or harsh the treatment from those masters might be, and the emphasis is on the latter situation. This dimension of 1 Peter's command is especially difficult for many twenty-first-century ears to hear.

It must be seen, however, that 1 Peter gives no validation of harsh treatment by slave masters; 2:19 makes explicit that the slaves' suffering is unjust. First Peter's advocacy of nonretaliatory behavior is not an endorsement of slavery and is also not an indication of the weakness of slaves. Peaceful submission to even the harshest of masters is evidence of genuine Christian faith. The point is to grasp what Christlike behavior looks like in one of the most difficult

---

23. Stephen C. Barton, "Social Setting of Early Non-Pauline Christianity," in *Dictionary of the Later New Testament and Its Developments*, ed. Ralph P. Martin and Peter H. Davids (Downers Grove, IL: IVP Academic, 1997), 1108.

24. Karen H. Jobes, *1 Peter*, BECNT (Grand Rapids: Baker Academic, 2005), 187. See also Bechtler, *Following in His Steps*, 167.

25. Paul J. Achtemeier, *1 Peter*, Hermeneia (Minneapolis: Fortress, 1996), 190.

26. The more common word for slave, *doulos*, occurs in 1 Pet. 2:16 and is used metaphorically for all Christians in service to God. Achtemeier, *1 Peter*, 194, alleges that even though the word *oiketai* refers to household slaves, "it can also be used generically for slaves and is probably to be understood in that way here [1 Pet. 2:18]."

situations imaginable. Slaves, though in a horrible, unenviable position, have the peculiar honor of serving as living examples of what Jesus is like.

The early Christians—especially slaves—were not in the position to overturn Roman society's oppressive and hierarchical social structure. However, as Miroslav Volf contends, "The call to follow the crucified Messiah was, in the long run, much more effective in changing the unjust political, economic, and familial structures than direct exhortations to revolutionize them would ever have been. For an allegiance to the crucified Messiah—indeed, worship of a crucified God—is an eminently political act that subverts a politics of dominion at its core."[27] Volf proceeds with the following recommendation:

> What we should learn from the text [1 Peter] is not, of course, to keep our mouths shut and hands folded, but to make our rhetoric and action more modest so that they can be more effective. As we strive for social change, 1 Peter nudges us to drop the pen that scripts master narratives and instead give account of the living hope in God and God's future (3:15; 1:5), to abandon the project of reshaping society from the ground up and instead do as much as we can from where we are at the time we are there (2:11), to suffer injustice and bless the unjust rather than perpetrating violence by repaying "evil for evil or abuse for abuse" (3:9), and to replace the anger of frustration with the joy of expectation (4:13).[28]

Volf's admonition might find an easier reception among the dominant culture, but even as a person of color, I find a measure of hope that allegiance to Christ can be a subversive act within a culture that depends on violence and intimidation in order to maintain social order.

I am part of a generation of African Americans who were regularly admonished by parents and other authority figures to be especially well-behaved because the dominant culture expected otherwise. My white classmates did not feel the same pressure to conform; their misbehavior was not attributed to their racial identity. African Americans needed to be model citizens so as not to draw the ire of those in authority. Outright resistance brought danger, or at least negative scrutiny. The stress of conforming to an inequitable way of life was compounded by resisting the strictures of society. Smith sees a similar phenomenon facing the readers of 1 Peter. She argues that "the letter constructs diaspora Christianity as a double-duty routine. It exhorts Christian readers to balance the precepts of the Christian community with the

27. Miroslav Volf, "Soft Difference: Theological Reflections on the Relation between Church and Culture in 1 Peter," *ExAud* 10 (1994): 22.

28. Volf, "Soft Difference," 23.

imperatives of civil society. Instead of distinguishing Christian life as a posture of either withdrawing or opposing the world, 1 Peter envisions Christianity—particularly diaspora Christianity—as a balancing act between integration and segregation, presence and difference, conformity and distinction."[29]

David Balch advises that "the most relevant social-scientific resources for appreciating the community-world relationship in 1 Peter are likely to be those which concern themselves specifically with contexts of imperial/colonial domination and with the ways in which subaltern groups produce and sustain their identity in such contexts."[30] Balch interacts with social-scientific literature and points out that those living under oppressive regimes may conform to society's expectations while simultaneously seeking out ways to affirm their identity and even subversively undermine the power structures: "Certainly there is no attempt to obscure the extent to which the dominant and powerful wield the big sticks, and are able to exercise power through a range of ideological and physical means, not least the brute force to subdue and coerce by terror. But the weak also exercise agency and power through the multifarious means by which they resist their domination, whether in hidden or overt ways, and whether through linguistic means (such as jokes, gossip, parody, etc.) or by physical acts (such as poaching, concealment, evasion, etc.)."[31] African Americans have long negotiated the tension inherent in conformity versus resistance, employing the "multifarious means" that Balch delineates, such as the tradition of African American comedians lampooning the dominant American culture.

Submission is perhaps an intensification of conforming. In other words, African Americans, as well as immigrants to the US, face pressure not only to conform to expectations of the dominant culture but also to submit, displaying obvious signs of deference, so as not to provoke those in authority. Submission to authority is not only a way that diaspora people imitate Jesus but also a strategy that increases the chance of preserving life in hostile territory. First Peter's commands to "conduct yourselves honorably" (2:12), "accept the authority of every human institution" (2:13), and "honor the emperor" (2:17 NRSV) are intended to lessen suspicion from unbelievers. The advice is meant not to sanction injustice but to keep the community relatively safe. The same idea is behind Peter's words to household servants. Smith comments on the "power dynamics between human masters and servants (1 Pet.

29. Smith, *Strangers to Family*, 45.
30. David L. Balch, "Hellenization/Acculturation in 1 Peter," in *Perspectives on First Peter*, ed. Charles H. Talbert, NABPR Special Studies Series 9 (Macon, GA: Mercer University Press, 1986), 117.
31. Balch, "Hellenization/Acculturation," 118–19.

2:18–20a)."[32] She rightly observes that "the letter does not want its readers to take a combative and conspicuous stance of self-defense," noting that the author's priority is "survival, not reprisal."[33] African Americans may cringe at 1 Peter's command to "accept the authority of your masters with all deference" (2:18 NRSV) but can also appreciate the wisdom of nonretaliation. Smith well summarizes the situation:

> First Peter is not a divine mandate defining a hierarchal social order that places white American males on top and female physiology and brown bodies at the bottom. Rather, it is a private prescription, supplying multicultural and vulnerable Christian populations with a strategy for functioning and surviving in environments prone to violent and aggressive reprisals for cultural difference and social deviance. The author of 1 Peter was not persuading his Christian sisters and brothers to see their plight as domestic slaves, inferior people, and subjects of imperial control as God's created order. Rather, the First Letter of Peter conveys just *one* out of several options available to a leader of a dispersed population that is exposed, vulnerable, and defenseless. The author commands submission not because it was God's way but because it was his way of mitigating the conspicuousness of his community and keeping members alive.[34]

Conclusion

Not only should we laud the Christians who first read 1 Peter, but we should also see them as teachers. And, by extension, we still find teachers among those who are dishonored in society because of their diaspora status. Despite that marginal status—or rather *because* of such status—diaspora Christians often embody the values and virtues of Jesus in a way that the dominant culture might not. The USA's history is replete with stories of immigrants, slaves, and women whose faith not only sustained them through suffering but also served to be a testimony to others. In my pulpit ministry, I often share the story of my own family members, especially that of my great-aunt, a member of the African diaspora who, in her youth, picked cotton in South Carolina. Flossie Glenn, as part of the Great Migration, eventually moved to Washington, DC, met the man who would become her husband, and remained married to Clifton Johnson for sixty-five years, until his death. For seventeen years I lived in Washington, DC, not too far from Aunt Flossie. She once responded to one of my questions by saying, "Don't you know all the females in your family did domestic work for white people?" She endured the Jim Crow South and

32. Smith, *Strangers to Family*, 73.
33. Smith, *Strangers to Family*, 74.
34. Smith, *Strangers to Family*, 165.

worked most of her life as a maid and cook, caring for other people's children while raising her own. At her funeral, the eulogist, a sixty-eight-year-old retired federal judge who rested in my great-aunt's arms shortly after he was born, regaled us with stories of her great faith and love toward others. My great-aunt, a victim of a racist, patriarchal society, a second-class citizen all her life, nevertheless taught many a way of life consistent with the Golden Rule.

Diaspora Christians are not merely inspirational; they are educational. They are our teachers. Biblically, the best teachers for Christians are to be found not among the powerful in society but largely among those diaspora Christians whose association to the state has been questioned and scrutinized because of their lowly position in society. The church would do well to increase its attention to those on the margins because it is there that we often see Christ most clearly.

20

An Appeal to Holiness in 2 Peter and Jude

Reading from an Indian Perspective

LANUWABANG JAMIR

India is a dynamic country with a population of 1.3 billion with diverse cultures and multireligious traditions. Hinduism, with its millions of gods and goddesses, is the largest religion, with around 80 percent of the population professing to be Hindus. It is a religion preoccupied with ritual purity and holiness. A multitude of religious and cultural practices, ceremonies, and festivals cover every aspect of life, seeking to maintain purity and holiness. From daily rituals, ablutions, and meditations to extreme ascetic practices, the sole aim is to attain and maintain holiness. Even during the pandemic, people flocked in millions to the Ganges, considered to be the holiest river, to take a holy dip for the ablution of sins. The theme of holiness appears prominently in 2 Peter and Jude, as the writers deal with the issues of false teachings and unholy living. This chapter looks at how the letters can relate to the Indian context, where the concept of holiness remains central in both society and the church.

Holiness in the Indian Context

According to the major religious tradition in India, holiness can be understood as the realization of "oneness or submergence with the divine."[1] Unlike communion, this is considered an *advaitic* union or nondual oneness.[2] The holy person becomes conscious of the divine immanence and radiates the presence of God.[3] It involves an inner experience and apprehension of the divine presence in every material and immaterial object in the universe. So divinity occupies the center of the Indian holiness tradition. To achieve this holiness or oneness with *Brahman* or God, renunciation or asceticism and other spiritual practices are indispensable for a seeker, and materialism is believed to be the main barrier to spiritual attainment.[4] Personal appropriation is required to achieve purity and holiness, done through self-control over human passions and attachments through renunciation, mediation, prayers and other religious rituals and practices, spiritual disciplines, mediation, yoga,[5] repetitive recitation of divine names or mantra, sacrifices, and penance.[6]

However, the pursuit of holiness is not open to everyone. There is a rigid framework centered on the notion of *karma*, or fate, based on one's actions. One must be in a position to pursue holiness, which may involve a series of rebirths. Finally, one has to be born a Brahmin, which is the highest caste in the social ladder, for whom this holiness is attainable. People from other, lower social castes, including women, are denied or have restricted accessibility to holiness.[7] Thus, the issue of pollution and purity becomes an important aspect of the caste system, whose ultimate aim is to attain a pure state. This also impacts one's work. Groups in the lowest strata of society are assigned to do menial jobs, which are considered to cause impurity or pollution, affecting one's holy status.

This concern to maintain holiness in turn affects interpersonal and restricts societal relationships. There is endemic discrimination on the basis of caste, manifested in the way the caste system is structured and maintained, such

1. Tapas Ghosh, "The Mark of Holiness (*Punyatva*) in Hinduism," *Allahabad Bible Seminary Journal* 2 (August 2010): 37.

2. Michael Amaladoss, "Holiness in the Indian Tradition," *Khristu Jyoti* 3 (September 2003): 229–30.

3. Holiness in this lifetime is attainable, and such people are called *Jivanmuktas*. Such holy people become role models and teachers to guide others to attain this holiness. Cf. Amaladoss, "Holiness in the Indian Tradition," 231.

4. Ghosh, "Mark of Holiness," 38; Amaladoss, "Holiness in the Indian Tradition," 229–30.

5. Mediation and yoga are considered important means of controlling both body and mind in order "to elevate one's mind into the highest level of spiritual reality." Ghosh, "Mark of Holiness," 43.

6. Cf. Ghosh, "Mark of Holiness," 39–40; Amaladoss, "Holiness in the Indian Tradition," 228–29.

7. Amaladoss, "Holiness in the Indian Tradition," 231.

as separate wells for drinking purposes, separate temples for worship and prayers, restrictions on women participating in rituals, and social distancing and branding of certain groups of people as "untouchables." A higher caste member will not even let the shadow of a lower caste member fall on him or her, for it would cause impurity and pollution. There is strict taboo about intercaste and interreligious marriages. This in turn has led to violence and even killing for breaking the holiness code and rules of the society.

Though holiness is to be achieved through personal appropriation,[8] it is also maintained in the group or community, because a person gets his or her identity and status by belonging to a certain caste. Moreover, there are collective actions to guard the community's holy status through prevention and protection, since impurities are contagious.

According to the latest census of 2011, Christians make up less than 3 percent of the total population.[9] Many are first- or second-generation Christians. So the religious and cultural traditions, observed for so long, continue to exert their influence on believers and their attitude toward holiness. This has in turn affected the church: tension between people belonging to different castes or preferential treatment based on caste, churches or fellowships catering exclusively to people belonging to a particular social group or caste, and the discrimination against women. All these issues are based on the idea of holiness maintained through the caste system. This has a detrimental effect on the life of the church and its witness to society.

There are other implications based on the dichotomous understanding of ritual and nonritual purity. For instance, should one participate with family members in non-Christian rites and rituals or partake in the food or sweets that were offered to idols? How should one engage the prevalent corruption and court cases related to church properties? Along with this comes the issue of persecution of Christians, which can be linked with the disruption of the social structure, because conversion can affect the whole system of maintaining the holiness and purity code in society.

Holiness in the Bible

Holiness in the Bible plays an important role in defining the relationship between God and his people. In the Old Testament, *qadosh* (set aside) is derived

---

8. Amaladoss rightly remarks that emphasis on individualistic holiness has led to inertia regarding the welfare of others. Cf. Amaladoss, "Holiness in the Indian Tradition," 230.

9. "Census Tables," https://censusindia.gov.in/census.website/data/census-tables. See also "Religious Composition of India," Pew Research Center, September 21, 2021, https://www.pewresearch.org/religion/2021/09/21/population-growth-and-religious-composition/.

from the Hebrew root *qdsh*, which implies separation. It refers to the holiness of God and his separateness from creation, and it represents the inherent nature—the very essence—of God. At the same time, God chooses people to reflect his holiness on earth and to be his witness (Lev. 20:8). So being "holy" means "set apart" as God's and for God's use.[10] However, God's people are also to consecrate themselves (20:7) by obeying the moral law, observing the cleanness codes, and carrying out rituals and sacrifices.[11] Holiness is meant to be a way of life for the people of Israel as they represent themselves as God's people.[12] This corporate idea of holiness entails a separation from all that is unclean and defiling, as impurity is contagious (cf. 13:45–46; 15:25; 21:11). Similarly, holiness of the holy items from the temple can be transferable (Ezek. 42:14; 44:19; 46:20), but people are to avoid them for they can cause death (Num. 4:15).[13]

In the New Testament, this concept of holiness referring to God's people as a distinctive community is carried over and becomes a mark of the early church identity and conduct. Jesus transcends the understanding about holiness and its practices. All the categories of things that cause pollution and impurities are taken care of when Jesus heals and cleanses the sick and the impaired (cf. Mark 5:27, 39–41; 14:3).[14] By his actions, Jesus opens the way for people to be restored into the community, for his holiness is "transferable" and has the positive outcome of life and wholeness.[15] Jesus comes as holiness personified and sets the standards of a holy life, as indicated when he proclaims that he has come to fulfill the law, which regulated the life of the people to maintain purity and holiness. Holiness is now based on one's "union with Christ by the power of the Holy Spirit."[16]

10. See the discussion of the word in N. H. Snaith, *The Distinctive Ideas of the Old Testament* (Philadelphia: Westminster, 1946), 24–62.

11. In the Old Testament, the prophets emphasize that trying to be holy through rituals but without moral uprightness is detestable to God. Cf. V. M. Sinton, "Holiness," in *New Dictionary of Christian Ethics and Pastoral Theology*, ed. David J. Atkinson and David H. Field (Leicester, UK: Inter-Varsity, 1995), 443–44.

12. The laws of Leviticus pertain to this understanding of holy: "be holy, because I am holy" (e.g., Lev. 11:44–45 NIV; cf. 19:3–10).

13. Hanna Stettler observes that this contagious character of holiness in the Old Testament occurs only in a few cases. Stettler, "Sanctification in the Jesus Tradition," *Biblia* 85 (January 2004): 160.

14. Dwight Swanson rightly observes that in Jesus "holiness does not withdraw, it reaches out." Swanson, "Holiness in the Dead Sea Scrolls: The Priorities of Faith," in *Holiness and Ecclesiology in the New Testament*, ed. Kent E. Brower and Andy Johnson (Grand Rapids: Eerdmans, 2007), 38.

15. Cf. Stettler, "Sanctification in the Jesus Tradition," 160.

16. Bernie A. Van De Walle, *Rethinking Holiness: A Theological Introduction* (Grand Rapids: Baker Academic, 2017), 150.

Theme of Holiness in 2 Peter and Jude

Second Peter and Jude are studied together, as there is some interdependence,[17] although background study of the epistles indicates that the contexts and situations are different.[18] Both of these letters were written by people closely associated with Jesus (cf. 2 Pet. 1:1; Jude 1), and both writers incorporated similar events from Old Testament traditions and applied their interpretations to deal with the issue at hand—namely, false teachers who were twisting God's word for their own gain (2 Pet. 2:3, 19; Jude 14–15)—and to serve as a warning to those who promoted false teachings and lifestyle.[19]

An overview reading clearly shows that the central theme of the letters is holiness.[20] Both authors were concerned that believers should keep themselves holy, despite being bombarded with heresies and the accompanying unholy lifestyles of the false teachers. This theme is indicated in the number of words and motifs related to holiness as well as the structural pattern used in the letters.

A Holy Status and Assurance of Holiness

First, the writers remind the readers of their holy status and shared identity in Christ. Similar to the Old Testament concept, recipients are described as the called community (2 Pet. 1:3; Jude 1).[21] It is an imputed status because God has chosen them, making them holy.[22] They are addressed as the "beloved,"

17. Similarity is seen especially between 2 Pet. 2:1–18; 3:1–3 and Jude 4–13, 16–18. They were dealing with similar issues, like the false teachers (2 Pet. 3:3; Jude 17–18). On the relationship between 2 Peter and Jude, see Richard Bauckham, *Jude, 2 Peter*, WBC 50 (Waco: Word, 1983), 141–43.

18. In both cases the false teachers have misled the church through their false teaching and licentious lifestyle, causing dissension (2 Pet. 2:1; Jude 18). But there are differences: in 2 Peter they are questioning the second coming of Christ (2 Pet. 3:1–10) and the reality of future judgment (2:3b; 3:4), but in Jude they are distorting the doctrine of grace (Jude 4) and claiming divine inspiration for their heretical teachings. Cf. Gene L. Green, *Jude and 2 Peter*, BECNT (Grand Rapids: Baker Academic, 2008), 40.

19. Cf. Bauckham, *Jude, 2 Peter*, 142–43; Richard B. Vinson, Richard F. Wilson, and Watson E. Mills, *1 & 2 Peter, Jude*, SHBC (Macon, GA: Smyth & Helwys, 2010), 271.

20. Along with honor and shame, patronage, and social status, people in the Greco-Roman society were preoccupied with the whole notion of purity, impurity, and holiness. See Bruce J. Malina, *The New Testament World: Insights from Cultural Anthropology* (Louisville: Westminster John Knox, 2001), 161–65.

21. The usage of the pronoun "our" to address God and Jesus Christ indicates that belongingness to a shared belief and identity. Likewise, the benedictions remind them of this oneness with God as a community (2 Pet. 3:18; Jude 25). This communitarian emphasis, based on the relational nature of God, is a trademark of the church in the New Testament. Cf. Ruth Anne Reese, *2 Peter and Jude*, THNTC (Grand Rapids: Eerdmans, 2007), 78–79.

22. Cf. Peter Oakes, "Made Holy by the Holy Spirit: Holiness and Ecclesiology in Romans," in *Holiness and Ecclesiology in the New Testament*, ed. Kent E. Brower and Andy Johnson (Grand Rapids: Eerdmans, 2007), 177; and Bruce W. Winter, "Carnal Conduct and Sanctification

emphasizing God's love for them (2 Pet. 1:17; 3:1, 8, 14, 15; Jude 1, 3, 20; cf. Luke 3:22). They now have a righteous standing before God, shared by other Christians (who are called "saints" or "holy ones," Jude 3), obtained through their faith in the redemptive work of God in Christ (2 Pet. 1:1; Jude 25).[23] Moreover, in 2 Peter, an explicit description of holiness is given: they have become partakers of the divine nature (1:4).[24]

After the reminder of their holy status, mediated through Jesus Christ (2 Pet. 1:1; Jude 25), the readers are assured that God will keep their holy status. Amid the impurities and corruption around them, they are reassured about "God's ability to preserve" them from falling so that they will stand in perfection before him (2 Pet. 1:4; 2:9; Jude 1, 24).[25]

Their holy status is a result of God's initiative, and he continues to grant them the divine power for "godly living," a term that includes maintaining their holy status (2 Pet. 1:3).[26] Likewise, they are dependent on his mercy, which will lead them to eternal life (2 Pet. 3:9; Jude 21). Just as holiness is derived and bestowed by God, the writers conclude that God also sustains and completes it.[27] This assurance and hope are based on the character of the sovereign and relational God, who has the power and authority over all creation.[28] This is affirmed through the Old Testament traditions: God saved Noah (Gen. 6:9) and Lot (Gen. 19) and delivered his people out of Egypt (2 Pet. 2:5; Jude 5). Just as God delivered his people in the past, so he will save them from the present realities and the impending judgment and confer to them entrance into his eternal kingdom, reserved for the holy people.[29]

in 1 Corinthians: Simul sanctus et peccator?," in Brower and Johnson, *Holiness and Ecclesiology in the New Testament*, 184.

23. Bauckham, *Jude, 2 Peter*, 168. As Reese remarks: "Throughout the canon righteousness is connected with purity, blamelessness and justice. . . . It is by the suffering of Jesus as the righteous one that the way of God was opened to the unrighteous (1 Pet 2.18)." Reese, *2 Peter and Jude*, 132.

24. It is unlikely that divinization is meant here; perhaps the author is referring to the restoration of humans to the image of God, in which they were originally created, which will come to its culmination in the future. Cf. Bauckham, *Jude, 2 Peter*, 182.

25. On the theme of "keeping," see Reese, *2 Peter and Jude*, 83–84; Mariam Kamell Kovalishyn, "Kept for Faithfulness: Reading the Epistle of Jude," *CRUX* 50 (2014): 13–23.

26. Cf. Bauckham, *Jude, 2 Peter*, 178. Divine power for godly living and the knowledge of Christ are interrelated. Holy life is affected through knowing the Lord, who first called them to be his own. The importance of Scripture in this whole process is indicated when the writers make it the central focus to refute the false teaching and lifestyle. Cf. J. N. D. Kelly, *The Epistles of Peter and of Jude*, BNTC (1969; repr., Grand Rapids: Baker, 1993), 224–25.

27. The final destination is described by the usage of "at peace" and "eternal life" (2 Pet. 3:14; Jude 21). It refers to the objective reality and the culmination wherein all believers will be found acceptable before God. Cf. Green, *Jude and 2 Peter*, 279–80.

28. Cf. 2 Pet. 3:5–7; Jude 25; Bauckham, *2 Peter, Jude*, 122–23.

29. Both writers refer to this unchanging and enduring character of God for all eternity (2 Pet. 3:18; Jude 25). See Green, *Jude and 2 Peter*, 126.

Description of the Unholy

The writers then extensively describe the nature and character of the ungodly people who advocate false teaching and an unholy lifestyle. They deny the Lord through their teaching and lifestyle (2 Pet. 2:1; Jude 4), characterized as "licentiousness," in contradiction to the Christian faith (2 Pet. 2:2, 18; Jude 4).[30] They indulge in a lifestyle dominated by sexual immorality (2 Pet. 2:10, 14, 18; Jude 8, 18). Along with that, they lead people astray and exploit them, motivated by greed, power, position, and financial gain (2 Pet. 2:3, 14, 15, 19; Jude 11, 16). Even when they come together for worship and fellowship, they have selfish motives, thinking about their own good instead of that of others (2 Pet. 2:13; Jude 12).[31] In the process, they cause division in the community (Jude 19). Their greedy, impure, and licentious lifestyle disrupts the relationships in the communities.[32] Their speech betrays their true nature and intention. Their speech is empty and directed against God, just like in the exodus event. They are characterized by boasting in their own ability and flattery for their own gain and to misguide believers (2 Pet. 2:18; Jude 16).[33] A series of metaphors is used especially in Jude to further describe their ungodly character and actions, emphasizing their "unreliability, fruitlessness, lack of control, and worthless directions" (Jude 12, 13, 16; cf. 2 Pet. 2:17, 18).[34]

This behavior results from the false teachers trusting not in God's word but in their own self-devised knowledge and arrogance (2 Pet. 3:5; Jude 10). They then justify their actions by misinterpreting the biblical principle of God's grace as freedom to do whatever they like (Jude 4) and by deliberately ignoring the word of God (2 Pet. 3:5), indicating they rejected the authority of the Lord in their lives (2 Pet. 2:10; Jude 8). Therefore, they are compared to irrational animals without reasoning ability (2 Pet. 2:12; Jude 10).[35]

---

30. The Greek word describes giving oneself to debauchery and sensuality, and it also involves brutal acts. Cf. William F. Arndt and F. Wilbur Gingrich, *A Greek-English Lexicon of the New Testament and Other Early Christian Literature* (Chicago: University of Chicago Press, 1974), 114; H. G. Liddell and R. Scott, *An Intermediate Greek-English Lexicon* (Oxford: Clarendon, 1975), 123, s.v. *aselgeia*.

31. The imagery used in Jude of shepherding themselves is probably a reference to the evil leaders in Ezekiel. "You eat the fat and clothe yourselves with the wool . . . without feeding the flock . . . (Ezek 34.3–4)." Reese, *2 Peter and Jude*, 57–58.

32. Cf. Walter Brueggemann, "Vision for a New Church and a New Century, Part II: Holiness Become Generosity," *USQR* 54 (January 2000): 56–57.

33. Reese, *2 Peter and Jude*, 63–64, 158.

34. For the metaphors, see Reese, *2 Peter and Jude*, 62; see also Bauckham, *2 Peter, Jude*, 87–88, 274.

35. "But these folks have neglected their rationality and followed their passions. Very well, their end will be like an animal's too." Green, *2 Peter and Jude*, 119.

The writers then proceed to show the consequences in terms of the holiness code. They are "blots and blemishes," meaning that they are now unacceptable and unholy people before God (2 Pet. 2:13; cf. Jude 12). Their state is bondage, as they are enslaved to their evil practices, with no freedom of their own (2 Pet. 2:19). They have no means of redemption, for they have rejected the only means of getting freedom and becoming the holy ones (2:20).[36] Not only that, but their actions make the whole community impure and damage their witness.[37] They are also capable of leading astray some in the community in this dangerous path of unholiness by enticing them with false promises (2:18). The word "blemish/spot" (*spilas*) can also refer to hidden rocks or a reef that can cause shipwreck (Jude 12; cf. 2 Pet. 2:13).[38] Or like wandering stars they mislead people from their path (Jude 13).[39] Nonetheless, the readers are not to be taken by surprise or be discouraged, as this was already foretold by the prophets and the apostles (2 Pet. 3:2, 3; Jude 17, 18). This reveals the sovereignty of God over history and all consequent events, so they should affirm their faith in the teachings of the Lord through the apostles and not give in to these false teachers.

God's Judgment on the Unholy

God's wrath and judgment inevitably follow. Peter and Jude refer to several events in the history of God's people to show the unchangeable character of a holy God who deals with ungodly people. These serve as a warning to all, especially to those who go astray. Jude begins with the exodus event, in which God destroyed all those who rebelled in the wilderness (Jude 5). Second Peter begins with the time of Noah, when the flood destroyed all the ungodly people in the world (cf. Gen. 6–8; 2 Pet. 2:5; 3:6). Both writers refer to the destruction of Sodom and Gomorrah in Genesis 18–19, which was the epitome of God's judgment on unholiness.[40] Likewise, other infamous characters from the Old Testament are set as an exemplary of God's judgment on the unholy. Cain, Balaam, and Korah are referred to in Jude 11, and Balaam in 2 Peter 2:15. The first murderer, a prophet who was after financial gain, and a prophet who rebelled against God's the authority of Moses and Aaron are examples that the false teachers have been imitating through their actions, implying

---

36. They think of themselves as holy but no longer are. Their lifestyle shows the rejection of that God-given status. Cf. 2 Pet. 2:21, 22; Jude 19.

37. The community is stained through their deceit and immorality. See Reese, *2 Peter and Jude*, 155–56.

38. Reese, *2 Peter and Jude*, 59–60.

39. Cf. Reese, *2 Peter and Jude*, 62.

40. Cf. Deut. 29:23; Isa. 3:9; Jer. 23:14. See also Reese, *2 Peter and Jude*, 166–67.

that the same judgment will befall them.[41] If God did not spare the angels who disobeyed him but cast them into hell for judgment, how much less will he spare humans who disobey his holy commandments (2 Pet. 2:4; Jude 6)?[42]

The surety and certainty of God's judgment on the false teachers even at the present time is emphasized, foretold by the prophets (2 Pet. 2:1, 3, 9; 3:7, 10; Jude 10, 13–15). These events show that God, who has saved his people before, also has the authority to destroy them if they do not conform to his holiness, a sobering judgment against apostasy.[43] The writers balance between assurance of holiness and judgment on those who go astray.

Holiness Ethics

The writers of 2 Peter and Jude also balance the imputed holiness from God with the demand for a life of holiness. In the Old Testament, people were holy by virtue of belonging to God. But this entailed that they observe and follow the laws and regulations, which included ritual and moral laws, marking them as belonging to God. The emphasis on ethics in both 2 Peter and Jude refers to this understanding. Believers are to live out their relationship with the Lord.[44]

To achieve this, two sets of actions are to be taken—namely, action to safeguard themselves and action toward others. Both writers exhort the readers to live holy and godly lives in keeping with their holy status and in light of impending parousia and judgment (cf. 2 Pet. 3:11, 12; Jude 23).[45] Unlike the false teachers, who are spots and blemishes, believers are directed in Old Testament terminology to be presented without blemish or spot before God (2 Pet. 3:14; Jude 24).[46] The two words suggest that believers are to be morally and ethically pure, as perfect sacrifices before the Lord at the final judgment.[47] They are to conduct their lives conforming to the holiness of God revealed in

41. For an explanation of these characters and their downfall, see Bauckham, *2 Peter, Jude*, 79–91; Reese, *2 Peter and Jude*, 53–57.

42. The reference to angels is based on Gen. 6:1–4 and 1 Enoch. Cf. Reese, *2 Peter and Jude*, 45, 151.

43. Cf. Reese, *2 Peter and Jude*, 45.

44. According to John Wesley, along with "imputed" righteousness, God also wants to "impart" righteousness. Don Thorsen, "Holiness in Postmodern Culture," *WTJ* 43, no. 2 (2008): 131.

45. Judgment by fire is a recurring image in the Old Testament. It will ultimately destroy everything, except that which is pure and righteous. Cf. Isa. 33:14–15; Zech. 13:9; Mal. 3:2; 1 Cor. 3:13–15; Reese, *2 Peter and Jude*, 171.

46. This refers to the cultic practice of sacrificing animals to God without blemish (Exod. 29:38; Lev. 1:3; 3:1). In later writings, "without spot and blemish" came to denote ethical and moral purity (Job 15:15; Ps. 25:2–3; Prov. 11:5); see Friedrich Hauck, "ἀμώμητος," *TDNT* 4:831; Bauckham, *2 Peter, Jude*, 122, 327. Likewise, in the New Testament, holiness is frequently paired or interchangeable with justice/righteousness or with purity/cleansing. Cf. Sinton, "Holiness," 444.

47. Cf. Bauckham, *2 Peter, Jude*, 327.

the teachings and embodied in the person of Jesus.[48] The demand to be without blemish or spot encompasses their whole conduct of life, as individuals and as a community. They must stand against everything the false teachers advocate for. And from the context, we see that the demand pertains not just to sexual purity but to all aspects of life, including greed and corruption.

The virtues that will safeguard their holiness are defined in 2 Peter 1:5–7 and Jude 2, 20, 21.[49] These virtues culminate in the practice of love for others (2 Pet. 1:7; Jude 2).[50] As in other New Testament writings, love is the encompassing virtue that "coordinates and unites all the other virtues."[51] A holy lifestyle exhibits itself in concern and love for those who have gone astray. Peter and Jude base their exhortation on the teachings of Jesus, who redefined holiness based on love of God and neighbor.[52] The virtues must be practiced with the goal of restoring those who have fallen short. As a holy community, believers are to love one another, building each other up in faith (Jude 20). Ruth Anne Reese observes that the pronoun "each other" indicates that it is the responsibility of everyone in the community, not just the leaders of the church, to uplift each other.[53] This relational engagement is to be based on justice, mercy, faith, and love.

Certain actions are recommended to believers so that the unholy ones might be saved. They are to show compassion to those who are in doubt (Jude 21, 22). They are to reach out to those who are on the verge of destruction and save them by rebuking and warning them, or by influencing them through their holy lifestyle (2 Pet. 1:7; Jude 23).[54] At the same time, they are to safeguard their holiness so that they are not tainted themselves and fall into the ways of the false teachers, made impure by sin and its corruption (2 Pet. 3:14; Jude 23).[55] Just like impurity was seen as polluting the whole community and

48. Cf. Peter H. Davids, *The Letters of 2 Peter and Jude*, PNTC (Grand Rapids: Eerdmans, 2006), 336; Daniel Keating, *First and Second Peter, Jude*, CCSS (Grand Rapids: Baker Academic, 2011), 208.

49. For an explanation of the catalog of virtues in Jude 20, 21, see Reese, *2 Peter and Jude*, 67–69; and for 2 Pet. 1:5–7, see Bauckham, *2 Peter, Jude*, 176–87.

50. Bauckham, *2 Peter, Jude*, 176; Reese, *2 Peter and Jude*, 201.

51. Bauckham, *2 Peter, Jude*, 187; cf. Reese, *2 Peter and Jude*, 34.

52. The old holiness code was no longer relevant, for it was no longer material or physical contaminations but distortion of neighborliness and what comes from within that defile a person (Matt. 23:23–26). Cf. Brueggemann, "Vision for a New Church and a New Century," 54–55.

53. Reese, *2 Peter and Jude*, 67–68.

54. This is reminiscent of the Old Testament events where the presence of even a single righteous person could have saved the entire city from being destroyed. Cf. Bauckham, *2 Peter, Jude*, 119; Reese, *2 Peter and Jude*, 70–71.

55. Most likely Zech. 3:2–5 is the background to Jude 23. Kelly suggests that social relations are to be restricted so that they are not influenced by their false teaching. Nonetheless they are to admonish them and intercede for them. Kelly, *Epistles of Peter and of Jude*, 289.

not just the offender, so, they are reminded, their holiness can be contagious and redemptive.

Moreover, this reminder keeps them on track and defends against temptation.[56] They ought to live in holiness and godliness (2 Pet. 3:11), motivated by the surety of the coming judgment along with the coming of God's kingdom and its culmination in the new heavens and new earth (3:12, 13). Unlike the false teachers, who interpret the delay of the parousia as an excuse for immoral living, they are to see the delay as God's forbearance for repentance and salvation. This holy living is to coincide with their knowledge of the Lord (1:2; 3:18). There is a close link between their holy status, their knowledge of Jesus, and their holy living.

The holiness presented shows that, though it is a status given to individuals, the whole community is also part of it; thus, believers are exhorted to care for one another. This communitarian emphasis of maintaining holiness corresponds with the New Testament understanding of the church as the body of Christ. This communitarian responsibility was an effective persuasion, since the readers of 2 Peter and Jude lived in a society in which the community played an important role in dictating the behavior of an individual.[57] The call to holiness is not about following a code of exclusiveness but about helping one another to grow in faith, purity, and holiness to conform to the image of God. The writers call for active participation in the life of others so that they are liberated from the oppressive forces or lifestyle to which they have been enslaved. This is the proper response to God's work of imputing to them his holiness through the work of Christ.[58]

Finally, the readers are reminded of one important aspect relating to those in the community who have gone astray. They are not to revile, condemn, or judge anyone, no matter what their actions are. Both writers refer to the angelic beings in biblical tradition who, though they are greater and more powerful than humans, restrain themselves from passing judgment against the devil or others (2 Pet. 2:11; Jude 9).[59] Judgment is the prerogative of God, and thus one leaves it to God to judge whether one is holy or unholy. Believers are to humble themselves lest they also fall and be judged.

56. Ruth Anne Reese, "Holiness and Ecclesiology in Jude and 2 Peter," in Brower and Johnson, *Holiness and Ecclesiology in the New Testament*, 339–40.

57. Bruce J. Malina and Jerome H. Neyrey, *Portraits of Paul: An Archaeology of Ancient Personality* (Louisville: Westminster John Knox, 1996), 186–87. Also, Green, *Jude and 2 Peter*, 117.

58. Reese, "Holiness and Ecclesiology," 339–40.

59. See the explanation about this allusion to the tradition behind the story of Michael the archangel in Jude 9, in Bauckham, *2 Peter, Jude*, 65–76; Reese, *2 Peter and Jude*, 49–51.

The Message of Holiness in 2 Peter and Jude for the Indian Context

The theme of holiness presented throughout these epistles indicates that it was an issue close to the hearts of the readers in the Christian communities in the Roman Empire. They came from a multiplicity of cultures and traditions and had a newfound identity in Christ; nonetheless, there were problems in the church. The theology of holiness presented to them was the core response to the issues at hand. The context of 2 Peter and Jude and the context of the church in India may differ, but the underlying motif of holiness has similar relevance. Holiness is central to the understanding of faith in the Indian churches. Many of the issues and problems in the churches are interconnected with the idea of holiness. These letters can help believers understand the proper concept of holiness, which in turn can rectify many of the issues in churches at times influenced by other religious traditions in the society.

First, the imputed holiness that is spoken about in these epistles can be liberative in the Indian context, as holiness is based on the redemptive work of God and not based on the observance of rites and rituals or *karma*. One need not be born into the higher-caste society but can be "born again" to attain this status. Rather than determined by birth and restricted to some, holiness is here and now, and available to all men and women irrespective of race, caste, status, position, or profession. Holiness, previously a dividing factor, can be a uniting factor, just as in the early church, which brought together Jews and gentiles. This is an important reminder to the readers in India to overcome the cultural barriers based on purity that divide the community, to embrace a holiness that brings people together. Moreover, like in the religious traditions of India, they become partakers of the divine and enter communion or relationship, but they do so not in terms of assimilation but with their own distinct identities.

Second, the assurance of holiness for believers in the midst of the hard realities of life, suffering, persecution, and attacks, based on the sovereignty and grace of God, is a comfort. The epistles remind believers in India that amid all the present sufferings and problems they may face, their holy status points to the fact that a future glory or judgment awaits all. The need of the hour is to stand firm and depend on the hope and grace of God, who has declared them holy.

Third, the description of the unholy in the letters should challenge believers in India to reflect on the concept of holiness prevalent today. Many times the focus is just on sexual immorality, while corruption, greed, position and power struggles, and litigations and court cases over church properties and finance are ignored. Such things pollute the whole community. Similarly, many false teachers who promote alternative gospels, such as prosperity gospels, are a danger to the life and witness of the church. As the letters indicate, unholy living stains the community and its Christian witness. This understanding comes close to the Indian concept of holiness, in which the community can be polluted by the actions of some in the community. These epistles appeal to all to reexamine the biblical concept of holiness and reaffirm it for the future of the church. The harsh words implying that the false teachers deny Jesus through their actions can be an eye-opener for those who live with a false sense of security and false perspective on holiness.

Fourth, just like the cultural and religious understanding in the Indian context that sees impurity and anything that causes pollution as a danger that must always be purged, the theme of judgment on the unholy and impure in the letters is relevant for the church in India. The experience of shame and exclusion associated with pollution and practiced in the communities can be expected in similar ways when God acts on those who live unholy lives.[60]

Fifth, the epistles remind the readers in Indian churches that they are to live according to the holiness standards set by the gospel, not as prescribed by earlier traditions and beliefs. This holy way of life is in response to God electing his people for himself, in contrast with fate in the major religious tradition of India. This study shows that though the context, the community, and their issues may be different, there is only one solution to all the crises that confront the church. Believers need to be firm and steadfast in the word of God to withstand the forces and influences that will lead them astray. The word of God is relevant to all situations and contexts, and believers are to live accordingly. The holiness expected from them pertains not just to sexual morality but to all matters of life, including status, position, wealth, and money.

Sixth, the emphasis on communitarian holiness in the epistles is similar to the Indian context, in which community is integral to the holiness of an individual. The church consists of people from different walks of life, a reminder that the gospel can overcome barriers and differences and bring unity and shared identity. Moreover, the emphasis on a collective identity is essential to overcoming some of the prejudices that exist within and outside the church. The biblical emphasis on shared or contagious holiness can be reclaimed in the Indian context as the community is involved in maintaining that social identity and holiness. Believers are to encourage, build up, and help one another to be found blameless and without blemish at the coming of the Lord.

60. Cf. Jerome H. Neyrey, *2 Peter, Jude: A New Translation with Introduction and Commentary*, AB 37C (New York: Doubleday, 1993), 201.

In a context in which community comes first, the ideas of shared identity and shared holiness in the epistles touch a central nerve for the church in India.

Seventh, the directives to reach out to unholy ones or those on the margins can challenge those in the church, as the orientation is often to safeguard one's own holiness. The gospel demands a radical change in worldview and behavior based on the concept of holiness that is contagious, relational, and redemptive. As Christ has made them holy who were earlier considered unclean, likewise believers are to reach out to those who have gone astray and try to restore them. They are to serve as God's agents to transmit his holiness in the society they live in. The idea of holiness in relation to neighborliness is an important message for a society in which communal tension and fights are frequent.

Eighth, a major issue in India is corruption in society.[61] Many churches are silent or inactive in regard to politics or societal engagements, or they are embroiled in them. This is partly due to the distinction that is made between the sacred and the secular. The epistles convey a very relevant message for the church to be proactive in holiness as a way of life. The Christian community should bring about individual as well as community transformation.

Finally, the reminder in the epistles to abstain from judging others, especially in the context of holiness, is relevant for the Indian church, where caste issues are still prevalent, leading to discrimination and other forms of injustice. Since holiness is derived from God, one is not to judge anyone based on background, caste, or status but to accept everyone as an equal, as God has done in Christ.

Conclusion

The epistles of 2 Peter and Jude were written to churches struggling with issues related to holiness, a central concern of both the church and the society at that time. The writers address these issues and provide the solutions to rectify them, based on the biblical concept of holiness. The message of these epistles is relevant for the church and society in India, where holiness matters. Amid challenges both internal and external, the church in India can find meaning and hope in its endeavor for holiness. Moreover, the call to holiness is the need of the hour, to transform the church and society for the kingdom of God.

---

61. According to Transparency International, India ranks 86th of 180 countries in "Corruption Perceptions Index, 2023," https://www.transparency.org/en/cpi/2023/index/ind.

21

Being the Church in Post-apartheid South Africa

Theological Perspectives from 1 John

CAROLINE SEED

On May 25, 2020, in the US city of Minneapolis, the death of George Floyd at the hands of white police officers unleashed what the *New York Times* suggested "may be the largest movement in US history."[1] Mass protests erupted in the United States, followed by extensive demonstrations around the world under the banner of the Black Lives Matter movement. The themes were quickly taken up by protesters in post-apartheid South Africa.[2] In some evangelical churches, twenty-six years after the first democratic elections in South Africa, the Black Lives Matter movement resulted in protests over long-standing grievances. Emergency meetings were called, and churches were plunged into crisis. It was as if a volcano of anger had erupted, and no one knew how to address it. The crisis called urgently for people of all races to come together around the word of God to learn how to address the problems

1. Larry Buchanan, Quoctrung Bul, and Jugal K. Patel, "Black Lives Matter May Be the Biggest Movement in US History," *New York Times*, July 3, 2020, https://www.nytimes.com /interactive/2020/07/03/us/george-floyd-protests-crowd-size.html.
2. "'Black Lives Matter' Protest Hits South Africa," Africa News, July 4, 2020, https://www .africanews.com/2020/06/04/black-lives-matter-protest-hits-south-africa/.

and live together in a truly biblical way. But there was little material to draw on, little theological work done.

In 2015, South African theologian Marilyn Naidoo wrote, "Race, ethnicity and national identity are important discussions that are unfinished ecclesial business for churches in South Africa. Churches remain monocultural to a large extent; . . . churches still largely reflect the social divisions of society."[3] Her purpose was to highlight the potential for reconciliation in the few truly multicultural churches that have purposively developed in the years since the ending of apartheid in 1994. In September 2021, she again called on the South African churches to "consider how to deepen social interaction as religious communities" and to "truly transform by being visionary challengers of the status quo."[4] The purpose of this chapter is to contribute in a small way toward thinking biblically about the task of being the church in the post-apartheid South African context.

The focus of this chapter is the First Epistle of John. This may seem an unusual route to take, given claims that the Johannine literature is sectarian and unsuited to addressing the needs of cultural pluralism in the twenty-first century.[5] However, far from providing evidence of exclusion and segregation in the Johannine community, 1 John displays a highly developed theological basis for unity and inclusivity within the limits of the true church. This unity is predicated on the "already" and "not yet" Johannine eschatological orientation in the light of the incarnation and resurrection, fellowship as *koinōnia* in the triune God, ethics as the manifestation of the *agapē* of God through "abiding in Christ," and continuous confession of sin. The basis for Christian unity is expressed as being "the children of God," or those who "practice righteousness" (1 John 3:7, 9–10) and who do not walk in the way of Cain, who murdered his brother (3:12).[6] This use of a familiar "collective memory" of the Cain and Abel narrative from the Jewish Scriptures provides an interpretative framework for Christian unity in the epistle (see 3:11–15).[7]

---

3. Marilyn Naidoo, "The Potential of Multicultural Congregations in Supporting Social Reconciliation," *HvTSt* 73, no. 4 (2017): 1, https://doi.org/10.4102/hts.v73i4.4622.

4. Marilyn Naidoo, "How Multicultural Churches in South Africa Are Breaking Down Race Barriers," *The Conversation*, September 22, 2021, https://theconversation.com/how-multicultural-churches-in-south-africa-are-breaking-down-race-barriers-167014.

5. Miroslav Volf, "Johannine Dualism and Contemporary Pluralism," *Modern Theology* 21, no. 2 (2005): 189–211; S. C. Barton, "Johannine Dualism and Contemporary Pluralism," in *The Gospel of John and Christian Theology*, ed. Richard Bauckham and Carl Mosser (Grand Rapids: Eerdmans, 2008), 3–18.

6. Unless otherwise indicated, all Scripture quotations in this chapter are from the ESV.

7. Caroline G. Seed, "Religious Belief, Conflict, and Violence: Theological Basis in 1 John for Being Passionate about What We Believe and Passionate about Loving Those Who Disagree with Us," *TImp* 5 (2016): 3–10; Tom Thatcher, "Cain the Jew the AntiChrist: Collective Memory

Method

As the task of this chapter is to determine how 1 John might speak theologically into race relations within the contemporary South African church situation, a hermeneutical method is needed. To move directly from ancient text to contemporary context without acknowledging the interpretative process is to act irresponsibly. This chapter provides a reading of 1 John that first seeks to understand the message in its original time and context before applying its theological principles to today's context.[8] This assumes the Bible to be the Word of God, through which God spoke to his people at the time in which it was written and through which he speaks to his church today.[9] Through reading the text theologically and then bringing the theological principles to bear in our current context, we attempt to understand how the Word of God speaks to the challenges of being the church in South Africa in the twenty-first century. In what follows, four theological principles are discussed and then applied to the church in South Africa.

Principle 1: The Church Lives in the "Last Hour"

The task of finding the theological principles that serve the intended audience as well as the church in South Africa begins with the eschatological framework. First John commences with a powerful reminder of the most recent event in salvation history, the incarnation and resurrection of the Messiah, who is introduced in 1:1 as the "Word of life" (*tou logou tēs zōēs*). The significance of the use of *logos* in Johannine theology is widely debated. Arguments range from the *logos* as a substitute for the Old Testament concept of the "Word of the Lord" through which God accomplishes his will in the world, to concepts of wisdom, to the influence of Greek philosophy in Philo's writings.[10] Daniel Boyarin argues, however, that far from being a Greek concept, Johannine *logos* theology is thoroughly Jewish, reflecting the substitution of the Aramaic *Memra* for the "Word of the Lord" in the Palestinian Targums.[11] John Ronning

---

and the Johannine Ethic of Loving and Hating," in *Rethinking the Ethics of John: "Implicit Ethics" in the Johannine Writings*, ed. Jan G. van der Watt and Ruben Zimmermann, CNNTE 3, WUNT 291 (Tübingen: Mohr Siebeck, 2012), 351.

8. J. Scott Duvall and J. Daniel Hays, *Grasping God's Word: A Hands-On Approach to Reading, Interpreting and Applying the Bible*, 4th ed. (Grand Rapids: Zondervan Academic, 2021).

9. Vern S. Poythress, *God-Centered Biblical Interpretation* (Phillipsburg, NJ: P&R, 1999), 110.

10. John Ronning, *The Jewish Targums and John's Logos Theology* (Peabody, MA: Hendrickson, 2010), 1–9.

11. Daniel Boyarin, "The Gospel of the Memra: Jewish Binitarianism and the Prologue of John," *HTR* 19, no. 3 (2001): 243–84.

further argues that the use of *logos* as the Greek translation of *Memra* in the Gospel and 1 John is a way of identifying Jesus with the God of Israel.[12] If this is the case, then the use of *logos* in 1 John 1:1 indicates a divine title, which makes the bold statement that the author and those with him have experienced the physical presence of God in the world in the person of his Son in fulfillment of the messianic prophecies of the Old Testament (1:3).

Commentators are generally in agreement that the opening section of 1 John, and indeed the whole of the epistle, refers to the incarnation of the Son.[13] Matthew Jensen, however, argues that the resurrection is in view in 1:1–4 as well as 4:2 and 5:6–7. Jensen's work has been criticized for going against the main findings of scholarship and producing weak arguments to substantiate his claims.[14] However, others have found Jensen's work "refreshing" because it "makes sense" that early Jewish Christians would need to be encouraged in their understanding of the resurrected Christ and not only the incarnate Christ.[15] Commentators such as Robert Yarbrough and Karen Jobes admit that the resurrection is in view in the opening section of 1 John.[16] Indeed, the incarnation, resurrection, and ascension must be in view as 1 John was written after the resurrection event. It is not, as Judith Lieu posits, only modern readers who find resonance with the resurrection in 1 John.[17]

It is the postresurrection church that is addressed in 1 John. This is the church that has believed the testimony of the eyewitnesses to the coming of the Son of God into the world and to his resurrection (1 John 1:1–4). Yarbrough notes that the coming of Jesus Christ signals something that is both "true" and "momentous" within the eschatological framework of 1 John.[18] In his work on the Danielic hour in 1 John 2:18–27, Stefanos Mihalios argues that the use of the "last hour" in 1 John 2:18 is an allusion to the "last hour" in Daniel 12:2. He proposes that the use of the Danielic concept introduces an inaugurated eschatology into the epistle because the world as it was previously

12. Ronning, *Jewish Targums*, 1, 204.

13. For an extensive list of commentators who hold this position, see Matthew D. Jensen, *Affirming the Resurrection of the Incarnate Christ: A Reading of 1 John* (Cambridge: Cambridge University Press, 2012), 56n23.

14. Daniel R. Street, review of *Affirming the Resurrection of the Incarnate Christ*, by Matthew Jensen, *JETS* 57 (2014): 201–4.

15. Matthew Y. Emerson, review of *Affirming the Resurrection of the Incarnate Christ*, by Matthew Jensen, *BBR* 23, no. 3 (2013): 445–46.

16. Robert W. Yarbrough, *1–3 John*, BECNT (Grand Rapids: Baker Academic, 2008), 40; Karen H. Jobes, *1, 2, and 3 John*, ZECNT (Grand Rapids: Zondervan, 2014), 42–43.

17. Judith M. Lieu, *1, 2 & 3 John: A Commentary*, NTL (Louisville: Westminster John Knox, 2008), 40.

18. Yarbrough, *1–3 John*, 37–38.

known is already "passing away" (1 John 2:17).[19] The events of the life, death, and resurrection of Jesus Christ signal a new movement in salvation history, as predicted in Daniel. The evidence for this is the multiplication of "antichrists" and "false prophets" in the current period (1 John 2:18–22; 4:1–3). The eschatological moment, therefore, has already come.

There is, therefore, a new eschatological order with soteriological implications already in place. Yet, there is also a future aspect to the eschatological moment. Eschatology is not fully realized.[20] The distinguishing mark of Daniel's "people" (Dan. 12:1) is that many who have died will awake to "everlasting life," and others will wake to "shame and everlasting contempt" (12:2). Likewise in 1 John, the people of Jesus Christ will receive eternal life in him (1 John 1:3; 2:25; 3:14; 5:11, 13, 20) at the parousia (2:28; 3:2; 4:17).[21] Those who reject him will remain in death (3:14; 5:16). Those who have received the "Word of life" (1:1) have already passed "out of death into life" (3:14) and in the future will receive eternal life. The momentous event of passing out of death into life creates a new community of those who live in the "truth" and "walk in the light" while they wait for future consummation (1:6–7; 5:20).

Principle 2: The Church Exists in Koinōnia with the Triune God

In his comments on "have fellowship" (*koinōnia*) in 1 John 1:3, Daniel Akin proposes that John could just as easily have written "we have eternal life," implying that "eternal life" and "fellowship" are interchangeable in the Johannine usage.[22] This proposal neglects the relational nature of communion between God and his people. The church is not just a people who inherit eternal life. It is specifically a people who inherit eternal life in fellowship with God. Yarbrough moves closer to the relational nature of fellowship in his comment that the purpose of the proclamation of eternal life (1:2) is to "nurture fellowship" between those who share knowledge of God and his Son (1:3).[23] However, Yarbrough's "shared knowledge" focuses more on the human aspect of fellowship than on the divine. Jobes, on the other hand, suggests a relational reading of fellowship in her observation that

19. Stefanos Mihalios, *The Danielic Eschatological Hour in the Johannine Literature* (London: T&T Clark, 2011), 161.

20. C. H. Dodd, *The Johannine Epistles*, MNTC (London: Hodder & Stoughton, 1946), xxvii.

21. Mihalios, *Danielic Eschatological Hour*, 162.

22. Daniel L. Akin, *1, 2, 3 John*, NAC (Nashville: Broadman & Holman, 2001), 57, 57n40. Although, Akin admits that it is possible that John used "fellowship" to add unspecified theological depth to his argument.

23. Yarbrough, *1–3 John*, 40–41.

John uses *koinōnia* with a greater theological depth than the common Greek usage of its time, where it was used for an association based on common interests and purposes. She writes, "John invites his readers to enter into a relationship with God the Father and his Son, Jesus Christ, by embracing God's redemptive purposes for the world in general and individual lives in particular."[24] The relationship the people of God enter into when they accept the proclamation of the "Word of life" is a relationship with the Father and the Son, put into effect by the Holy Spirit (2:27; 3:24; 4:13). In other words, this is divine-human communion. The true church exists in fellowship with the triune God.

In the Old Testament, the relationship between Yahweh and his people is regulated by covenant terms and stipulations. This enables the holy God to dwell among an unholy people. The covenant regulates the relationships between the people and God, and the people and one another (Lev. 19:2). There is, therefore, both a vertical (Godward) and a horizontal (humanward) aspect to living as the people of God. In the same way, in 1 John 1:1–7, there are both vertical and horizontal implications to fellowship with the triune God. First, in 1:3a, the purpose of the proclamation of the message about the Word of life is so that the hearer will enter into the same state of joy in Christ as John and the other apostolic witnesses (horizontal). Second, in 1:3b, the nature of this fellowship, as we have noted, is directed to the triune God (vertical). Third, in 1:6–7, fellowship is expressed vertically as "with him" and horizontally as "with one another." Thus, the new status of the people of God who have passed from death to life is that they live in fellowship with God, through his Son, and this means that they also live in fellowship with one another.

The clear ethical implications of living in fellowship with the triune God are necessitated by the character of God. John writes, "God is light, and in him is no darkness at all" (1 John 1:5). In 1 John 1:6, the concept of living outside a covenant relationship with God is expressed as "walk[ing] in darkness" (cf. Isa. 9:2). In 1 John 1:7, it is made clear that those who live in fellowship with God cannot walk in the darkness, precisely because God is light and there is no darkness in his character. Light is intimately associated with God's holiness, and those who walk with a holy God must also be holy.[25] In John's Gospel, Jesus Christ proclaims that he is the "light of the world" (John 8:12), thereby fulfilling the predictions of Isaiah 9:2. Therefore, the person who claims to live in union with Christ ("in him" and who "abides

---

24. Jobes, *1, 2, and 3 John*, 53.
25. Yarbrough, *1–3 John*, 49.

in him," 1 John 2:5–6) will prove it by the evidence of the holiness of God shining through them.[26] In 1 John, this is through keeping the commandment to love one another (2:7–11; 3:11–24; 4:7–21).

Principle 3: The Church Abides in Agapē

The commandment to "love one another" brings us to what is apparently the central theological concern of 1 John. In his exegetical study on *agapē* in 1 John, Fernando Segovia points out that the noun *agapē* is used eighteen times and the verb form *agapan* is used twenty-six times. He also observes that the use of these terms is concentrated in the middle of the letter, in chapters 3 and 4.[27] The repetition of *agapē* in this way in the center of the message suggests that it is a key theological concept. When considered with the possibility that the Cain and Abel allusion (1 John 3:11–15) provides the central pivot idea for a larger macrochiasm of ideas that governs the whole theological argument of 1 John, it is clear that John intends his hearers to take note.[28]

John introduces the allusion negatively: "We should not be like Cain, who was of the evil one and murdered his brother. And why did he murder him? Because his own deeds were evil and his brother's righteous" (1 John 3:12). This is used to prove the point made in 3:10 that the children of the devil are evident to all because they do not "practice righteousness" and do not love their brothers and sisters. The collective memory of the story of the first brothers is thus a case in point to connect the hearers with the familiar pattern of the "righteous" and the "unrighteous" in the Hebrew Bible.[29] The governing concept in 3:11 is the repetition of the message that "you have heard from the beginning, that we should love one another," linking righteousness and love of the other. Whether "the beginning" refers to the reception of the Christian gospel or to the creation of the world is not important.[30] The point made is that the command to love is as much a central concept in the New Testament as it is in the Old Testament. Stephen Smalley writes, "The biblical concept of love . . . is distinctive, in as far as it is associated with a God who enters into a covenant relationship with his people and maintains it with undeserved 'steadfast love' (Deut. 7:9). God's essential activity is saving love . . . , and in NT terms we find this activity centered in the person and work of Jesus. God

---

26. John Calvin, *Commentary on the First Epistle of John*, ed. and trans. John Owen (Grand Rapids: Baker, 1999), 164.

27. Fernando F. Segovia, "Agape and Agapan in 1 John and the Fourth Gospel" (PhD diss., University of Notre Dame, 1978), 62, 63.

28. Seed, "Religious Belief," 3–10.

29. Related to concepts of the "wise" and the "foolish" in Wisdom literature.

30. Stephen S. Smalley, *1, 2, 3 John*, WBC 51 (Waco: Word, 1984), 182.

has loved us in Christ, and we are therefore called to love others in and through him (cf. John 3:16; 1 John 4:8, 16)."[31] Smalley summarizes the core message of 1 John as the covenant love of Yahweh in the Old Testament fulfilled in his saving love through the giving of his Son in the New Testament and carried by the disciples into the world by obeying the new commandment to "love one another" in the same way that Christ has loved them (John 13:34; 1 John 2:7–8). In this way, *agapē* expresses the whole content of the Christian faith[32] and is central to the message of 1 John.

In 1 John, the noun *agapē* and its verb form *agapaō* are used specifically to refer to the love of God. When they are used of believers, they refer to the way believers reflect the love of God in their lives as a result of living in fellowship with him. "God is love" (1 John 4:8), and therefore those who "abide" in his fellowship "abide" in his love (4:16). God demonstrated his love by sending his Son into the world to lay down his life (3:16; 4:10). This was entirely his initiative, flowing out of the mutual perichoretic love of the ontological Trinity.[33] This shows the nature of *agapē*. It originates in the triune God and therefore must characterize the lives of children of God, who live in union with him. Christians know they have "passed out of death into life" (3:14) because they exude the *agapē* of the one who is "the eternal life" (1:2). Therefore, John writes quite confidently, "If anyone says, 'I love God,' and hates his brother, he is a liar" (4:20).

In 1 John, *agapē* expresses itself in action that imitates the love of God in sending Christ (3:18). Such love for others is seen in the imitation of the sacrifice of Jesus Christ on behalf of the world (3:16). Believers display the love of God, lay down their lives "for the brothers" (3:16), give to those in need (3:17), pray for the weak (5:16), and proclaim the gospel (1:3). In this, they show that they have the "love of the Father" in them (2:15).

In our attempt to apply core theological principles from 1 John to race relations in the churches in post-apartheid South Africa, we have so far considered the common eschatological moment and the shared fellowship with God in Christ through the Holy Spirit. In this third section, we have added the central theological principle of *agapē* as the self-giving love of God that is replicated in the people of God as the church of Christ. Those who are truly "born of God" (1 John 4:7) live in fellowship with him and keep the old commandment that has been made new in Jesus Christ by loving one another.

31. Smalley, *1, 2, 3 John*, 61.
32. W. Günther and H.-G. Link, "Love," *NIDNTT* 2:542.
33. Thomas F. Torrance, *The Christian Doctrine of God: One Being, Three Persons* (Edinburgh: T&T Clark, 1996), 185–94.

However, before we can attempt to apply these three principles to the problem of racial integration in the churches of post-apartheid South Africa, a fourth principle needs to be brought to bear. That is how the church maintains its fellowship in the love of God as it waits for the parousia (1 John 2:28).

Principle 4: The Church Lives by Confession of Sin

We have seen that the ethical implication of living in fellowship with the triune God is to obey the commandment to love one another. John makes it clear that the one who is born of God does not keep on sinning (1 John 3:6, 9; 5:18), but equally, he states that those who claim to be free of sin are not being truthful to themselves or God (1:8, 10). Sin is a reality in the fallen world. Christians are to "keep [them]selves from idols" (5:21) and to ensure that they "do not love the world or the things in the world" (2:15). They are surrounded by temptation and fall into various types of sin (5:16–17). Therefore, there is a need for cleansing from sin so that the relationship of fellowship with God and with one another in *agapē* can be restored.

Jobes comments that denying one's sin is counter to walking in the light.[34] Therefore, God has provided a way that Christians in the church can be restored to fellowship through cleansing in the blood of Jesus (1 John 1:7–2:2). This is predicated on the confession of sin, which is the opposite of trying to hide it behind false claims of sinlessness (1:9). Georg Strecker comments that it is not clear whether John indicates private or public confession, but either way, the confession is to God.[35] Christians who confess their sin receive cleansing because God is "faithful and just" (1:9). He remembers his covenant promises in the Old Testament, which point forward to the inauguration of the new covenant through the sacrifice of Jesus Christ for the sins of the world in the New Testament (2:2). Therefore, even though Christians fall into sin, God promises restoration and reconciliation, providing that they acknowledge their sin with true repentance.[36]

Nonetheless, this provision for the forgiveness of sin is not a license to sin (1 John 2:1a). The epistle has been written so that Christians do not fall into sin. This is qualified by a condition: "But if anyone does sin, we have an advocate with the Father, Jesus Christ the righteous" (2:1b). Thus, holiness as sinlessness is required of believers who walk in fellowship with the triune God. Any failure to walk in the light of God's holiness must be confessed

---

34. Jobes, *1, 2, and 3 John*, 71.
35. Georg Strecker, *The Johannine Letters*, ed. Harold Attridge, trans. Linda M. Maloney, Hermeneia (Minneapolis: Fortress, 1996), 32.
36. Calvin, *First Epistle of John*, 166.

before God and brought by faith to Jesus Christ, "the righteous" through whom forgiveness is obtained in two ways, first as an "advocate" and second as "propitiation" for sin.

First, Christ is the *paraklētos* ("advocate"), meaning one who comes alongside to help another.[37] The use of *paraklētos* is unique to the Johannine literature in the New Testament.[38] In 1 John 2:1, it is used of Christ. In John's Gospel, it is used of the Holy Spirit (John 14:16, 26; 15:26; 16:7). Martin Culy notes that the usage in 1 John 2:1 indicates not so much the ability of the advocate to intercede for a defendant but the status of the *paraklētos* that enables him "to bring about a good outcome for the one being accused."[39] Jobes argues that it is Christ's unique status as the one who gave himself for the sins of the world that enabled him to act as the paraclete for his disciples when he was on earth and to promise that the Holy Spirit will assume that role when he is glorified.[40] This indicates, once again, the full participation of the triune God in the cleansing of the sinner and their restoration to fellowship with God and others. Christ is the one through whom right standing with God is restored.

Second, Christ is the *hilasmos* ("propitiation") for the sins of all people (1 John 2:2). Scholars have debated whether the term in antiquity was used for propitiation or expiation or both.[41] Culy favors "the means by which sins are dealt with," meaning that Christ, in himself, provides the sacrifice of atonement for sin.[42] This accords with the reading of *paraklētos* as a status rather than an action. Christ is the one who has the status to bring about forgiveness and reconciliation because he is, in himself, the atoning sacrifice.

Thus, we have come full circle. Fellowship with God and one another, described as "walking in the light," can be maintained only by ongoing cleansing from sin.[43] Sin is essentially not loving one another. Jesus Christ himself is the means of cleansing and reconciliation, and this is the gracious gift of God's love as believers wait for his return in eschatological expectation.

Conclusion: Being the Church in Post-apartheid South Africa

Based on the four theological principles examined above, we now turn to the previously stated task of applying them to the church context in post-apartheid

---

37. David Jackman, *The Message of John's Letters*, BST (Leicester, UK: Inter-Varsity, 1988), 44.
38. Jobes, *1, 2, and 3 John*, 78.
39. Martin M. Culy, *1, 2, 3 John: A Handbook on the Greek Text*, BHGNT (Waco: Baylor University Press, 2004), 22.
40. Jobes, *1, 2, and 3 John*, 78.
41. See Akin, *1, 2, 3, John*, 82–83, for example.
42. Culy, *1, 2, 3 John*, 23.
43. Jobes, *1, 2, and 3 John*, 78.

South Africa. The first principle sought to establish an eschatological frame-work for the application, acknowledging the postresurrection milieu for the epistle through the allusion to the Danielic "last hour." This indicates a shared inaugurated eschatology because the world before the momentous events of the incarnation and resurrection of Jesus Christ is "passing away" (1 John 2:17), and the new era has arrived in which the postresurrection new community of believers lives in "truth" and "walks in the light." However, it also indicates a "not yet" eschatological aspect, as those who are walking in the light wait for the coming of Jesus Christ, the judgment, and eternal life. In terms of the message of the Word of God for future generations, we note that the church in South Africa is found in the same eschatological moment of salvation history as the Johannine community of the first century AD.[44] Although two millennia have passed and salvation is nearer for us than it was then (cf. Rom. 13:11), those in the contemporary South African church who have "passed from death into life" exist in Christ under the same ethical implications of being the people of "eternal life" as the community to which the epistle is addressed.

The second theological principle considered the implications of living in fellowship (as *koinōnia*) with God in Christ. This was seen on a deeper theological level to indicate a relationship with the triune God. In the Old Testament, communion with God is regulated by covenant. In the New Testament, it is put into effect by faith in Jesus Christ. First John does not use the term "covenant," but the new covenant is implied in the vertical (Godward) and horizontal (humanward) dimensions of fellowship in the first chapter. Those who have believed in Christ are born of God and share fellowship with God and one another. In addition, ethical implications flow out of living in fellowship with the triune God. These are derived from his character, which John describes in terms of the biblical images of light and darkness. God is utterly holy, and from that, it follows that those who live in fellowship with him must also be holy. In 1 John, this is expressed as "walking in the light." This principle helps us to establish a foundation for racial unity in the church. It is predicated on the status of all true believers who have received the apostolic witness about Jesus Christ (1 John 1:1–3) as those who, through Christ, live in fellowship with a holy God and for whom the ethical implications are the same.

This observation led to the third principle, which suggested that the key theological concern of the epistle is love (*agapē*) expressed as the ontological

44. It is beyond the scope of this chapter to engage in the debate regarding the composition and dating of the "Johannine Community." See Raymond E. Brown, *The Epistles of John*, AB 30 (New York: Doubleday), 1982.

nature of the triune God and the ethical response of his children who "abide in him." This ethical response flows out of the indwelling of the believer in the fellowship of the triune God but is expressed in covenantal terms as the "old" and yet "new" commandment. The old commandment to love one another has been made new in Christ through the expression of the love of God in the sacrifice of his Son for the sins of the world. This commandment requires a practical response. All believers must "practice righteousness" by expressing love for God and one another in the church by laying down their lives "for the brothers" (1 John 3:10, 16). This concept is pegged to the Cain and Abel allusion at the center of the epistle, in which the example of the evil Cain, who hated his brother, is contrasted with the righteous Abel, encouraging believers to emulate the righteous Abel.

In the post-apartheid context of the church in South Africa, the centrality of the need to work out *agapē* in practical terms is paramount. First John 4:20–21 stresses the impossibility of loving God while hating fellow Christians. Indeed, claiming to be a Christian and yet living in hatred of other Christians is a contradiction. It implies that true faith does not exist. The question is whether the exclusion of the other from our churches, whether deliberately or otherwise, constitutes hatred. Although John does not answer this question explicitly, James does: "If you really fulfill the royal law according to the Scripture, 'You shall love your neighbor as yourself,' you are doing well. But if you show partiality, you are committing sin and are convicted by the law as transgressors" (James 2:8–9). When other Christians are excluded either actively or passively, both John and James attest to the seriousness of the sin.

The question is, What can be done to rectify the situation that some churches currently find themselves in? This leads to the fourth theological principle: the church lives by confession of sin. First John provides a way for the church to restore fellowship with God and with one another by the confession of sin and faith in the work of Christ, who is both the *hilasmos* and the *paraklētos*. Confession of sin acknowledges the sinfulness of human nature, the reality of temptation to sin, and the bias of human nature toward hatred (as in the allusion to Cain). The outcome of confessing sin and receiving forgiveness and cleansing is restoration to fellowship with the triune God. The ethical outcome is the commandment to love all fellow Christians in practical ways by imitating the sacrificial love of God in Christ.

Thus, it is impossible to walk in the light in fellowship with God and not love one another in practical ways. First John brings a theological imperative to the churches in South Africa to work for unity by deliberately seeking to incorporate all believers into the body of Christ that is the local church. This should happen not just in the megachurches (as per Naidoo's 2017 article) but at all levels of the church. A difficult task, given the historical heritage? Certainly. However, if we claim to be without sin in this area, we deceive ourselves. First John points us to the need for both private and public confession and gives us confidence that if we do this, God is "faithful and just to forgive us our sins and to cleanse us from all unrighteousness" (1:9). Restored to fellowship with God in Christ, we will be set free to "walk in the light" and experience fellowship across the races in mutual *agapē*.

22

Reading Revelation among the People Living with the Symbolic Emperor System

MASANOBU ENDO

The purpose of this chapter is to read Revelation (mainly chaps. 2–3) in contemporary Japanese social and religious contexts. The Christian communities in Asia Minor to which John addressed his letters were under the reign of the Roman emperor. Similarly, there was a time in Japan when the emperor had great power, backed by an army-led government, firmly supported by the Constitution of the Japanese Empire.[1] During World War II, the government forced the people to honor Emperor Showa as "a god appeared as a human" (*Arahitogami*). After the war, General Headquarters abolished the Constitution of the Japanese Empire and urged the emperor to declare his humanity to his people. In the new Constitution, which was promulgated in 1946, the emperor became the symbol of the state and the unity of the people. However, people's feelings toward the emperor seem not to have changed much. Even under the new Constitution, though he is not believed to be a living god anymore, people continue to have sentiment for the emperor.

1. The Constitution of the Japanese Empire was promulgated in 1889, in which the emperor was stipulated to be "sacred and inviolable" (article 3).

In 2019, the enthronement ceremony of Emperor Reiwa was held at the Imperial Palace, and it was broadcast all over the world. In the ceremony, he went up to the *Takamikura* (the imperial throne: 254-inch height) with three treasures that were believed to have come from *Amaterasu Ômikami* (the Sun Goddess, who is regarded as the emperor's ancestor), wearing the costume inherited from the Heian period (eighth century AD). After he got to the *Takamikura*, the curtain was opened slowly, and the emperor appeared. After some silence, he spoke the words of blessing to the people and the world. In response, then prime minister Shinzo Abe raised his hands high and gave three cheers, which were an act of swearing loyalty to the emperor. These ritual steps were based on the Emperor's Coronation Act (*Tôkyokurei*), enacted in 1889. Because there had not been an emperor's coronation since the abolition of the old Constitution, the government intentionally adopted the old act. The Imperial Household Agency, which has inherited the imperial tradition since ancient times, naturally welcomed the decision of the government. The problem is that the ceremony was held as a religious ceremony of Shintoism.[2] Even if some noticed that it risked breaking the Principle of Separation of Religion and Politics (article 3, paragraph 20 of the Japanese Constitution), they didn't dare raise questions, and the media, too, refrained from raising objections on this matter, showing deference to the authorities. To express this attitude toward authority, a word that has recently gained attention in Japan is *sontaku*, which means "conjecture," the choice to do something voluntarily by reading between the lines or guessing the intention of the person with power. This paper seeks to read the text of the book of Revelation by using this concept.

Context: Religious Crisis in the Symbolic Emperor Era

Japanese churches were swallowed by the empire system during the Second World War. The National Christian Council was held in Aoyama Gakuin in 1940,[3] in response to the government making the law (*Shûkyôdantaihô* in 1939) to govern all religious groups in Japan. All denominations, except the Japan Holiness Church and some nondenominational churches, were organized into one.[4] At the meeting, worship was held in the morning, during which *Kimigayo* (a hymn for the emperor) was first sung, and *Kyûjôyôhai* (a

2. The ruling party (Liberal Democratic Party) tends to value Shintoism.
3. Aoyama Gakuin was founded as a mission school with the help of the Methodist Episcopal Church in 1874.
4. The churches belonging to this denomination continued to be severely persecuted by the government; see W. Yamazaki, ed., *Passion of the Holiness Church during the War* [in Japanese] (Tokyo: Shinkyô Shuppan, 1990).

salute to the Imperial Palace) was done by all attendees. Rev. Yoshimune Abe (also the president of Aoyama Gakuin and chair of the new organization the United Church of Christ in Japan) preached from Revelation 21:1 as follows:

> This is a meeting to celebrate *Kôki* [emperor's reign] 2600th, but we should call this meeting "Pentecost" in the history of Japanese churches. What comes to my mind on such a great day is the Apocalypse that John saw and wrote, "I saw a new heaven and a new earth (Rev. 21:1)." . . . John was active in 90 A.D. when Roman Emperor Domitianus reigned. . . . God has given revelations according to the different circumstances of each country. In the 16th century, God raised Luther and started the Protestant movement in Germany. Likewise, it is the revelation that God gave us this opportunity for all denominations to be united in Japan. What is the reason? That is because here we see a unique revelation God gave to us. Our country has an unbroken line of the Japanese Imperial Family, and its prestige roars around the world, and now it is 2600 years. . . . It is the time to carry the destiny of the East Asian peoples and strive to establish the Great East Asia Co-Prosperity Sphere so that we can establish true peace to heaven and earth of the East Asia.[5]

Abe interpreted "a new heaven and a new earth" (Rev. 21:1)[6] by overlapping it with the vision of "the Great East Asia Co-Prosperity Sphere." He did *Sontaku* to the government at that time. After the meeting was closed with three cheers, most of the participants went to Meiji Shrine and bowed to the former emperor. In 1967, twenty years after the end of the war, the National Christian Council of Japan confessed the guilt of participating in the war and expressed repentance for their sin.[7]

So what about Japan today? Of particular interest are the issues in the field of education. The Ministry of Education has one policy to integrate the people with values based on Japanese culture and tradition, and they are trying to incorporate the historical view of *Kôkoku Shikan* (emperor-centered historiography, which is also based on Shintoism). In 1999, the government enacted a law that established *Nishôki* (which was later called *Hinomaru*) as the national flag and *Kimigayo* as the national anthem. The red circle drawn in the center of *Nishôki* symbolizes the *Amaterasu Ômikami* (Sun Goddess), and *Kimigayo* (Your World) is a hymn for the emperor. During the war, both vowing to *Nishôki* and singing *Kimigayo* demonstrated more than just respect for the emperor. After the emperor's humanity declaration, these may have lost

---

5. National Christian Council of Japan, ed., *Kôki 2600 and Church United* [in Japanese] (Tokyo: The Board of Publications—The United Church of Christ in Japan, 1941), 46–48, my translation.
6. Unless otherwise indicated, English translations of the Bible are my own.
7. The full confession text is available on the website (https://uccj.org/confession) in both English and Japanese.

their religious nature, but some Christians are reluctant to use them because historically they were used for worshiping the emperor. After the enactment of the law (since 1999), the government issued a notice to schools (elementary, junior high, and high school) to display *Nishôki* and sing *Kimigayo* at every school ceremony and warned of punishment for anyone who does not follow the instructions. Some teachers did not obey and were reprimanded. Christians living in Japan have difficulties in the symbolic emperor system, even though the current situation is not as severe as before.

Religious Crises in the Context of Asia Minor (Late First Century AD)

Two Major Crises

The letters to the seven churches in Revelation have a common form: depiction of Christ, church evaluation, encouragement for the church, and rewards to the saints. Particular attention is given to the religious crises that the churches were facing. Figure 22.1 is a list of troublemakers mentioned in each letter.

Figure 22.1

Ephesus	1 Self-proclaimed apostles	2 Nicolaitans
Smyrna	3 Self-proclaimed Jews,[a] the "Synagogue of Satan" Accused Christians (*blasphēmia*[b]) who would be imprisoned and receive hardship (*thlipsis*).	
Pergamum		4 Those who hold to the teaching of Balaam = Nicolaitans: they misled others to *phagein eidōlothyta kai porneusai*.
Thyatira		5 Jezebel, self-proclaimed prophet: she misled others into *porneusai kai phagein eidōlothyta*.
Sardis		
Philadelphia	6 Self-proclaimed Jews: "Synagogue of Satan" Christian had to be patient with them.	
Laodicea		

a. The reflections on self-proclaimed Jews are based on the author's research presentation ("Self-Proclaimed Jews in Rev. 2:9 and 3:9") at the 60th Annual Academic Conference of the Japan New Testament Society (2020).

b. Generally, *blasphēmia* means any kind of speech that is defamatory or abusive (BDAG, 178). Aune listed various historical events in which the Jews accused Christians (D. Aune, *Revelation 1–5*, WBC [Nashville: Nelson, 1997], 162–63).

Figure 22.2

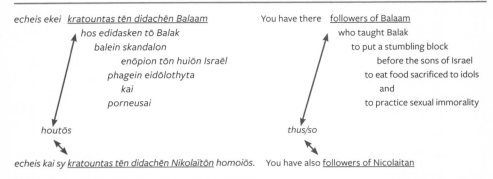

Here are six references (1 to 6) concerning the crises the churches were facing. The self-proclaimed Jews of Smyrna (3) and Philadelphia (6) are probably the same kinds of groups, and both are called the "synagogue of Satan" (Rev. 2:9; 3:9). In Smyrna, the Christians are blamed by them, and some will be imprisoned because of their accusations (2:9–10). In Philadelphia, their accusations will prove false, and they will apologize to the Christians (3:9–10).[8]

Those who hold to the teaching of Balaam in Pergamum (4) and Thyatira's false prophet, Jezebel (5), are also the same because their wrong guidance is the same (Rev. 2:14, 20). Balaam was a gentile fortune teller who is depicted as a troublesome person for the Israelites in 2 Peter 2:15 and Jude 11. Jezebel was the gentile princess who tempted Israel to idolatry. The word order of the infinitive clauses of Revelation 2:14 and 20 is inverted to emphasize the parallelism in both clauses.

Revelation 2:14   *phagein eidōlothyta kai porneusai*   A // B

Revelation 2:20   *porneusai kai phagein eidōlothyta*   B′ // A′

Additionally, the conjunction "likewise" (*houtōs*) at the beginning of Revelation 2:15 connects two sentences and indicates that those who hold to the teaching of Balaam and the Nicolaitans are similar groups (see fig. 22.2).

"Those who self-proclaim to be apostles" (*tous legontas heautous apostolous*, Rev. 2:2) in Ephesus is not used in the sense of "the apostles" (e.g., 1 Cor. 12:28) but rather is used in the general meaning, like "sent ones" (*pempsas*; e.g., John 13:16; Phil. 2:25; Heb. 3:1). They insisted that they were chosen and sent by God,

---

8. "Fall to the feet" (*proskynēsousin enōpion tōn podōn sou*, Rev. 3:9) means "apology for the previous wrong accusations" or "the reversal of position between them."

as did the self-proclaimed Jews in Smyrna and Philadelphia. But John knew the latter were not such and called their groups a "synagogue of Satan" (*synagōgē tou satana*, Rev. 2:9; 3:9). What we can see from these observations, concerning the religious crises that John envisaged in chapters 2–3, is summarized in the following two categories: (1) the "hardship" (*thlipsis*, 2:9) suffered because of the self-proclaimed Jews or apostles; and (2) the "temptation" (*peirasmos*, 3:10) received from those who hold to the teaching of a pseudo-prophet.

Regarding the Jews, Martin Karrer proposes to see the self-proclaimed Jews literally as "non-Jews" (gentiles) who were attracted to Judaism and respected the Jewish traditions so much that they were not satisfied with the way Christians lived.[9] When the author of Acts depicts the Jews who were relentlessly interfering with Paul's ministries (Acts 13:45, 50; 14:2, 5, 19; 17:5, 13; 18:13; 21:27), he gives two main reasons: first, they were filled with jealousy (*zēlos*, 13:45; cf. 17:5); second, they thought that Paul was against the Mosaic law and Jewish customs (18:13; 21:27).[10] Interestingly, in the latter case, the Roman authorities dismissed the Jewish accusations.[11] Thus, the Jews had to perjure themselves regarding Christians' infidelity to the Roman emperor (17:7; cf. Luke 23:1–2 [perjury against Jesus]).

Many scholars believe that the accusations of self-proclaimed Jews in the seven letters relate to the Mosaic law.[12] Certainly that was what caused their jealousy. But they had learned that they could not involve citizens in Asia Minor or persuade the Roman authorities for that reason alone. They had to prove Christians' infidelity to the Roman emperor.[13] When John calls this group "the synagogue of Satan," he may have observed not only Satan behind this group but also the Roman emperor. However, the real threat to Christians was not simply the Roman emperor but "the Jews" who set themselves on the Roman side and persecuted Christians. David deSilva comments that Domitian's attitude toward his own divinity is less relevant than the enthusiasm of the local elites in Asia Minor to demonstrate their loyalty.[14]

---

9. M. Karrer, *Johannesoffenbarung 1:1–5:14*, EKKNT 24.1 (Göttingen: Vanderhoeck & Ruprecht, 2017), 299–305.

10. Acts does not state the reason in the following cases: 13:50; 14:2, 5, 19; 17:13.

11. Concerning the Roman legal system, see A. N. Sherwin-White, *The Letters of Pliny: A Historical and Social Commentary* (Oxford: Clarendon, 1966), 779.

12. E.g., Stephen S. Smalley, *The Revelation to John* (Downers Grove, IL: InterVarsity, 2005), 66; D. Aune, *Revelation 1–5*, WBC 52A (Nashville: Nelson, 1997), 162–65.

13. Grant Osborne rightly comments that the Jews denounced Polycarp and the church before the Roman authorities for defaming the emperor and the Roman religion by refusing to worship the emperor (Osborne, *Revelation*, BECNT [Grand Rapids: Baker Academic, 2002], 131). See also A. Yarbro Collins, "Vilification and Self-Definition in the Book of Revelation," *HTR* 79 (1986): 308–20.

14. David A. deSilva, *Seeing Things John's Way: The Rhetoric of the Book of Revelation* (Louisville: Westminster John Knox, 2009), 52.

Concerning the self-proclaimed Jews, Gregory Beale comments that they sometimes had no qualms in semi-revering other deities along with their Old Testament God.[15] He identifies the self-proclaimed Jews with the pseudo-prophets (see fig. 22.1). However, the Jews in John's day were not so easy to lead to idolatry. Emil Schürer examined Josephus's and Philo's works concerning this issue. In Josephus's *Jewish War*, the Jews in the middle of the first century AD offered sacrifices for the Roman emperor.[16] But Schürer carefully distinguishes between sacrifices "for" the emperor and sacrifices "to" the emperor. In other words, it is unclear whether it was emperor worship or worship dedicated to Yahweh on behalf of the emperor. Schürer highlights this story:[17] "The Jews said, 'We offer sacrifices twice every day *for Caesar, and for the Roman people*' . . . ; but that if *he would place the images among them*, he must first sacrifice the whole Jewish nation; and *that they were ready to expose themselves*, together with their children and wives, to be slain" (*J.W.* 2.10.4).[18] This record suggests that the emperor's statue was not in the place of worship and that they were worshiping Yahweh on behalf of the emperor. The Roman emperor treated the Jews generously in those days and permitted them to form a Jewish community (*synagōgē*).[19] Philo records in *On the Embassy to Gaius* about his mission trip to Rome to complain about the Greeks who persecuted Alexandrian Jews. Why did the Greeks persecute them? It may be because the Greeks thought that the Jews were not loyal to the emperor. Therefore, Gaius called the Jews "the haters of God" (*hoi theomiseis*) because they did not intend to worship the emperor. Then the Jews responded to the accusation as follows:

O Lord Gaius, we are falsely accused; for *we did sacrifice, and we offered up entire hecatombs, the blood of which we poured in a libation upon the altar*, and the flesh we did not carry to our homes to make a feast and banquet upon it, as it is the custom of some people to do, but *we committed the victims*

15. G. K. Beale, *The Book of Revelation*, NIGTC (Grand Rapids: Eerdmans, 1998), 240. He relies on S. R. F. Price, *Rituals and Power: The Roman Imperial Cult in Asia Minor* (Cambridge: Cambridge University Press, 1984), 220–21; J. Massyngberde Ford, *Revelation*, AB 38 (New Haven: Yale University Press, 1995), 393. Price had relied on Emil Schürer, *The History of the Jewish People in the Age of Jesus Christ*, 2 vols. (Edinburgh: T&T Clark, 1973–79), 1:486, 2:360–62.

16. Josephus, *J.W.* 2.10.4. See Schürer, *History of the Jewish People*, 1:484.

17. In Schürer, *History of the Jewish People*, 2:76.

18. The translation is from *The Works of Flavius Josephus*, trans. W. Whiston (Peabody, MA: Hendrickson, 1987) (consulted via Accordance Bible software, emphasis added).

19. Josephus, *Ant.* 14.213–16, 256–58; Philo, *Legat.* 311–12. See also P. Trebilco, *Jewish Communities in Asia Minor*, SNTSMS 69 (Cambridge: Cambridge University Press, 1991), 8–12.

entire to the sacred flame as a burnt offering: and we have done this three times already, and not once only; on the first occasion when you succeeded to the empire, and the second time when you recovered from that terrible disease with which all the habitable world was afflicted at the same time, and the third time we sacrificed in hope of your victory over the Germans. (*Legat.* 356)[20]

This text can be taken as if the Jews worshiped the emperor. But Gaius was unimpressed and replied, "'Grant,' said he, 'that all this is true, *and that you did sacrifice; nevertheless you sacrificed to another god and not for my sake* [*tethykate all' heterō*]; and then what good did you do me? *Moreover you did not sacrifice to me* [*ou gar emoi tethykate*]'" (*Legat.* 357). These records indicate that the Jews did not participate in idol worship.

The next line of argument follows William Tarn and Guy Griffith, who assert that there were Jews in Asia Minor and Syria who incorporated Greco-Oriental cults.[21] An inscription of the Jewish tomb found in an Egyptian archaeological site has "God the highest" (*theos hypistos*) instead of Yahweh.[22] Tarn also speculates that the Jews probably used *hypistos* in the meaning of Zeus, when they had a ceremony to celebrate the establishment of the new synagogue in Athribis, because the prefect of police was there. Tarn adds that *Sabazios* was also used as a substitute for Yahweh (*Zeus Sabazios* = Lord Sabaoth).[23] However, must this be evidence for religious syncretism?[24] The Japanese people call Yahweh "Kami," initially drawn from Shintoism because they had no equivalent god's name when the missionaries brought Christianity to Japan. These titles also fail, therefore, to be support for Beale's claim.[25]

To summarize the research so far, John warns his readers concerning at least two crises: one is the fear of being "blamed" (*blasphēmia*) by the "false Jews" (*pseudo-Ioudaioi* or *pseudo-apostoloi*), and the other is a temptation (*peirasmos*) from those who hold to the teaching of the false prophet (*kratountes tēn didachēn*).

---

20. The translation is from *The Works of Philo*, trans. C. D. Young (Peabody, MA: Hendrickson, 1993).

21. W. W. Tarn and G. T. Griffith, *Hellenistic Civilization*, 3rd ed. (London: Arnold, 1959), 225.

22. Franz Cumont, "Les mystères de Sabazius et le judaïsme," *CRAI* 50, no. 1 (1906): 63–79, https://doi.org/10.3406/crai.1906.71756. But Philo uses the same words (*Leg.* 3.24, 82, 89; *Ebr.* 105; *Flacc.* 46; *Legat.* 157, 278, 317).

23. Tarn refers to Cumont, "Les mystères de Sabazius et le judaïsme," 76.

24. Tarn and Griffith, *Hellenistic Civilization*, 212.

25. In b. Avod. Zar. (teaching on "idolatry" in the Babylonian Talmud), it is shown how the Jews were cautious about Roman emperor worship and local pagan festivals. In *Dialogue with Trypho* (written by Justin [ca. AD 160]), Trypho (a diaspora Jew) is surprised that gentile Christians eat *eidōlothyta* (*Dial.* 8.4; 10.3).

Suspicious Eyes from the Local Citizens

In the late first century AD in Asia Minor, Christians faced various diffi-culties in religious life.[26] Ancient Ephesus was the city that had long boasted of being "the guardian of Artemis." In the days of Emperor Domitian, the Ephesians were trying to win the honor of being "a Roman emperor's guard-ian," competing with other cities. Two religions (Artemis and the emperor as living gods) never conflicted in a polytheistic world.[27] The Ephesians ex-pected both to benefit sthem: Artemis may bring the harvest, and the emperor may bring political advantage and economic prosperity. Simon Price cites a photo of a coin symbolizing a temple dedicated to the emperor.[28] Some coins have a pattern in which the temple of the emperor is drawn with temples of other gods (Zeus, Goddess Rome, and Artemis), and some coins have only the temple of the emperor. A coin from Ephesus (third century AD) depicts people sacrificing cattle in front of the emperor's temple. Because the coin has the word *Vota* (vows) in the triangle of the temple pediment, distinguish-ing between "to worship" and "to vow," Price argues that the worship was dedicated not to the emperor but to other gods on behalf of the emperor.[29] But for the ancient Greeks who lived in a polytheistic world, how clear was such a distinction?

And what about the diaspora Jews? According to Josephus, the Roman emperor Augustus initially regarded the Jews as an "ally" and was gener-ous with them (*Ant.* 14.10.1 and after), and he even exempted them from military service. The emperor allowed them to exercise autonomy within the Roman Empire, to keep the Sabbath, and to perform rituals according to their law in Laodicea (*Ant.* 14.10.20), Sardis (*Ant.* 14.10.24), and Ephesus (*Ant.* 14.10.25). At least until the middle of the first century AD, the Roman Empire did not force the Jews to worship the emperor. The residents of Asia Minor also recognized the Jews' autonomy there because they had to comply with Roman decrees. But they must have had no good impression of the Jews who benefited from Rome and yet lived their unique customs

---

26. Cf. J. A. Kelhoffer, "The Relevance of Revelation's Date and the Imperial Cult for John's Appraisal of the Value of Christians' Suffering in Revelation," in *Die Johannesapokalypse: Kontexte—Konzepte—Rezeption*, ed. J. Frey, J. A. Kelhoffer, and F. Tóth, WUNT 287 (Tübin-gen: Mohr Siebeck, 2012), 570–73.

27. Cf. M. Immendörfer, *Ephesians and Artemis*, WUNT 436 (Tübingen: Mohr Siebeck, 2017), 116–22; S. Friesen, "The Cult of the Roman Emperors in Ephesos: Temple Wardens, City Titles, and the Interpretation of the Revelation of John," in *Ephesos, Metropolis of Asia: An Interdisciplinary Approach to Its Archaeology, Religion, and Culture*, ed. H. Koester, HTS 41 (Cambridge, MA: Harvard University Press, 1995), 229–50.

28. Price, *Rituals and Power*, between pp. 198 and 199.

29. Price, *Rituals and Power*, 214–15.

and religion.[30] The Jews feared that such citizens would become skeptical of their loyalty to the emperor and would file suit against them to the town officers (e.g., *politarchēs*, Acts 17:6), the ceremonial officials (e.g., *Asiarchēs*, 19:31), or the governors (e.g., *anthypatos*, 19:38). In the latter half of the first century AD, Jewish immigrants must have been aware of Rome's tax-evasion hunting and the expulsion of Jews from the cities, triggered by the Jewish rebellion against Rome.[31]

Due to these circumstances, the correlated position of Jewish immigrants in the community in Ephesus can be summarized as follows (see fig. 22.3): (1) Jewish immigrants tried to maintain friendly relations with Rome (mainly through tax obligations and an attitude of obedience); (2) Rome granted religious privileges to Jewish immigrants; (3) gentile residents expected political and economic rewards from Rome; (4) gentile residents showed an attitude of obedience and took the initiative in worshiping the emperor; (5) gentile residents accepted Jewish immigrants because they were aware of Roman authority behind the Jews; and (6) Jewish immigrants engaged in ritual activities in the community using Rome's religious privileges and tried to maintain Jewish identity by separating themselves from pagan customs.[32]

We should assume a correlation diagram of at least four parties (Rome, gentile residents, Jewish immigrants, and the Christian community) to consider why the self-proclaimed Jews persecuted the Christian community. For Jews who first immigrated to Asia Minor, built friendly relations with Rome, and built a stable religious life in the community, the Christian community was at risk of disrupting their stability.[33] They blamed the Christian community for differentiating themselves, considered them a dangerous group that ridiculed Rome as "Babylon the Destruction," and accused them of

30. Philo was sent to Gaius to defend the Alexandrian Jews against the charges from the Greeks (*Legat.* 353). Josephus also mentions how the Greeks despised and hated the Jews (*Ag. Ap.* 2.80–144). A Philippian accuses Paul and Silas to the magistrates (*stratēgos*) and says, "These men are *Jews*, and they are disturbing our city. They *advocate customs that are not lawful for us as Romans to accept or practice*" (Acts 16:20–21 ESV). This saying shows how the local Greeks viewed the Jews. See also Trebilco, *Jewish Communities in Asia Minor*, 8–12.

31. J. Walters, "Romans, Jews, and Christians: The Impact of the Romans on Jewish/Christian Relations in First-Century Rome," in *Judaism and Christianity in First-Century Rome*, ed. K. Donafried and P. Richardson (Grand Rapids: Eerdmans, 1998), 175–89.

32. In b. Avod. Zar. 2.1 and 10.3–5 (although they are later documents), it is shown that the Jews were wary of Roman society's immorality and that they were trying to maintain their ethnic identity by adhering to the law.

33. Romans hated and persecuted Christians because they did not participate in local religious rituals and denied Roman gods. See W. Frend, *Martyrdom and Persecution in the Early Church* (Garden City, NY: Doubleday, 1967), 123.

Figure 22.3

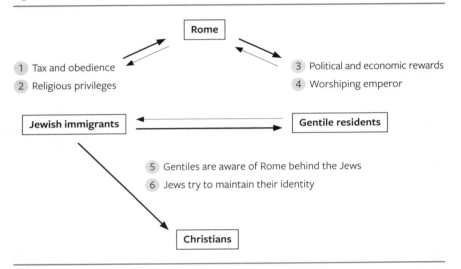

making a noise around the world and disobeying the Roman emperor's edict (Acts 17:6–7). The Jews needed to remind their gentile neighbors that they were legitimate immigrants recognized by the Roman Empire. However, from John's viewpoint, it is the Roman Empire (secular power, not God) that admits that they (the self-proclaimed Jews) are true Jews. John calls them "the synagogue of Satan" not because they participate in idolatry but because they are under Roman rule and even under Satan's control.[34] Curiously, the Roman Empire does not appear directly in the seven letters in Revelation. The tribulation was brought about by self-proclaimed Jews and temptation by self-proclaimed prophets, and this brought them imprisonment and poverty. However, if we trace the root cause in the dual world depicted in Revelation 13 and 19, we know of Rome under Satan's control. John warns the Christians not to lose sight of the real enemies behind them amid immediate difficulties.

Eidōlothytos *(Idolatry)* and Porneia *(Adultery, Idolatry, Trade Relations)*

John summarizes another crisis with two infinitive clauses: *phagein eidōlothyta* and *porneusai* (Rev. 2:14). Animals were dedicated to gods in

34. See the battle between Satan and the saints depicted in the drama's intermission in Rev. 13 and 19.

idol worship.[35] The meat and wine dedicated to the idols were sometimes served at festivals and sometimes sold by priests to the local markets at low prices. The talmudic tractate Avodah Zarah (teaching on "idolatry" in the Babylonian Talmud) teaches to avoid any foods (meat and wine) involved in "idol worship."[36] The same policy was confirmed in the early Christian churches (Acts 15:20, 29). Regarding "fornication" (*porneia*), the Talmud teaches as follows: "They do not leave *cattle* in gentiles' inns, because they are suspect in regard to *bestiality*. And a *woman* should not be alone with them, because they are suspect in regard to *fornication*. And a man should not be alone with them, because they are suspect in regard to *bloodshed*" (b. Avod. Zar. 2.1).[37] Here, "fornication" means "bestiality with cattle" and "adultery with the woman." This indicates that the Jews at the time were quite vigilant about the immorality of the pagan society. "Fornication" (*porneia*), one of "the things to abstain" from when the Jerusalem Council was held (Acts 15:20, 29), seems to indicate specific misconduct. John may mention it in a broader sense because, in the Old Testament, idol worship is often described as an act of infidelity to Yahweh (Ps. 106:39; Wis. 14:12; Isa. 47:10; Nah. 3:1–4 [cf. 1:14]).[38] It is possible to take the two infinitive clauses as a synonymous parallelism (*phagein eidōlothyta // porneusai*). Further, context suggests the broader meaning here.

Between the second and third of the three visions of apocalyptic judgments in Revelation (seven seals [A], seven trumpets [B], and seven bowls [C]; see the outline below), a drama (X1) depicting the realities of this world as a battle of evil power with God's people is arranged as an interlude. The sequel (X2) unfolds as a drama of the battle of the kingdom of the Lamb with the kingdom of the beast after the vision of the third judgment (C).

A: Seven Seals (6:1–8:1)
 B: Seven Trumpets (8:2–11:19)
   X1: Battle: God's People vs. Evil Power (12:1–14:5)
 C: Seven Bowls (15:1–16:21)
   X2: Battle: Kingdom of the Lamb vs. Kingdom of the Beast (17:1–19:5)

The correlation between the actors of these dramas is shown in figure 22.4.

---

35. Price, *Rituals and Power*, 198–99, 214–15.
36. See b. Avod. Zar. 10.3–5.
37. Translation from J. Neusner, *The Babylonian Talmud: A Translation and Commentary* (Peabody, MA: Hendrickson, 2005) (consulted via Accordance Bible software, emphasis added).
38. Cf. Beale, *Revelation*, 250.

Figure 22.4

Dragon (= Satan)
▼
Beast out of the sea (Rom. 13:1 = 17:3,
= Roman emperors or Roman Empire)

Beast out of the earth (pseudo-prophets; cf. 19:20)
They make the people worship the Beast (13:12)
They make an image for the Beast (13:14)
They kill those who do not worship the image of the Beast (13:15)
They restrict commercial transactions to idol worshipers only (13:17)
▼
Great Prostitute (= metropolis of Roman Empire)
▼
Kings and people of the earth worshiping the Dragon and Beast

---

The image of "the beast out of the earth" represents the false prophets. They entice the people to worship the beast (the emperors), cast a statue of the beast, and cause those who would not worship the image of the beast to be slain. They have the role of making people be imprinted on the right hand or the forehead to get permission for commerce. Merchants of the nations accumulate wealth through commercial dealings with the Great Prostitute (*pornē megalē*, Rev. 17:1; 19:2) and drown in luxurious life (18:3, 9, 11–15). These acts are expressed as "fornication" (*porneia*), and their commercial counterpart is called the "Great Prostitute" (*pornē megalē*; cf. 17:2; 18:3, 9). In Revelation 18:3, the political relations of all the nations and kings with the Great Prostitute and the commercial relations of the merchants with the Great Prostitute are juxtaposed (see fig. 22.5). These types of relations expand the meaning of *porneia*.

The Old Testament frequently speaks of God's judgment on the cities that have accumulated wealth in trade with gentile countries.[39] In Isaiah 23:17–18, Tyre's merchandise and wages earned through transactions with all the kingdoms are described as a reward for prostitution.[40] Avodah Zarah stipulates that the Jews should not be involved in idolatry or gain any benefit when they

39. E.g., 1 Chron. 14:1; 2 Chron. 2:12–13; Neh. 13:16; Isa. 23:1–18; Jer. 51:6–9; Ezek. 16:15–17; 27:1–36.
40. See these studies for theological insights into Babylon's prosperity: R. Bauckham, *The Bible in Politics: How to Read the Bible Politically* (London: SPCK, 1989), 85–102; Bauckham, *The Climax of Prophecy: Studies on the Book of Revelation* (Edinburgh: T&T Clark, 1993), 338–83.

Figure 22.5. Revelation 18:3

ek tou oinou tou thymou **tēs porneias autēs**	of the wine of the wrath of **her fornication**
pepōkan _panta ta ethnē_	all the nations have drunk
kai	and
hoi basileis tēs gēs	the kings of the earth
met' autēs	with her
eporneusan	**have committed fornication**
kai	and
hoi emporoi tēs gēs	the merchants of the earth
ek tēs dynameōs tou strēnous autēs	through the abundance of her luxury
eploutēsan.	have become rich.

are doing business with the gentiles.[41] The religious crisis that the diaspora Jews and Christians faced was not only the imposition of emperor worship but also all activities that might have been related to idolatry. The Jewish communities (_synagōgē_) existed in Asia Minor long before the Christians formed communities there. There were likely Jews who made considerable money in commerce with residents and Rome.[42] Their influence on the Christian life must not have been small.

Conclusion: How Japanese Churches Today Face These Religious Crises

We considered the two crises that Christians faced in the late first century AD: one is the fear of being blamed (_blasphēmia_) from the false Jews (_pseudo-Ioudaioi_ or _pseudo-apostoloi_), and the other is temptation (_peirasmos_) from those who hold to the teaching of the false prophet (_kratountes tēn didachēn_). And we assume a correlation diagram of four parties (Rome, gentile residents, Jewish immigrants, and the Christian community; see fig. 22.3). Various forces were working within the diagram, and there were various temptations and battles. Even though the Roman Empire might not have been a direct enemy, Christians faced difficulties with earlier immigrant Jews (persecution) and gentile residents (temptation). Christians were encouraged not to compromise their faith in the Lord, as self-proclaimed Jews did in their behavior toward the Roman emperor and the gentile residents.

41. E.g., b. Avod. Zar. 1.5–6; 2.3–5.
42. See G. M. A. Hanfmann, _Sardis from Prehistoric to Roman Times: Results of the Archaeological Exploration of Sardis 1958–1975_ (Cambridge, MA: Harvard University Press, 1983), 65.

During World War II, the most influential Christian leaders in Japan led the churches to a compromise in faith as a false prophet. In Japan today, churches are not suffering as they once were, but they are still under the influence of the symbolic emperor system. In particular, the problems in school education are not small. We must continue to nurture the spiritual eyes to see through the little deceit (Rev. 2:2) to prevent "a small flame from burning down the entire forest" as the Japanese churches failed once. John on Patmos encouraged us to "be faithful unto death" (Rev. 2:10 ESV; cf. 2:13).

Kyrie eleison

APPENDIX

Pew Research Data

Religious Landscapes of the Countries Represented

Chapter 1: Brazil

Population: 194,950,000
Percent Christian: 88.9
Percent Unaffiliated: 7.9
Percent Folk Religion: 2.8

Chapter 2: Kazakhstan and Russia

Kazakhstan

Population: 16,030,000
Percent Christian: 24.8
Percent Muslim: 70.4

Russia

Population: 142,960,000
Percent Christian: 73.3
Percent Muslim: 10

Chapters 3 and 5: Indonesia

Population: 239,870,000
Percent Christian: 9.9

The information in this appendix (excepting chapters 10 and 19) is from the 2010 Pew Research demographic study on the global religious landscape. See https://assets.pewresearch.org/wp-content/uploads/sites/11/2012/12/globalReligion-tables.pdf.

Percent Muslim: 87.2
Percent Hindu: 1.7

Chapter 4: Hong Kong

Population: 7,050,000
Percent Christian: 14.3
Percent Unaffiliated: 56.1
Percent Buddhist: 13.2
Percent Folk Religion: 12.8

Chapter 6: China

Population: 1,341,340,000
Percent Christian: 5.1
Percent Unaffiliated: 52.2
Percent Buddhist: 18.2
Percent Folk Religion: 21.9

Chapter 7: South Korea

Population: 48,180,000
Percent Christian: 29.4
Percent Unaffiliated: 46.4
Percent Buddhist: 22.9

Chapter 8: Nigeria

Population: 158,420,000
Percent Christian: 49.3
Percent Muslim: 48.8
Percent Folk Religion: 1.4

Chapter 9: Kenya

Population: 40,510,000
Percent Christian: 84.8
Percent Muslim: 9.7
Percent Folk or "Other" Religion: 2.9

Chapter 10: Latino/a American

"This [Latino/a American] ethnic group includes any person of Cuban, Mexican, Puerto Rican, South or Central American, or other Spanish culture or origin, regardless of race. According to 2020 Census data, there are 62.1 million Hispanics living in the United States. This group represents 18.9 percent of the total U.S. population, the nation's second-largest racial or ethnic group after non-Hispanic whites."[1]

Chapter 11: The Philippines

Population: 93,260,000
Percent Christian: 92.6
Percent Muslim: 5.5
Percent Folk Religion: 1.5

Chapter 12: Colombia

Population: 46,290,000
Percent Christian: 92.5
Percent Unaffiliated: 6.6

Chapter 13: Egypt

Population: 81,120,000
Percent Christian: 5.1
Percent Muslim: 94.9

Chapter 14: Zimbabwe

Population: 12,570,000
Percent Christian: 87.0
Percent Unaffiliated: 7.9
Percent Folk or "Other" Religion: 4.2

Chapter 15: Australia

Population: 22,270,000
Percent Christian: 67.3

    1. "Hispanic/Latino Health," OMH: U.S. Department of Health and Human Services Office of Minority Health, accessed January 12, 2024, https://minorityhealth.hhs.gov/hispaniclatino -health.

Percent Muslim: 2.4
Percent Unaffiliated: 24.2

Chapter 16: Ethiopia

Population: 82,950,000
Percent Christian: 62.8
Percent Muslim: 34.6
Percent Folk Religion: 2.6

Chapter 17: Guatemala

Population: 14,390,000
Percent Christian: 95.2
Percent Unaffiliated: 4.1

Chapter 18: Sri Lanka

Population: 20,860,000
Percent Christian: 7.3
Percent Muslim: 9.8
Percent Hindu: 13.6
Percent Buddhist: 69.3

Chapter 19: African American

"In 2021, 40.1 million people in the United States were non-Hispanic black alone, which represents 12.1 percent of the total population of 331.9 million."[2]

Chapter 20: India

Population: 1,224,610,000
Percent Christian: 2.5
Percent Muslim: 14.4
Percent Hindu: 79.5
Percent Buddhist: 0.8

2. "Black/African American Health," OMH: U.S. Department of Health and Human Services Office of Minority Health, accessed January 12, 2024, https://minorityhealth.hhs.gov/blackafri can-american-health#:~:text=Overview%20(Demographics),total%20population%20of%20 331.9%20million.

Chapter 21: South Africa

Population: 50,130,000
Percent Christian: 81.2
Percent Muslim: 1.7
Percent Unaffiliated: 14.9

Chapter 22: Japan

Population: 126,540,000
Percent Christian: 1.6
Percent Unaffiliated: 57.0
Percent Buddhist: 36.2

CONTRIBUTORS

EDITOR

Mariam Kamell Kovalishyn (associate professor of New Testament, Regent College, Vancouver) grew up in Western New York. Her research focuses on the General Epistles (James–Jude) and their interconnection with broader biblical theology. She coauthored the *Zondervan Exegetical Commentary on James*, has authored numerous articles and book chapters, and cares deeply for global biblical studies and for training the laity to read the Bible well. She holds a PhD from the University of St. Andrews.

AUTHORS

J. Ayodeji Adewuya (professor of New Testament, Pentecostal Theological Seminary, Cleveland, Tennessee) was born and raised in Nigeria and was a resident missionary in the Philippines for eighteen years, where he continues to travel regularly and minister. He holds a PhD from the University of Manchester, England.

Davinson Kevin Bohorquez (sessional lecturer, Regent College, Vancouver, BC) was born in New York City, was raised in Bogotá, Colombia, and currently lives in Vancouver, BC, Canada, with his wife, Halyna, and two kids. He is an elder with the Church of the Nazarene, serving as the associate pastor of Christian formation at Vancouver First Church of the Nazarene, and he teaches as a sessional lecturer in Koine Greek at Regent College. He holds a MATS and ThM from Regent College.

Gabriel J. Catanus (affiliate assistant professor of theology and ethics, Fuller Theological Seminary, Pasadena, California) is the director of the Filipino American Ministry Initiative at Fuller and pastor of Garden City Covenant

Church in Chicago, where he serves immigrant families and young professionals. He received his PhD in theological ethics from Loyola University Chicago.

Bernardo Cho (professor of New Testament and biblical theology and director of the DMin program, Seminário Teológico Servo de Cristo, São Paulo, Brazil) was born and raised in Brazil and is of Korean descent. In addition to teaching, he serves as the founding pastor of a multiethnic church in the São Paulo city center. He is a Langham graduate and also works with the Langham Scholar program as the scholar care coordinator for Latin America and the Caribbean. He holds a PhD from the University of Edinburgh.

Dany Christopher (lecturer in biblical studies, Amanat Agung Theological Seminary, Jakarta, Indonesia) is from Indonesia. More recently, his research focuses on understanding the Holy Spirit in light of other spirit phenomena in Luke-Acts. Beside teaching, he is also a pastor who regularly preaches and leads bible study groups. He holds a PhD from Durham University, UK, and is a Langham Scholar.

David A. deSilva (Trustees' Distinguished Professor of New Testament and Greek, Ashland Theological Seminary, Ashland, Ohio) is of Sri Lankan descent and has traveled to Sri Lanka frequently to teach and to visit family. He has contributed several books to the publishing program of Colombo Theological Seminary, including *Reading Paul through Asian Eyes: A Sri Lankan Commentary on Galatians* (Colombo Theological Seminary, 2014) and *Reading Revelation: From Ancient Asia Minor to Modern South Asia* (Colombo Theological Seminary, 2017), both published in English and Sinhalese. He holds a PhD from Emory University.

Miguel G. Echevarría (associate professor of New Testament and Greek, Southeastern Baptist Theological Seminary, Wake Forest, North Carolina) grew up in South Florida and is of Cuban descent. He has taught and ministered in the US and in Latin America. His publications include *40 Questions about the Apostle Paul, Engaging the New Testament: A Short Introduction for Students and Ministers*, and *Reading the Bible Latinamente: Latino/a Interpretation for the Life of the Church*. He holds a PhD from Southern Baptist Theological Seminary.

Dennis R. Edwards (dean, North Park Theological Seminary, Chicago, Illinois) is African American and was born and raised in New York City. He has served as a pastor and educator for over three decades. He holds a PhD in biblical studies from the Catholic University of America in Washington, DC, and is the author of *1 Peter* in The Story of God Bible Commentary series (Zondervan) and *Humility Illuminated* (IVP Academic).

Masanobu Endo (professor of Christian studies and chair of the Religious Affairs Committee, Tokyo Woman's Christian University, Tokyo, Japan) grew up in Japan. He is an ordained pastor of The Evangelical Alliance Mission (TEAM). He holds a PhD from the University of St. Andrews.

Lanuwabang Jamir (dean of the New Testament Department, Union Biblical Seminary, Pune, India) is from the small state of Nagaland in Northeast India. He is the author of *Exclusion and Judgment in Fellowship Meals: The Socio-historical Background of 1 Corinthians*. He holds a PhD from London School of Theology and is a Langham Scholar.

Lyn M. Kidson (independent scholar and honorary research fellow at Macquarie University, Sydney, Australia) grew up in New South Wales, Australia. She is currently working in academic administration and regularly speaks and writes on early Christianity, the Pastoral Epistles, numismatics, and gender. She holds a PhD from Macquarie University.

Jin Hwan Lee (academic supervisor, Canada School of Theology, Toronto) was born in South Korea. He holds a PhD from the University of St. Michael's College, the University of Toronto.

Elizabeth W. Mburu (associate professor of New Testament and Greek, Africa International University, Nairobi, Kenya) was born and raised in Nairobi, Kenya. She is Kenyan by nationality and has also experienced being part of the African diaspora community in the US. In addition to teaching, she is also the Langham Literature Regional Coordinator, Anglophone Africa, and is on the NIV Committee for Bible Translation and the Lausanne Global Diaspora Network. Her recent book is titled *African Hermeneutics* (Carlisle, UK: Langham, 2019). She holds a PhD from Southeastern Baptist Theological Seminary.

Fady Mekhael (sessional instructor in New Testament and Second Temple Judaism at McMaster University in Hamilton, Ontario; Tyndale University in Toronto, Ontario; and the European School of Theology and Culture in Germany) is a native Copt-Arab Egyptian, who has taught in different capacities at Middle Eastern seminaries. He also worked as a Bible Translation Officer with the Bible Society of Egypt and has been trained as a Bible Translation Advisor with the United Bible Societies to oversee Bible translation projects in the Middle East and North Africa region. He holds a Master of Arts in Theology from the Evangelical Theological Seminary in Cairo and a Master of Theology from Duke University, and his undergraduate degree in Egyptology and archaeology is from Alexandria University. He holds a PhD from McMaster University.

Nelson Morales (professor of hermeneutics and New Testament and provost, Seminario Teológico Centroamericano, Guatemala City, Guatemala) was born in Chile but has lived in Guatemala for more than thirty years. He and his wife are involved in theological education and in Langham preaching. He holds a PhD in New Testament from Trinity International University.

Gift Mtukwa (senior lecturer and dean of the department in the School of Religion and Christian Ministry, Africa Nazarene University, Nairobi, Kenya) was born and raised in Harare, Zimbabwe, and currently lives in Nairobi, Kenya. His main areas of research include the social and economic world of early Christianity. He is the author of *Work and Community in the Thessalonian Correspondence* (Langham Creative Projects, 2021). He holds a PhD from the University of Manchester.

Viktor Roudkovski (professor of biblical studies and chair of the Department of Theology, LeTourneau University, Longview, Texas) grew up in Kazakhstan, a former republic of the USSR, and is ethnically and culturally Russian. He travels there frequently to visit family, teach, and do mission work. He holds a PhD from New Orleans Baptist Theological Seminary.

Chakrita M. Saulina (affiliated scholar/life member, Clare Hall, University of Cambridge, UK) is a native of Jakarta, Indonesia, who has taught, studied, and ministered in four different countries on three continents. Currently, she lives in the US. She serves on the editorial board for the Logia monograph series (sponsored by Asia Theological Association and Langham Publishing) and on the steering committee of Interrelations of the Gospels program unit at the Society of Biblical Literature Annual Conference. She holds a PhD in New Testament studies from the University of Cambridge, UK.

Caroline Seed (lecturer at George Whitefield College, Cape Town and extraordinary researcher North-West University) was born in the UK and raised in southern Africa. A mission partner with the Church Mission

Society (Britain), she taught Bible and theology in five African countries. She is now a theological education consultant focusing on postgraduate studies and academic leadership. She holds a PhD in dogmatics from North-West University, South Africa.

Josaphat Tam (associate professor of biblical studies and academic dean, Evangel Seminary, Hong Kong, China) was born and grew up in Hong Kong. Like many other Hongkongers, his parents escaped from China and migrated to Hong Kong during the Cultural Revolution. Before teaching at Evangel, he pastored an evangelical Cantonese-speaking church. He is the author of *Apprehension of Jesus in the Gospel of John* (Mohr Siebeck, 2015) and *Reading the Old Testament with Peter: The Messianic "New Era" in 1 Peter* [Chinese] (Tien Dao, 2021). He holds a PhD from the University of Edinburgh and is a Langham Scholar.

Abeneazer G. Urga (department head for master's in biblical studies, Evangelical Theological College, Addis Ababa, Ethiopia; adjunct professor, Columbia International University in Columbia, South Carolina, and Ethiopian Graduate School of Theology in Addis Ababa) is a member of Equip International, Summer Institute of Linguistics in Ethiopia/International, and associate member of Studiorum Novi Testamenti Societas (SNTS). His recent book is *Intercession of Jesus in Hebrews* (Mohr Siebeck, 2023). He holds a PhD in biblical studies from Columbia International University.

Sze-kar Wan (professor of New Testament, Perkins School of Theology, Southern Methodist University, Dallas, Texas) was born in China, was brought up in Hong Kong, and emigrated to the US at age fifteen. He considers himself a one-point-fiver who straddles both Chinese and Western cultures. He is interested in Confucianism and Asian American hermeneutics as well as his own specialty in Pauline studies. Wan is an ordained Episcopal priest with the Diocese of Massachusetts (US) and holds a ThD from Harvard University Divinity School and an MDiv from Gordon-Conwell Theological Seminary.

NAME INDEX

SCRIPTURE AND ANCIENT WRITINGS INDEX